THE
NAO
OF BROWN

THE
NAO
OF BROWN

glyn dillon

First published 2012
by SelfMadeHero
5 Upper Wimpole Street
London W1G 6BP
www.selfmadehero.com

Copyright © 2012 Glyn Dillon

Written and Illustrated by: Glyn Dillon
Layout Designer: Kate McLauchlan

Editorial Assistant: Lizzie Kaye
Marketing Director: Doug Wallace
Publishing Director: Emma Hayley
With thanks to: Nick de Somogyi

A CIP record for this book is available from the British Library.

ISBN: 978-1-906838-42-3
10 9 8 7 6 5 4 3 2 1
Printed and bound in China

FOREWORD

So Siobhan said, 'I've met this man...' She and I have known each other since we were four and I have watched her navigate through the dating years with admirable grace and kindness, always staying friends, ALWAYS the one making sure that there were no hard feelings, whoever's fault it was, and never wallowing or losing faith. If it wasn't right, it wasn't right. This time, though, there was something different in her eyes – a vulnerability, a fear, almost as if she'd just eaten a pound of popping candy, drunk a can of coke and was trying to keep calm. I knew this was it.

At some point early on he gave me Isao Takahata's 'Grave of the Fireflies' to watch, which led to a Studio Ghibli revolution in our house – this man knew about really good stuff.

Two years later, my sister and I were making 100 origami cranes for their wedding guests and Glyn Dillon had become our little family's newest and most cherished friend.

He first told me about 'The Nao of Brown' in 2008 after he and Siobhan came to see me in a play. We were all walking along The Cut outside The Old Vic, propelled along somewhere, backs of coats and sideways chat along a buzzing London road. All I heard was 'washing machine' and 'meditation' but what I remember understanding, in spite of the fact that I couldn't really hear him and we didn't get to finish the conversation, was that he was going for the holy grail – the notes between the notes, the truth of our fumbling inconsequential lives, and endeavouring to make that truth beautiful. That he would be travelling effortlessly between our imagined reality, reality and fantasy seemed like a brilliant idea, tailor-made for his not-inconsiderable skills. At the time I remember thinking: if he does it, it will be astounding.

A year later, he sold the idea to SelfMadeHero and he and Siobhan began utilising and planning every spare minute so Glyn could write, draw and then colour each panel himself while still managing to see his sons in daylight and his wife across a dinner table. I occasionally checked into his website, but saw Glyn rarely – 'The Nao' had taken over. Was he writing it? Or was it writing him? Either way, the universe was conspiring to make it happen.

At one point he had strained his drawing hand so badly he couldn't pick up a pen. Siobhan said the frustration of him not being able to draw was far worse than any pain he was experiencing. I unhelpfully asked, 'Could he get someone else to come in and just, you know, take over for a bit?' She looked at me as if I had suggested he finish it in crayons. They were in it together: he, fearlessly pillaging his heart; she, fiercely protecting him while he was doing it.

Reading 'The Nao of Brown' is to experience the delicate ephemeral process of personal enlightenment. The panels often feel like memories. This is partly because it is set in an area of North West London I know and love but mostly because the honesty of the writing, the truthful recollection and depiction of felt and thought experience, is so acute that it's as if we, the reader, are Nao.

This book is a gift, a transcendental experience of love, hope and beauty in all its violence, despair and brutality. When I finished reading it for the first time, I remembered something I had forgotten and have now resolved never to forget:

The restless mind will make you believe that it is you, that *you* are it.

You are not.

Jessica Hynes

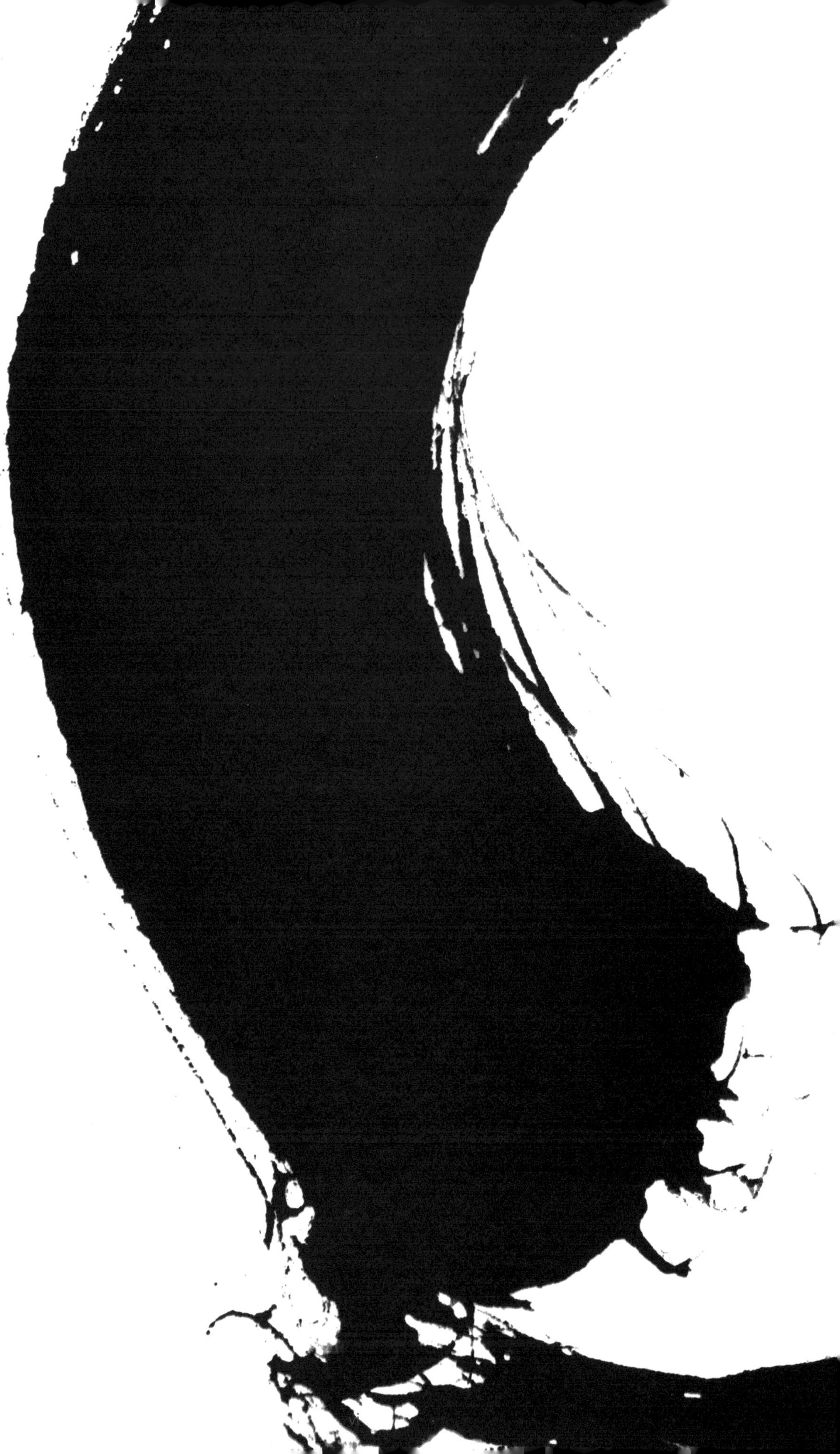

For Siobhan
x

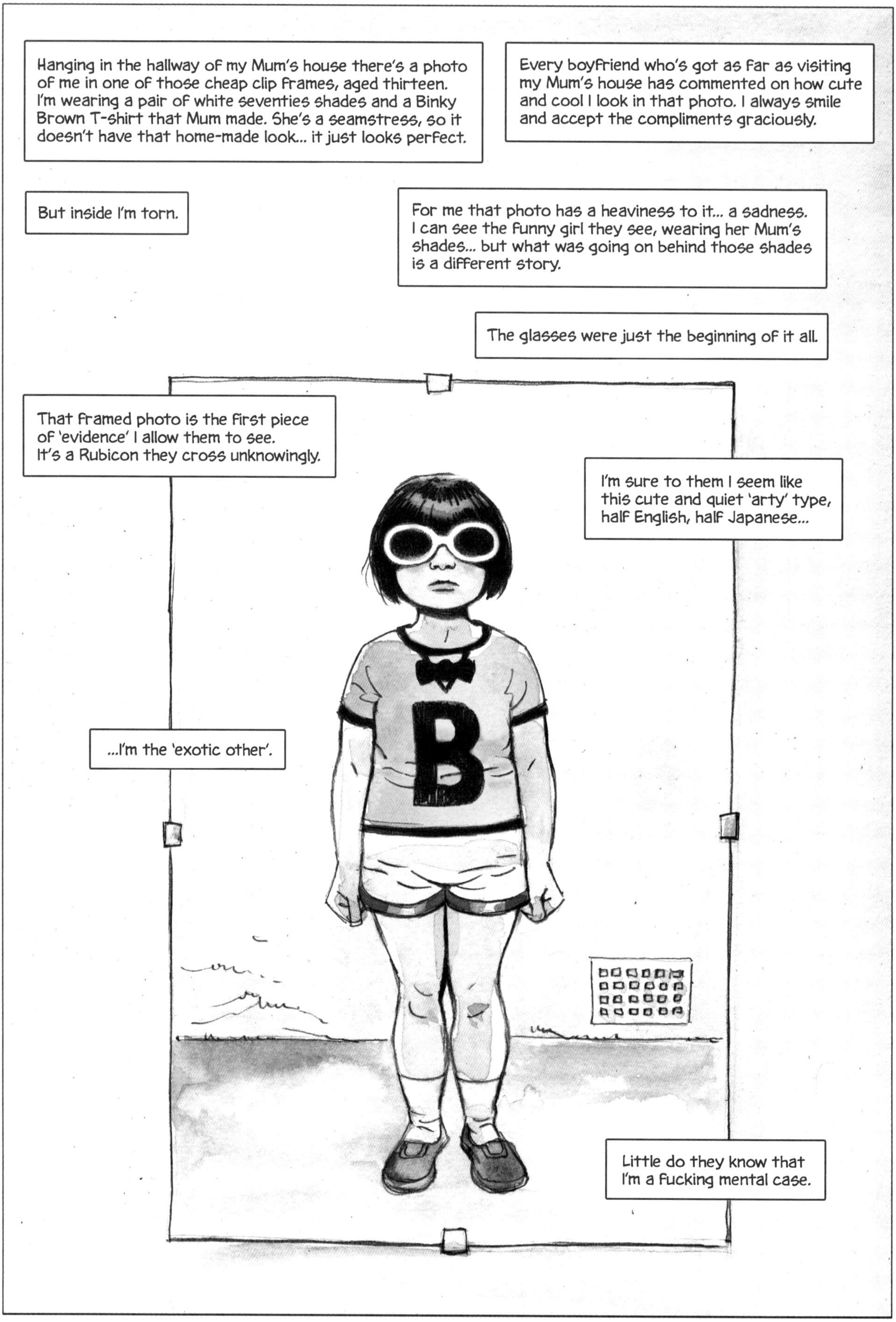
Hanging in the hallway of my Mum's house there's a photo of me in one of those cheap clip frames, aged thirteen. I'm wearing a pair of white seventies shades and a Binky Brown T-shirt that Mum made. She's a seamstress, so it doesn't have that home-made look... it just looks perfect.
Every boyfriend who's got as far as visiting my Mum's house has commented on how cute and cool I look in that photo. I always smile and accept the compliments graciously.
But inside I'm torn.
For me that photo has a heaviness to it... a sadness. I can see the funny girl they see, wearing her Mum's shades... but what was going on behind those shades is a different story.
The glasses were just the beginning of it all.
That framed photo is the first piece of 'evidence' I allow them to see. It's a Rubicon they cross unknowingly.
I'm sure to them I seem like this cute and quiet 'arty' type, half English, half Japanese...
...I'm the 'exotic other'.
B
Little do they know that I'm a fucking mental case.

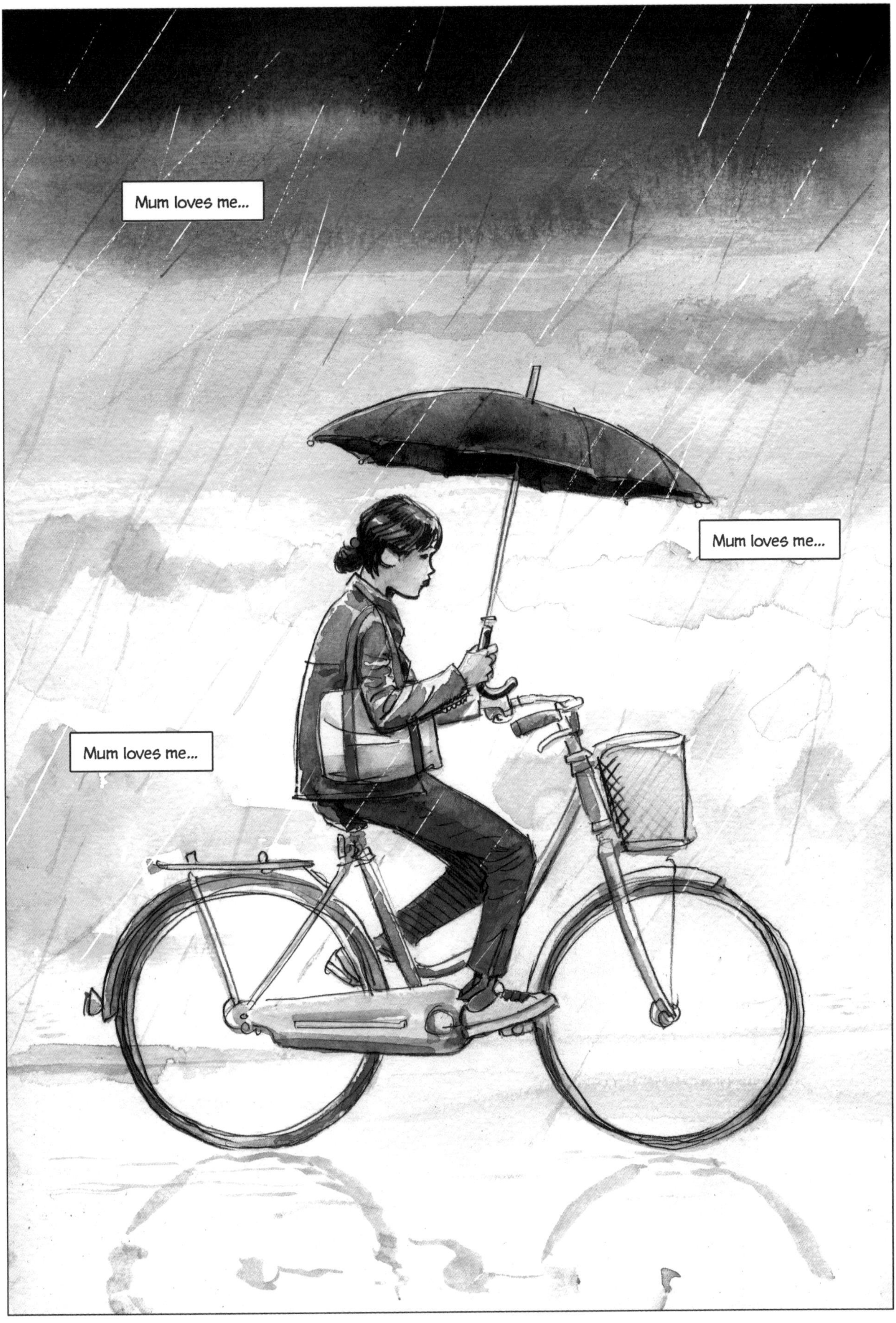
Mum loves me...
Mum loves me...
Mum loves me...

My Mum... the eldest daughter of a pub landlord... proper Paddington girl...

...and married in a kimono.

She's still got it, tucked away somewhere... 'in waiting'.

It's beautiful silk... deep purple with cranes on it, for fidelity and loyalty...

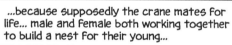

...because supposedly the crane mates for life... male and female both working together to build a nest for their young...

Maybe that's why they're an endangered species these days.

It's funny to think of Dad as the 'exotic other'.

10

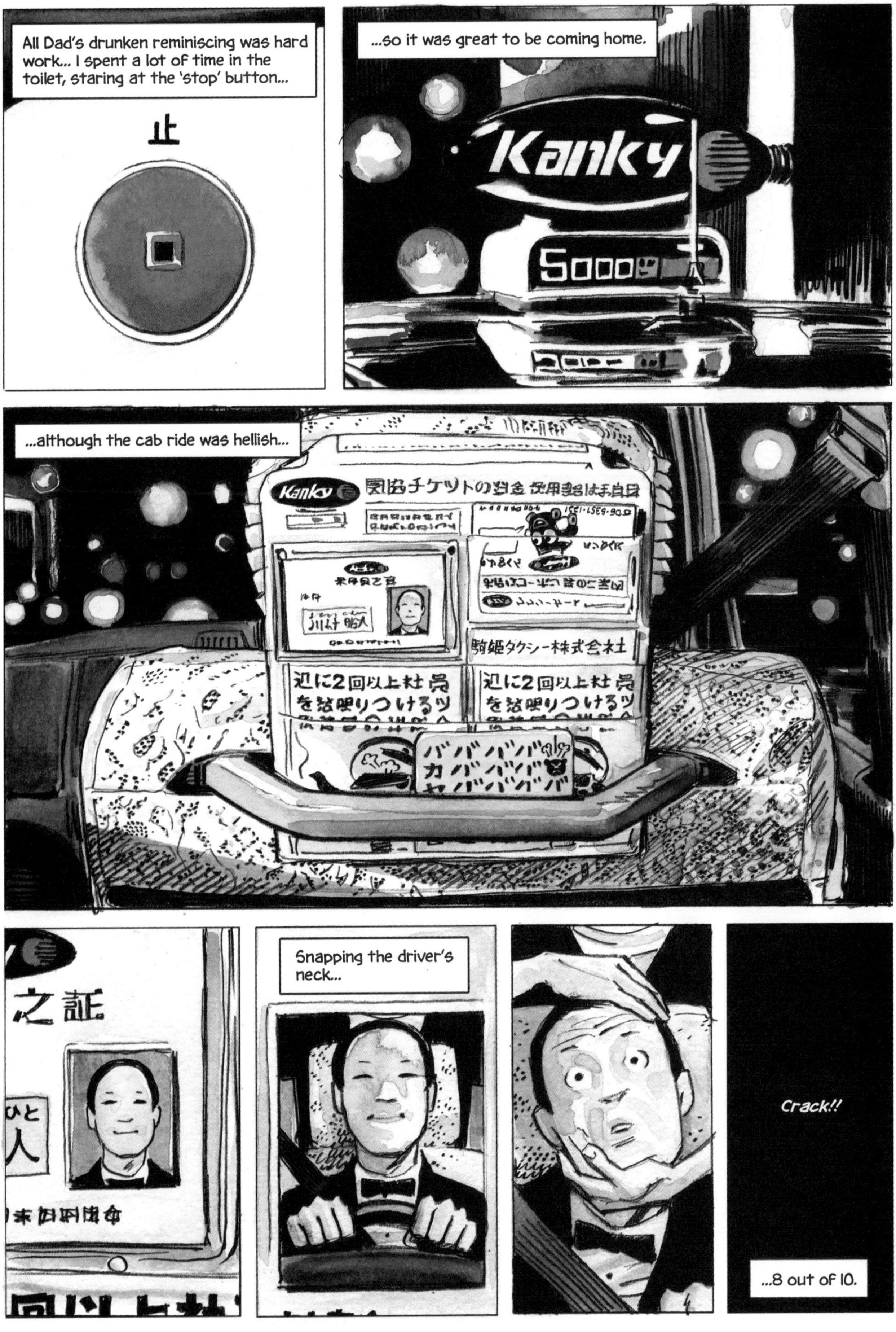
All Dad's drunken reminiscing was hard work... I spent a lot of time in the toilet, staring at the 'stop' button...
止
...so it was great to be coming home.
Kanky
5000
...although the cab ride was hellish...
Kanky
駒姫タクシー株式会社
Snapping the driver's neck...
Crack!!
...8 out of 10.

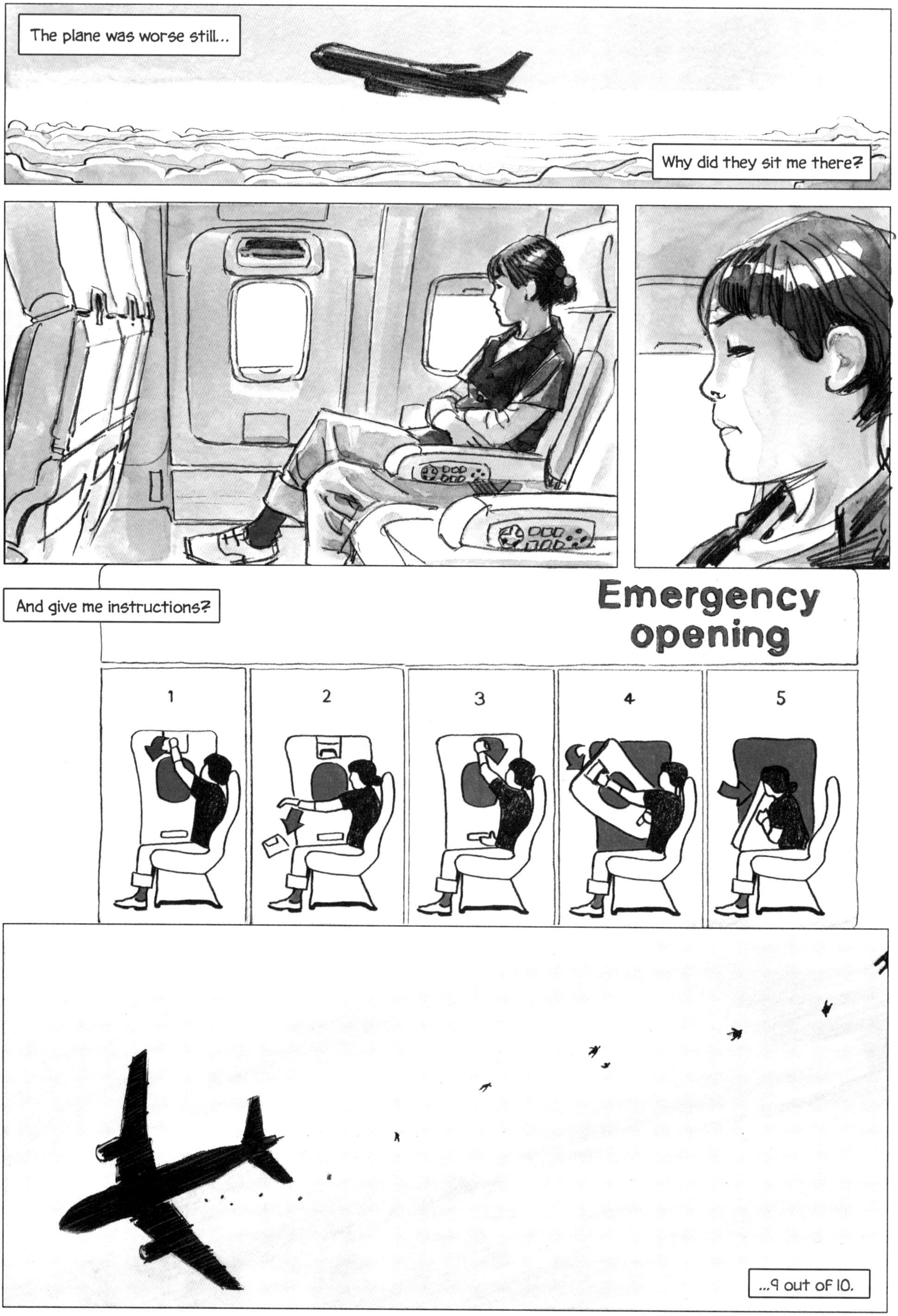

The plane was worse still...
Why did they sit me there?
And give me instructions?
Emergency opening
1
2
3
4
5
...9 out of 10.

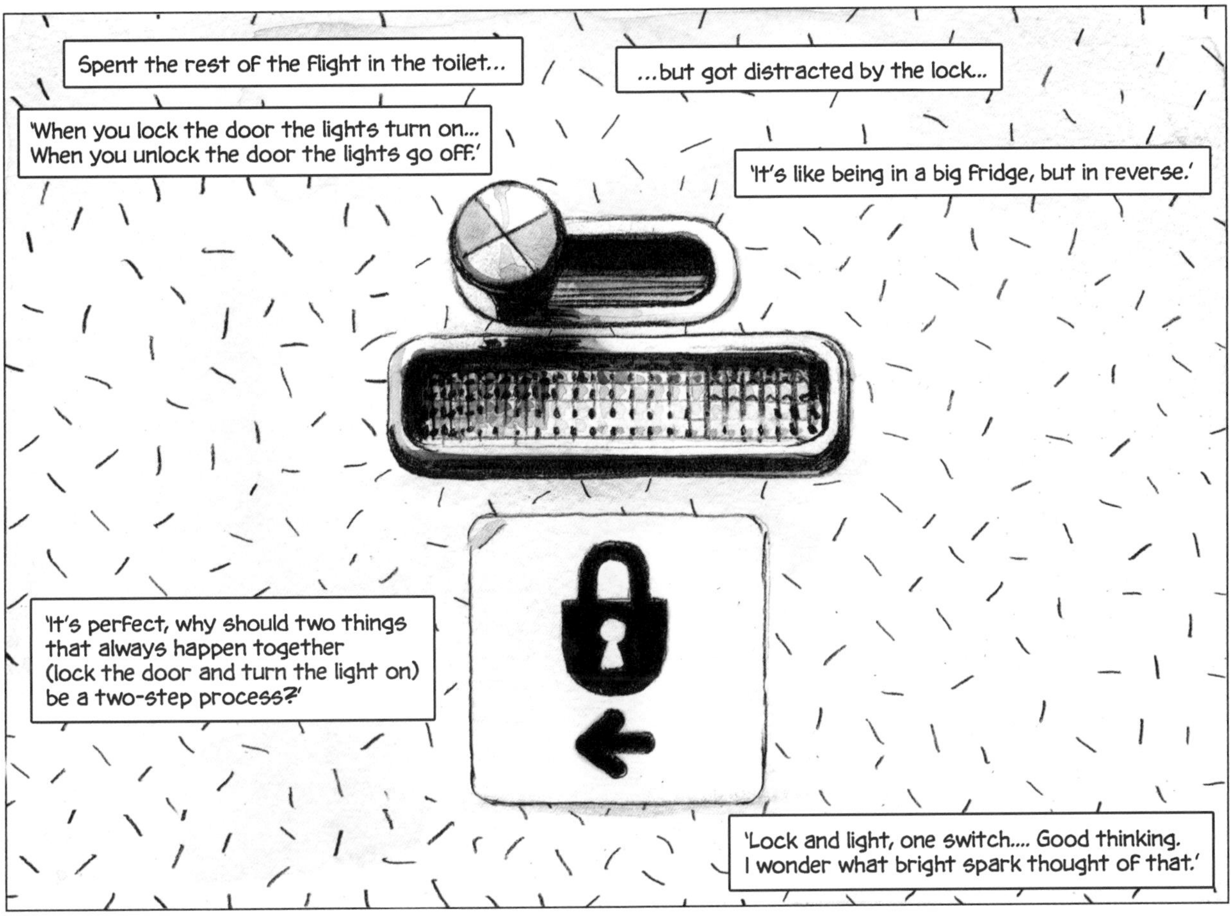
Spent the rest of the flight in the toilet...
...but got distracted by the lock...
'When you lock the door the lights turn on...
When you unlock the door the lights go off.'
'It's like being in a big fridge, but in reverse.'
'It's perfect, why should two things that always happen together (lock the door and turn the light on) be a two-step process?'
'Lock and light, one switch.... Good thinking. I wonder what bright spark thought of that.'

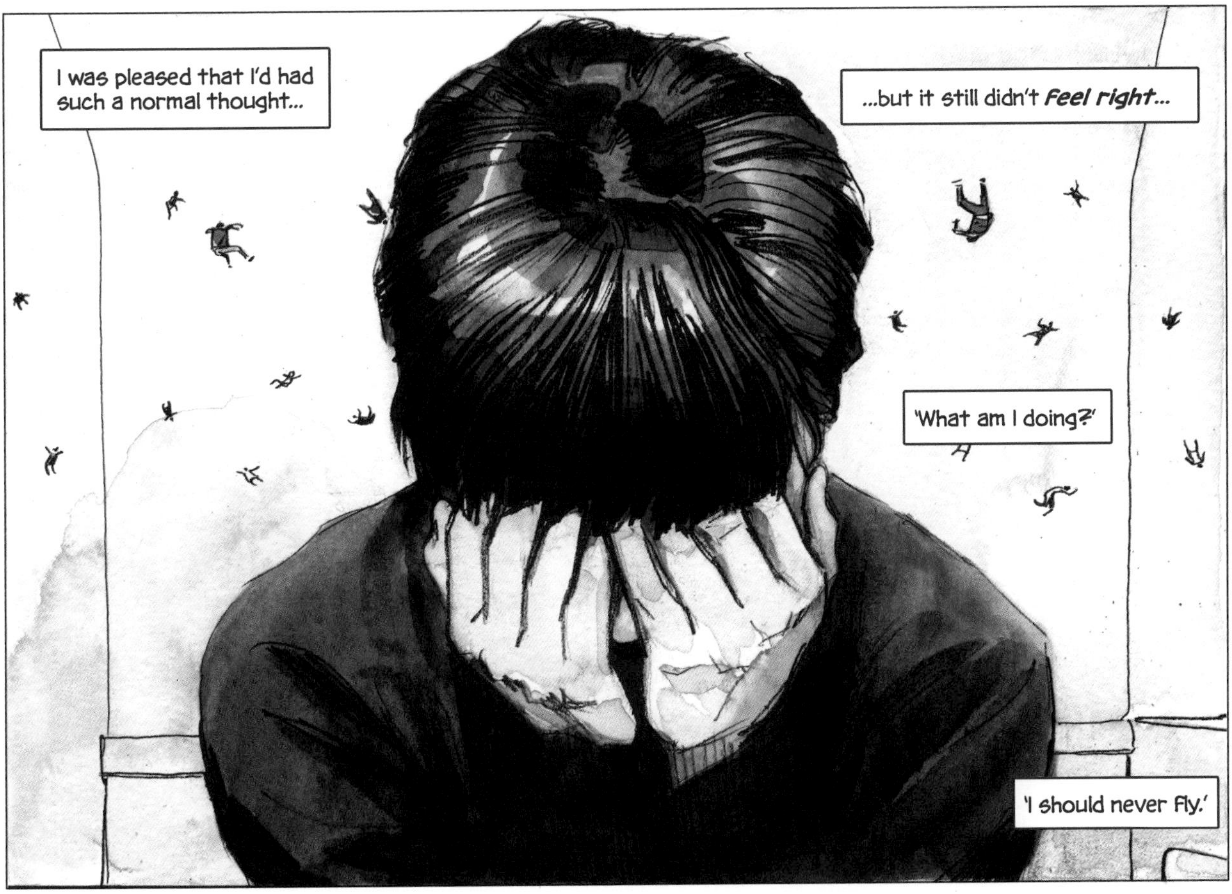
I was pleased that I'd had such a normal thought...
...but it still didn't *feel right*...
'What am I doing?'
'I should never fly.'

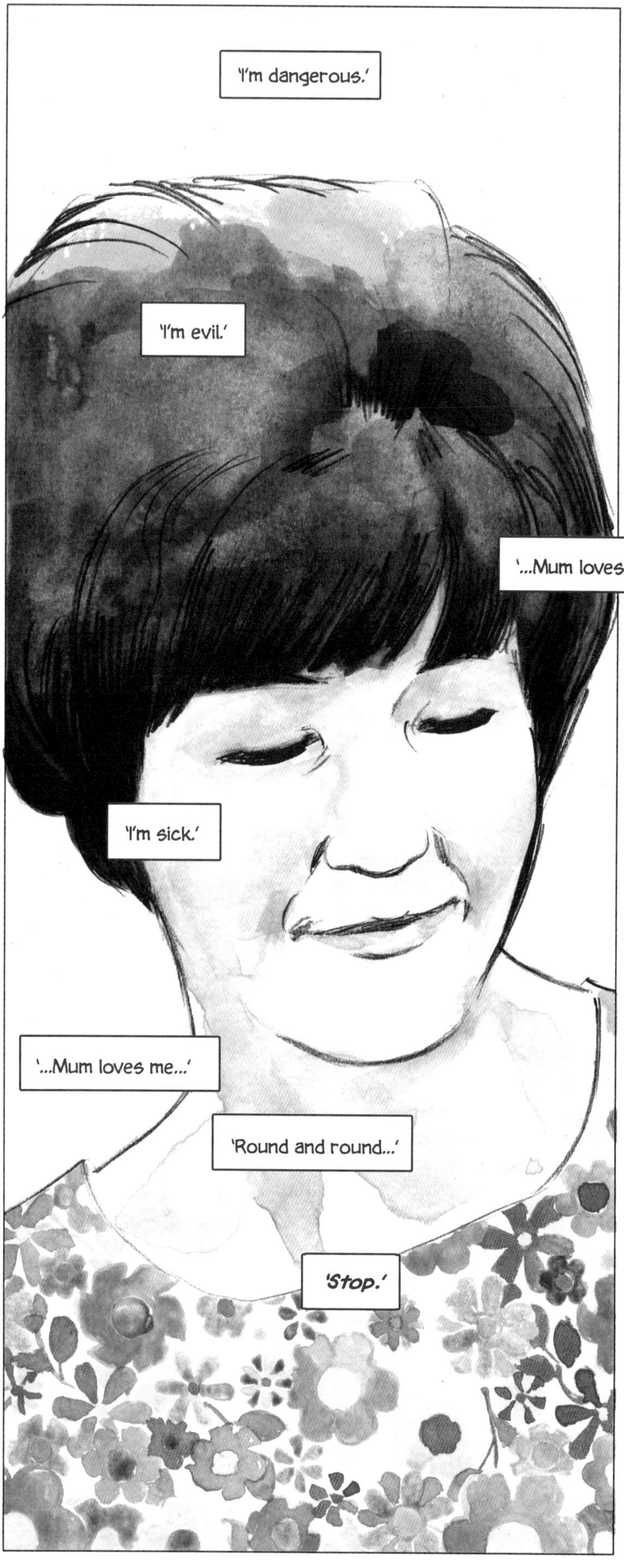
'I'm dangerous.'
'I'm evil.'
'...Mum loves me...'
'I'm sick.'
'...Mum loves me...'
'Round and round...'
'Stop.'

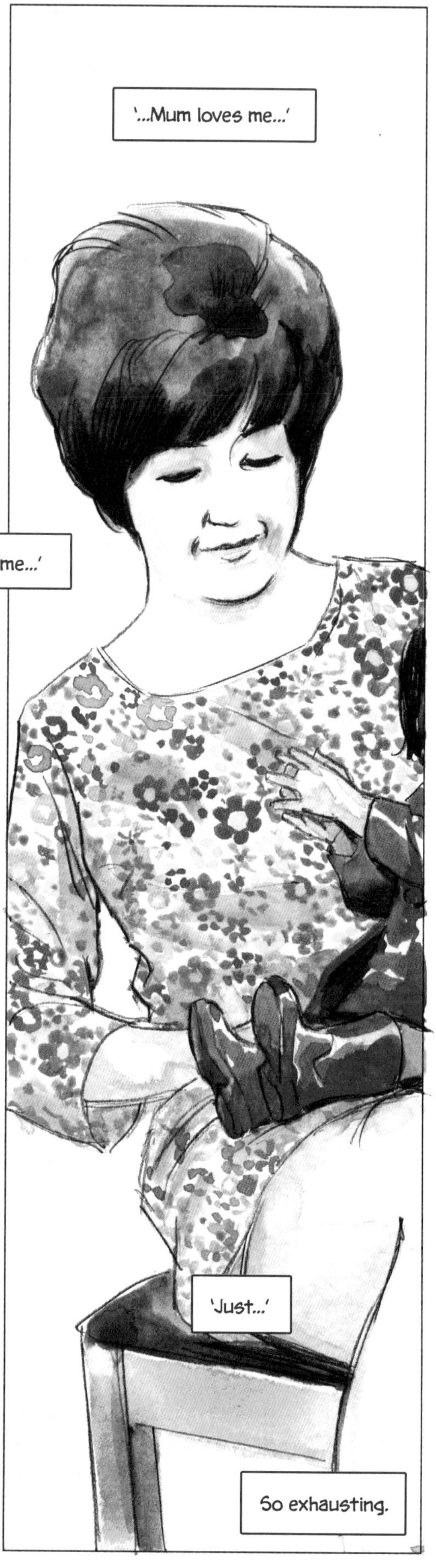
'...Mum loves me...'
'Just...'
So exhausting.

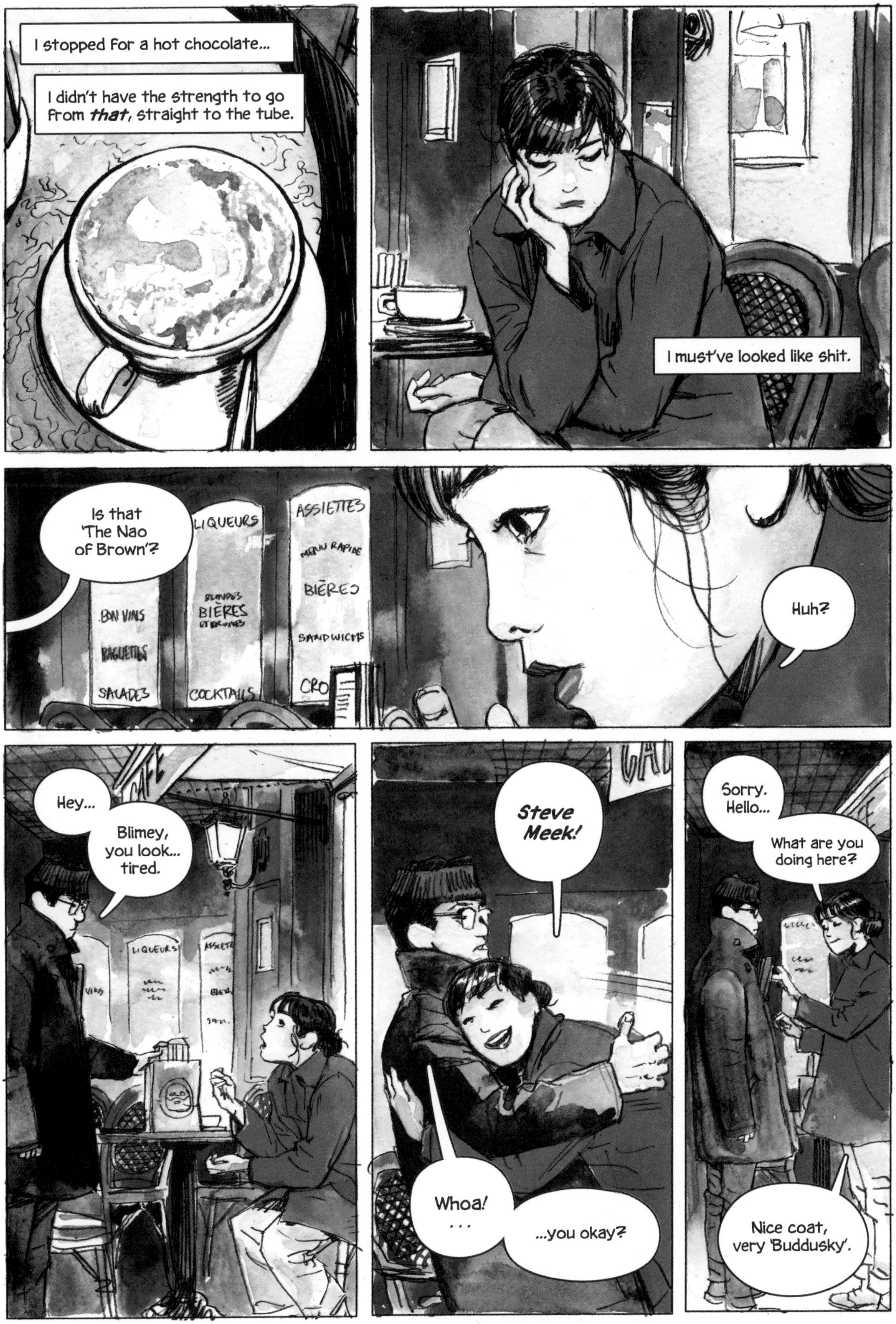
I stopped for a hot chocolate...
I didn't have the strength to go from *that*, straight to the tube.
I must've looked like shit.
Is that 'The Nao of Brown'?
LIQUEURS
ASSIETTES
MENU RAPIDE
BIÈRES
SANDWICHS
BON VINS
BAGUETTES
SALADES
COCKTAILS
Huh?
Hey...
Blimey, you look... tired.
Steve Meek!
Whoa!
. . .
...you okay?
Sorry. Hello...
What are you doing here?
Nice coat, very 'Buddusky'.

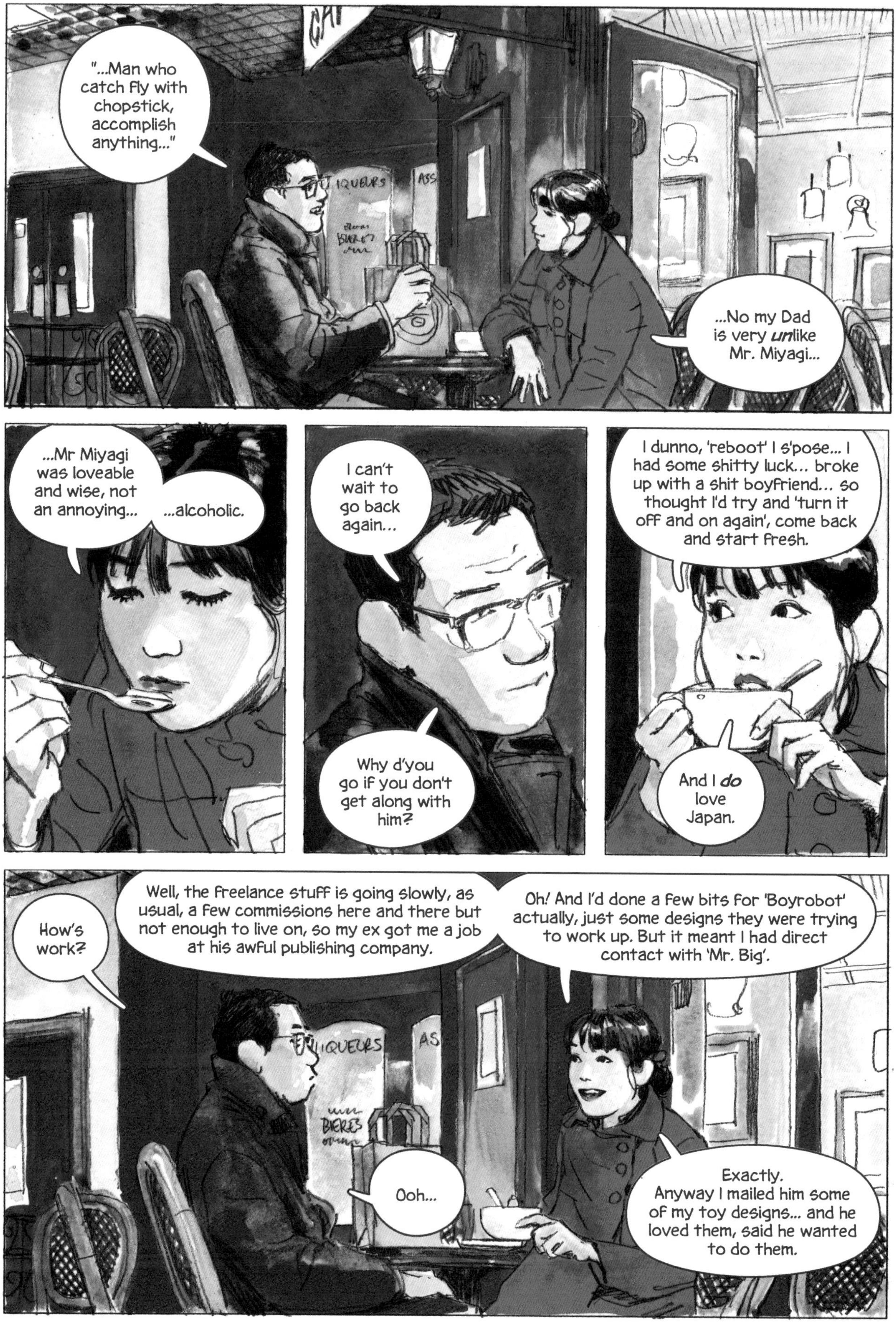
"...Man who catch fly with chopstick, accomplish anything..."
...No my Dad is very *un*like Mr. Miyagi...
...Mr Miyagi was loveable and wise, not an annoying...
...alcoholic.
I can't wait to go back again...
Why d'you go if you don't get along with him?
I dunno, 'reboot' I s'pose... I had some shitty luck... broke up with a shit boyfriend... so thought I'd try and 'turn it off and on again', come back and start fresh.
And I *do* love Japan.
How's work?
Well, the freelance stuff is going slowly, as usual, a few commissions here and there but not enough to live on, so my ex got me a job at his awful publishing company.
Oh! And I'd done a few bits for 'Boyrobot' actually, just some designs they were trying to work up. But it meant I had direct contact with 'Mr. Big'.
Ooh...
Exactly.
Anyway I mailed him some of my toy designs... and he loved them, said he wanted to do them.

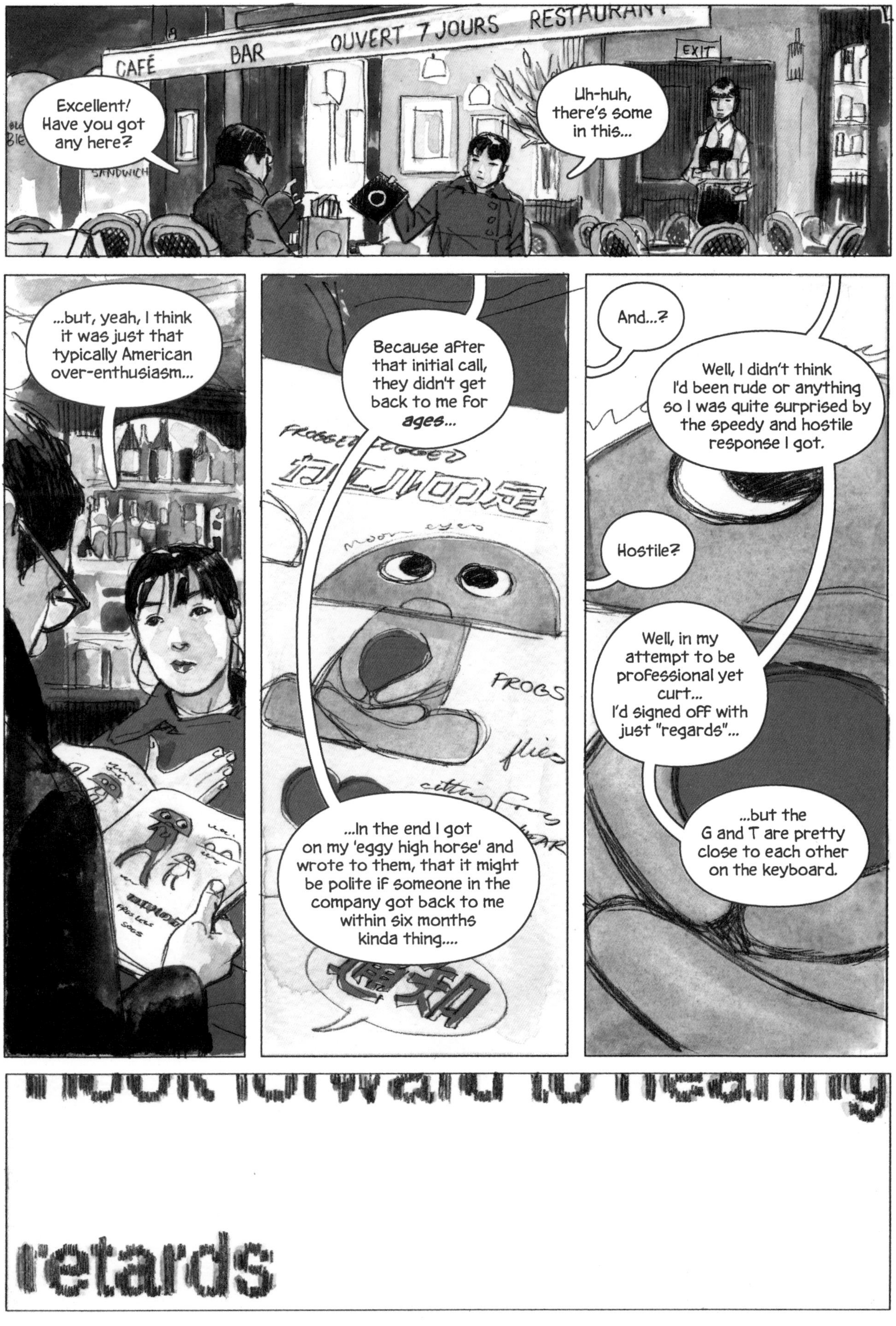

Excellent! Have you got any here?

Uh-huh, there's some in this...

...but, yeah, I think it was just that typically American over-enthusiasm...

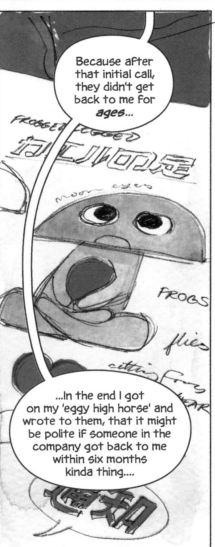

Because after that initial call, they didn't get back to me for *ages*...

...In the end I got on my 'eggy high horse' and wrote to them, that it might be polite if someone in the company got back to me within six months kinda thing....

And...?

Well, I didn't think I'd been rude or anything so I was quite surprised by the speedy and hostile response I got.

Hostile?

Well, in my attempt to be professional yet curt... I'd signed off with just "regards"...

...but the G and T are pretty close to each other on the keyboard.

~~I look forward to hearing~~

~~retards~~

17

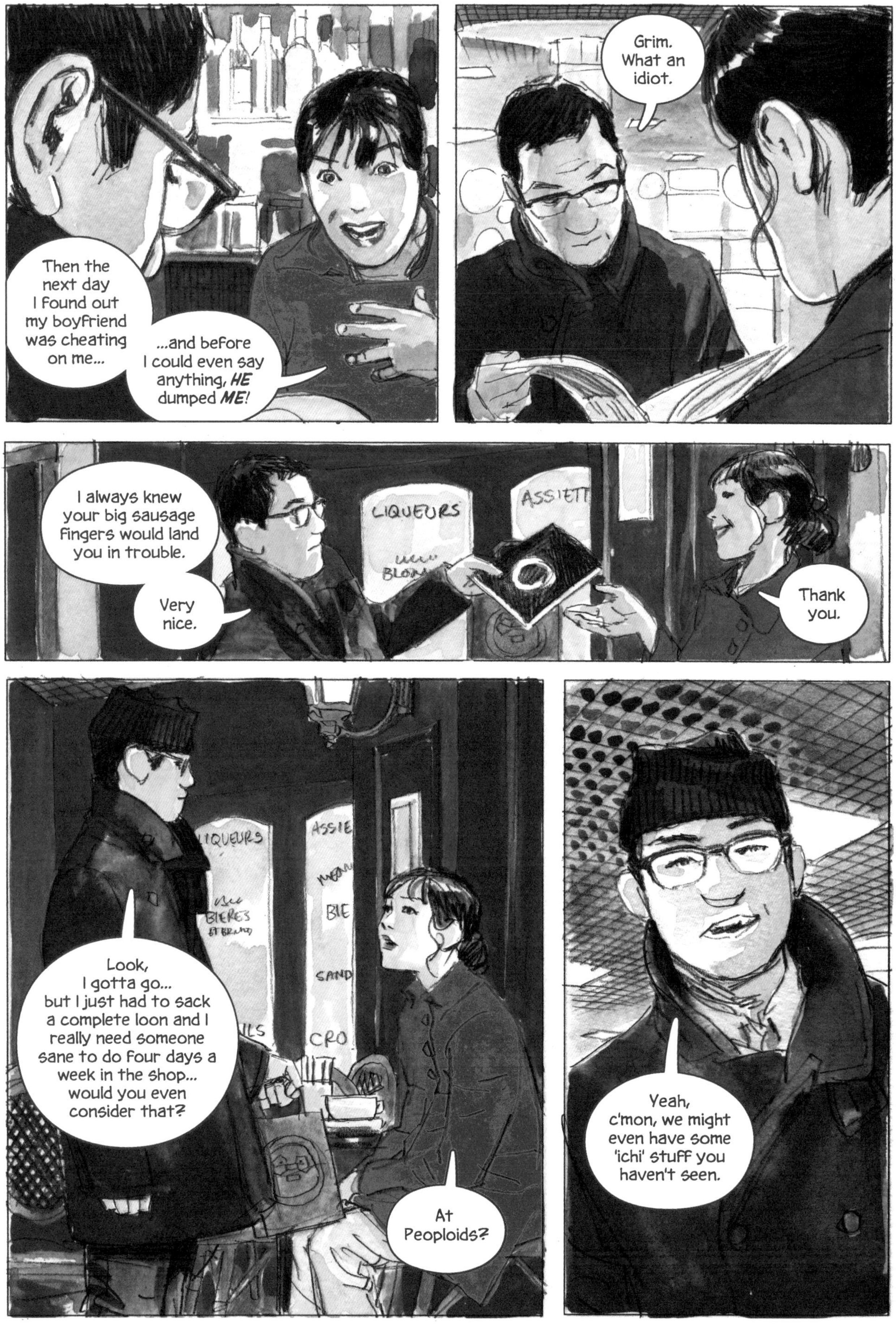
Then the next day I found out my boyfriend was cheating on me...
...and before I could even say anything, HE dumped ME!
Grim. What an idiot.
I always knew your big sausage fingers would land you in trouble.
Very nice.
Thank you.
LIQUEURS
ASSIETT
Look, I gotta go... but I just had to sack a complete loon and I really need someone sane to do four days a week in the shop... would you even consider that?
At Peoploids?
Yeah, c'mon, we might even have some 'ichi' stuff you haven't seen.

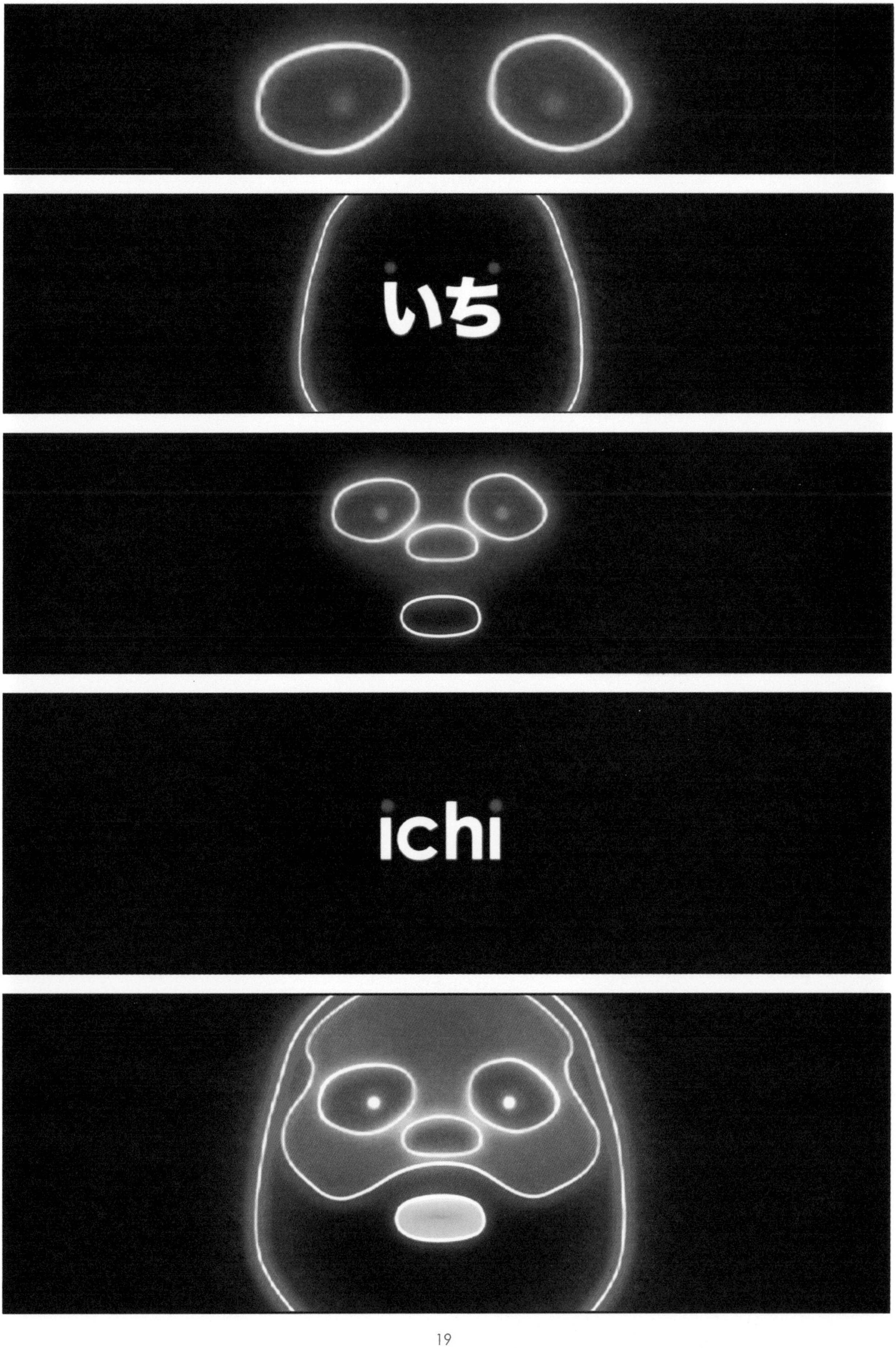
いち
ichi

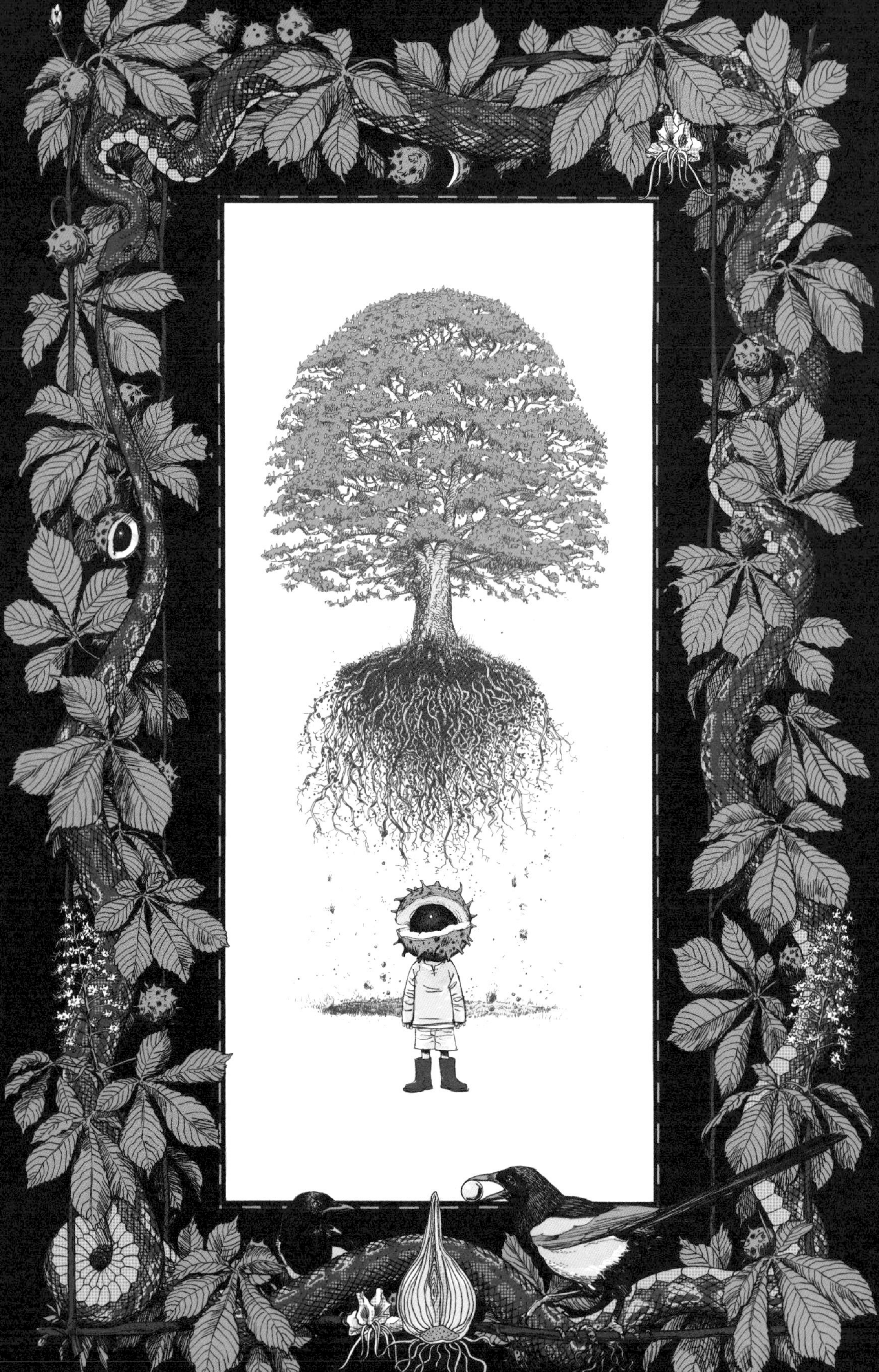

Once upon a time there was a warring family who possessed riches aplenty but had secured little happiness... One night, by the light of a full moon, the Nothing... disguised as a brown snake, came upon their house and turned them all into a single tree, all except the youngest son Pictor, who was good... he was playing down by the lake, with the fireflies, so as to avoid his squabbling brood.

But this clan was no ordinary clan and therefore the tree was no ordinary tree: it grew 'barbed nuts' across its boughs in order to continue its quarrel. The tree, whose branches now bickered amongst themselves, fought so hard it wrenched itself from the ground.

The good boy Pictor, on returning from the lake to find his family uprooted, fell to his knees broken hearted. He started eating the stones around him, in order to kill himself.

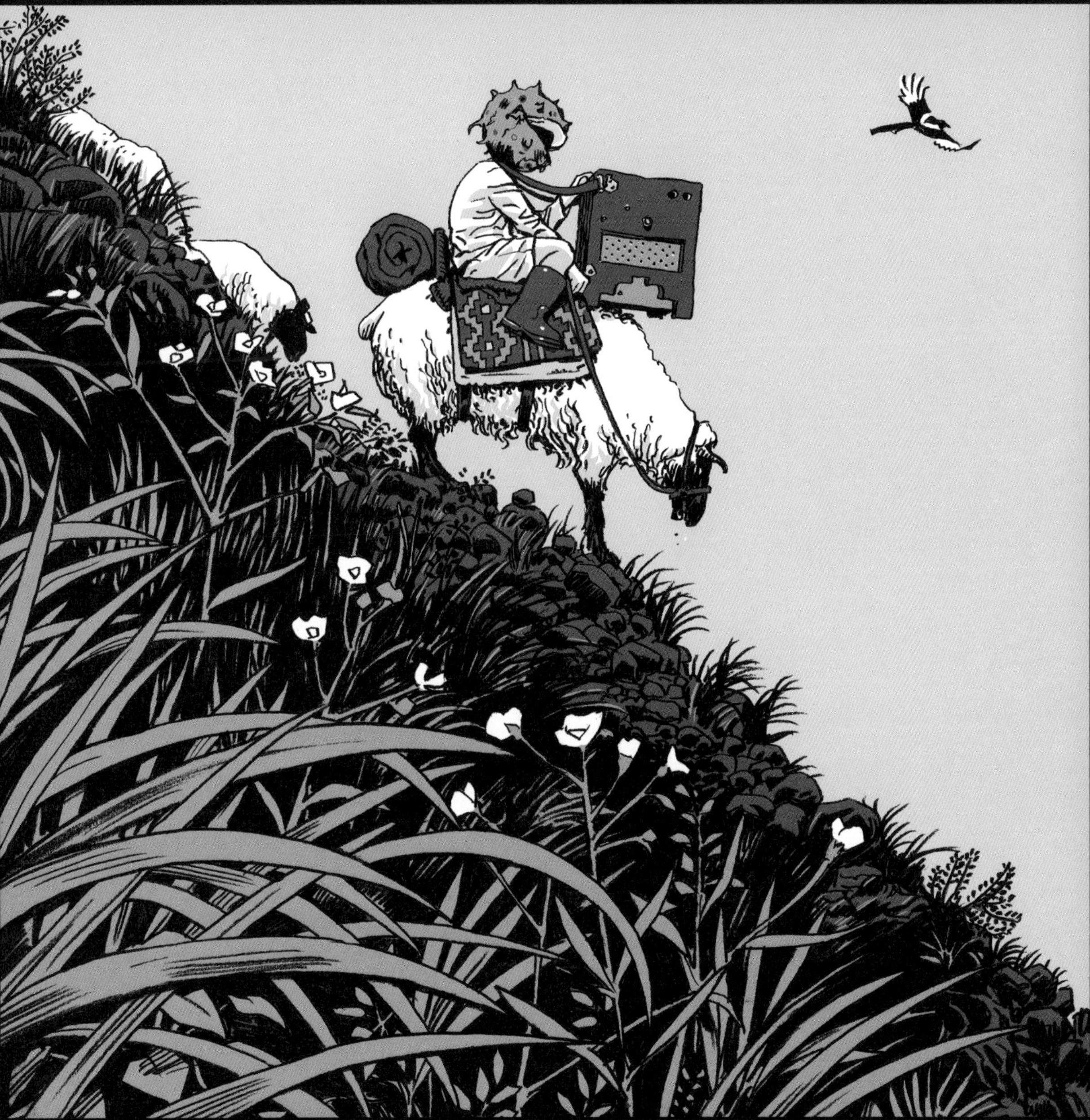

On seeing this, the Nothing became a pair of 'pies' and fetched the most perfect, small white stone. When Pictor ate this stone he turned part boy, part tree. Then the two birds said to Pictor "You will be half boy, half tree, for a long dozen and three more years and if during that time nobody falls in love with you... you and your family will stay this way forever..."

The tree was untroubled, knowing how good a boy Pictor was. It insisted he go find a wife as soon as he could... then it said, no, he must stay and look after the house... and so the quarrelling began anew.

Good Pictor turned from his tree saying, "I shall shoe my sheep and head for the woods. I promise to come back married..."

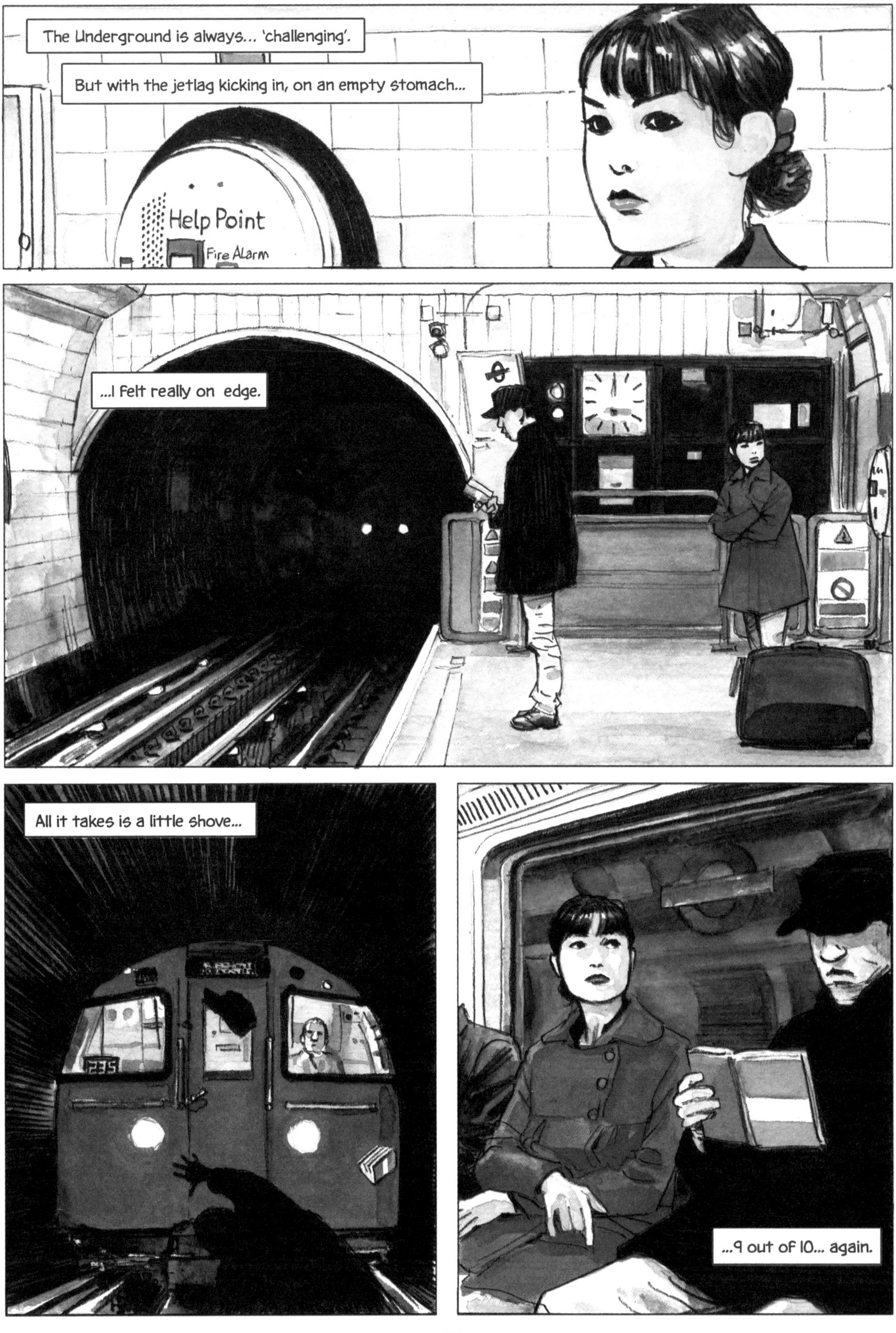
The Underground is always... 'challenging'.
But with the jetlag kicking in, on an empty stomach...
Help Point
Fire Alarm
...I felt really on edge.
All it takes is a little shove...
...9 out of 10... again.

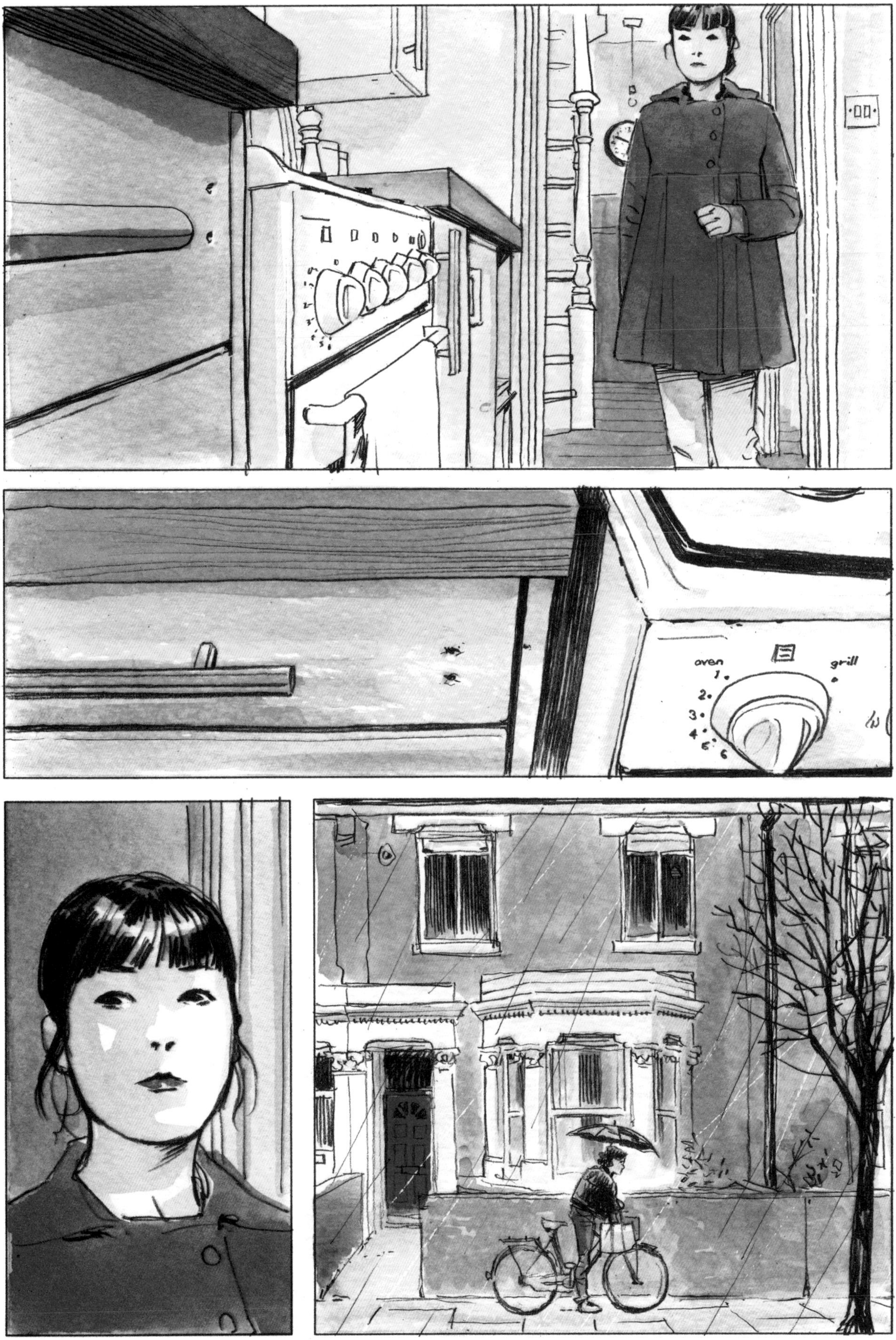
oven
grill
1
2
3
4
5
6

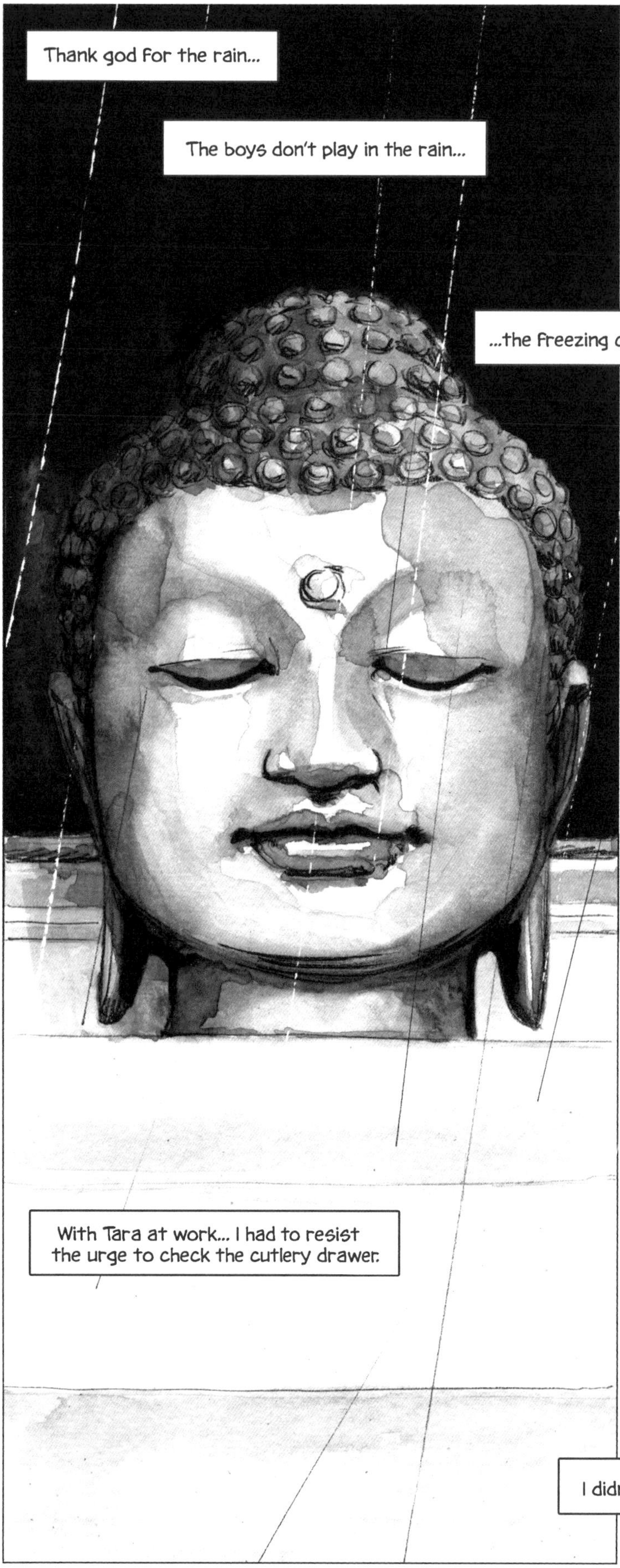
Thank god for the rain...
The boys don't play in the rain...
...the freezing cold, but not the rain.
With Tara at work... I had to resist the urge to check the cutlery drawer.

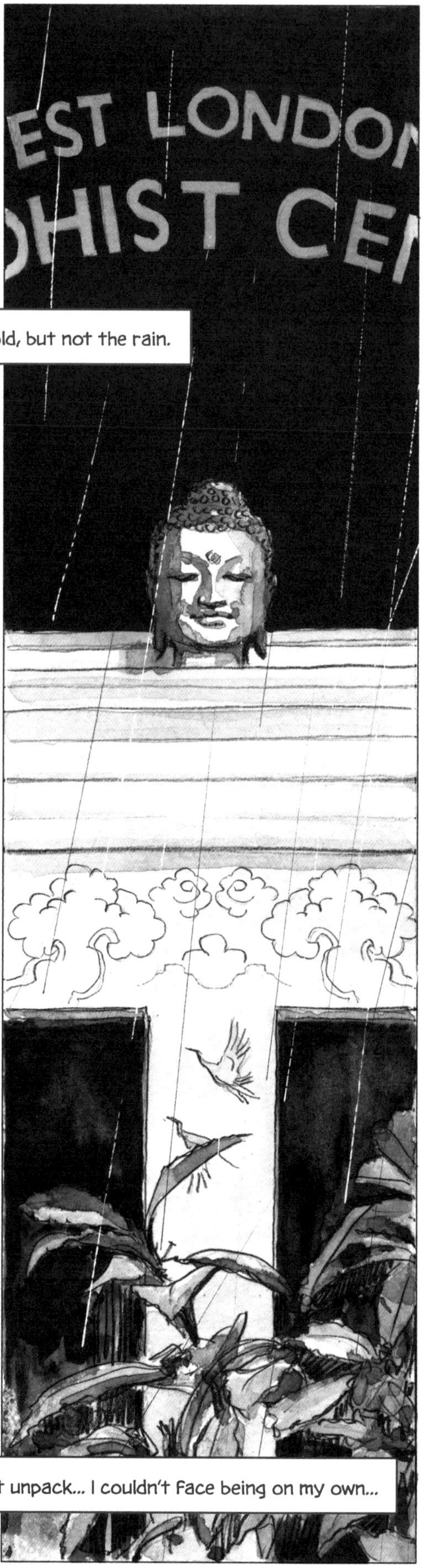
EST LONDON
DHIST CEN
I didn't unpack... I couldn't face being on my own...

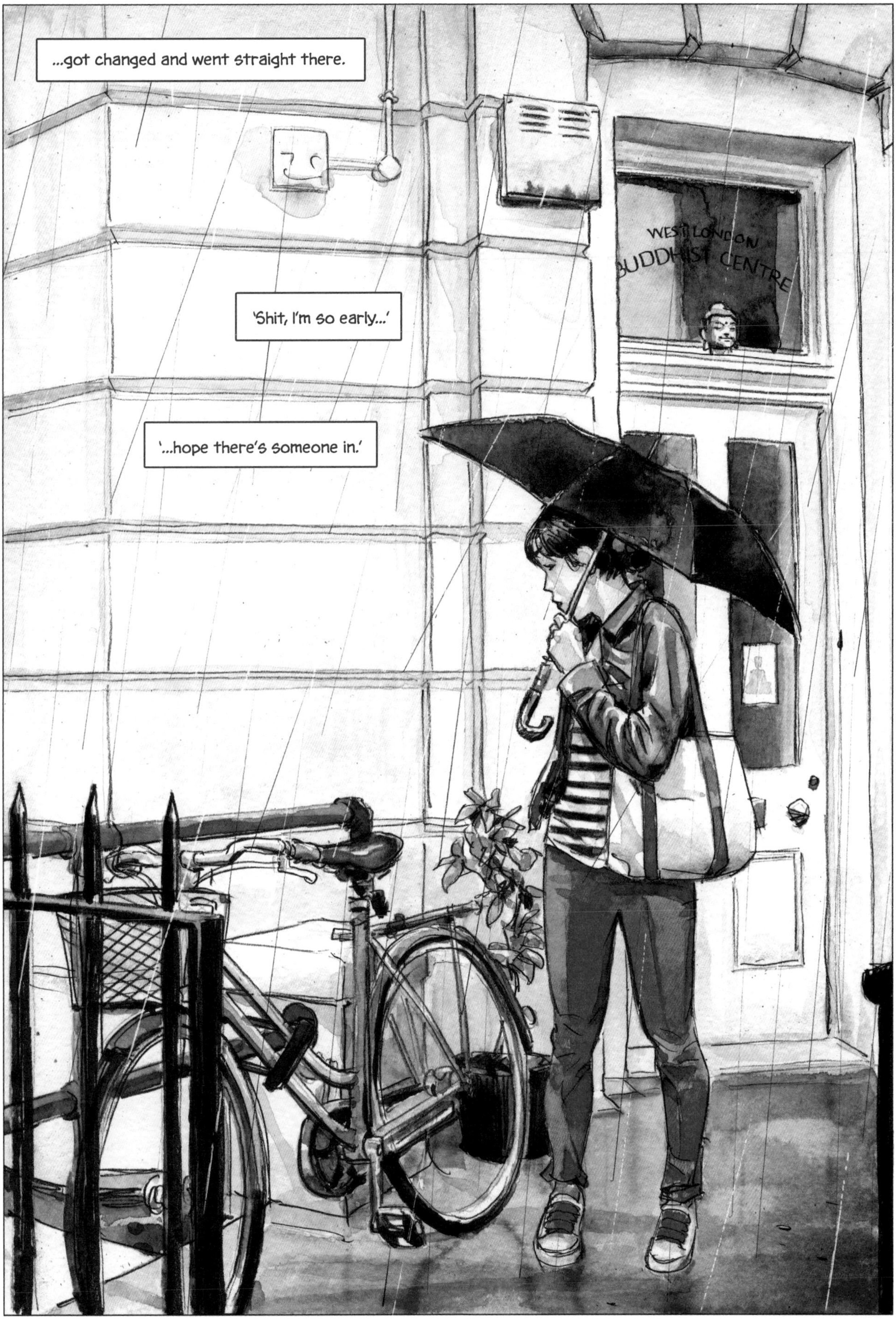
...got changed and went straight there.
WEST LONDON
BUDDHIST CENTRE
'Shit, I'm so early...'
'...hope there's someone in.'

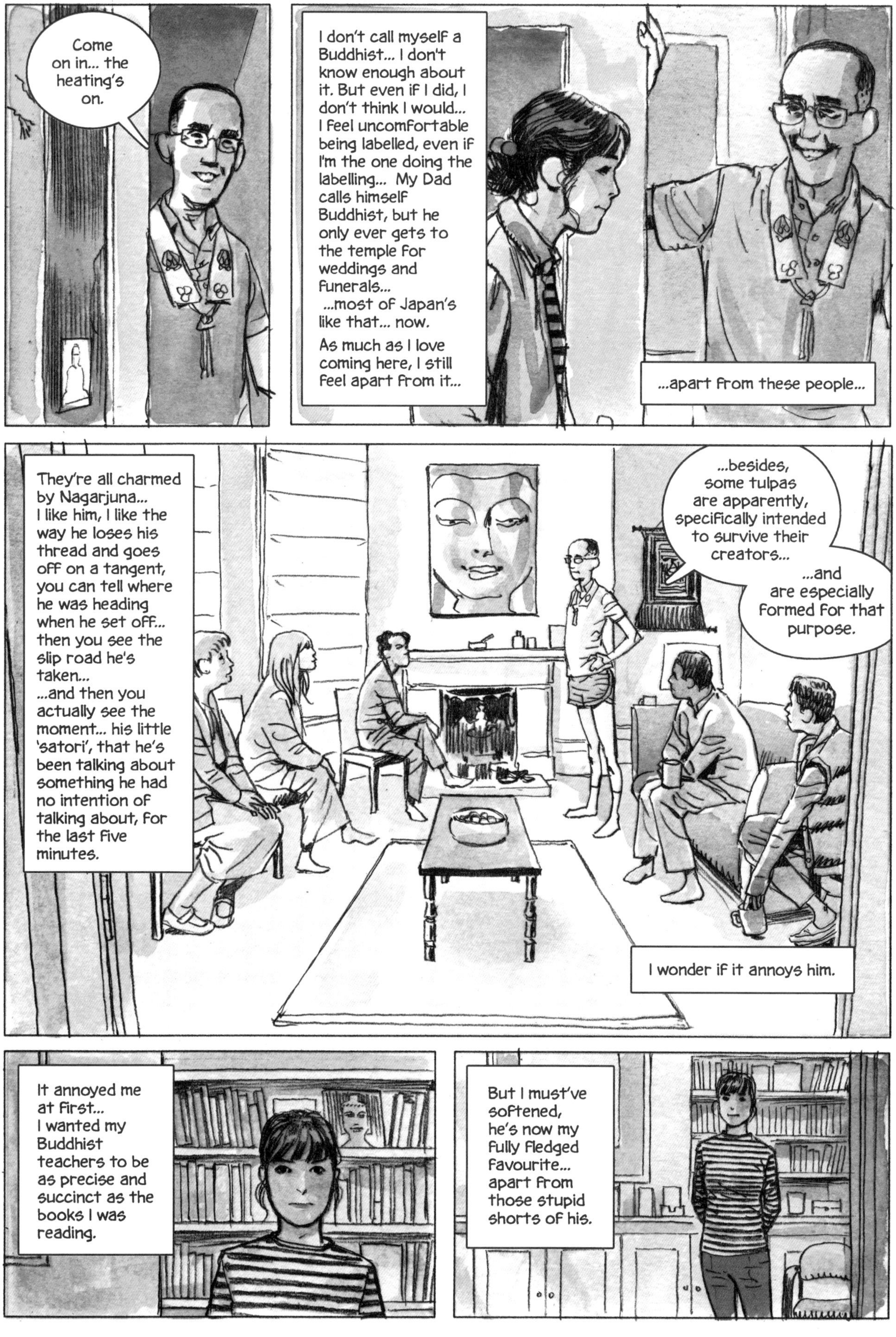
Come on in... the heating's on.
I don't call myself a Buddhist... I don't know enough about it. But even if I did, I don't think I would... I feel uncomfortable being labelled, even if I'm the one doing the labelling... My Dad calls himself Buddhist, but he only ever gets to the temple for weddings and funerals...
...most of Japan's like that... now.
As much as I love coming here, I still feel apart from it...
...apart from these people...
They're all charmed by Nagarjuna... I like him, I like the way he loses his thread and goes off on a tangent, you can tell where he was heading when he set off... then you see the slip road he's taken... ...and then you actually see the moment... his little 'satori', that he's been talking about something he had no intention of talking about, for the last five minutes.
...besides, some tulpas are apparently, specifically intended to survive their creators...
...and are especially formed for that purpose.
I wonder if it annoys him.
It annoyed me at first... I wanted my Buddhist teachers to be as precise and succinct as the books I was reading.
But I must've softened, he's now my fully fledged favourite... apart from those stupid shorts of his.

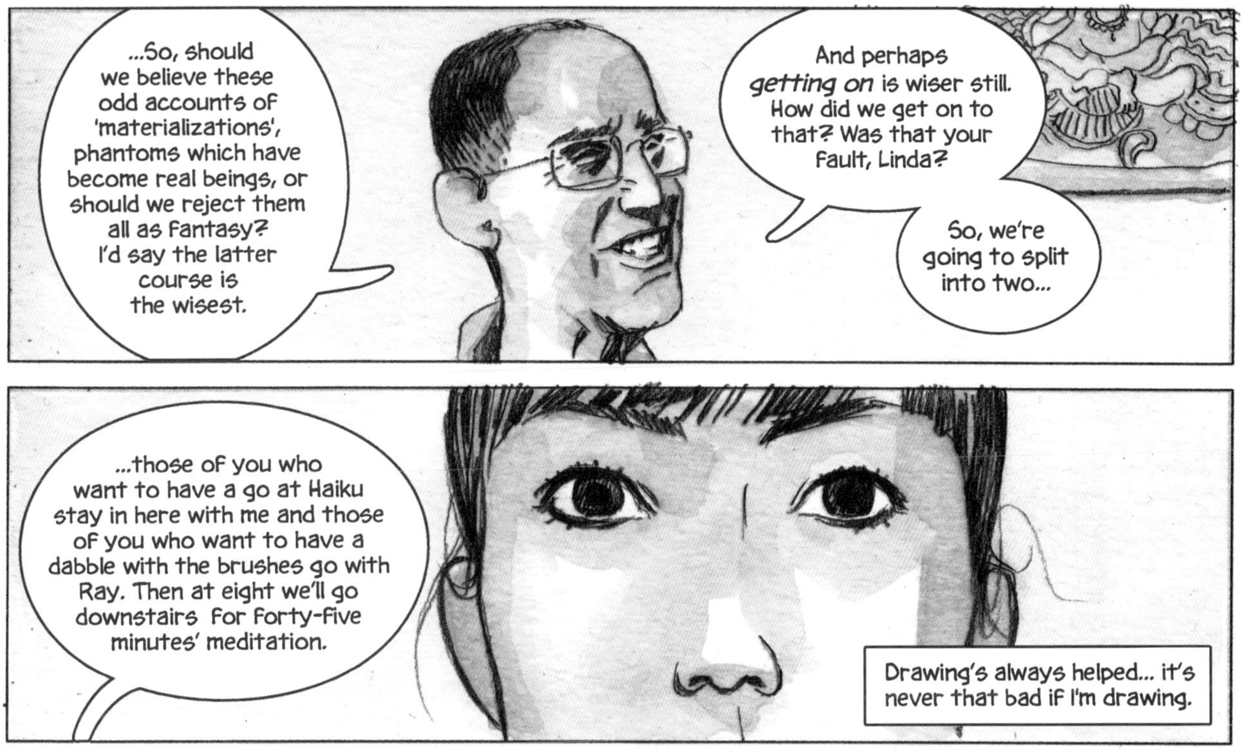
...So, should we believe these odd accounts of 'materializations', phantoms which have become real beings, or should we reject them all as fantasy? I'd say the latter course is the wisest.
And perhaps *getting on* is wiser still. How did we get on to that? Was that your fault, Linda?
So, we're going to split into two...
...those of you who want to have a go at Haiku stay in here with me and those of you who want to have a dabble with the brushes go with Ray. Then at eight we'll go downstairs for forty-five minutes' meditation.
Drawing's always helped... it's never that bad if I'm drawing.

Most of the men join me in heading for the end of the room with brushes and ink, only a few stay behind with the ladies to come up with something snappy in seventeen syllables.

The men who come here all seem really... well, nice, obviously Romantics... and one or two obviously gay.

...Dignaga, however, is a different story, he's got something about him, looks like an old punk or an ex-junkie, maybe it's his Shane MacGowan smile... and that 'doesn't suffer fools gladly' air he has about him...

The way he looks at me, I just feel stupid... I'm sure he knows I'm stupid... so naturally I dislike him... yet at the same time I feel the desperate need to please *him* more than anyone else.

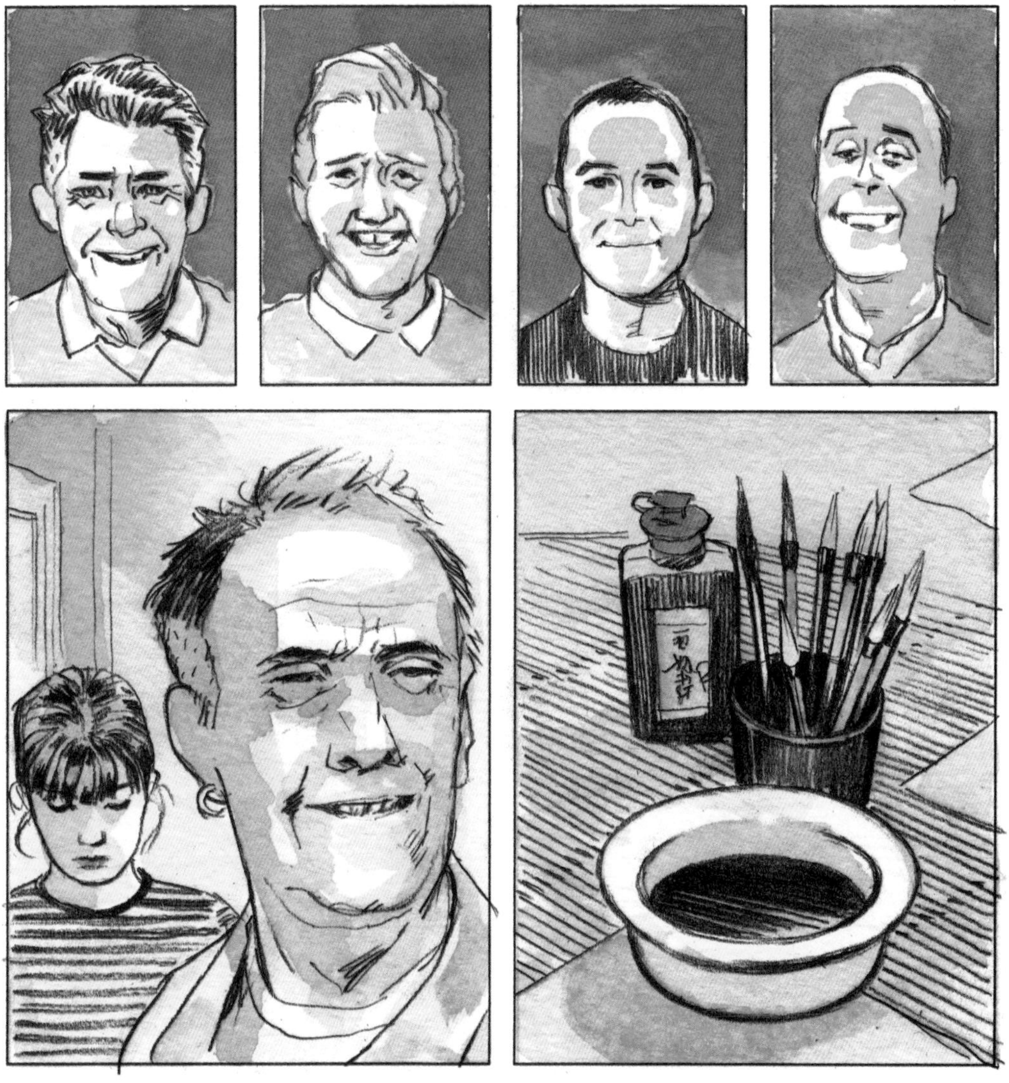

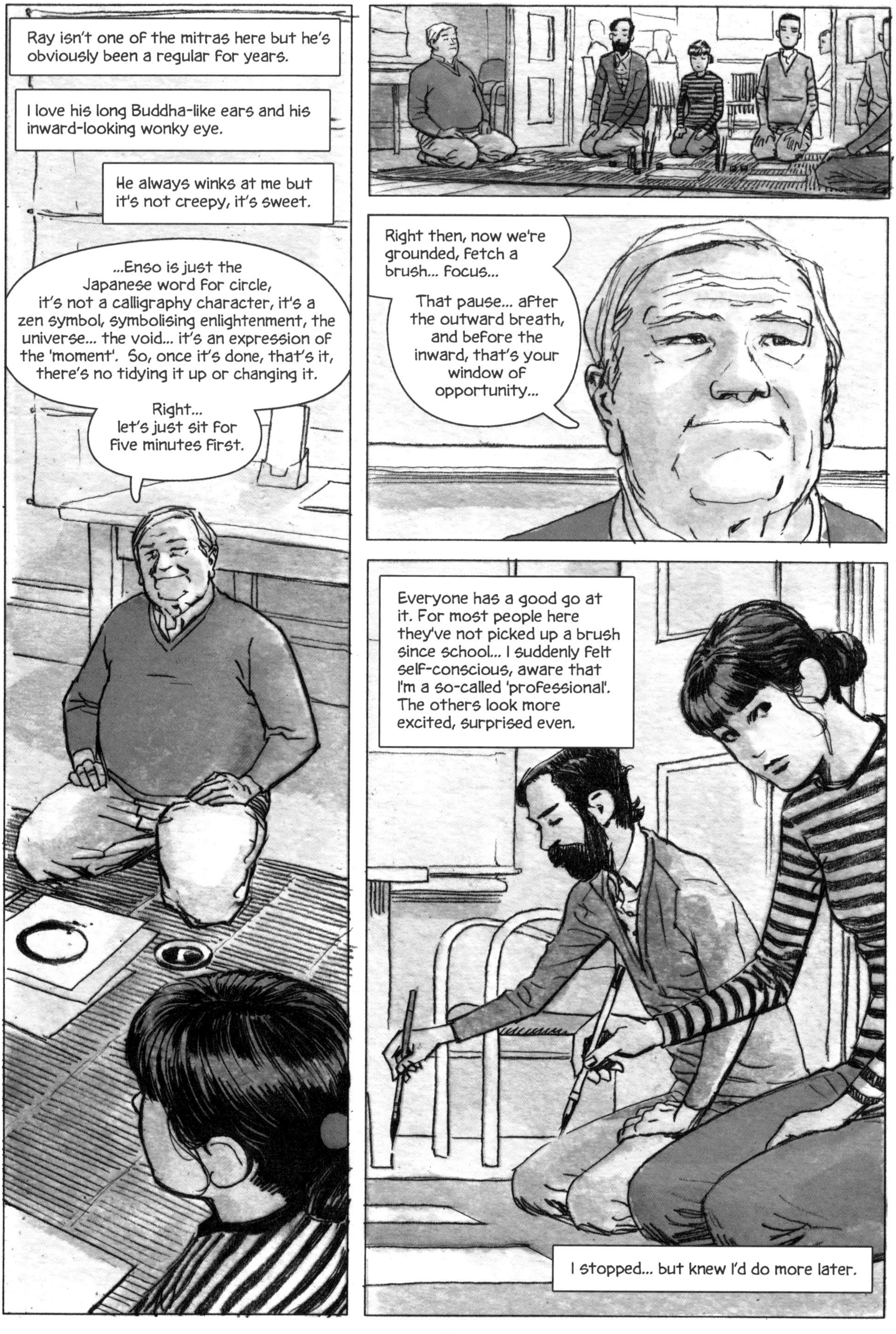

Ray isn't one of the mitras here but he's obviously been a regular for years.
I love his long Buddha-like ears and his inward-looking wonky eye.
He always winks at me but it's not creepy, it's sweet.
...Enso is just the Japanese word for circle, it's not a calligraphy character, it's a zen symbol, symbolising enlightenment, the universe... the void... it's an expression of the 'moment'. So, once it's done, that's it, there's no tidying it up or changing it.
Right... let's just sit for five minutes first.
Right then, now we're grounded, fetch a brush... focus...
That pause... after the outward breath, and before the inward, that's your window of opportunity...
Everyone has a good go at it. For most people here they've not picked up a brush since school... I suddenly felt self-conscious, aware that I'm a so-called 'professional'. The others look more excited, surprised even.
I stopped... but knew I'd do more later.

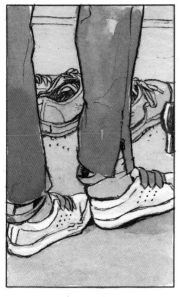

I secure the spot I've made my own... near the door, for air... next to Dignaga and opposite Nagarjuna, because I figure, if I can hear him properly, I'll be able to concentrate better.

But the incense was putting me on edge.

I've really got quite an aversion to incense...

...gets up my nose.

'Oh... *god*, his knob's poking out of those *stupid* shorts.'

'...again.'

...When you feel yourself drifting, just gently return yourself to 'one' and start over. Remember, be gentle, the thoughts will recede... we can't control what comes up... the best we...

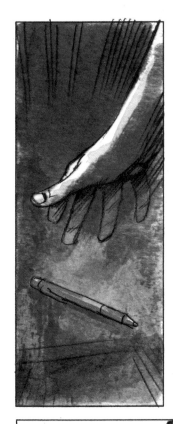

...to let it go...

Forty minutes... 'Mindfulness of breathing' ...

Donnnnnnnnnggggg

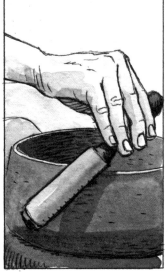

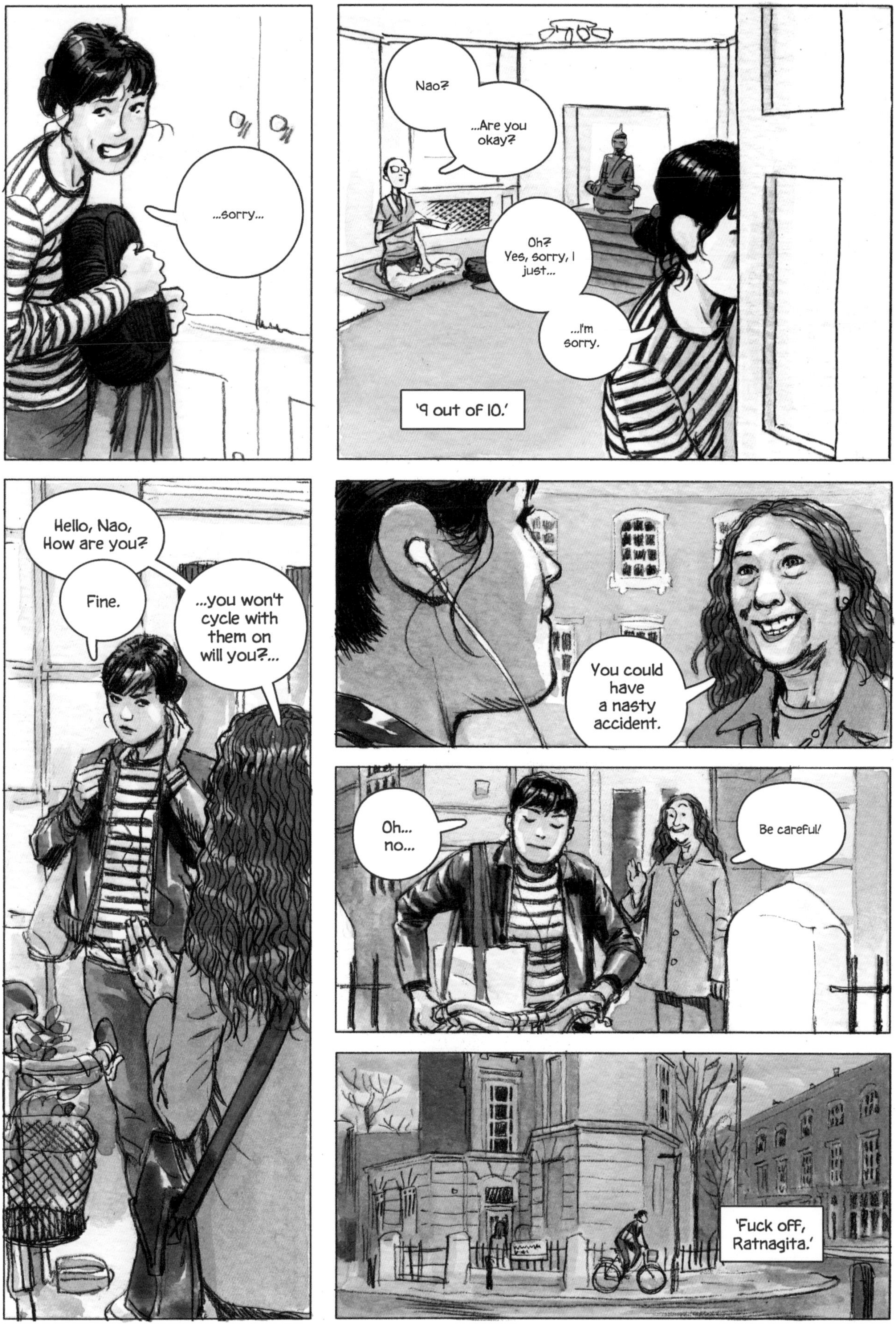
...sorry...
Nao?
...Are you okay?
Oh? Yes, sorry, I just...
...I'm sorry.
'9 out of 10.'
Hello, Nao, How are you?
Fine.
...you won't cycle with them on will you?...
You could have a nasty accident.
Oh... no...
Be careful!
'Fuck off, Ratnagita.'

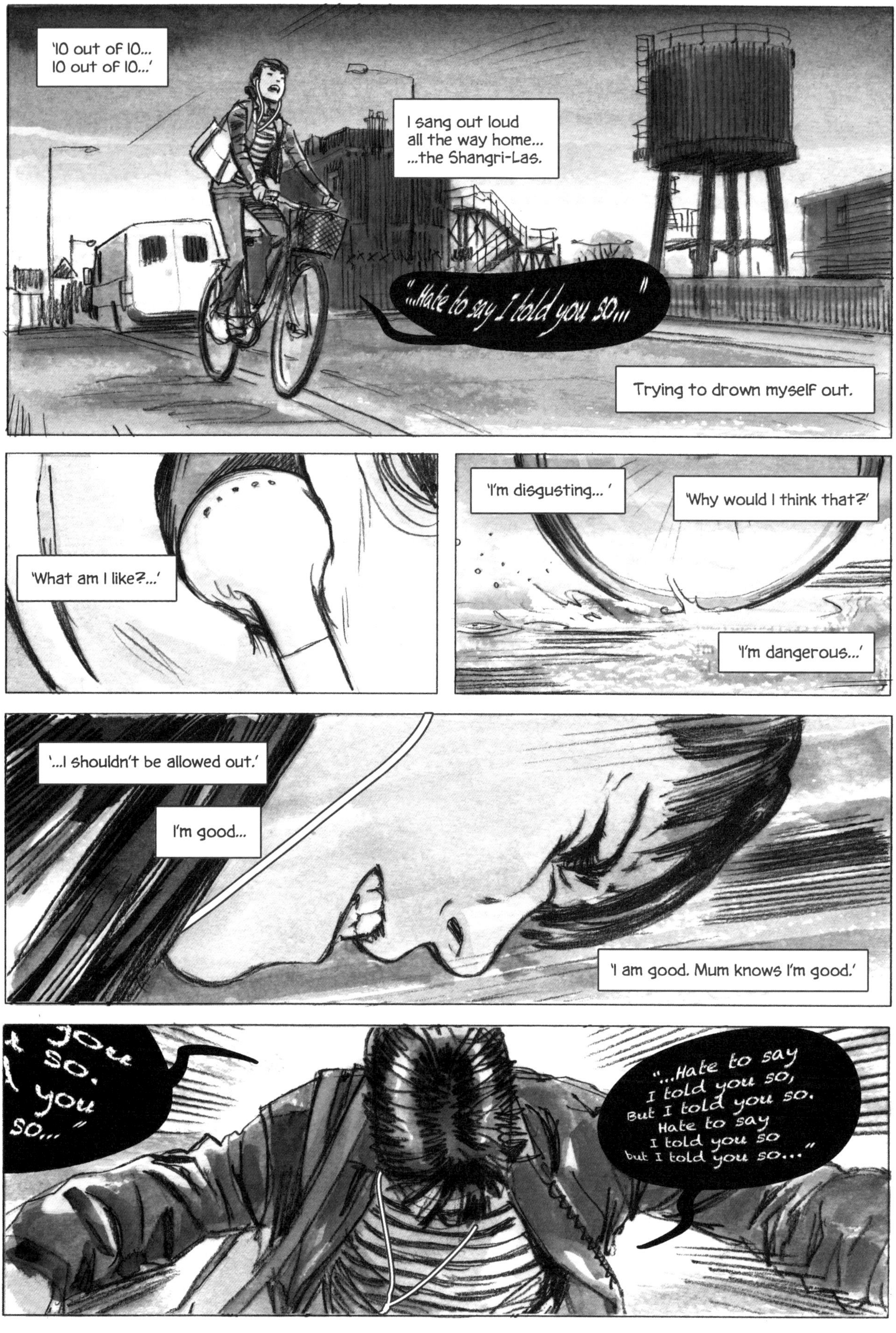
'10 out of 10... 10 out of 10...'
I sang out loud all the way home... ...the Shangri-Las.
"...Hate to say I told you so..."
Trying to drown myself out.
'What am I like?...'
'I'm disgusting... '
'Why would I think that?'
'I'm dangerous...'
'...I shouldn't be allowed out.'
I'm good...
'I am good. Mum knows I'm good.'
you so. you so..."
"...Hate to say I told you so, But I told you so. Hate to say I told you so but I told you so..."

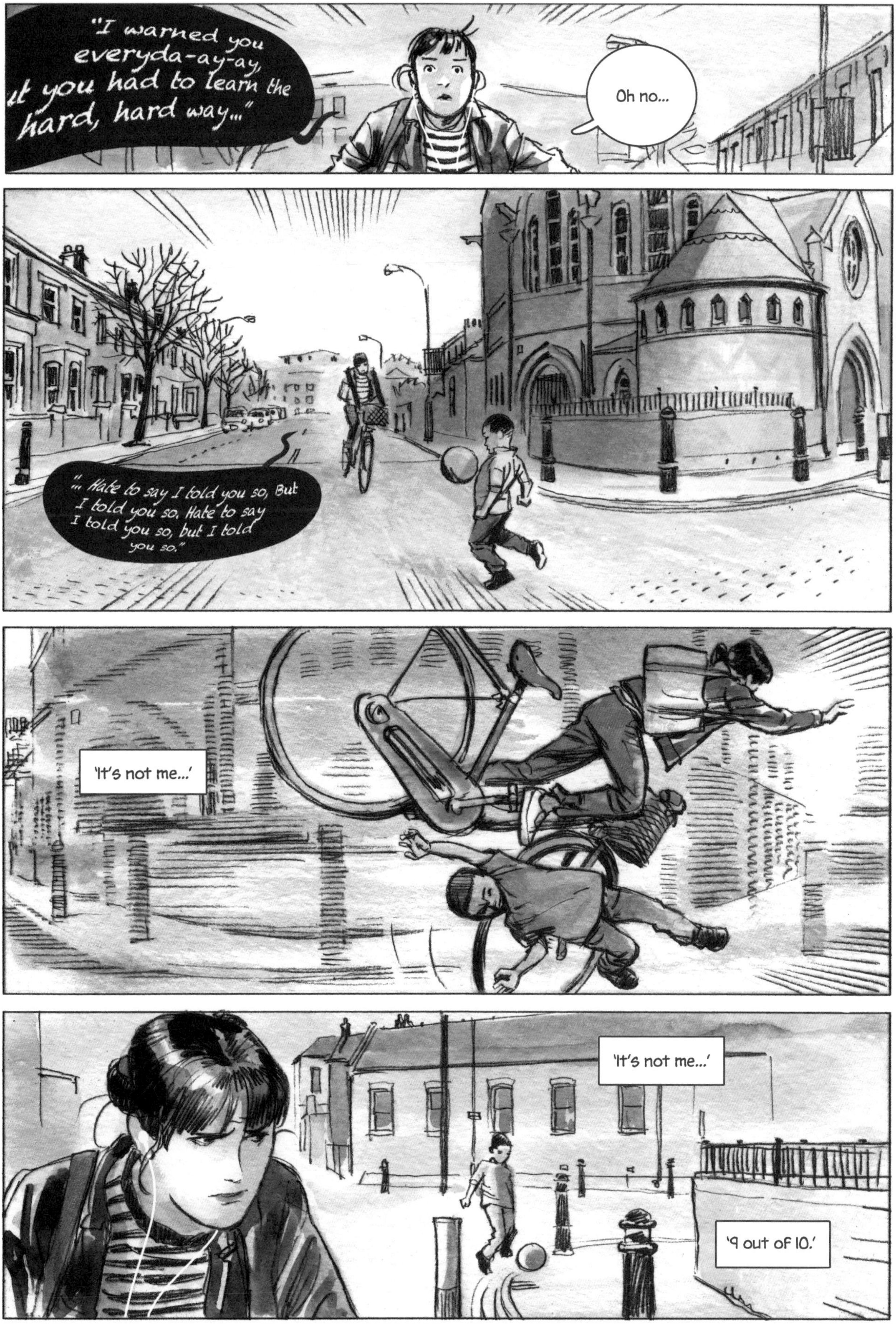
"I warned you everyda-ay-ay, ut you had to learn the hard, hard way..."
Oh no...
"... Hate to say I told you so, But I told you so. Hate to say I told you so, but I told you so."
'It's not me...'
'It's not me...'
'9 out of 10.'

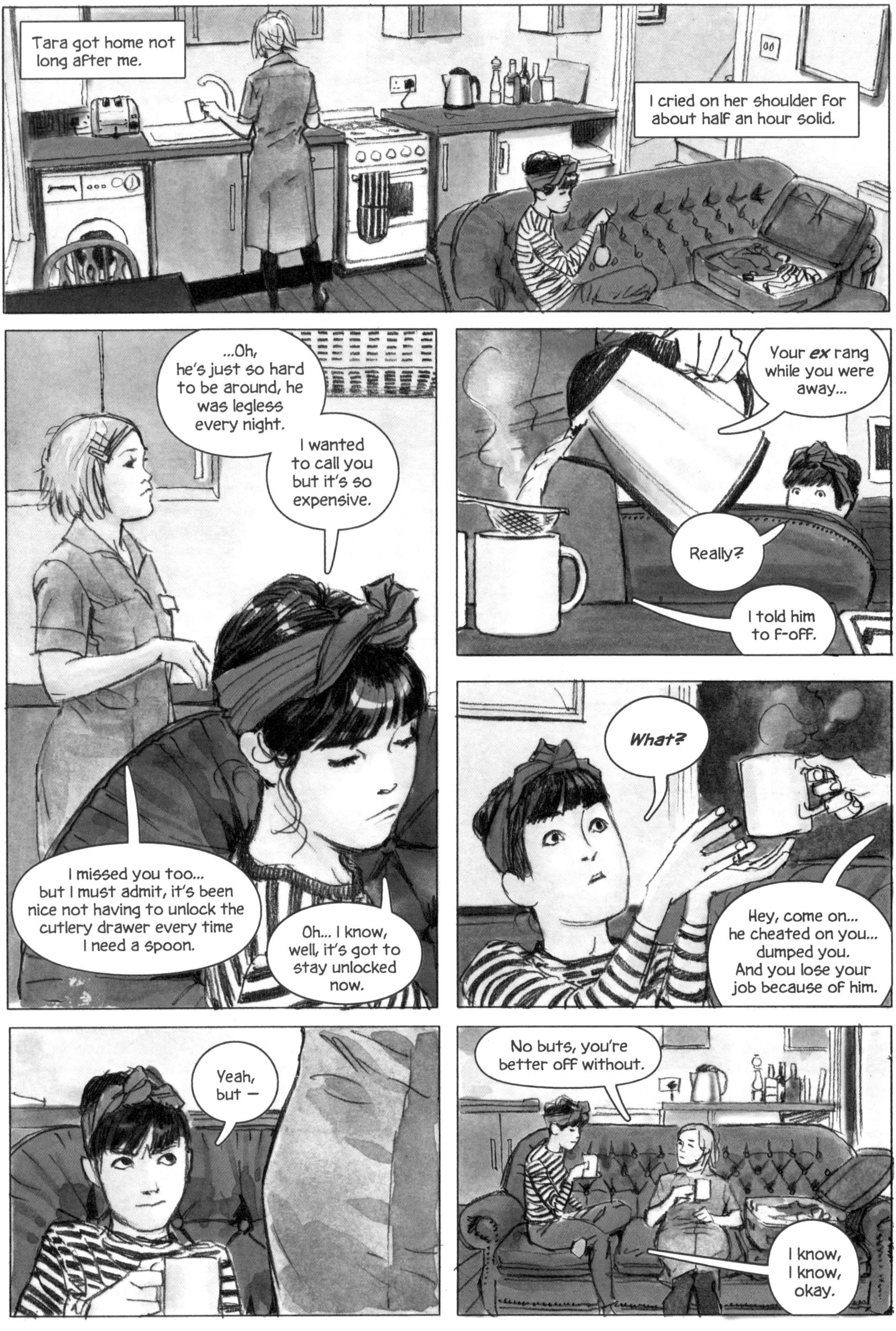
Tara got home not long after me.
I cried on her shoulder for about half an hour solid.
...Oh, he's just so hard to be around, he was legless every night.
I wanted to call you but it's so expensive.
I missed you too... but I must admit, it's been nice not having to unlock the cutlery drawer every time I need a spoon.
Oh... I know, well, it's got to stay unlocked now.
Your *ex* rang while you were away...
Really?
I told him to F-off.
What?
Hey, come on... he cheated on you... dumped you. And you lose your job because of him.
Yeah, but —
No buts, you're better off without.
I know, I know, okay.

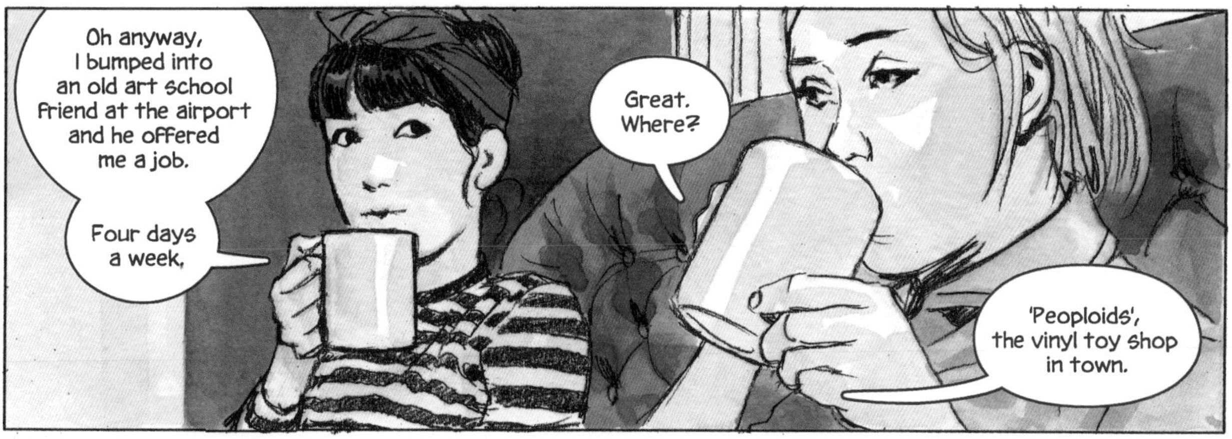
Oh anyway, I bumped into an old art school friend at the airport and he offered me a job.
Four days a week,
Great. Where?
'Peoploids', the vinyl toy shop in town.

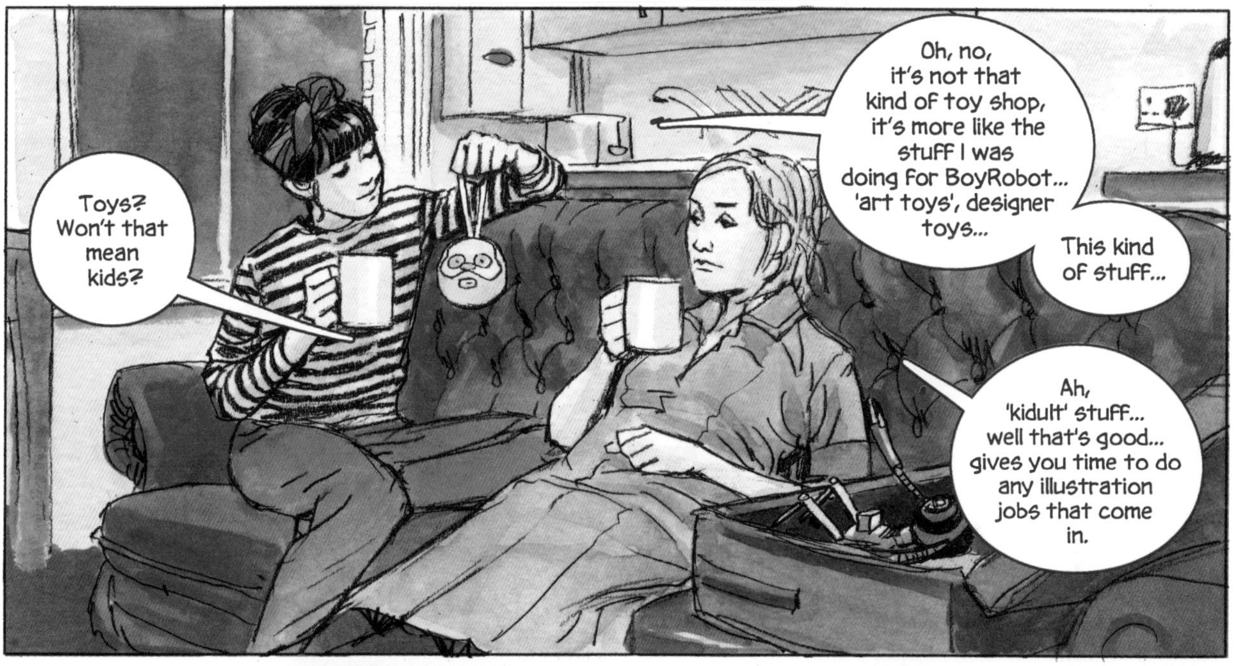
Toys? Won't that mean kids?
Oh, no, it's not that kind of toy shop, it's more like the stuff I was doing for BoyRobot... 'art toys', designer toys...
This kind of stuff...
Ah, 'kidult' stuff... well that's good... gives you time to do any illustration jobs that come in.

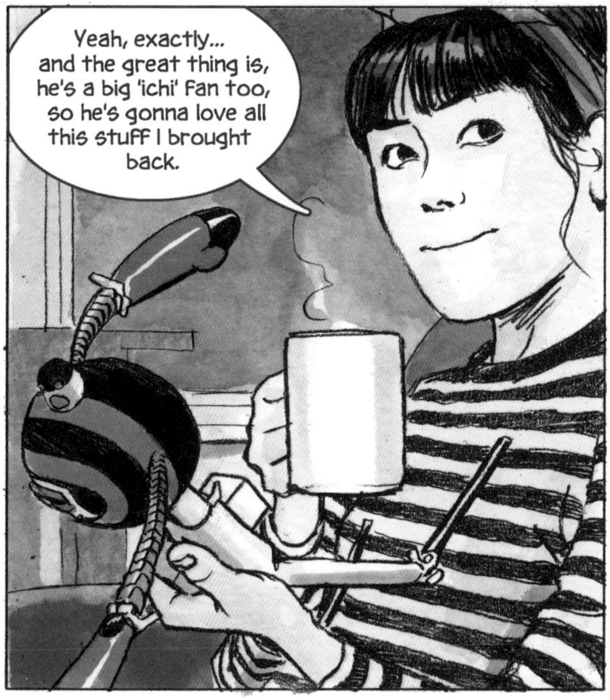
Yeah, exactly... and the great thing is, he's a big 'ichi' fan too, so he's gonna love all this stuff I brought back.

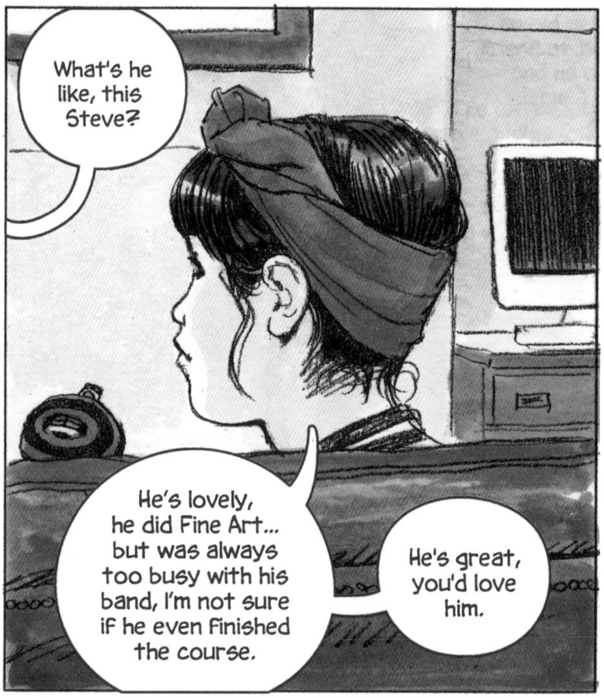
What's he like, this Steve?
He's lovely, he did Fine Art... but was always too busy with his band, I'm not sure if he even finished the course.
He's great, you'd love him.

"Oh, yeah, hey, you and him, maybe that could work..."

"...Zachaeus Stephen Meke, these days... Steve Meek."

"...He changed his name, or 're-arranged' it, as he would say, just before we started college..."

"I'm the only one who knows his secret identity."

peoploids

69

Nice hat, very 'Zizou'.

5

"...Oh, and he's the same height as me."

My first day at Peoploids was lovely... not very complicated. I followed Steve around, taking in the daily routine.

Okay, you need to read this...

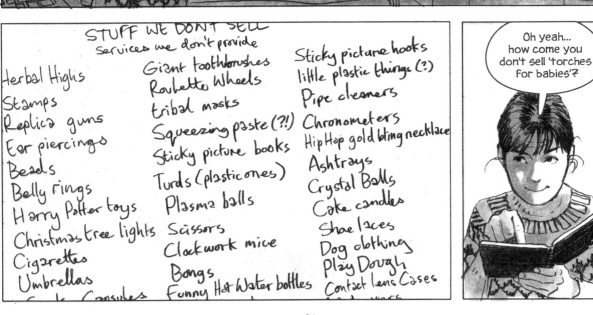

STUFF WE DON'T SELL
services we don't provide

Herbal Highs
Stamps
Replica guns
Ear piercings
Beads
Belly rings
Harry Potter toys
Christmas tree lights
Cigarettes
Umbrellas

Giant toothbrushes
Roulette Wheels
tribal masks
Squeezing paste (?!)
Sticky picture books
Turds (plastic ones)
Plasma balls
Scissors
Clockwork mice
Bongs
Funny Hot Water bottles

Sticky picture hooks
little plastic things (?)
Pipe cleaners
Chronometers
HipHop gold bling necklace
Ashtrays
Crystal Balls
Cake candles
Shoe laces
Dog clothing
Play Dough
Contact lens cases

Oh yeah... how come you don't sell 'torches for babies'?

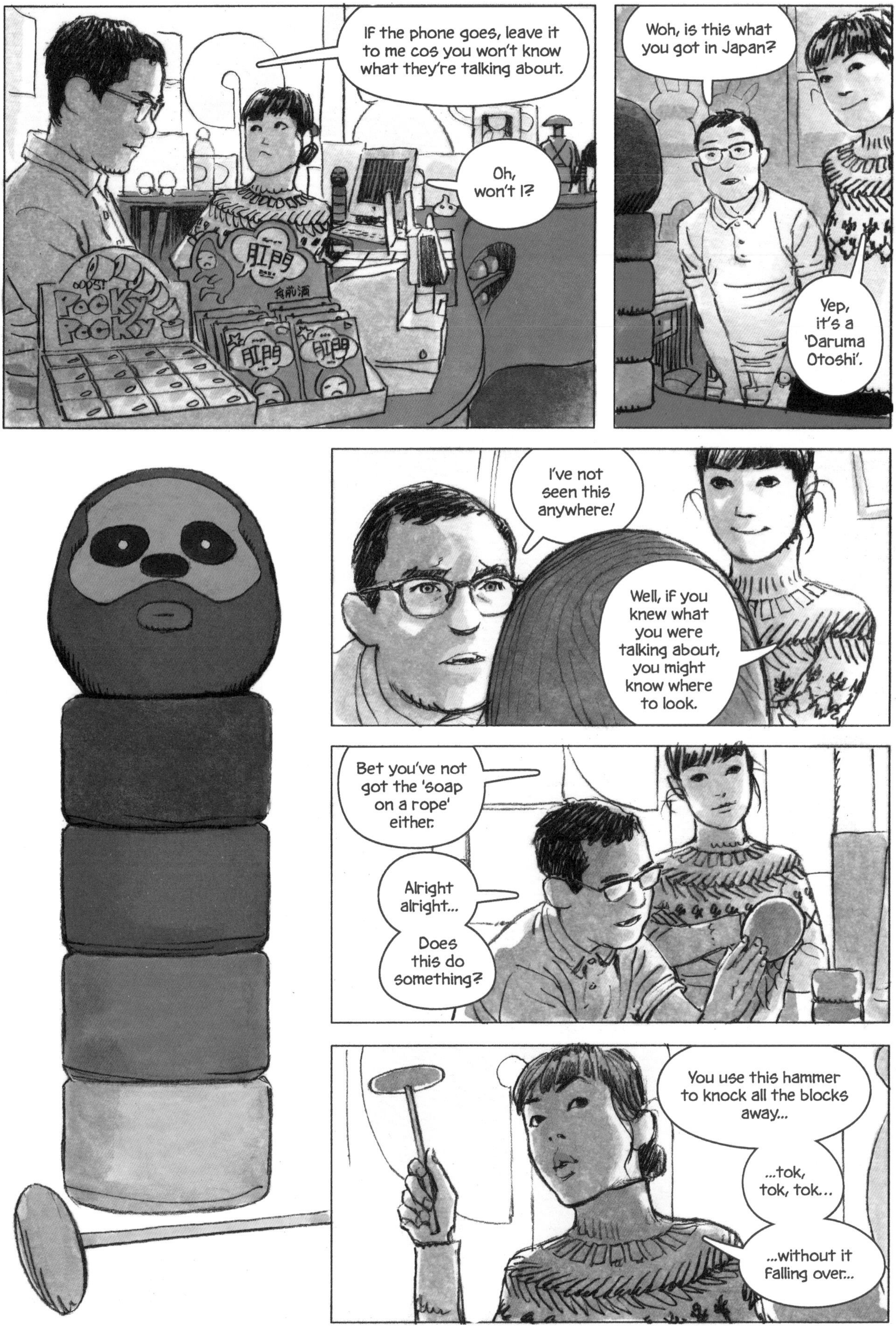
If the phone goes, leave it to me cos you won't know what they're talking about.
Oh, won't I?
肛門
Pocky Pocky
Woh, is this what you got in Japan?
Yep, it's a 'Daruma Otoshi'.
I've not seen this anywhere!
Well, if you knew what you were talking about, you might know where to look.
Bet you've not got the 'soap on a rope' either.
Alright alright...
Does this do something?
You use this hammer to knock all the blocks away...
...tok, tok, tok...
...without it falling over...

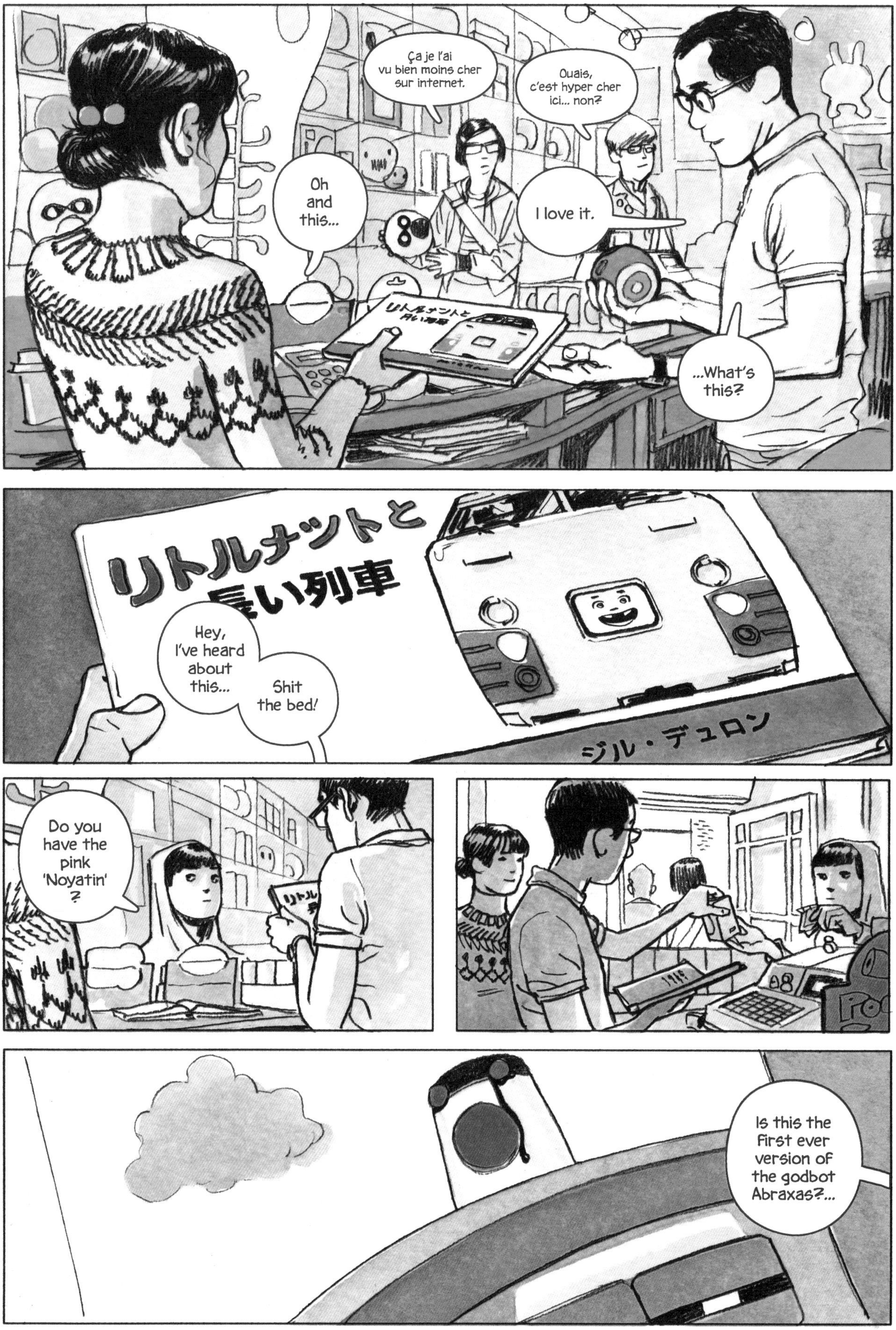
Ça je l'ai vu bien moins cher sur internet.
Ouais, c'est hyper cher ici... non?
Oh and this...
I love it.
...What's this?
リトルナットと
Hey, I've heard about this...
Shit the bed!
ジル・デュロン
Do you have the pink 'Noyatin'?
Is this the first ever version of the godbot Abraxas?...

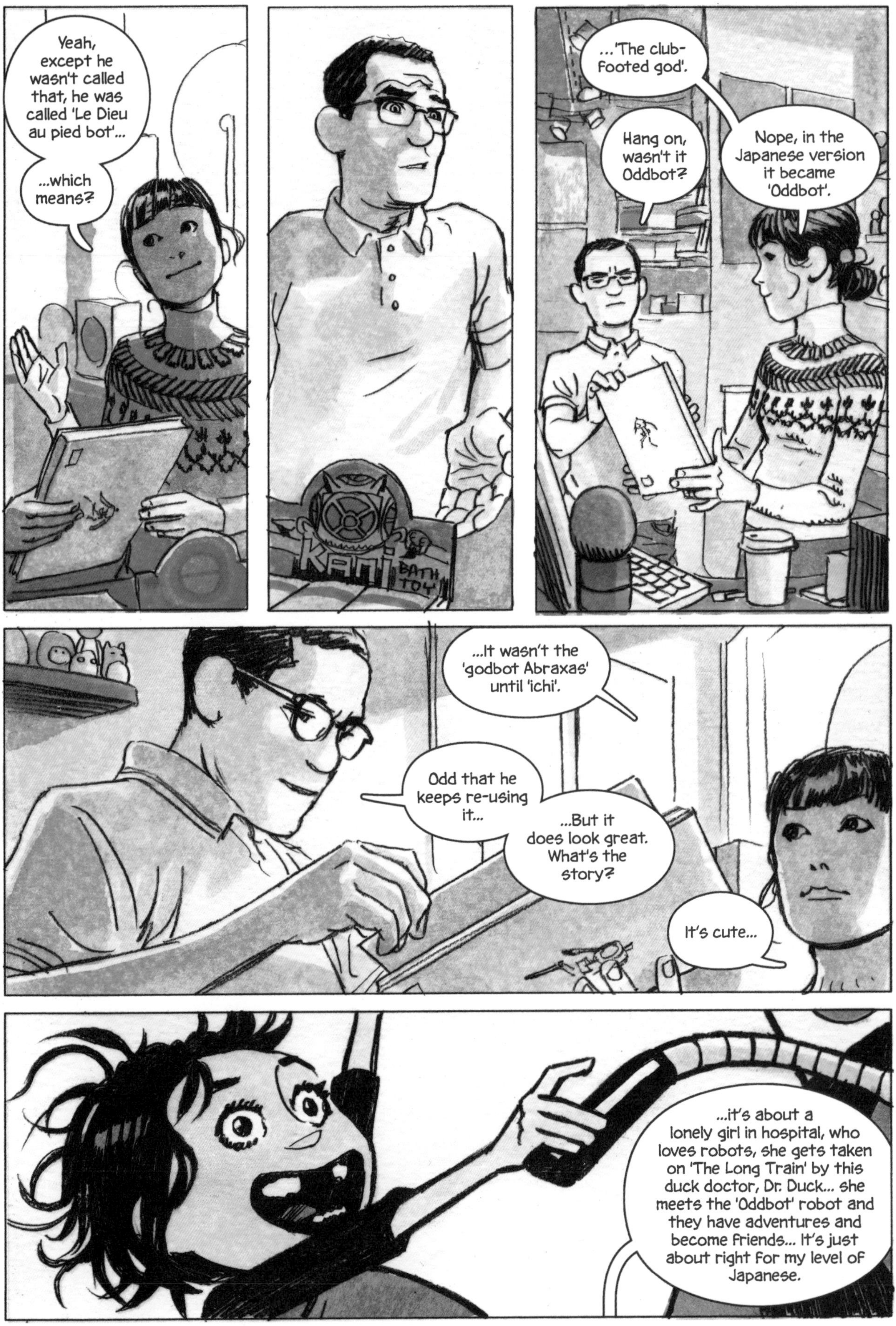
Yeah, except he wasn't called that, he was called 'Le Dieu au pied bot'...
...which means?
...'The club-footed god'.
Hang on, wasn't it Oddbot?
Nope, in the Japanese version it became 'Oddbot'.
KAMI BATH TOY
...It wasn't the 'godbot Abraxas' until 'ichi'.
Odd that he keeps re-using it...
...But it does look great. What's the story?
It's cute...
...it's about a lonely girl in hospital, who loves robots, she gets taken on 'The Long Train' by this duck doctor, Dr. Duck... she meets the 'Oddbot' robot and they have adventures and become friends... It's just about right for my level of Japanese.

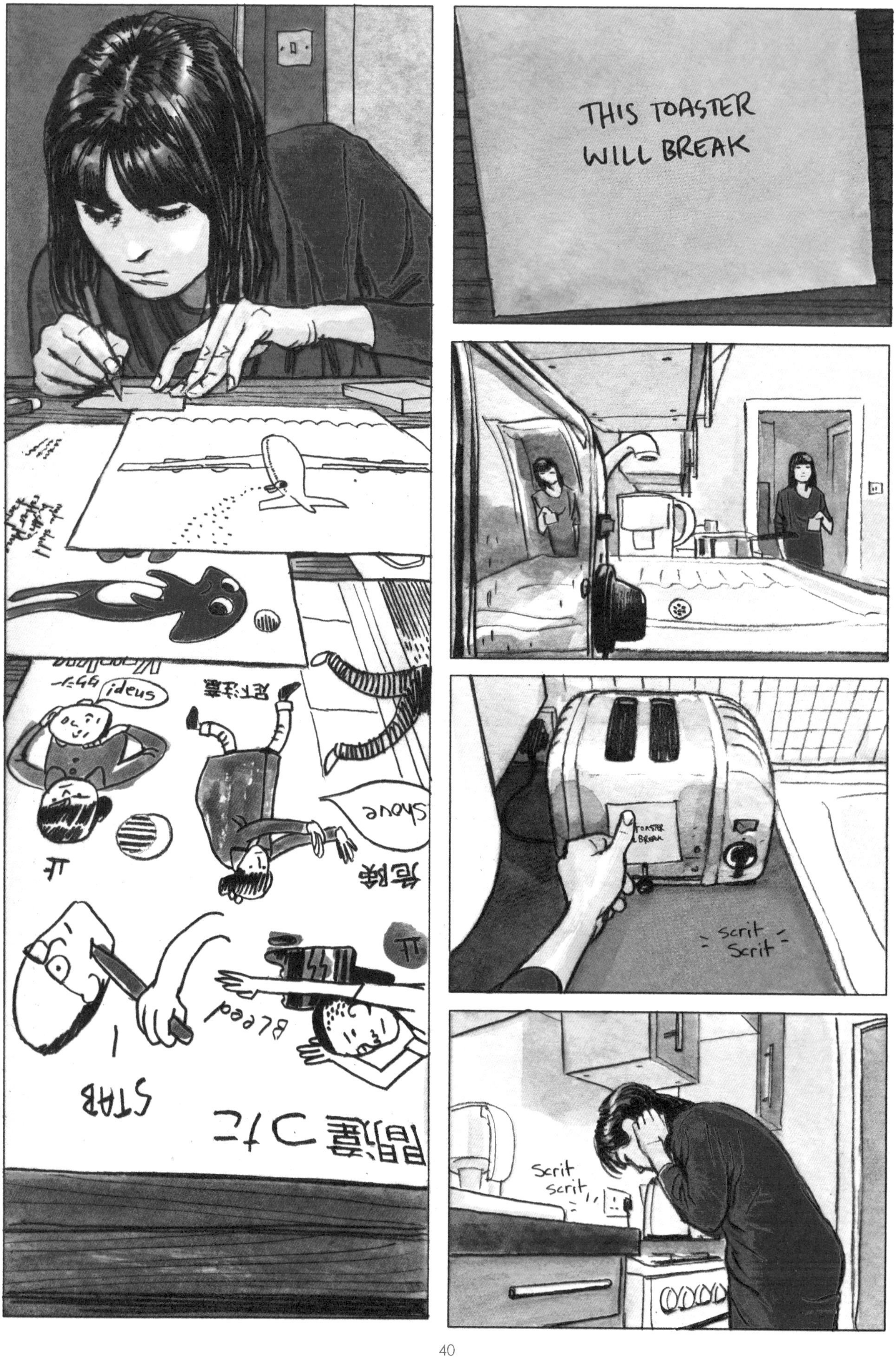

snap!
shove
危険
Bleed
STAB
間違った
THIS TOASTER WILL BREAK
scrit scrit
scrit scrit

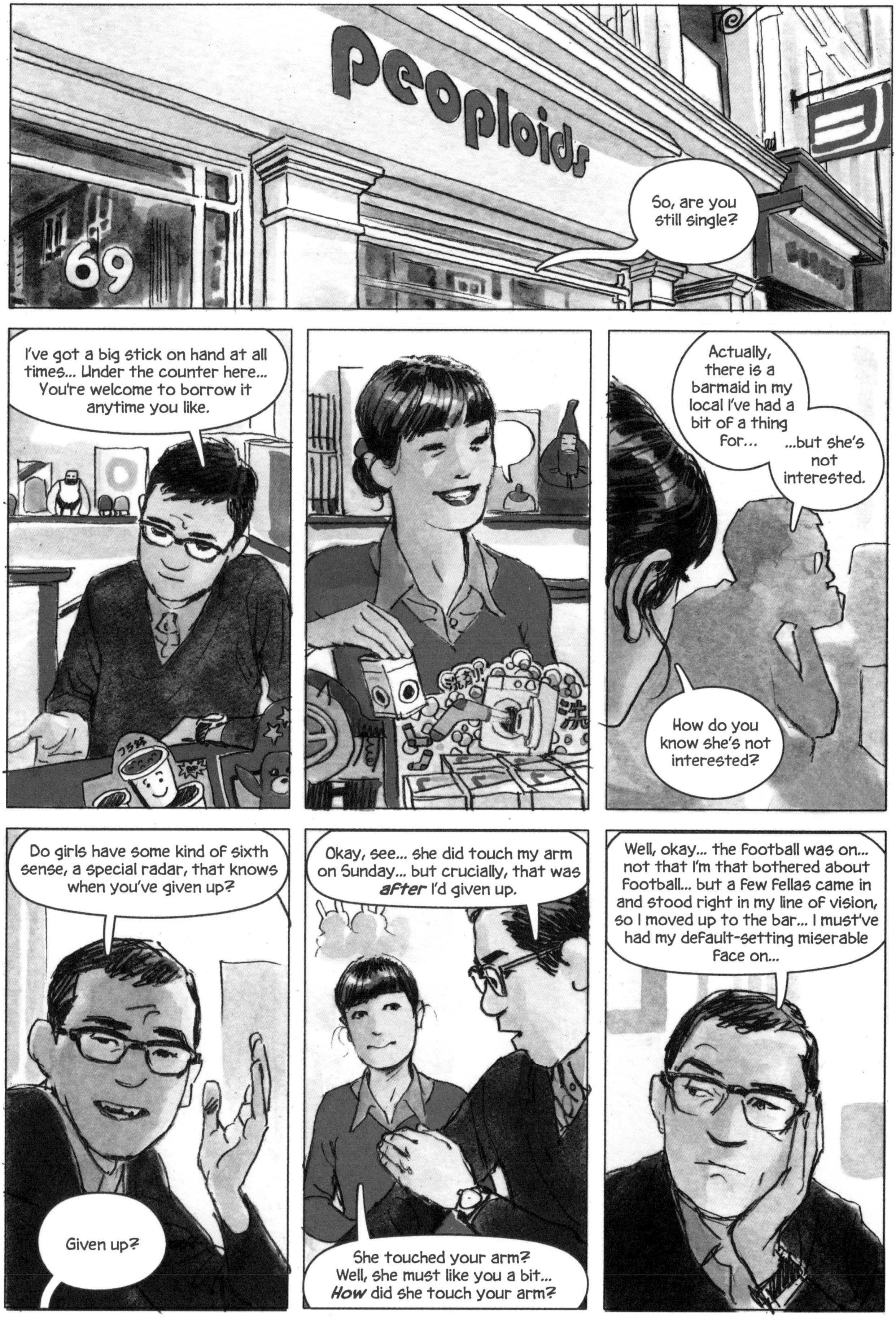
peoploids
69
So, are you still single?
I've got a big stick on hand at all times... Under the counter here... You're welcome to borrow it anytime you like.
Actually, there is a barmaid in my local I've had a bit of a thing for...
...but she's not interested.
How do you know she's not interested?
Do girls have some kind of sixth sense, a special radar, that knows when you've given up?
Given up?
Okay, see... she did touch my arm on Sunday... but crucially, that was *after* I'd given up.
She touched your arm? Well, she must like you a bit... *How* did she touch your arm?
Well, okay... the football was on... not that I'm that bothered about football... but a few fellas came in and stood right in my line of vision, so I moved up to the bar... I must've had my default-setting miserable face on...

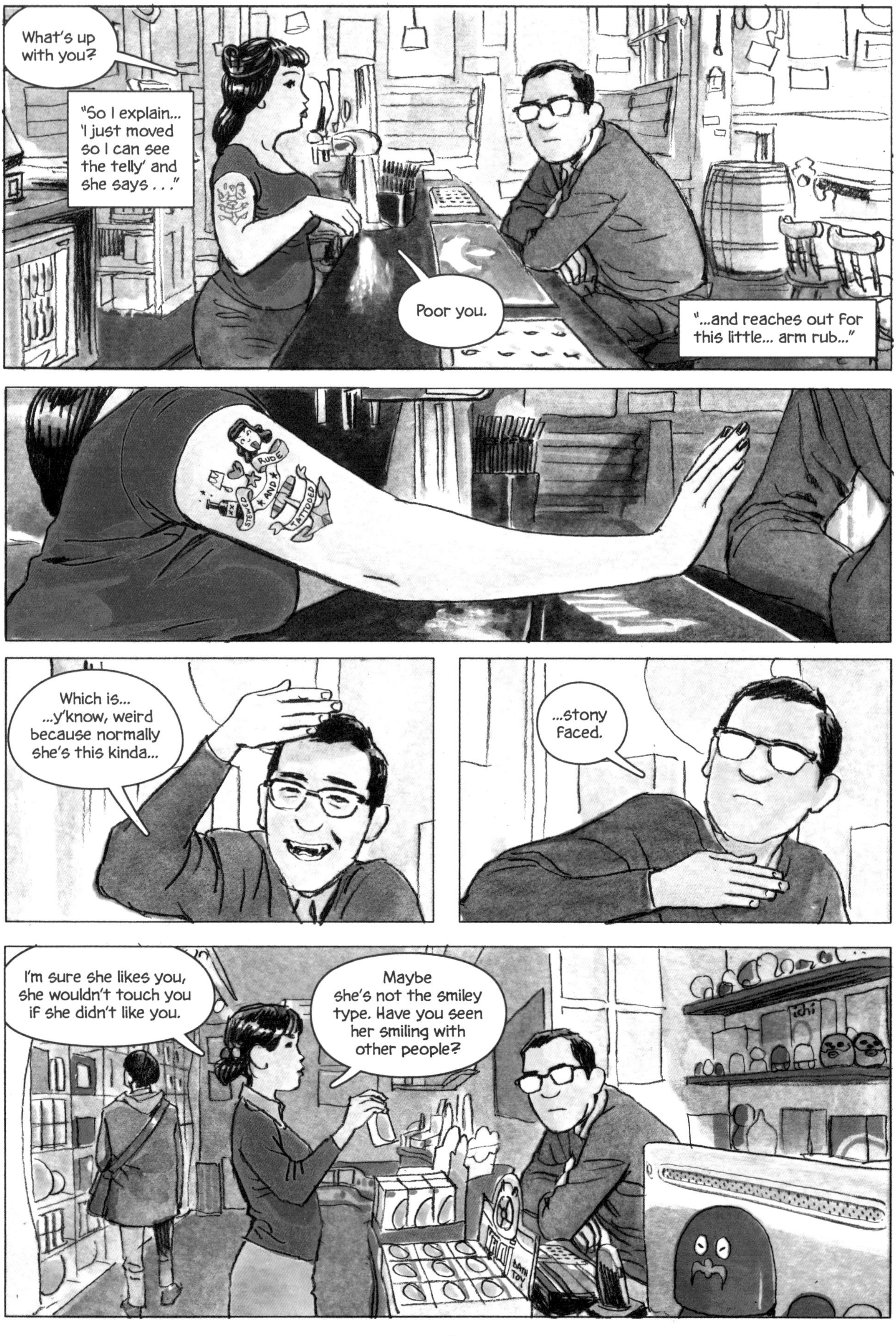
What's up with you?
"So I explain... 'I just moved so I can see the telly' and she says . . ."
Poor you.
"...and reaches out for this little... arm rub..."
RUDE
STEWED ★AND★ TATTOOED
Which is... ...y'know, weird because normally she's this kinda...
...stony faced.
I'm sure she likes you, she wouldn't touch you if she didn't like you.
Maybe she's not the smiley type. Have you seen her smiling with other people?
ichi

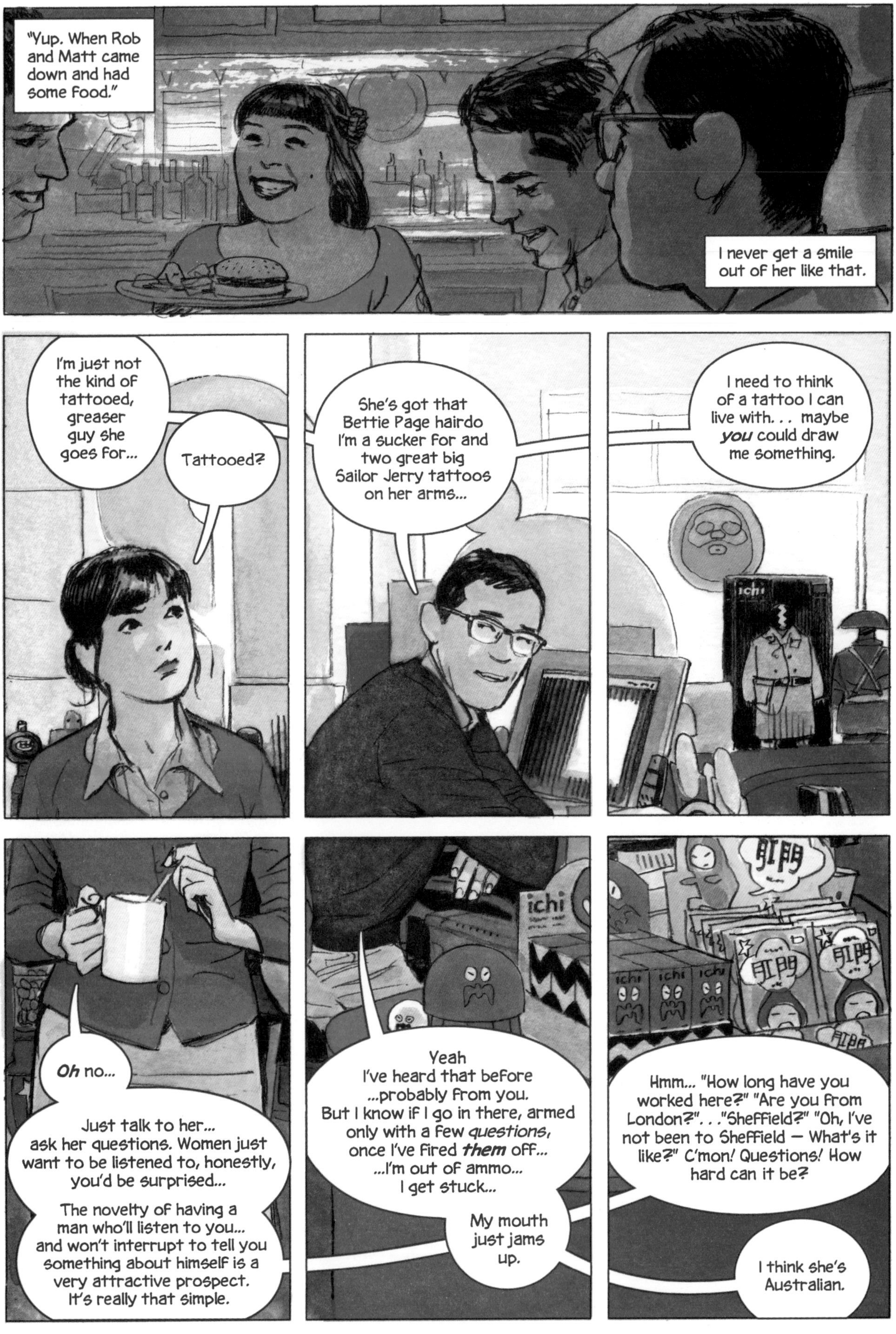
"Yup. When Rob and Matt came down and had some food."
I never get a smile out of her like that.
I'm just not the kind of tattooed, greaser guy she goes for...
Tattooed?
She's got that Bettie Page hairdo I'm a sucker for and two great big Sailor Jerry tattoos on her arms...
I need to think of a tattoo I can live with. . . maybe *you* could draw me something.
Oh no...
Just talk to her... ask her questions. Women just want to be listened to, honestly, you'd be surprised...
The novelty of having a man who'll listen to you... and won't interrupt to tell you something about himself is a very attractive prospect. It's really that simple.
Yeah I've heard that before ...probably from you. But I know if I go in there, armed only with a few *questions*, once I've fired *them* off... ...I'm out of ammo... I get stuck...
My mouth just jams up.
Hmm... "How long have you worked here?" "Are you from London?". . ."Sheffield?" "Oh, I've not been to Sheffield — What's it like?" C'mon! Questions! How hard can it be?
I think she's Australian.

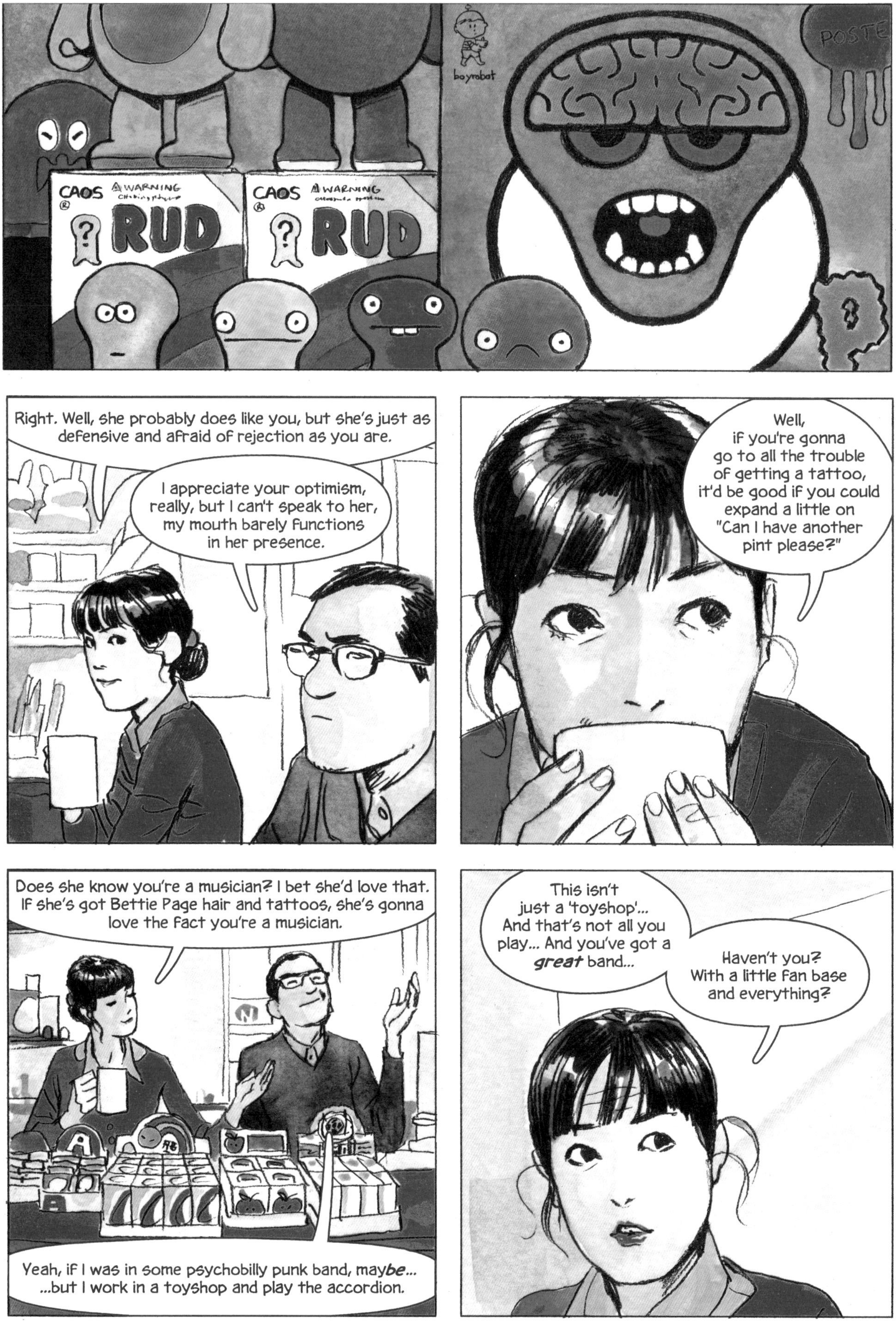
CAOS
WARNING
RUD
CAOS
WARNING
RUD
boyrobot
POSTE
Right. Well, she probably does like you, but she's just as defensive and afraid of rejection as you are.
I appreciate your optimism, really, but I can't speak to her, my mouth barely functions in her presence.
Well, if you're gonna go to all the trouble of getting a tattoo, it'd be good if you could expand a little on "Can I have another pint please?"
Does she know you're a musician? I bet she'd love that. If she's got Bettie Page hair and tattoos, she's gonna love the fact you're a musician.
Yeah, if I was in some psychobilly punk band, may*be*...
...but I work in a toyshop and play the accordion.
This isn't just a 'toyshop'... And that's not all you play... And you've got a ***great*** band...
Haven't you? With a little fan base and everything?

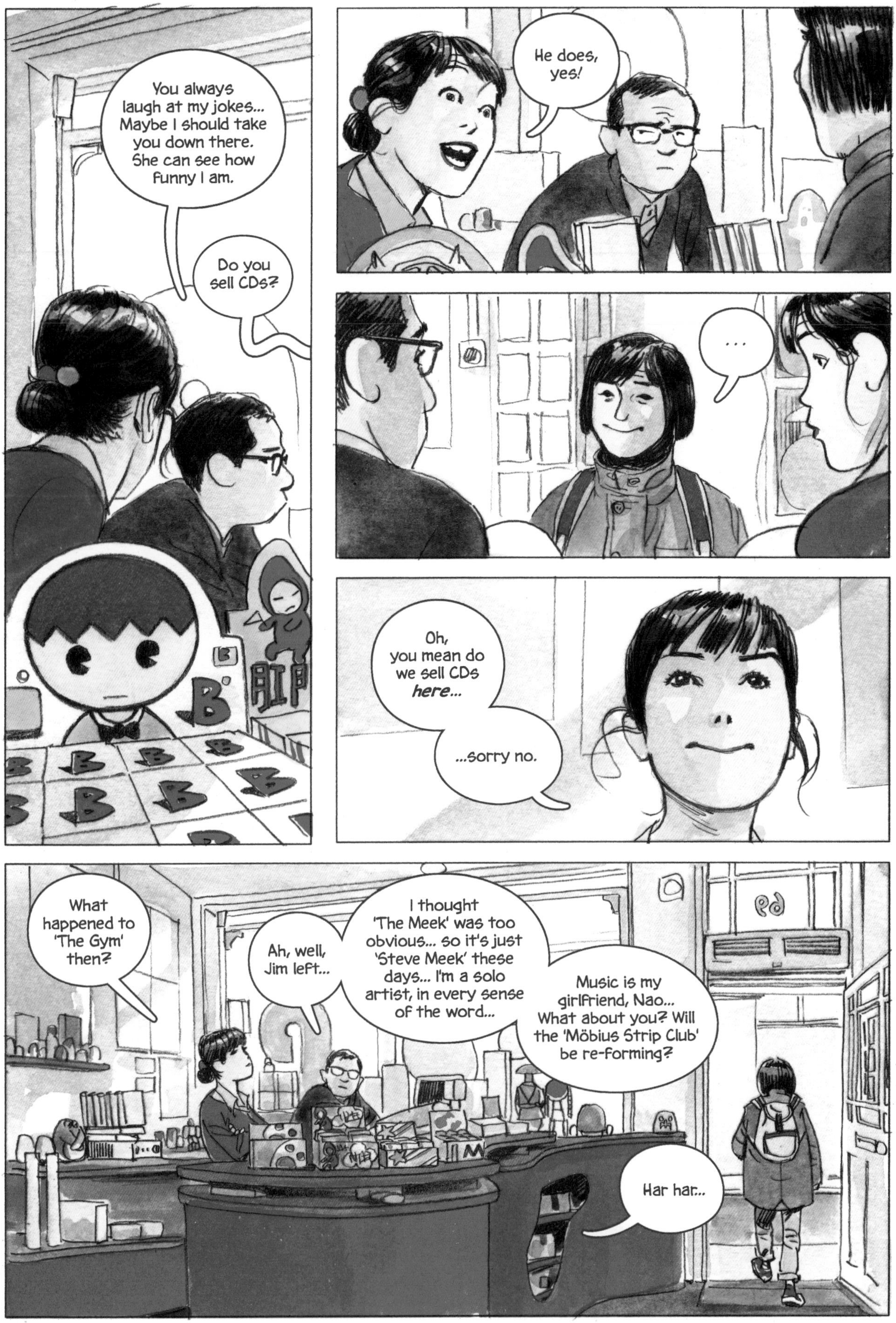
You always laugh at my jokes... Maybe I should take you down there. She can see how funny I am.
Do you sell CDs?
He does, yes!
...
Oh, you mean do we sell CDs *here*...
...sorry no.
What happened to 'The Gym' then?
Ah, well, Jim left...
I thought 'The Meek' was too obvious... so it's just 'Steve Meek' these days... I'm a solo artist, in every sense of the word...
Music is my girlfriend, Nao... What about you? Will the 'Möbius Strip Club' be re-forming?
Har har...

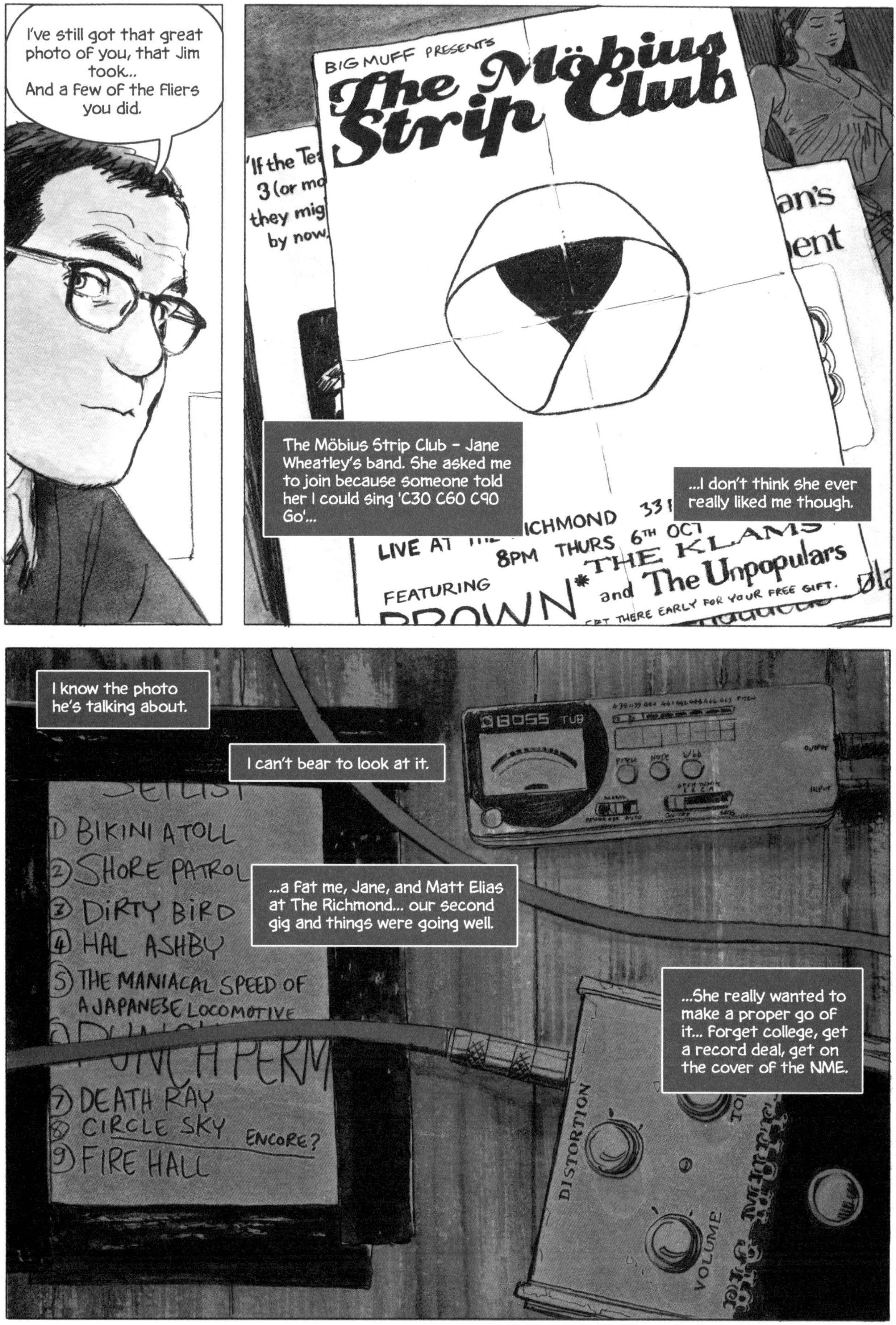
I've still got that great photo of you, that Jim took... And a few of the fliers you did.
BIG MUFF PRESENTS
The Möbius Strip Club
The Möbius Strip Club – Jane Wheatley's band. She asked me to join because someone told her I could sing 'C30 C60 C90 Go'...
...I don't think she ever really liked me though.
8PM THURS 6TH OCT
FEATURING
THE KLAMS
and The Unpopulars
I know the photo he's talking about.
I can't bear to look at it.
BOSS
1 BIKINI ATOLL
2 SHORE PATROL
3 DIRTY BIRD
4 HAL ASHBY
5 THE MANIACAL SPEED OF A JAPANESE LOCOMOTIVE
PUNCH PERM
7 DEATH RAY
8 CIRCLE SKY
ENCORE?
9 FIRE HALL
...a fat me, Jane, and Matt Elias at The Richmond... our second gig and things were going well.
...She really wanted to make a proper go of it... Forget college, get a record deal, get on the cover of the NME.
DISTORTION
VOLUME

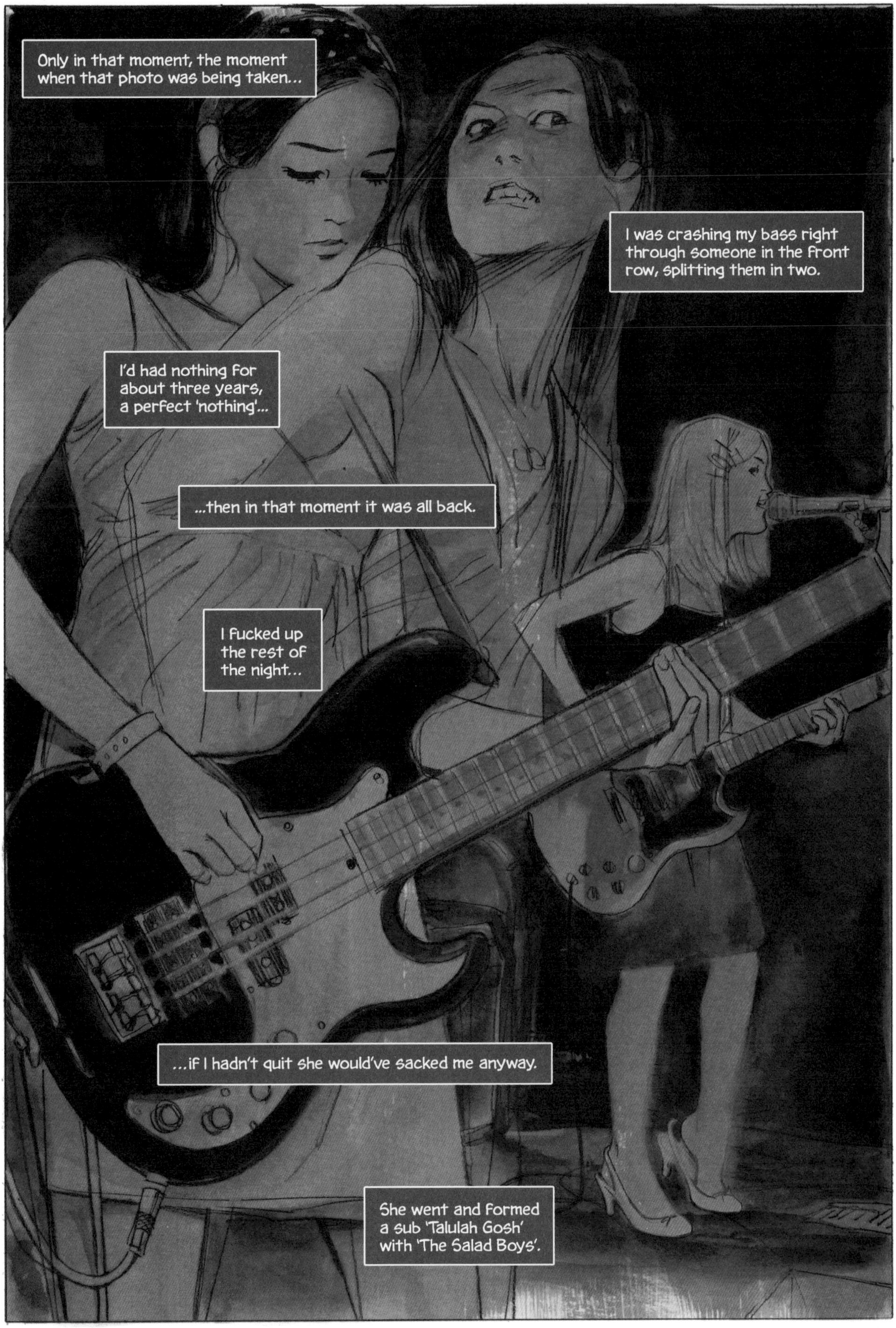
Only in that moment, the moment when that photo was being taken...
I was crashing my bass right through someone in the front row, splitting them in two.
I'd had nothing for about three years, a perfect 'nothing'...
...then in that moment it was all back.
I fucked up the rest of the night...
...if I hadn't quit she would've sacked me anyway.
She went and formed a sub 'Talulah Gosh' with 'The Salad Boys'.

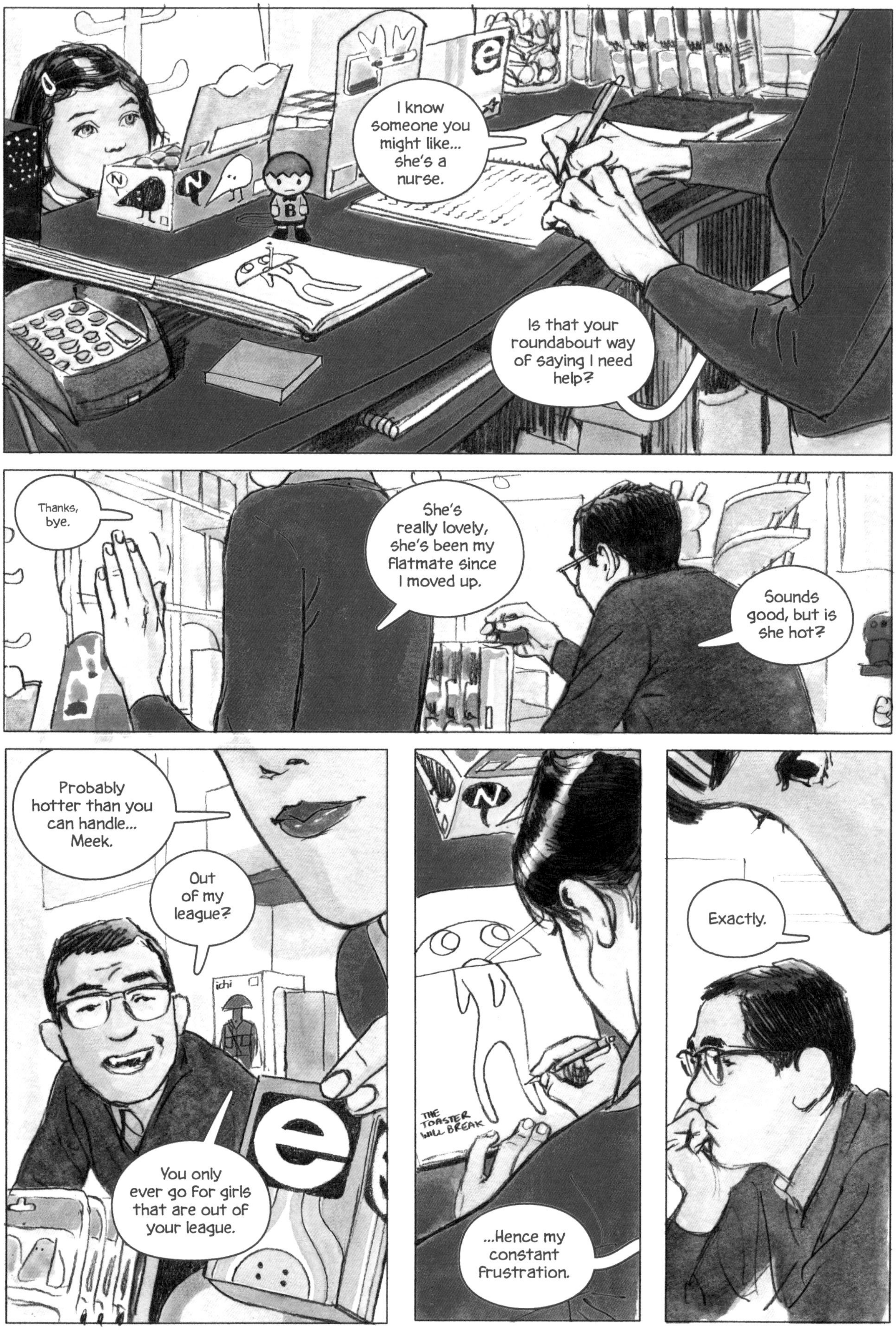

I know someone you might like... she's a nurse.
Is that your roundabout way of saying I need help?
Thanks, bye.
She's really lovely, she's been my flatmate since I moved up.
Sounds good, but is she hot?
Probably hotter than you can handle... Meek.
Out of my league?
ichi
You only ever go for girls that are out of your league.
THE TOASTER WILL BREAK
...Hence my constant frustration.
Exactly.

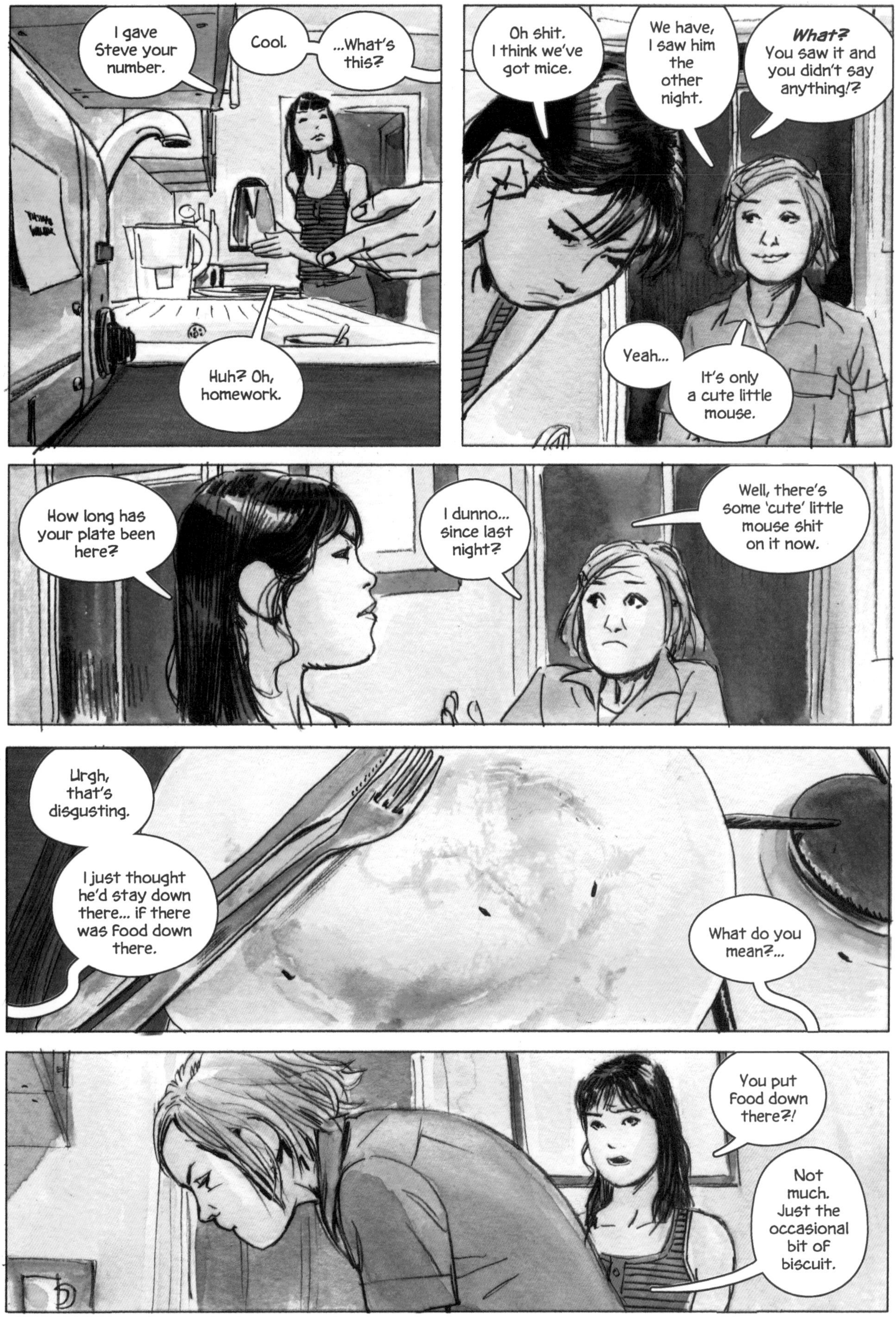

I gave Steve your number.
Cool.
...What's this?
Huh? Oh, homework.
Oh shit. I think we've got mice.
We have, I saw him the other night.
What? You saw it and you didn't say anything!?
Yeah...
It's only a cute little mouse.
How long has your plate been here?
I dunno... since last night?
Well, there's some 'cute' little mouse shit on it now.
Urgh, that's disgusting.
I just thought he'd stay down there... if there was food down there.
What do you mean?...
You put food down there?!
Not much. Just the occasional bit of biscuit.

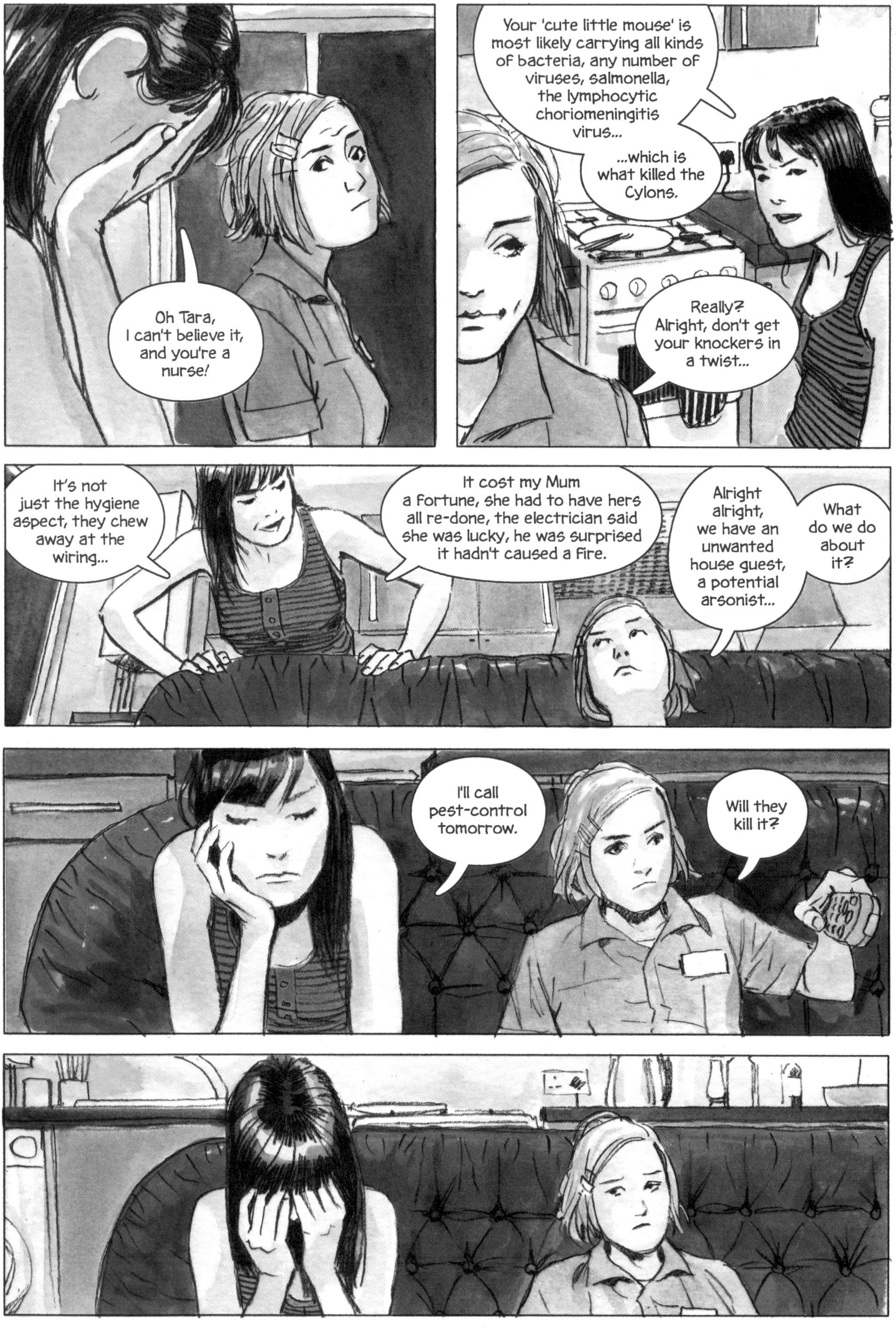
Oh Tara, I can't believe it, and you're a nurse!
Your 'cute little mouse' is most likely carrying all kinds of bacteria, any number of viruses, salmonella, the lymphocytic choriomeningitis virus...
...which is what killed the Cylons.
Really? Alright, don't get your knockers in a twist...
It's not just the hygiene aspect, they chew away at the wiring...
It cost my Mum a fortune, she had to have hers all re-done, the electrician said she was lucky, he was surprised it hadn't caused a fire.
Alright alright, we have an unwanted house guest, a potential arsonist...
What do we do about it?
I'll call pest-control tomorrow.
Will they kill it?

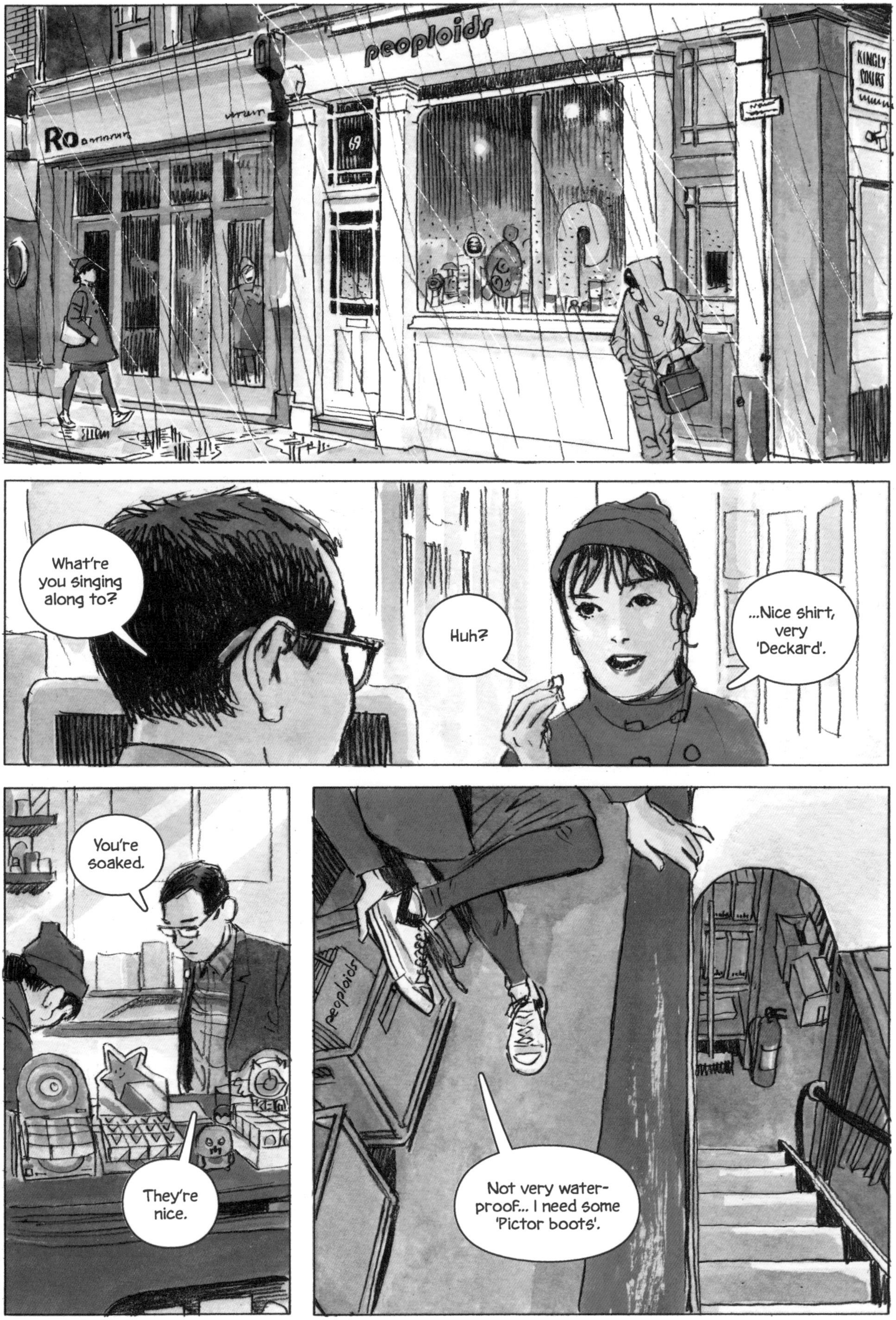
peoploids
KINGLY COURT
Ro
69
What're you singing along to?
Huh?
...Nice shirt, very 'Deckard'.
You're soaked.
They're nice.
peoploids
Not very water-proof... I need some 'Pictor boots'.

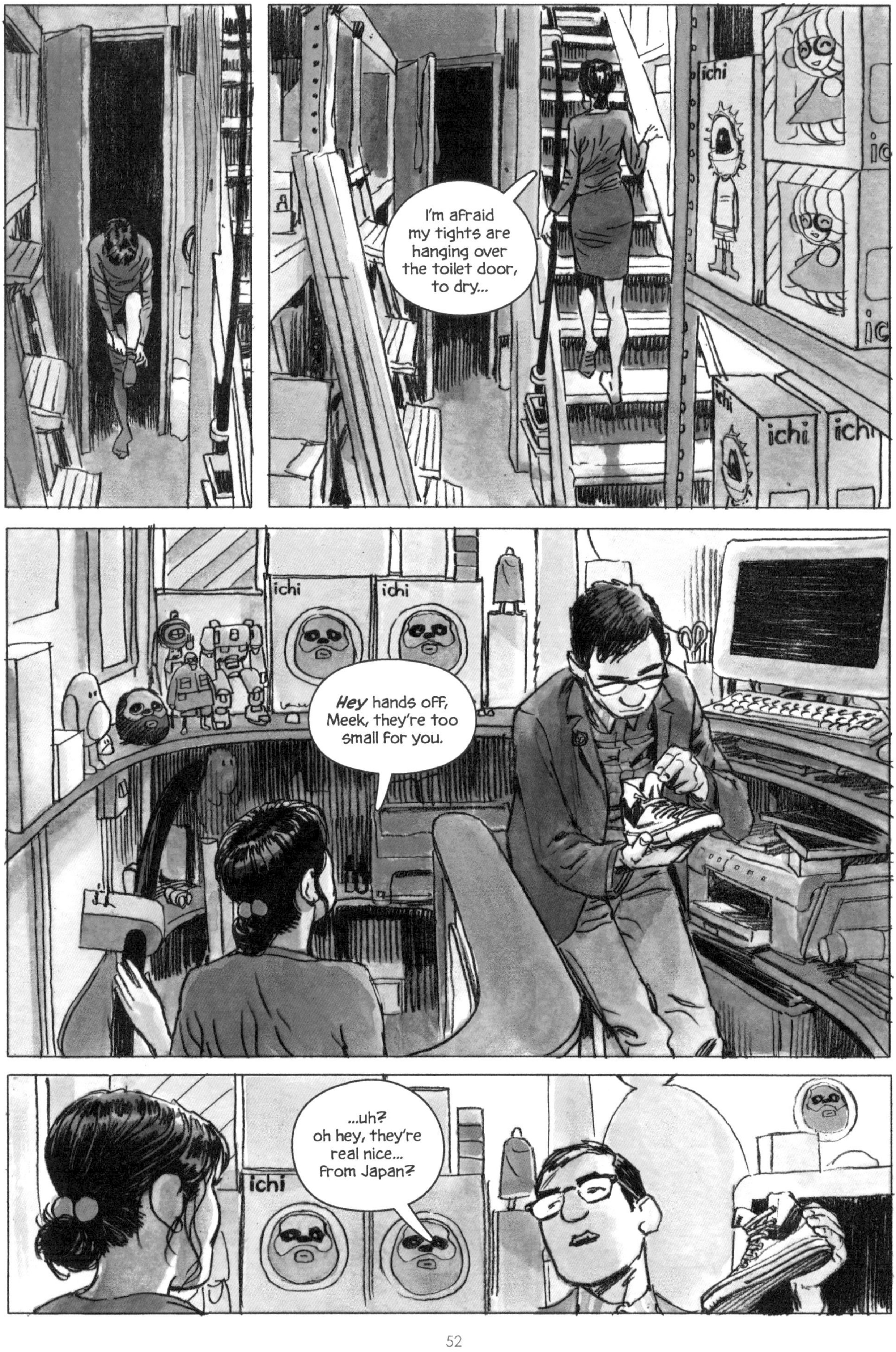
ichi
I'm afraid my tights are hanging over the toilet door, to dry...
ichi
ichi
ichi
ichi
ichi
Hey hands off, Meek, they're too small for you.
ichi
...uh? oh hey, they're real nice... from Japan?

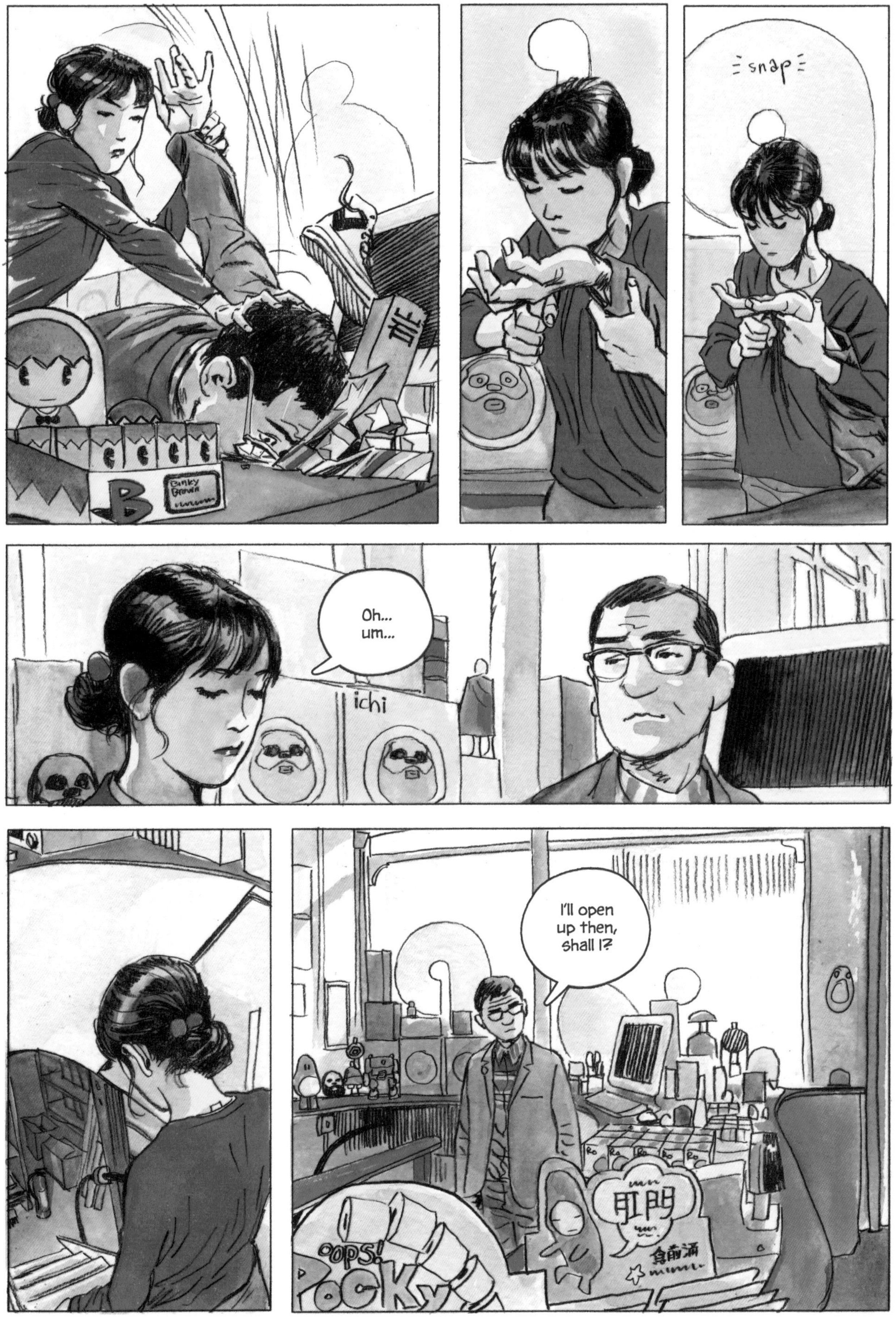
Binky Brown
snap
Oh... um...
ichi
I'll open up then, shall I?
OOPS!
POCKY

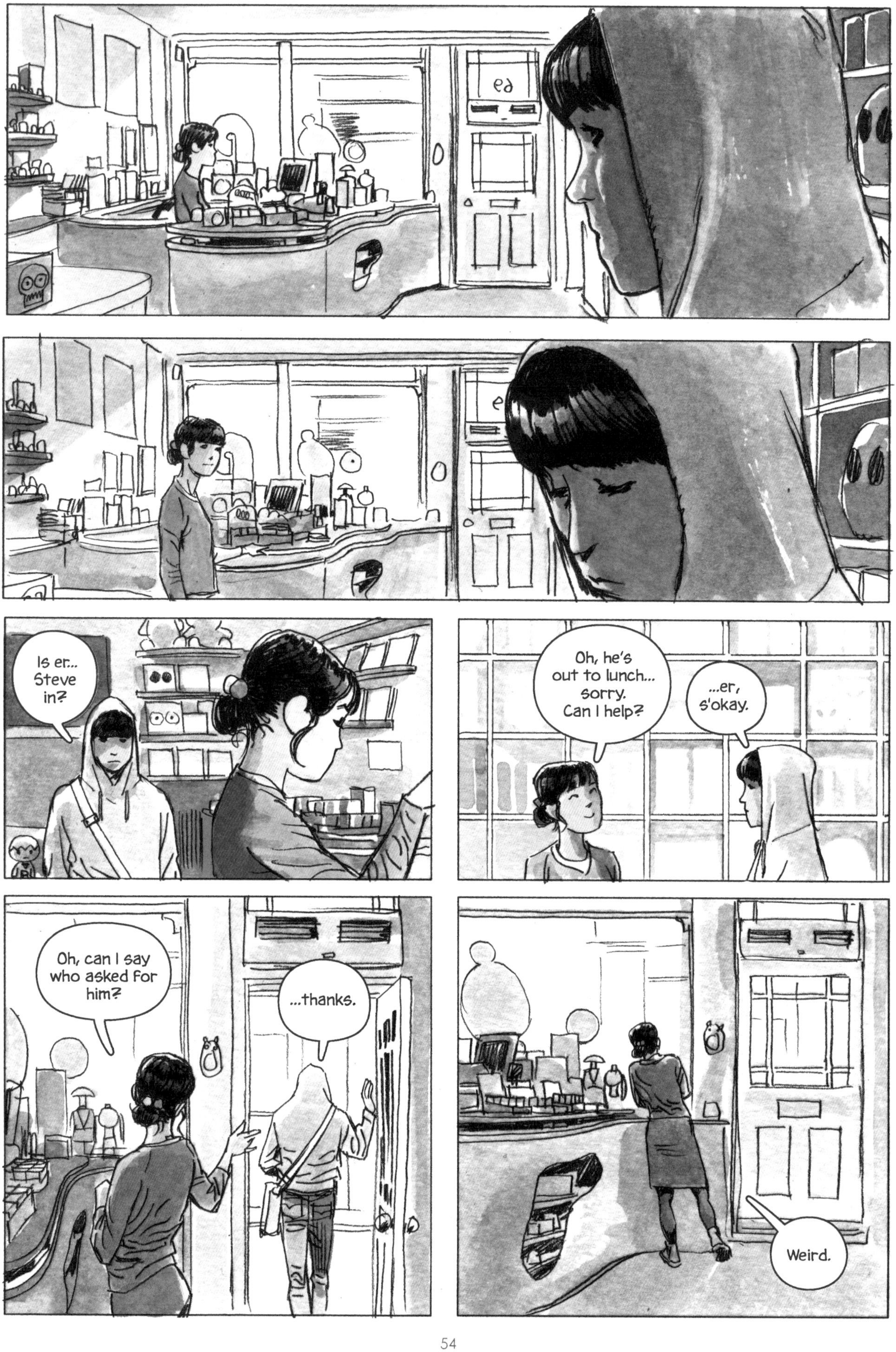
Is er... Steve in?
Oh, he's out to lunch... sorry. Can I help?
...er, s'okay.
Oh, can I say who asked for him?
...thanks.
Weird.

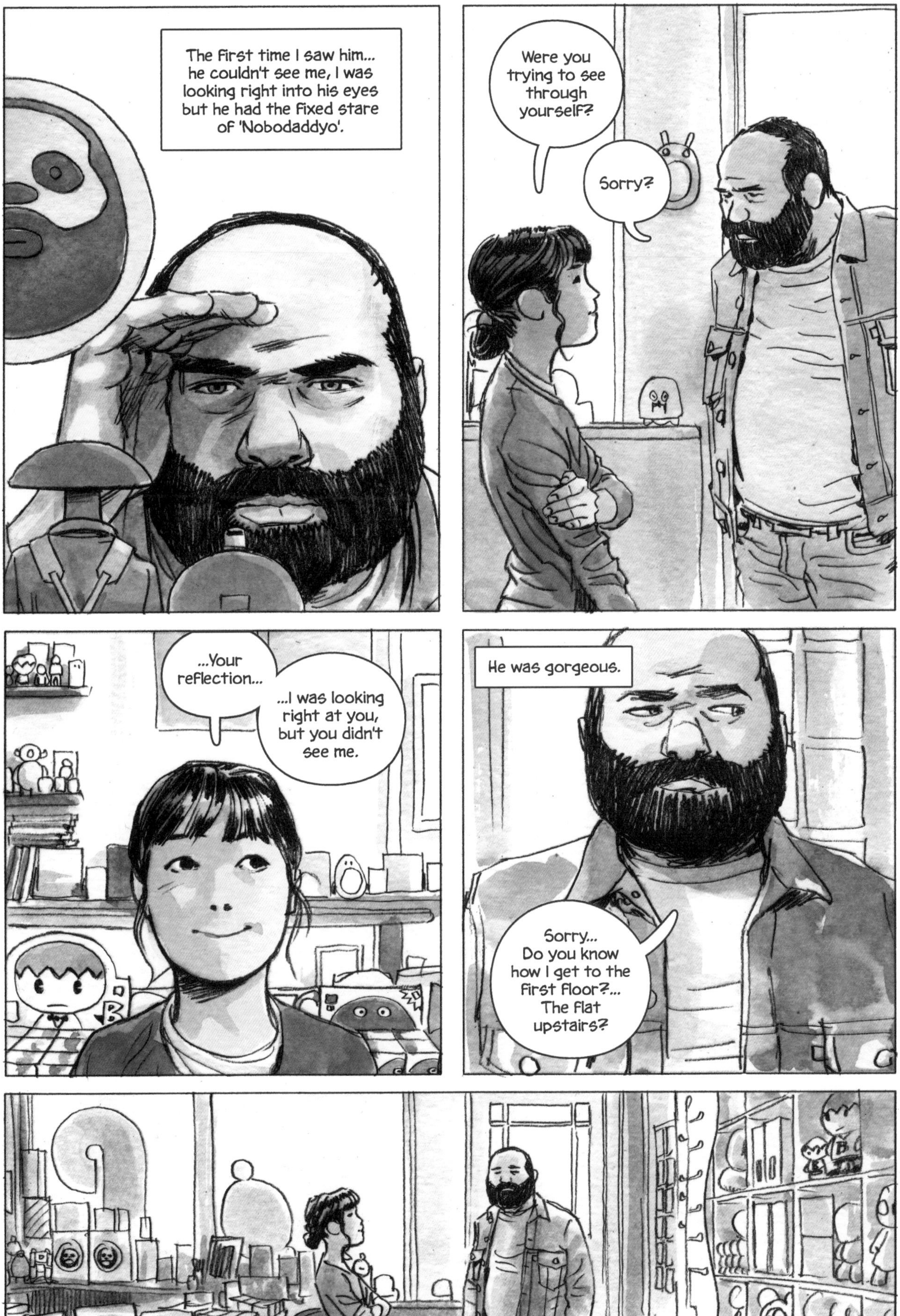

The first time I saw him... he couldn't see me, I was looking right into his eyes but he had the fixed stare of 'Nobodaddyo'.
Were you trying to see through yourself?
Sorry?
...Your reflection...
...I was looking right at you, but you didn't see me.
He was gorgeous.
Sorry... Do you know how I get to the first floor?... The flat upstairs?

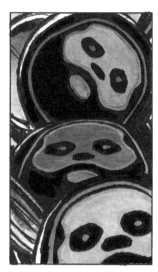

I'm sorry, I don't, my manager's not here right now.

Washing machine... repairs.

Oh right, yeah, it must be upstairs, we've not got a washing machine...

... just the kettle...

Would you like a tea?

Thanks, no... I better find upstairs.

'*Tea?!*... Why would he want a tea?!'

'...with a complete *stranger!*'

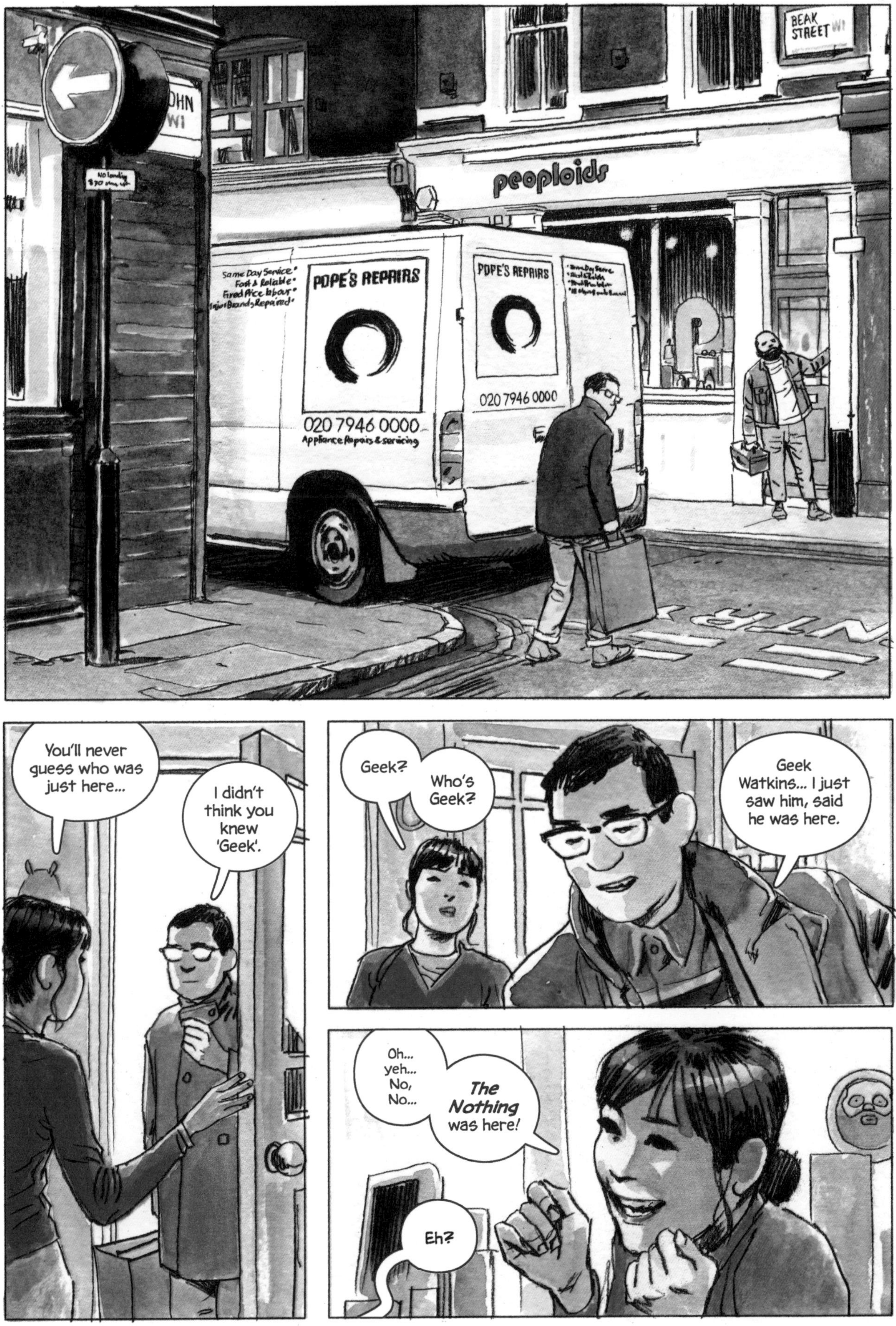
BEAK STREET W1
peoploids
Same Day Service*
Fast & Reliable*
Fixed Price labour*
Major Brands Repaired*
POPE'S REPAIRS
020 7946 0000
Appliance Repairs & servicing
POPE'S REPAIRS
020 7946 0000
You'll never guess who was just here...
I didn't think you knew 'Geek'.
Geek?
Who's Geek?
Geek Watkins... I just saw him, said he was here.
Oh... yeh... No, No...
The Nothing was here!
Eh?

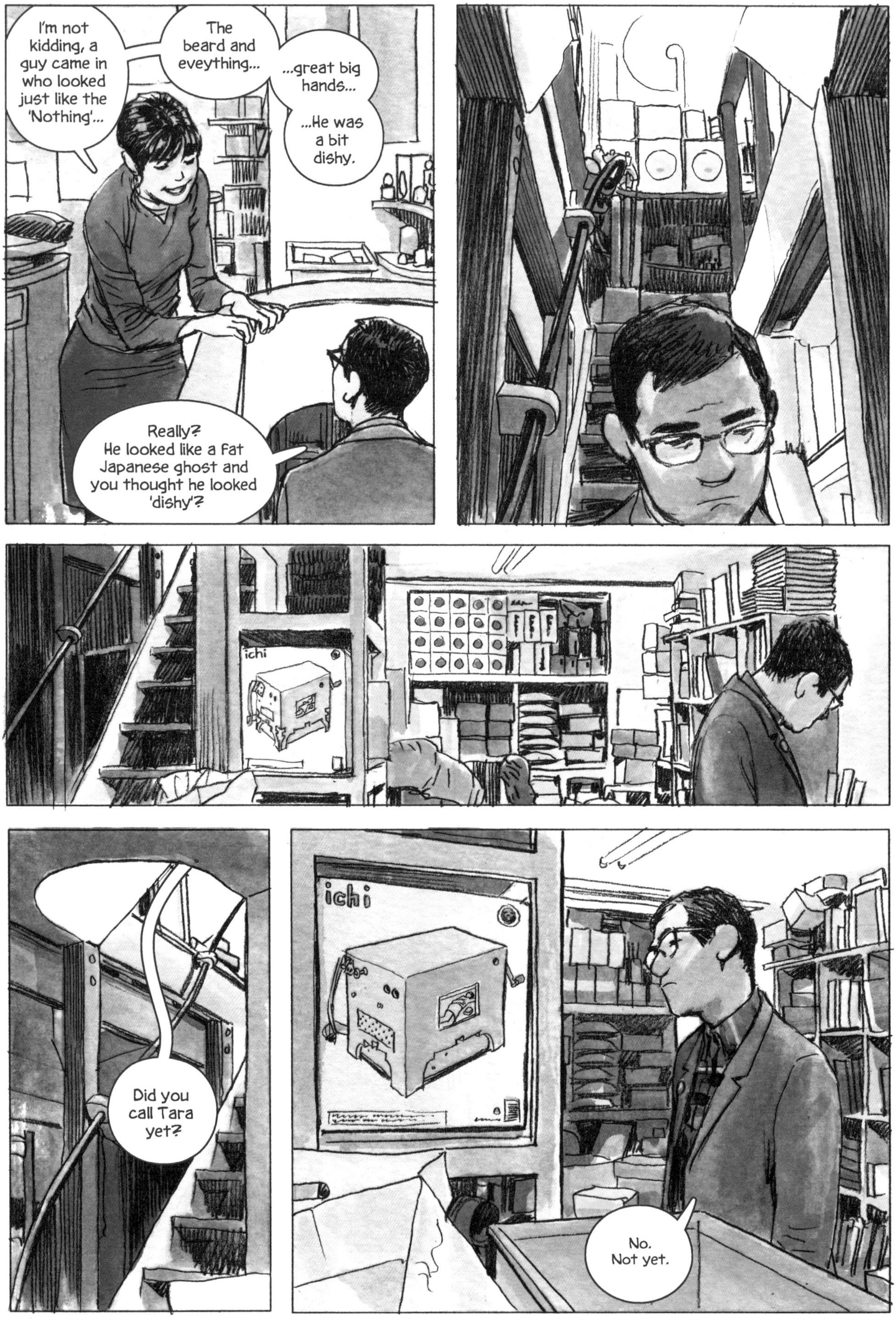
I'm not kidding, a guy came in who looked just like the 'Nothing'...
The beard and eveything...
...great big hands...
...He was a bit dishy.
Really? He looked like a fat Japanese ghost and you thought he looked 'dishy'?
ichi
Did you call Tara yet?
ichi
No. Not yet.

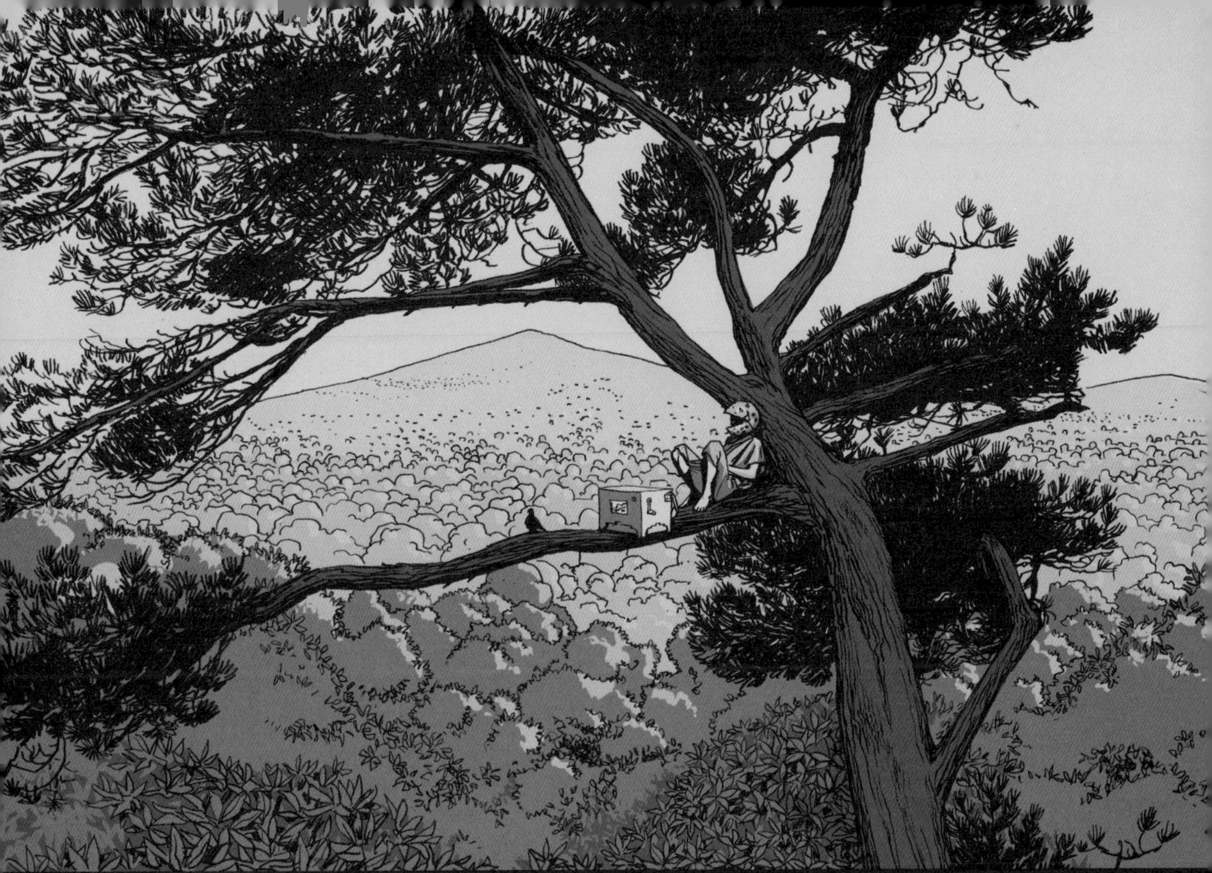

...He shod the sheep and rode away, taking his music box with him. Once he reached the giant woods he climbed up into a tall tree, where he sat tending his sheep and playing the music box. He fashioned a noble roost amidst the branches and sat there for many years until his herd grew quite large.

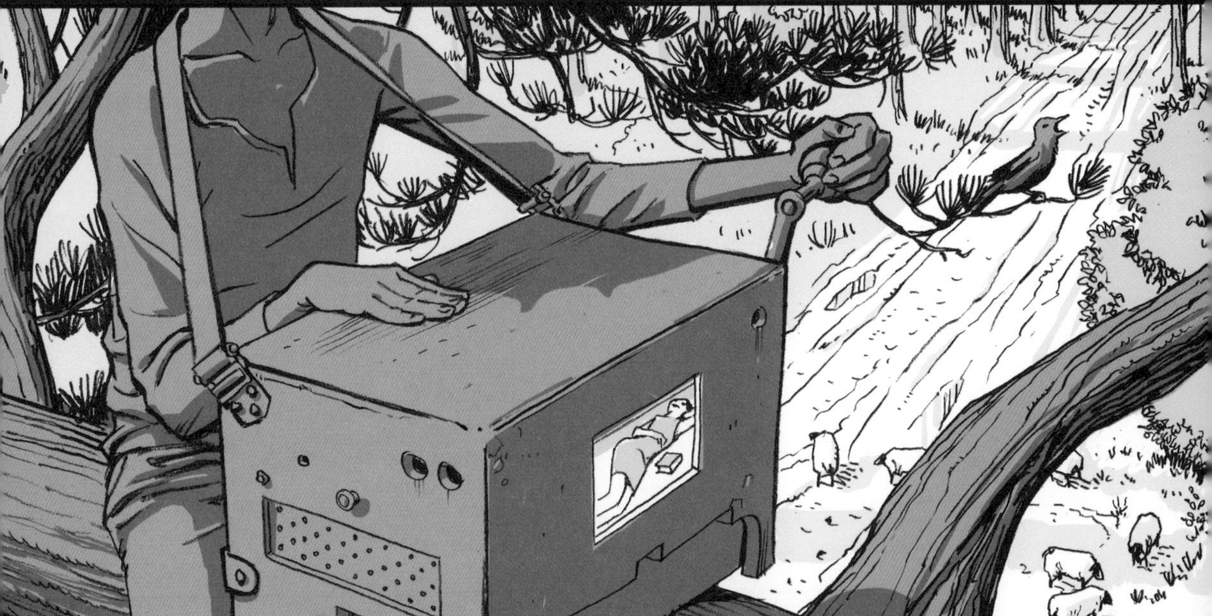

As he sat amidst the birds, he would play his music box, performing the most comforting of melodies. And one day a

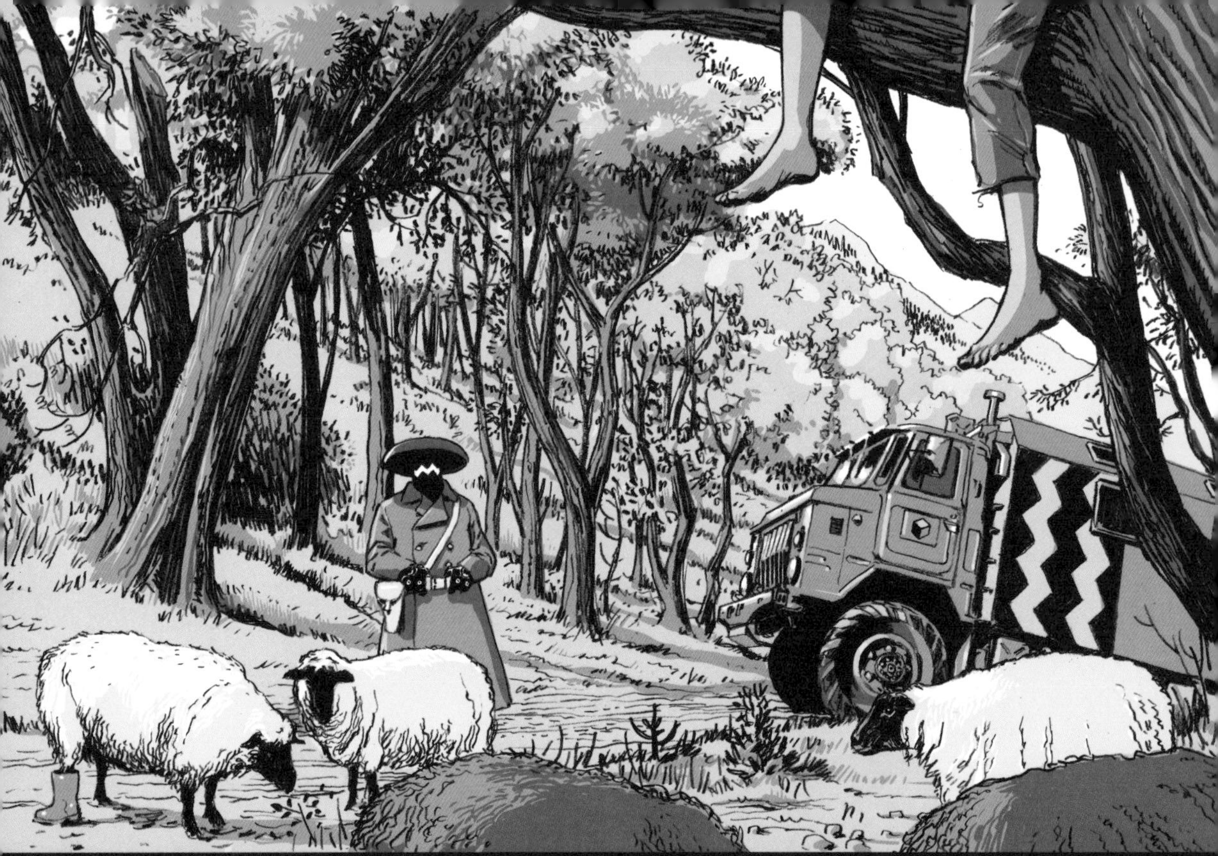

When he heard these most comforting of strains, he sent one of his privates to see where the music was coming from. Upon looking, the soldier found a small herd of sheep and the strange part-boy, part-tree creature sitting above them in the branches, playing a worn black music box.

The Captain told his private to ask the creature whether he knew the way out of the giant woods in order that they could return to their garrison. Pictor climbed down from his roost and said he would show him the way if the Captain promised to give him his daughter's hand in marriage.

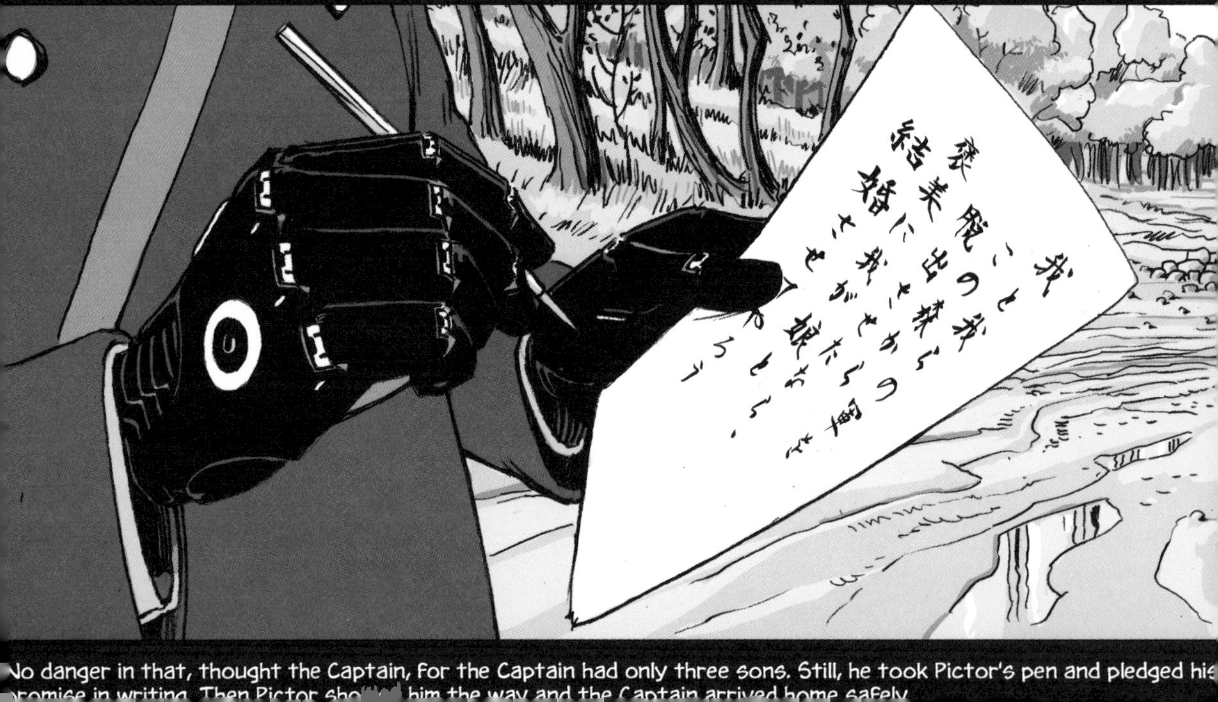

No danger in that, thought the Captain, for the Captain had only three sons. Still, he took Pictor's pen and pledged his promise in writing. Then Pictor showed him the way and the Captain arrived home safely.

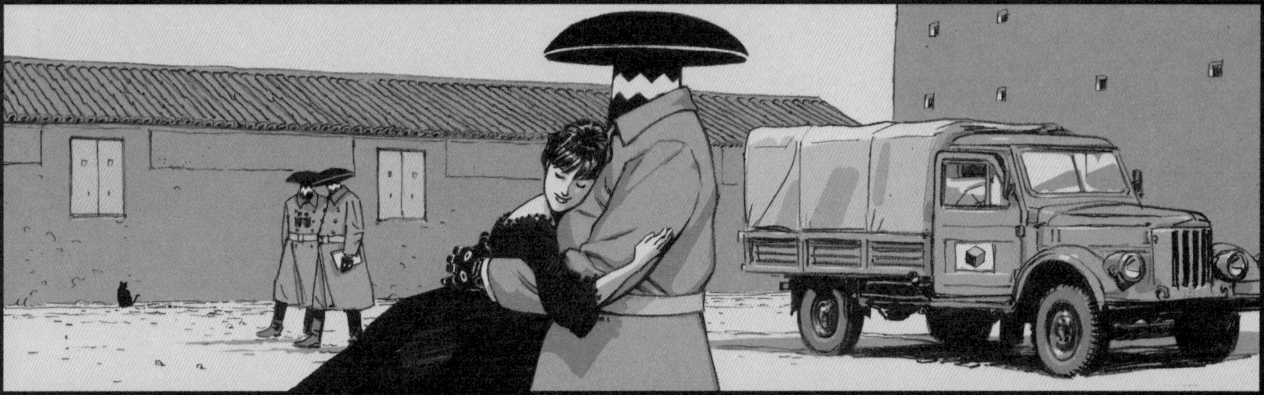

When his wife saw him coming from afar she was so overjoyed, she ran to him, kissed him and told him the good news that she was expecting their fourth child.

"Maybe this could be the daughter that we have longed for," said the happy wife. The Captain remembered Pictor and explained to her what had happened: how he had been forced to make a promise in writing to a wood creature that had demanded his daughter's hand in marriage. Then the Captain made another promise to his wife that he would never let the creature enter this garrison, let alone marry any child of theirs, and the wife was happy with that.

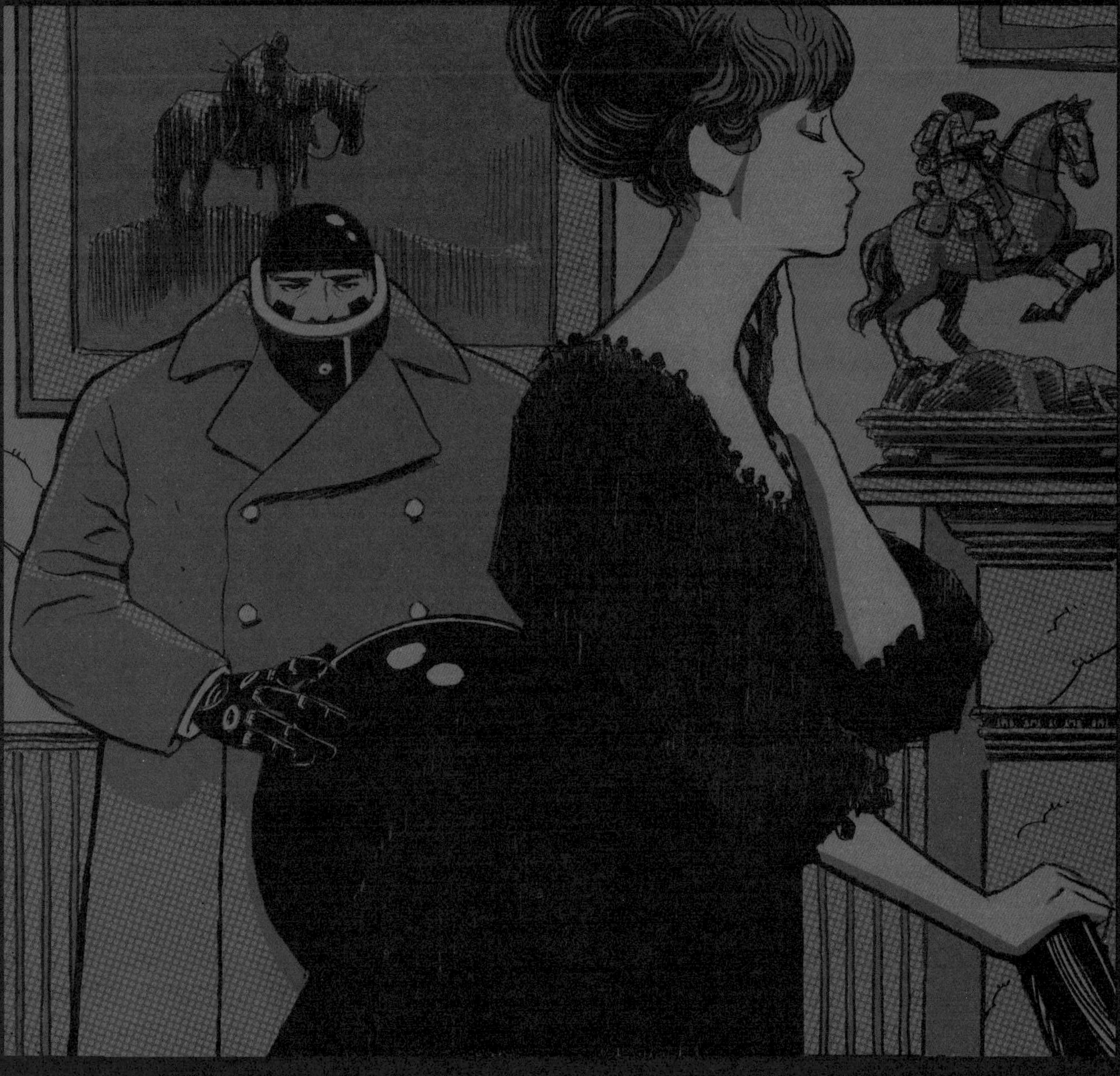

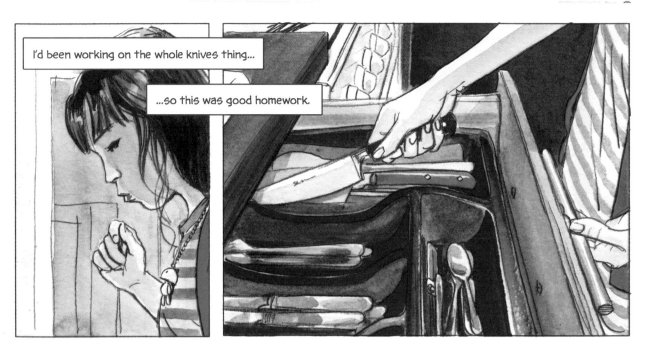

I'd been working on the whole knives thing...

...so this was good homework.

'No comfy grey...'

'... just the good stuff.'

'...and this.'

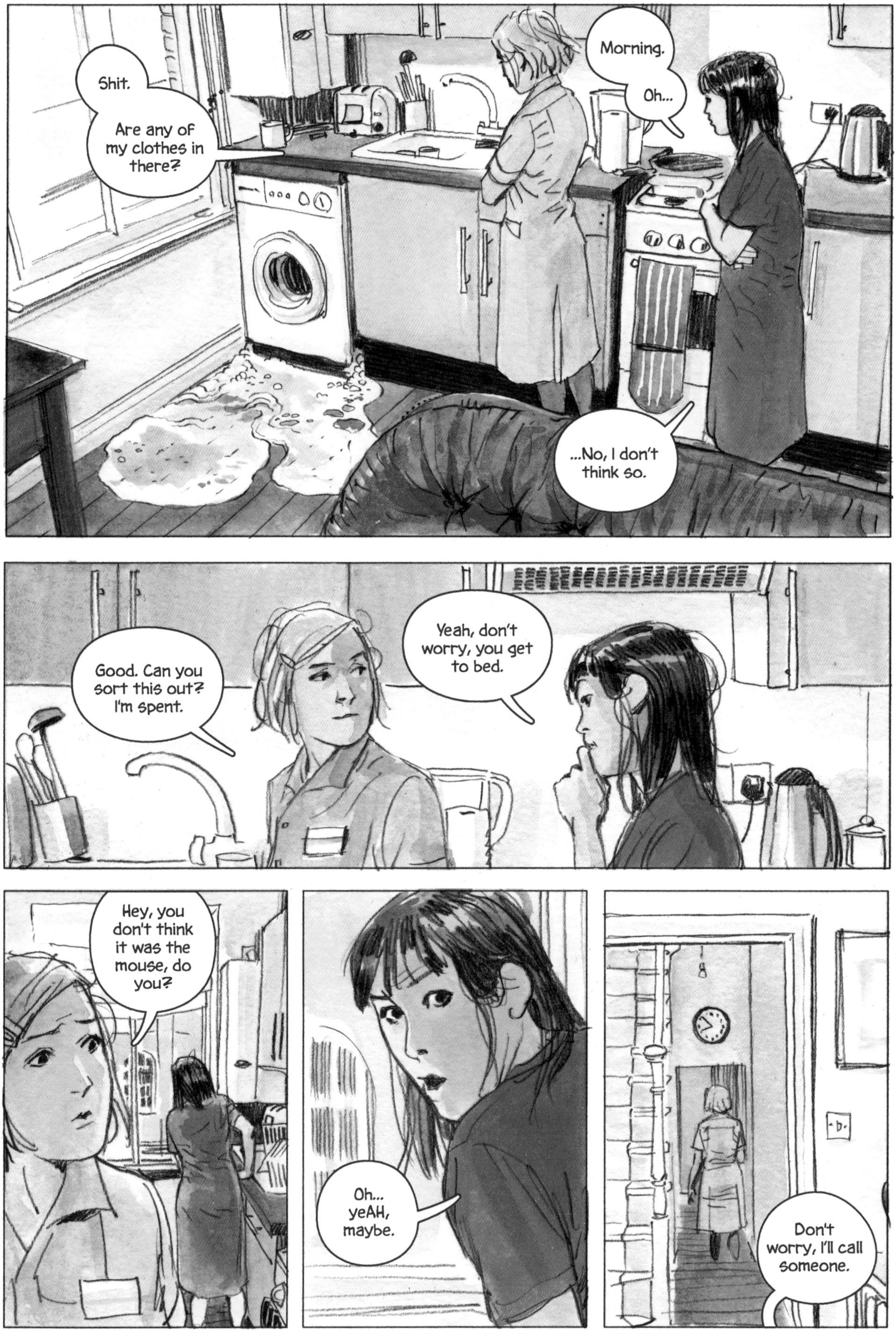
Shit.
Are any of my clothes in there?
Morning.
Oh...
...No, I don't think so.
Good. Can you sort this out? I'm spent.
Yeah, don't worry, you get to bed.
Hey, you don't think it was the mouse, do you?
Oh... yeAH, maybe.
Don't worry, I'll call someone.

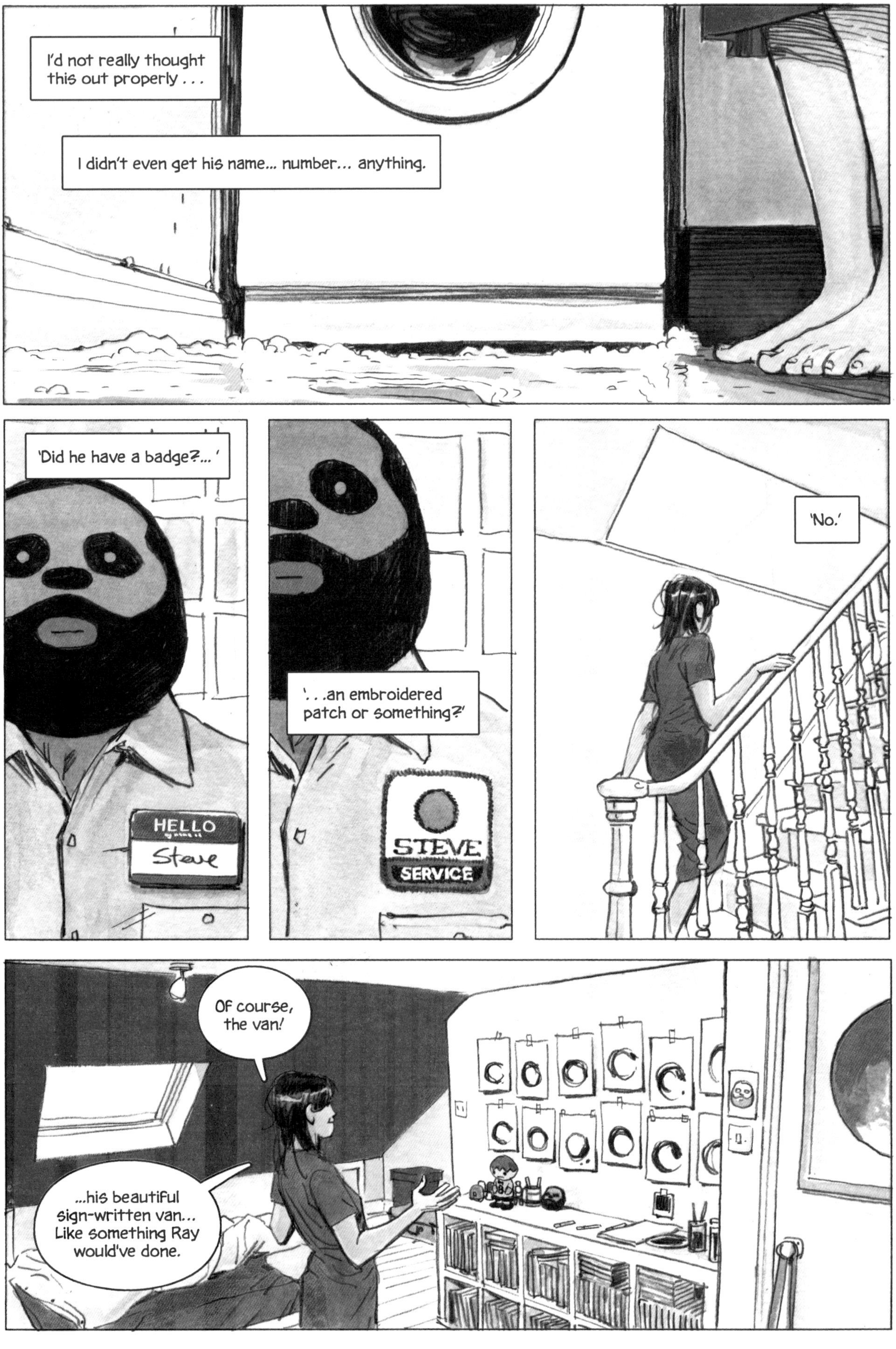
I'd not really thought this out properly . . .
I didn't even get his name... number... anything.
'Did he have a badge?...'
HELLO
Steve
'. . .an embroidered patch or something?'
STEVE
SERVICE
'No.'
Of course, the van!
...his beautiful sign-written van... Like something Ray would've done.

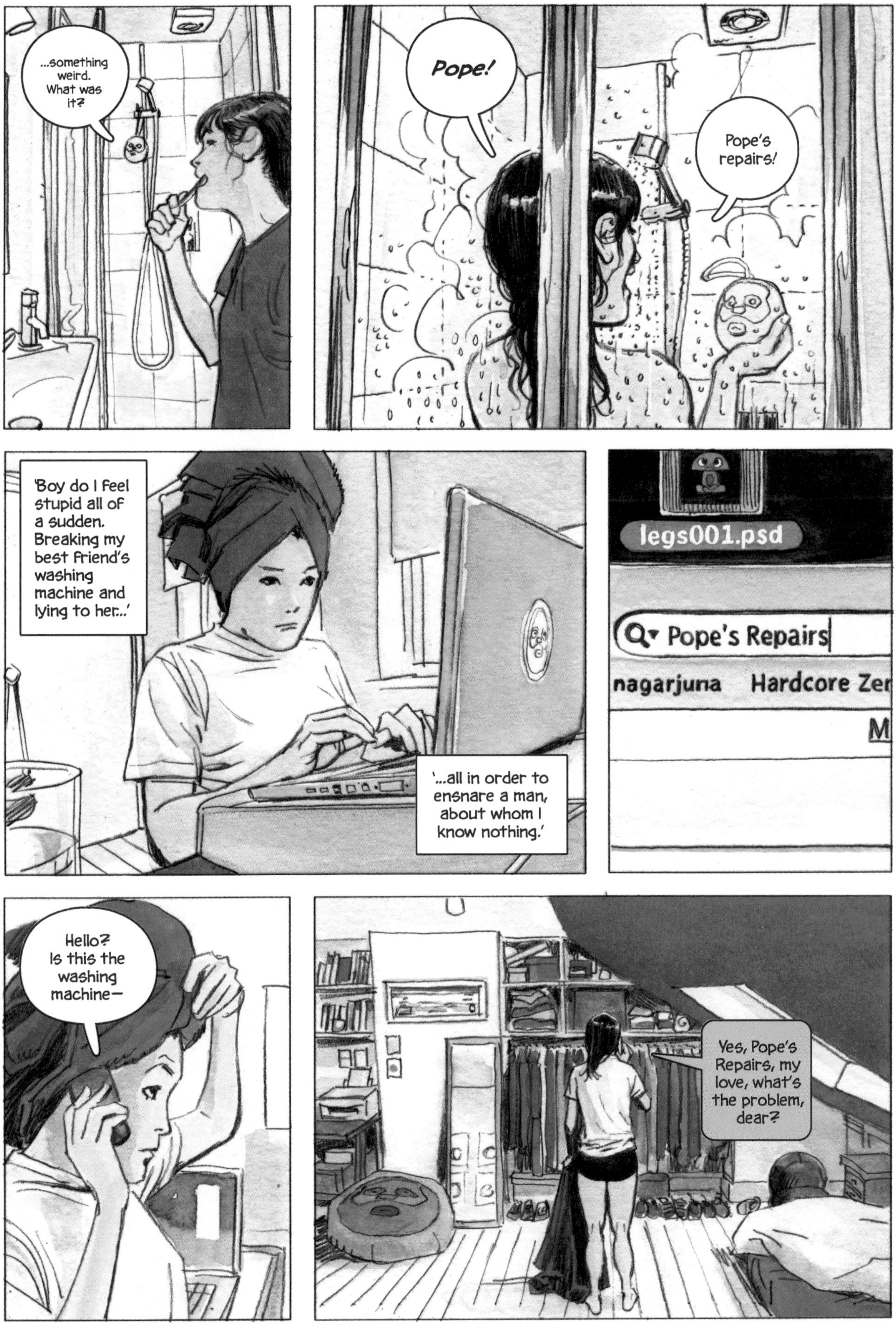

...something weird. What was it?
Pope!
Pope's repairs!
'Boy do I feel stupid all of a sudden. Breaking my best friend's washing machine and lying to her...'
'...all in order to ensnare a man, about whom I know nothing.'
legs001.psd
Pope's Repairs
nagarjuna
Hello? Is this the washing machine—
Yes, Pope's Repairs, my love, what's the problem, dear?

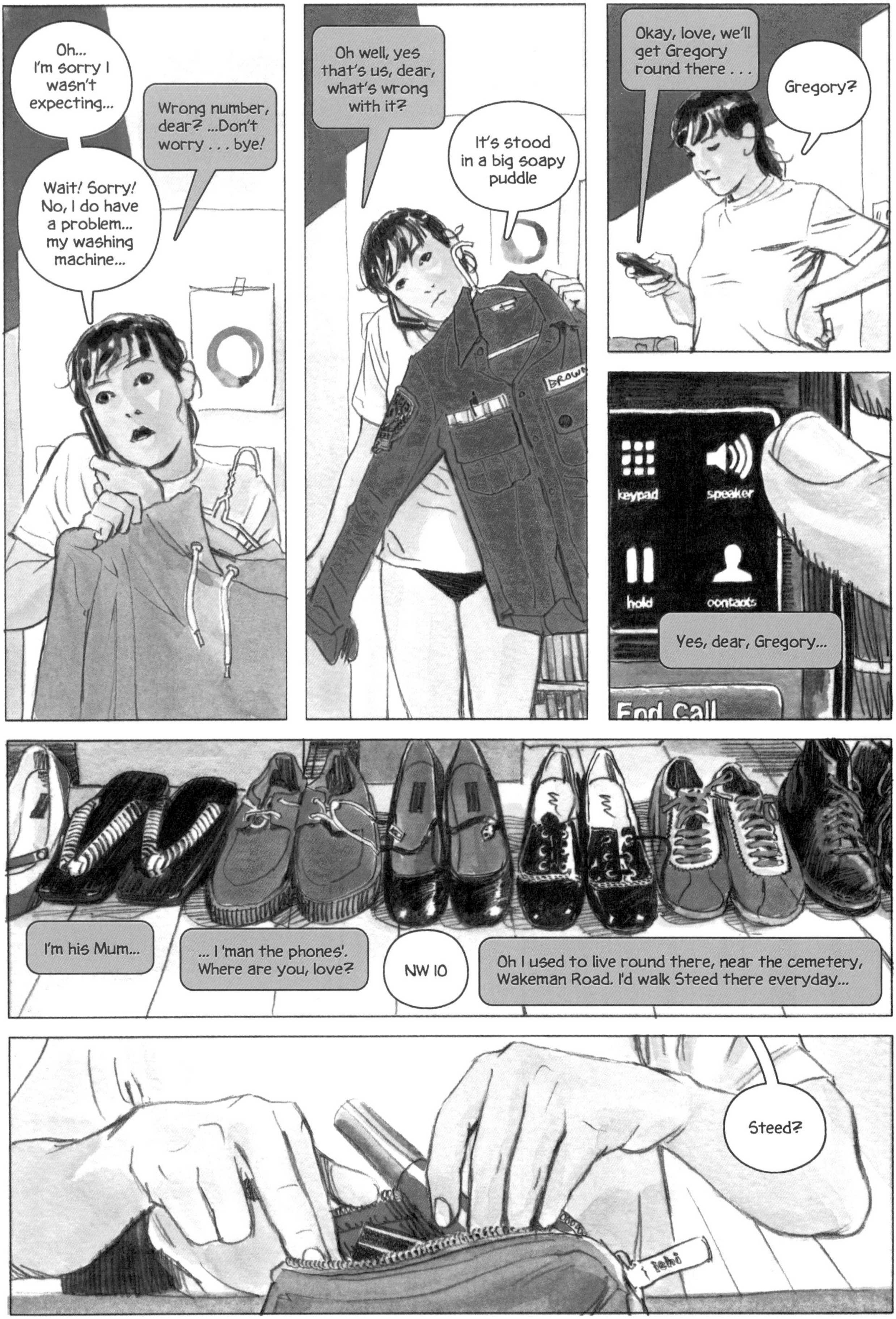
Oh... I'm sorry I wasn't expecting...
Wrong number, dear? ...Don't worry . . . bye!
Wait! Sorry! No, I do have a problem... my washing machine...
Oh well, yes that's us, dear, what's wrong with it?
It's stood in a big soapy puddle
Okay, love, we'll get Gregory round there . . .
Gregory?
keypad
speaker
hold
contacts
Yes, dear, Gregory...
End Call
I'm his Mum...
... I 'man the phones'. Where are you, love?
NW 10
Oh I used to live round there, near the cemetery, Wakeman Road. I'd walk Steed there everyday...
Steed?

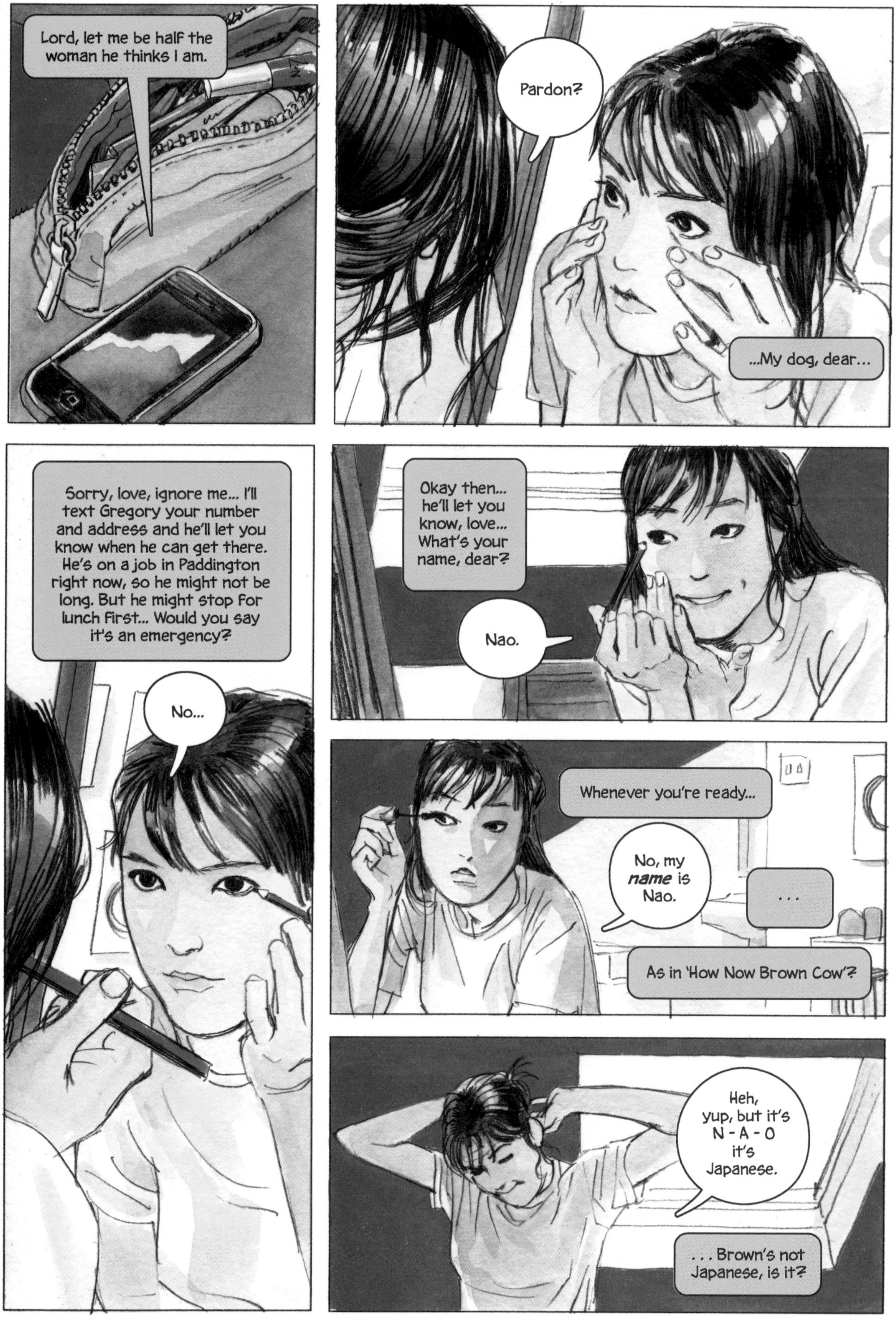

Lord, let me be half the woman he thinks I am.
Pardon?
...My dog, dear...
Sorry, love, ignore me... I'll text Gregory your number and address and he'll let you know when he can get there. He's on a job in Paddington right now, so he might not be long. But he might stop for lunch first... Would you say it's an emergency?
No...
Okay then... he'll let you know, love... What's your name, dear?
Nao.
Whenever you're ready...
No, my *name* is Nao.
. . .
As in 'How Now Brown Cow'?
Heh, yup, but it's N - A - O it's Japanese.
. . . Brown's not Japanese, is it?

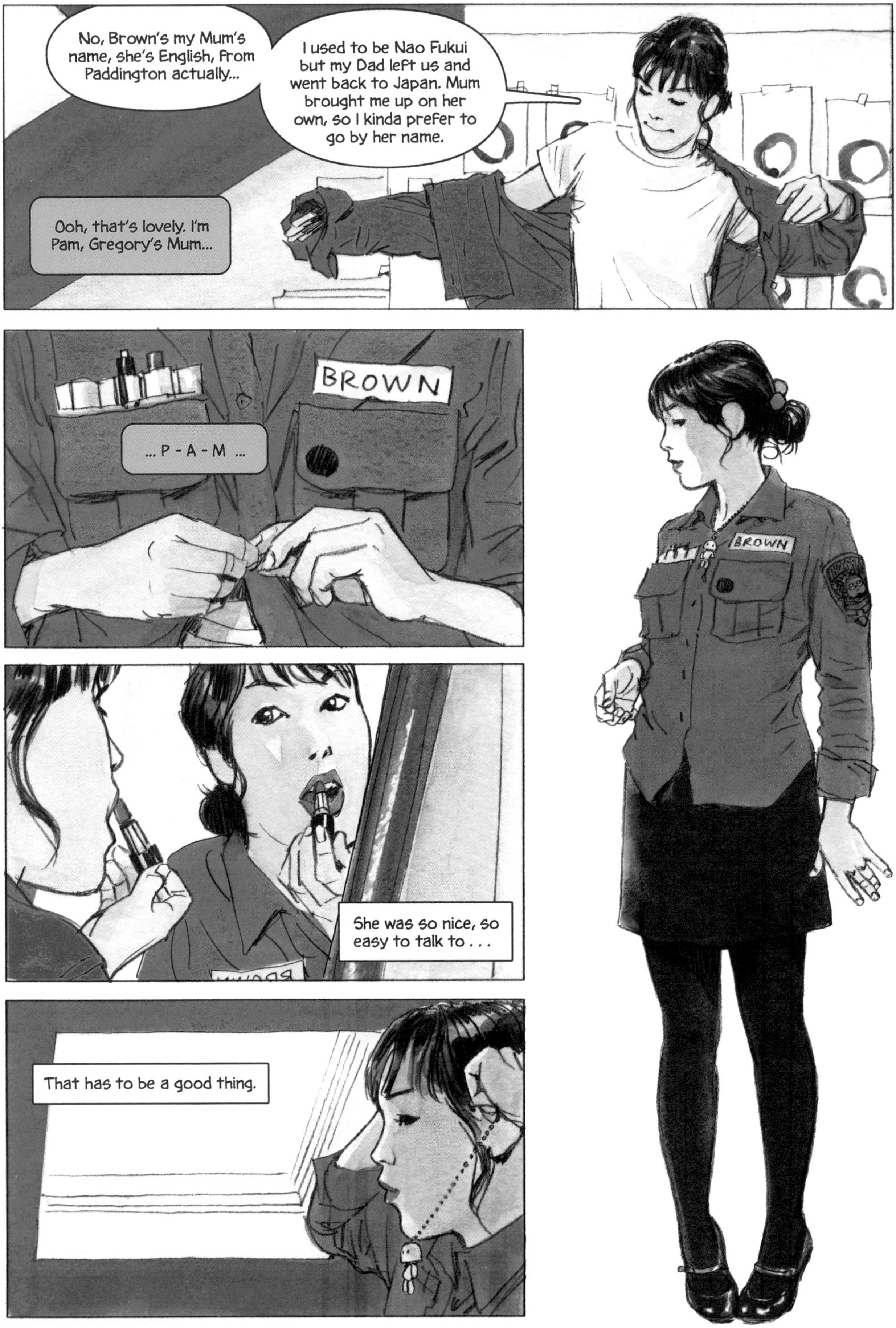
No, Brown's my Mum's name, she's English, from Paddington actually...
I used to be Nao Fukui but my Dad left us and went back to Japan. Mum brought me up on her own, so I kinda prefer to go by her name.
Ooh, that's lovely. I'm Pam, Gregory's Mum...
BROWN
...P-A-M...
She was so nice, so easy to talk to . . .
That has to be a good thing.
BROWN

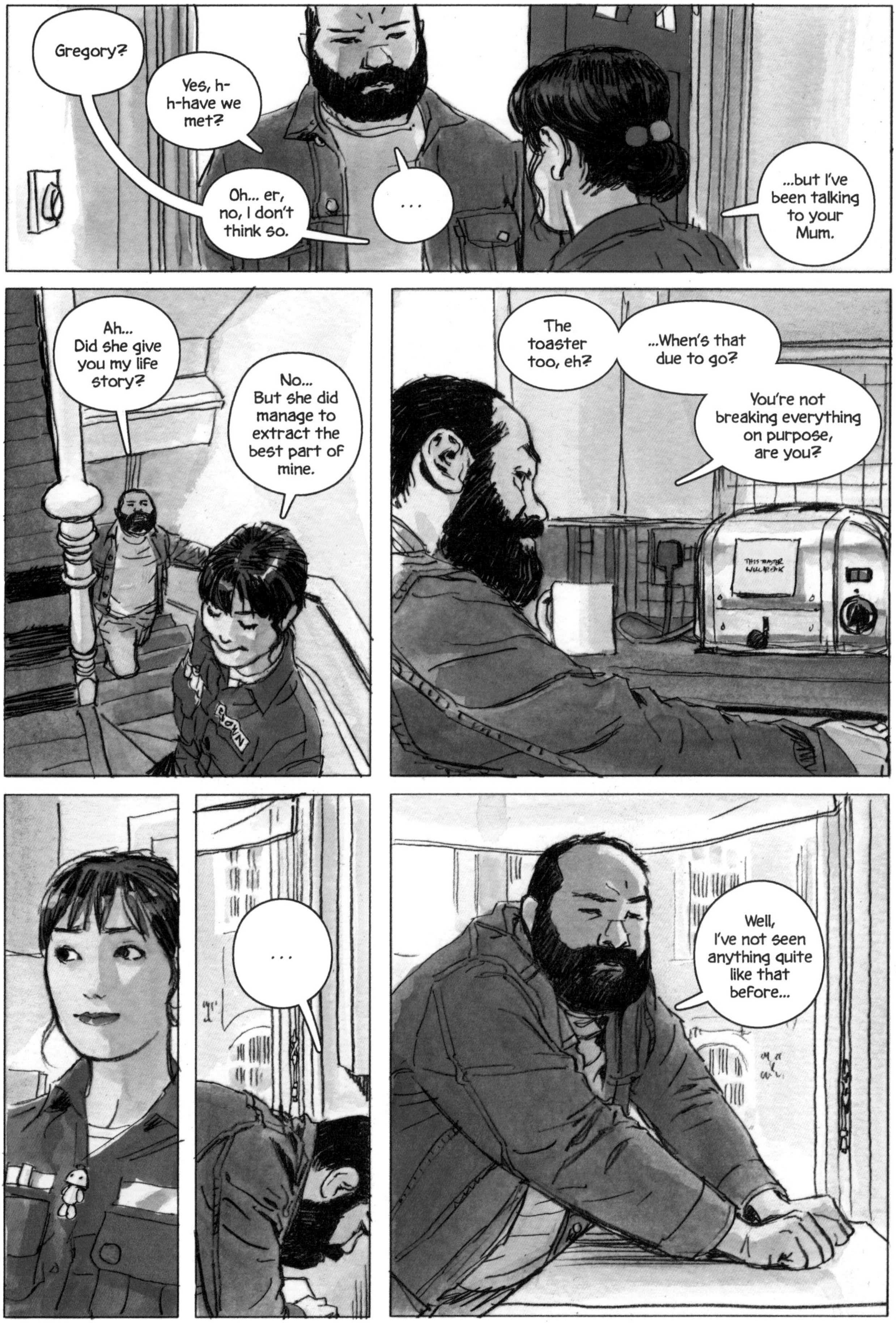
Gregory?
Yes, h-
h-have we
met?
Oh... er,
no, I don't
think so.
...
...but I've
been talking
to your
Mum.
Ah...
Did she give
you my life
story?
No...
But she did
manage to
extract the
best part of
mine.
The
toaster
too, eh?
...When's that
due to go?
You're not
breaking everything
on purpose,
are you?
...
Well,
I've not seen
anything quite
like that
before...

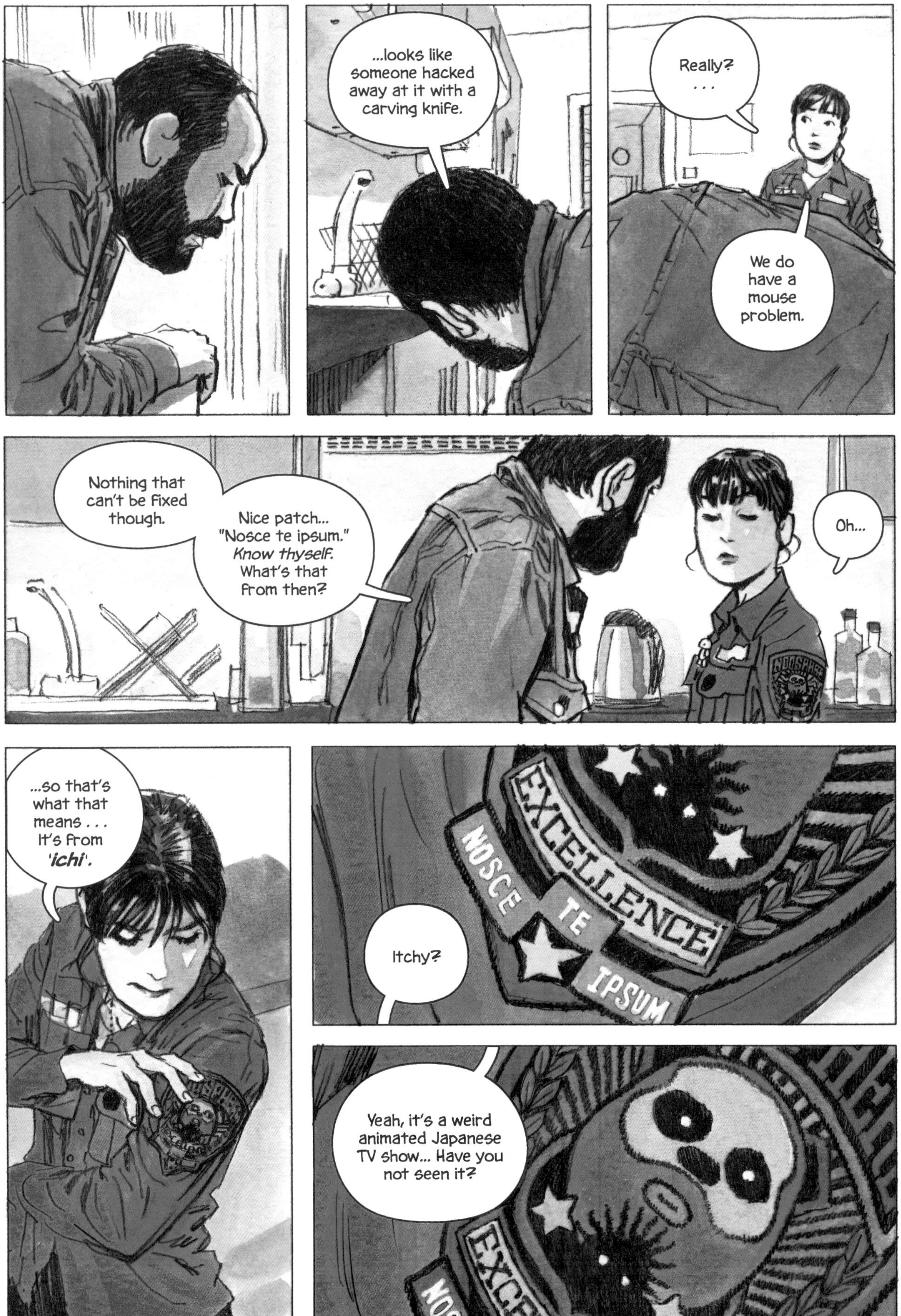
...looks like someone hacked away at it with a carving knife.
Really? . . .
We do have a mouse problem.
Nothing that can't be fixed though.
Nice patch... "Nosce te ipsum." *Know thyself.* What's that from then?
Oh...
...so that's what that means . . . It's from '*ichi*'.
EXCELLENCE
NOSCE TE IPSUM
Itchy?
Yeah, it's a weird animated Japanese TV show... Have you not seen it?

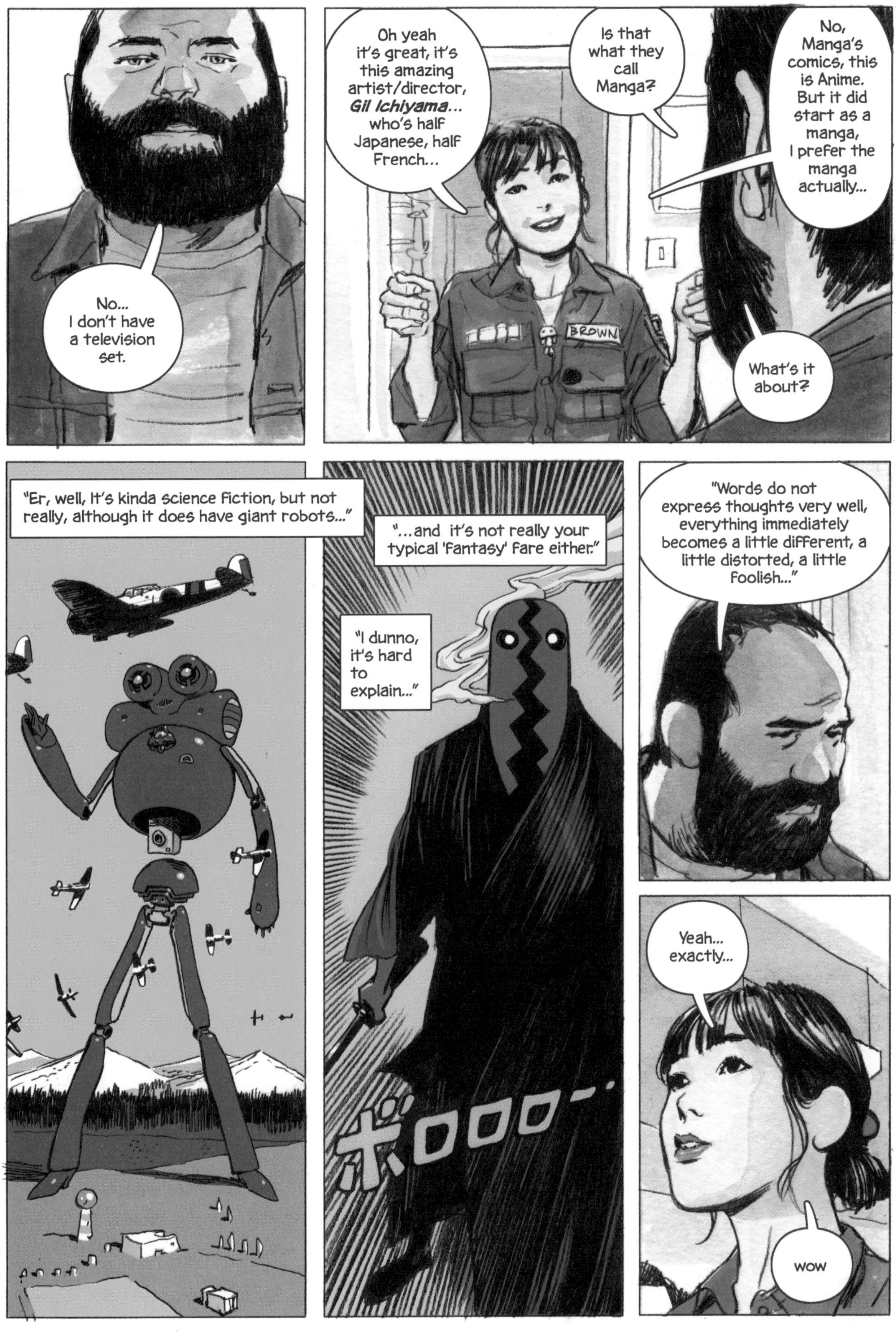
No... I don't have a television set.
Oh yeah it's great, it's this amazing artist/director, ***Gil Ichiyama...*** who's half Japanese, half French...
Is that what they call Manga?
No, Manga's comics, this is Anime. But it did start as a manga, I prefer the manga actually...
What's it about?
"Er, well, it's kinda science fiction, but not really, although it does have giant robots..."
"...and it's not really your typical 'fantasy' fare either."
"I dunno, it's hard to explain..."
ボロロロ--
"Words do not express thoughts very well, everything immediately becomes a little different, a little distorted, a little foolish..."
Yeah... exactly...
wow

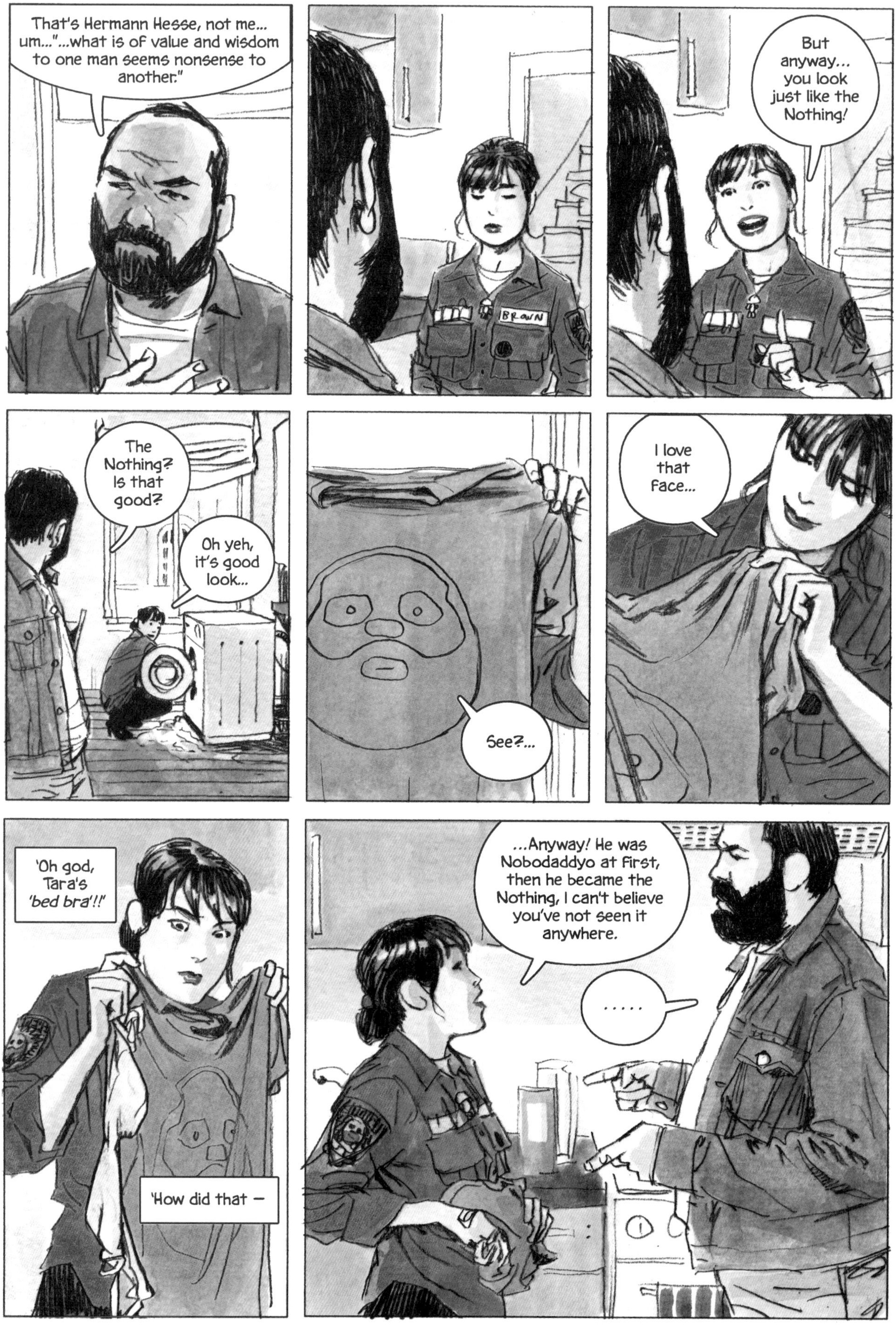
That's Hermann Hesse, not me... um..."...what is of value and wisdom to one man seems nonsense to another."
But anyway... you look just like the Nothing!
The Nothing? Is that good?
Oh yeh, it's good look...
See?...
I love that face...
'Oh god, Tara's *'bed bra'!!'*
'How did that —
...Anyway! He was Nobodaddyo at first, then he became the Nothing, I can't believe you've not seen it anywhere.
.....

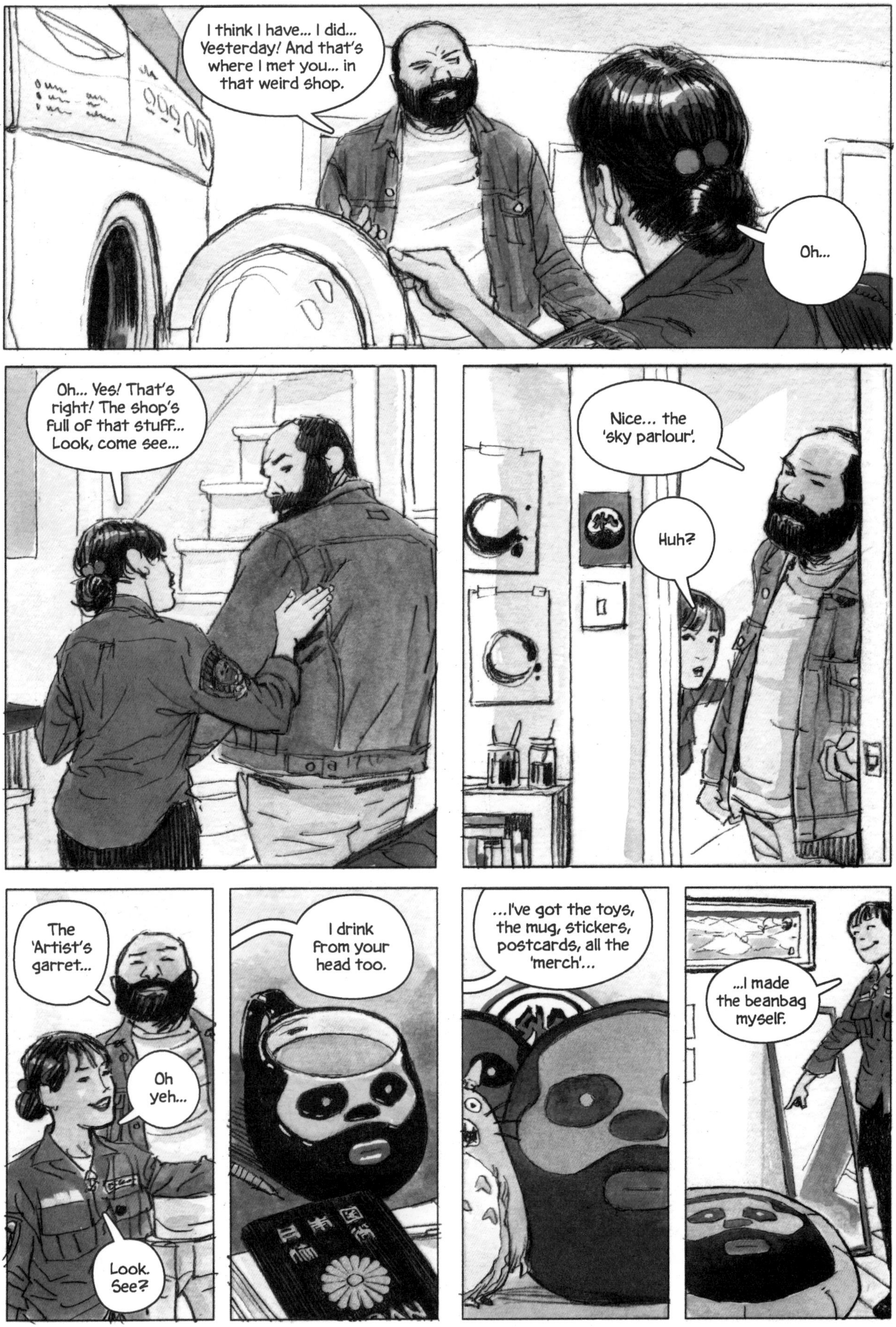

I think I have... I did... Yesterday! And that's where I met you... in that weird shop.
Oh...
Oh... Yes! That's right! The shop's full of that stuff... Look, come see...
Nice... the 'sky parlour'.
Huh?
The 'Artist's garret...
Oh yeh...
Look. See?
I drink from your head too.
...I've got the toys, the mug, stickers, postcards, all the 'merch'...
...I made the beanbag myself.

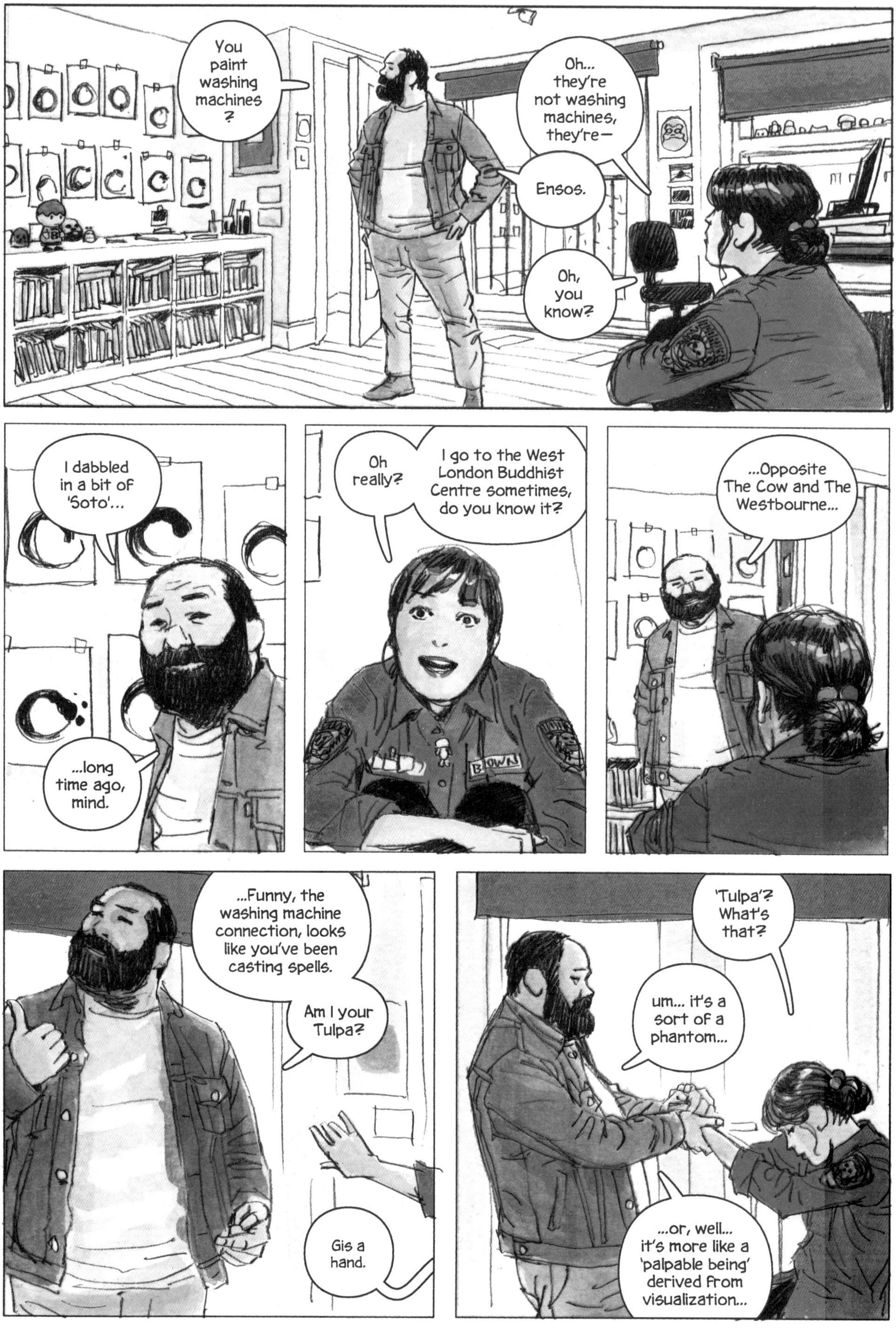
You paint washing machines?
Oh... they're not washing machines, they're—
Ensos.
Oh, you know?
I dabbled in a bit of 'Soto'...
...long time ago, mind.
Oh really?
I go to the West London Buddhist Centre sometimes, do you know it?
...Opposite The Cow and The Westbourne...
...Funny, the washing machine connection, looks like you've been casting spells.
Am I your Tulpa?
Gis a hand.
'Tulpa'? What's that?
um... it's a sort of a phantom...
...or, well... it's more like a 'palpable being' derived from visualization...

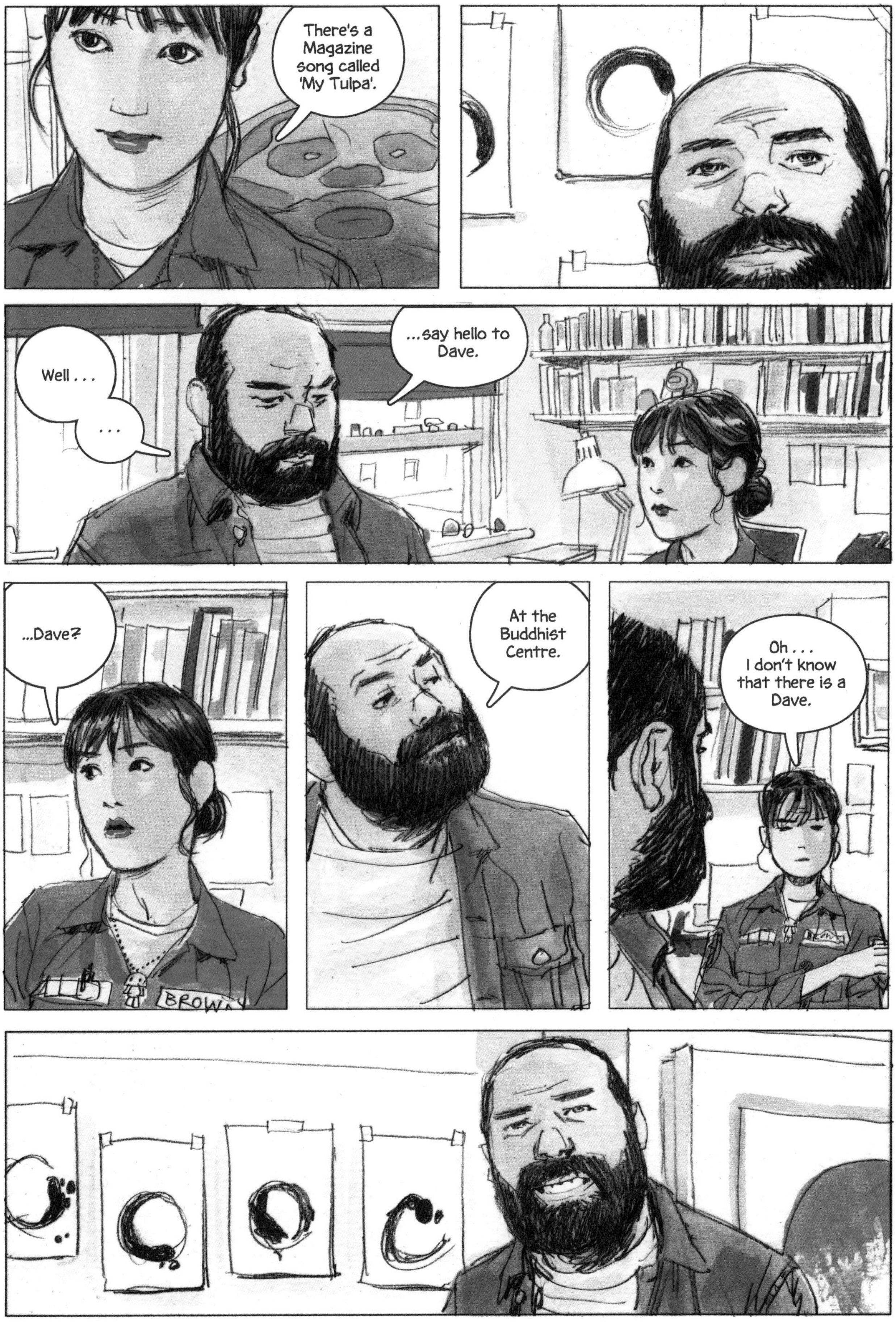
There's a Magazine song called 'My Tulpa'.
Well . . .
. . .
. . . say hello to Dave.
...Dave?
At the Buddhist Centre.
Oh . . . I don't know that there is a Dave.

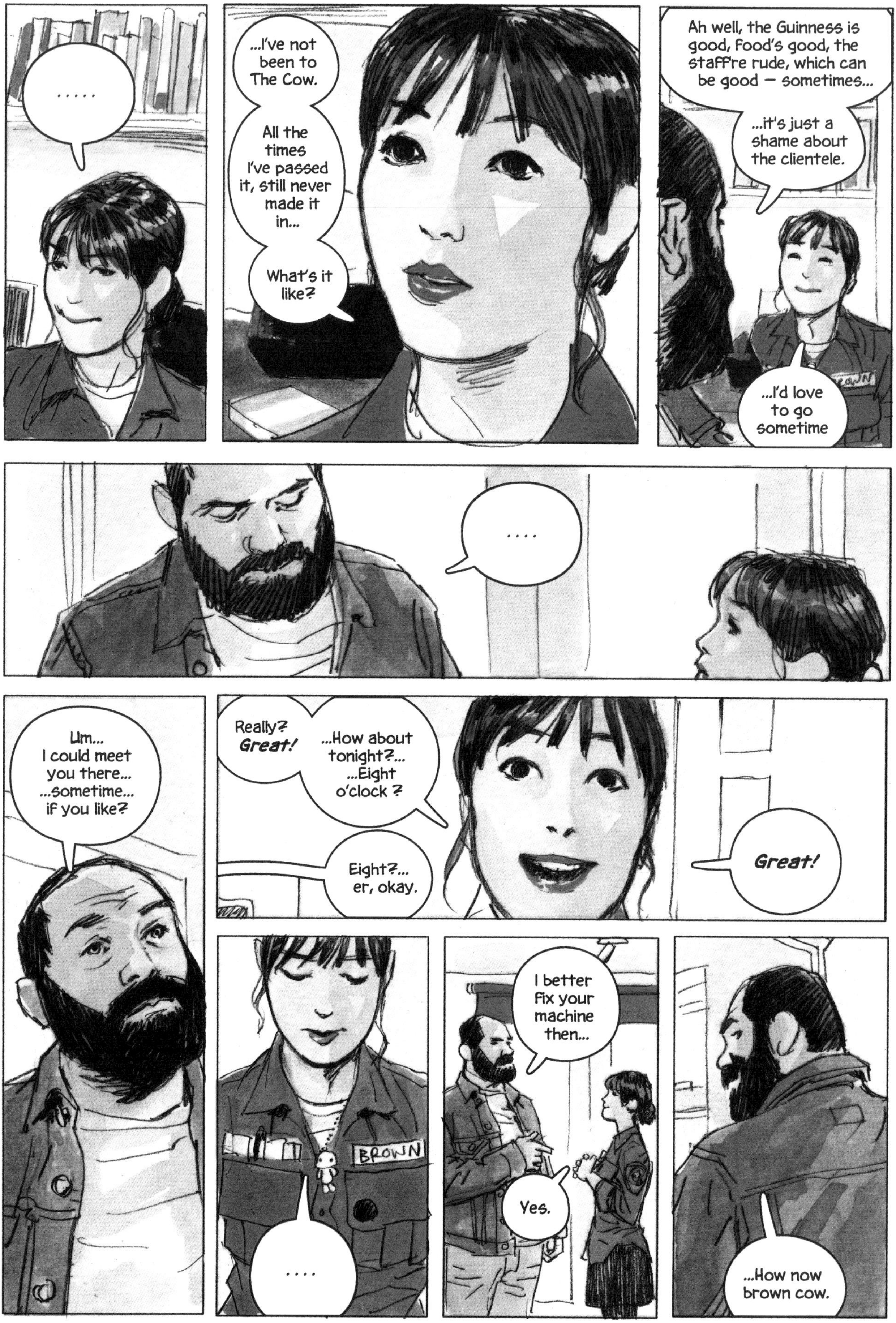
.....
...I've not been to The Cow.
All the times I've passed it, still never made it in...
What's it like?
Ah well, the Guinness is good, food's good, the staff're rude, which can be good — sometimes...
...it's just a shame about the clientele.
...I'd love to go sometime
....
Um... I could meet you there... ...sometime... if you like?
Really? *Great!*
...How about tonight?... ...Eight o'clock ?
Eight?... er, okay.
Great!
....
I better fix your machine then...
Yes.
...How now brown cow.

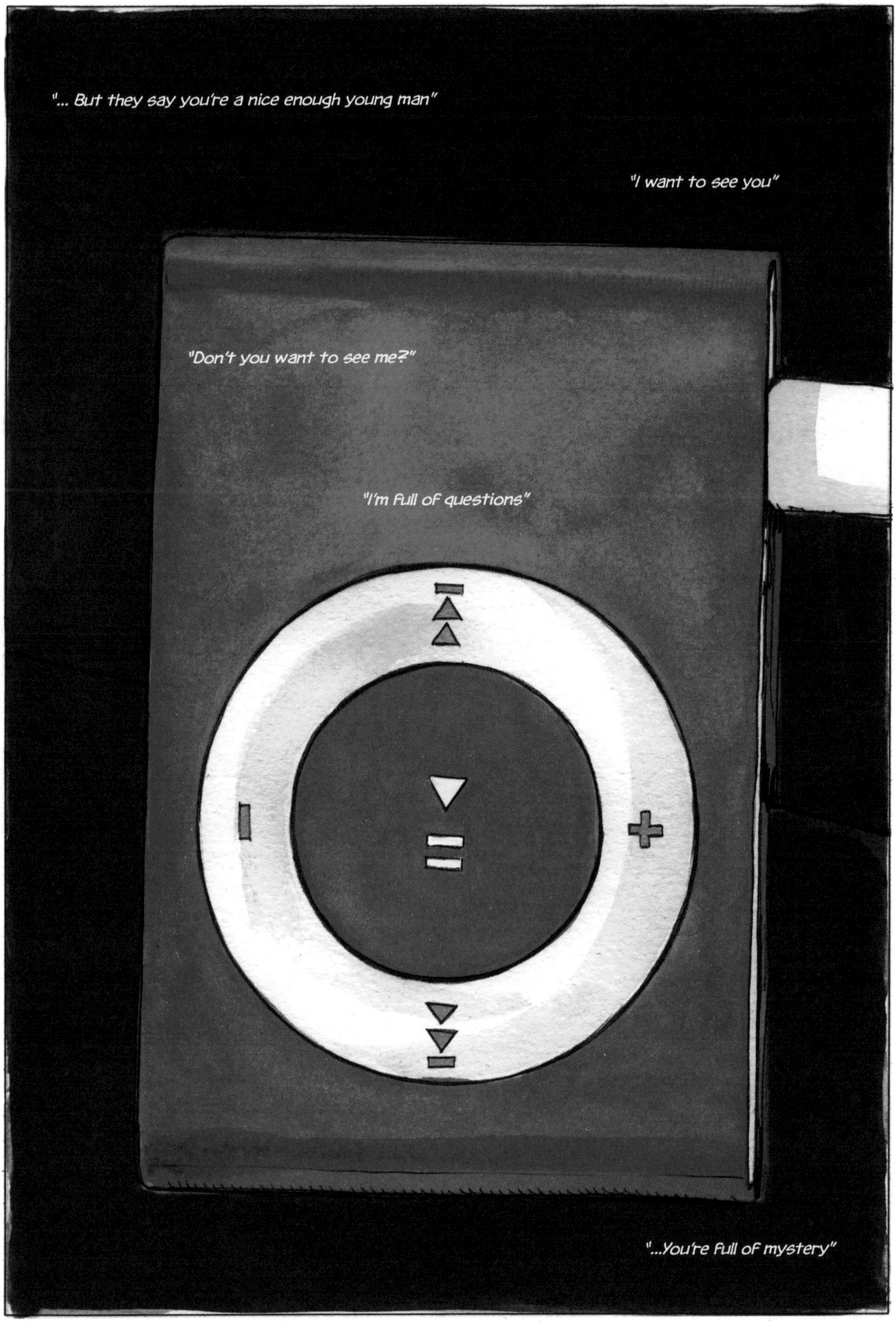
"... But they say you're a nice enough young man"
"I want to see you"
"Don't you want to see me?"
"I'm full of questions"
"...You're full of mystery"

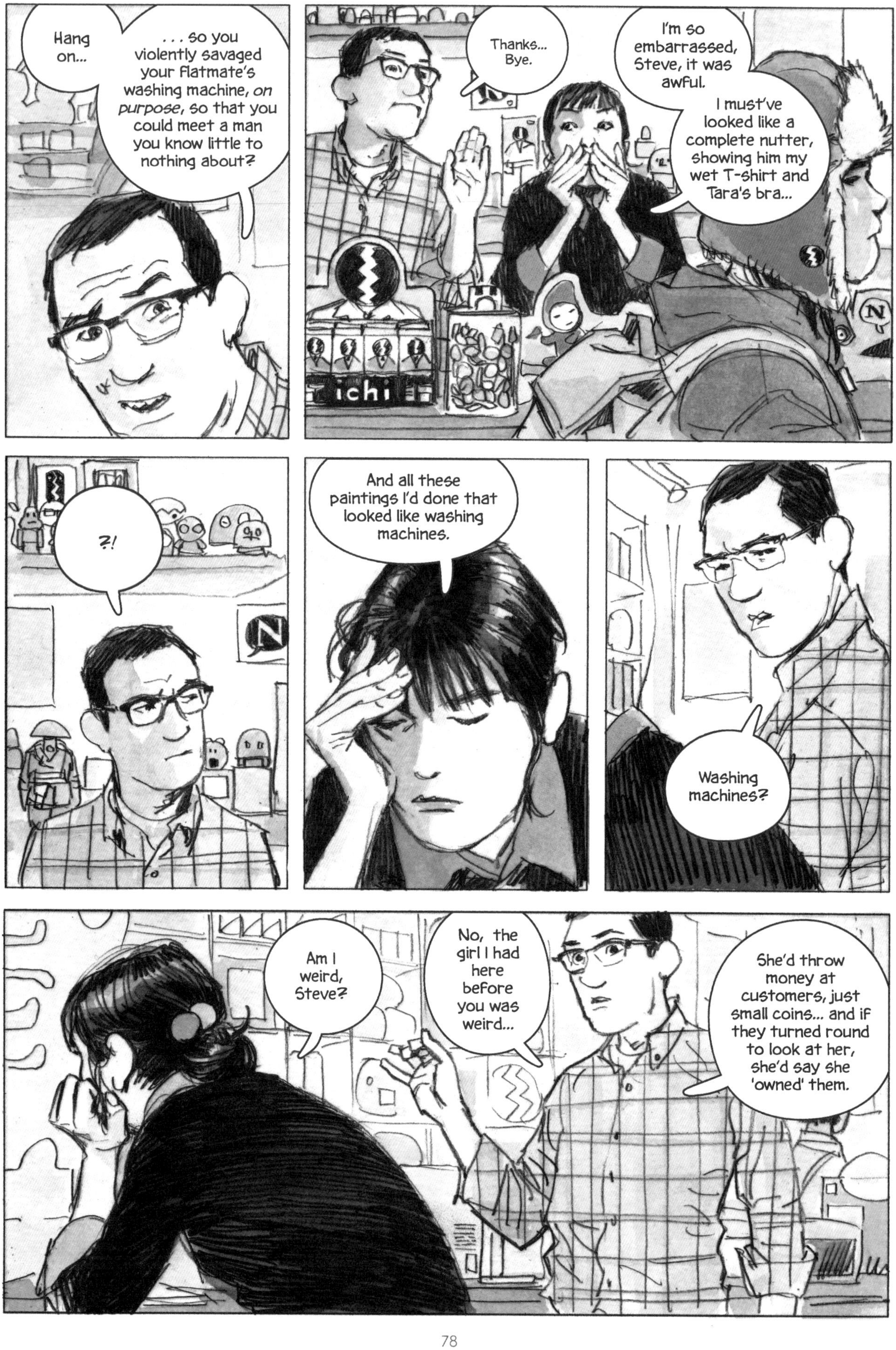
Hang on...
. . . so you violently savaged your flatmate's washing machine, *on purpose*, so that you could meet a man you know little to nothing about?
Thanks... Bye.
I'm so embarrassed, Steve, it was awful.
I must've looked like a complete nutter, showing him my wet T-shirt and Tara's bra...
ichi
?!
And all these paintings I'd done that looked like washing machines.
Washing machines?
Am I weird, Steve?
No, the girl I had here before you was weird...
She'd throw money at customers, just small coins... and if they turned round to look at her, she'd say she 'owned' them.

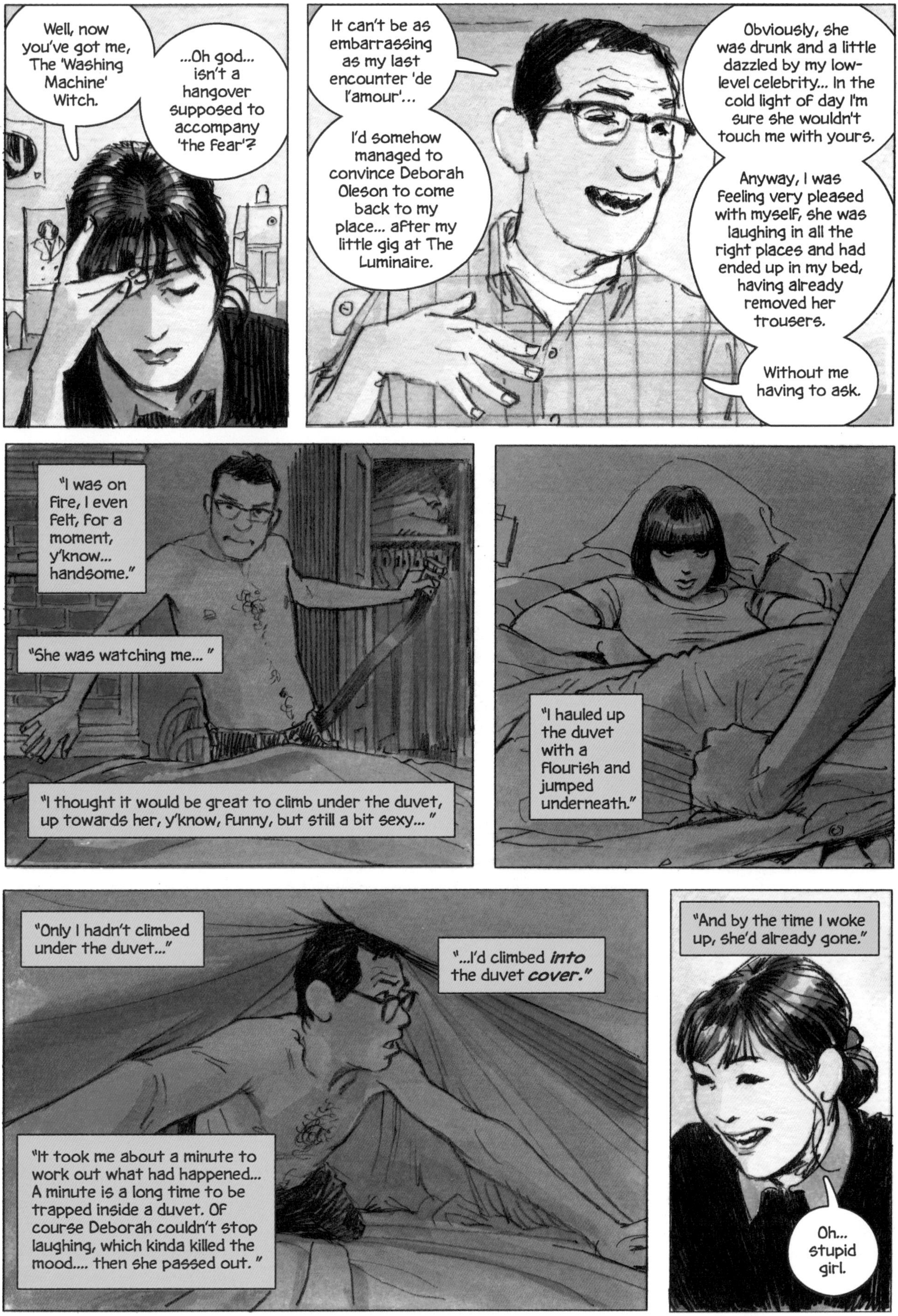
Well, now you've got me, The 'Washing Machine' Witch.
...Oh god... isn't a hangover supposed to accompany 'the fear'?
It can't be as embarrassing as my last encounter 'de l'amour'...
I'd somehow managed to convince Deborah Oleson to come back to my place... after my little gig at The Luminaire.
Obviously, she was drunk and a little dazzled by my low-level celebrity... In the cold light of day I'm sure she wouldn't touch me with yours.
Anyway, I was feeling very pleased with myself, she was laughing in all the right places and had ended up in my bed, having already removed her trousers.
Without me having to ask.
"I was on fire, I even felt, for a moment, y'know... handsome."
"She was watching me..."
"I thought it would be great to climb under the duvet, up towards her, y'know, funny, but still a bit sexy..."
"I hauled up the duvet with a flourish and jumped underneath."
"Only I hadn't climbed under the duvet..."
"...I'd climbed *into* the duvet *cover*."
"It took me about a minute to work out what had happened... A minute is a long time to be trapped inside a duvet. Of course Deborah couldn't stop laughing, which kinda killed the mood.... then she passed out."
"And by the time I woke up, she'd already gone."
Oh... stupid girl.

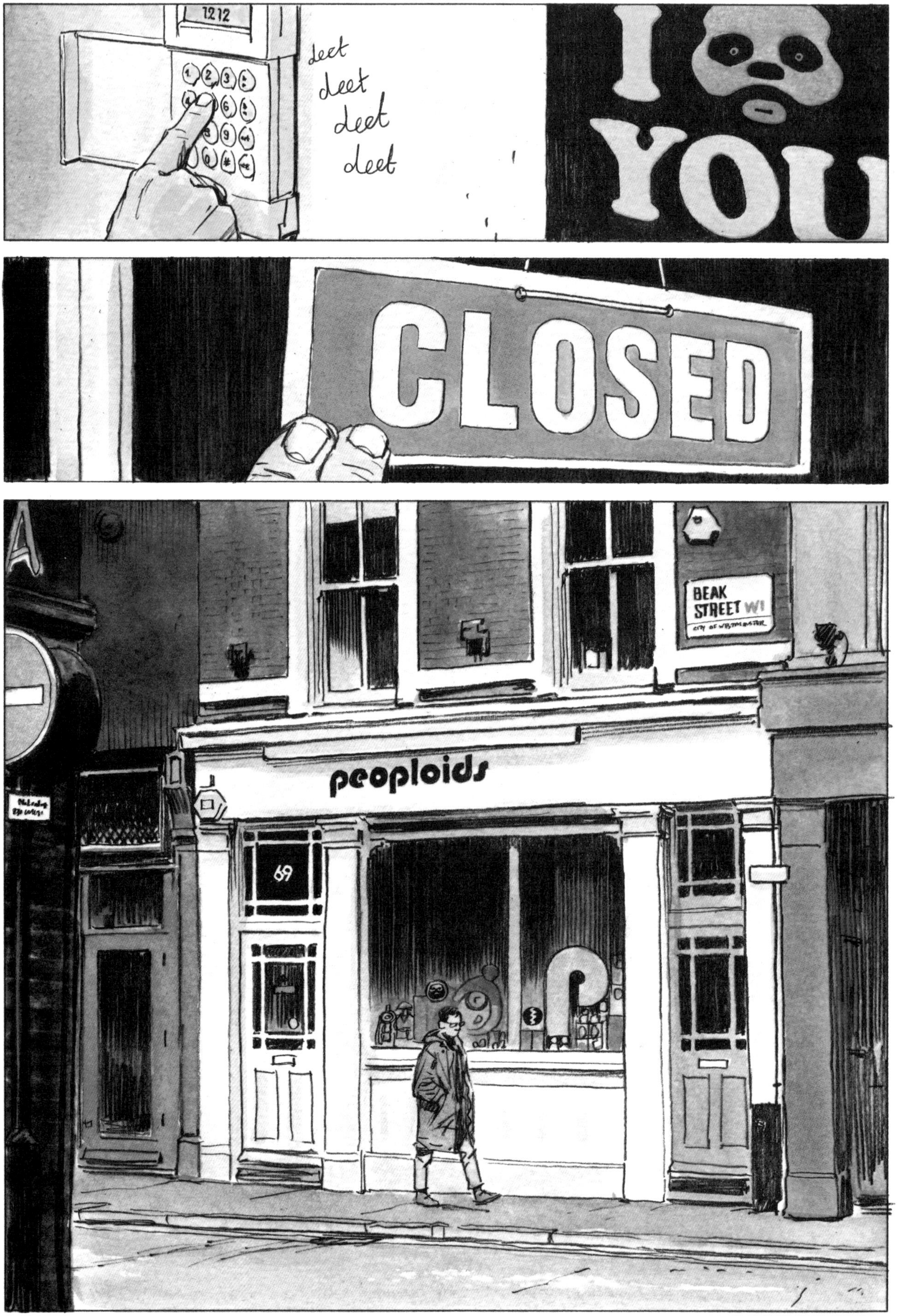
1212
deet
deet
deet
deet
I
YOU
CLOSED
BEAK
STREET W1
peoploids
69

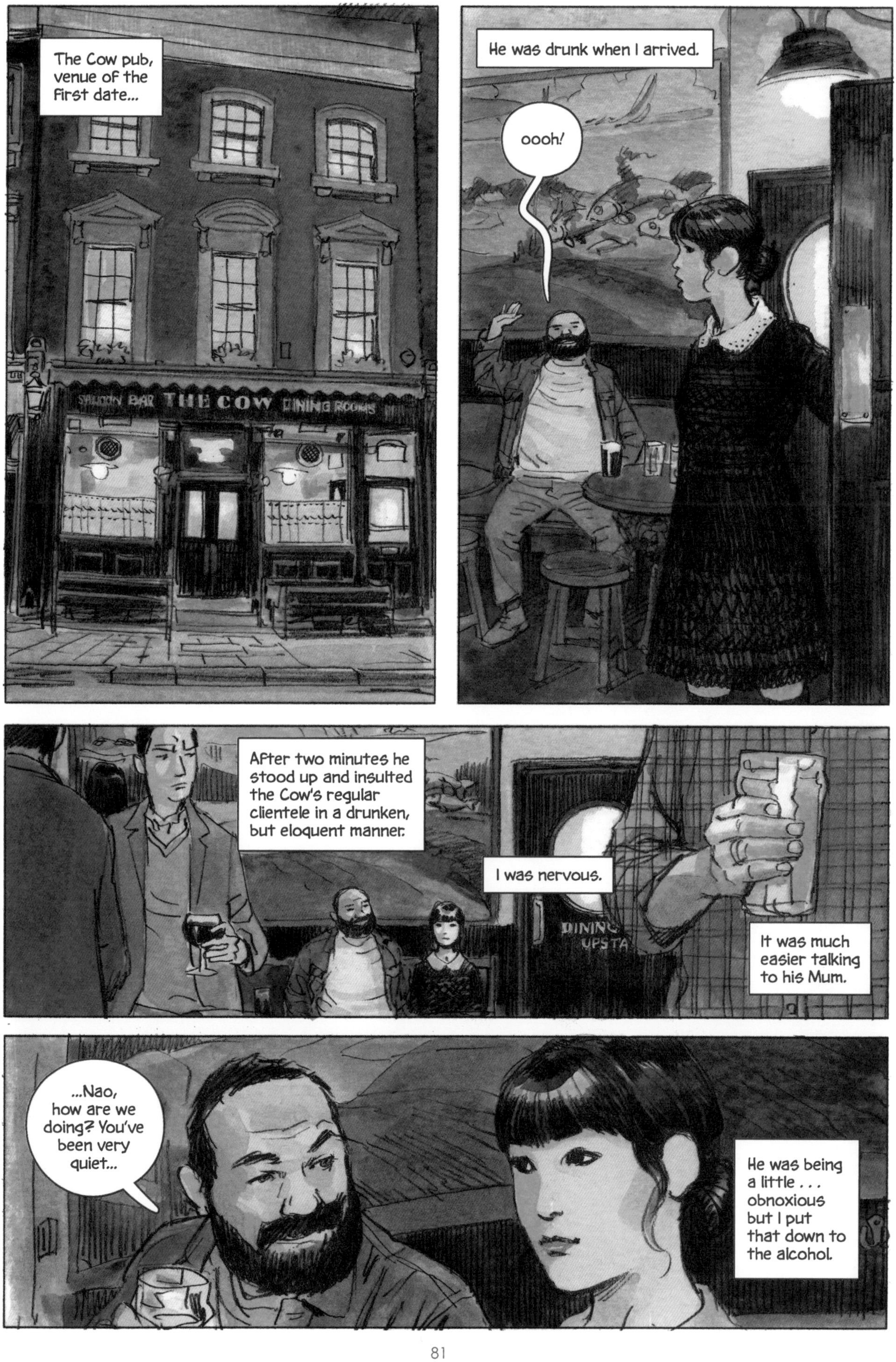

The Cow pub, venue of the first date...
SALOON BAR THE COW DINING ROOMS
He was drunk when I arrived.
oooh!
After two minutes he stood up and insulted the Cow's regular clientele in a drunken, but eloquent manner.
I was nervous.
DINING UPSTA
It was much easier talking to his Mum.
...Nao, how are we doing? You've been very quiet...
He was being a little . . . obnoxious but I put that down to the alcohol.

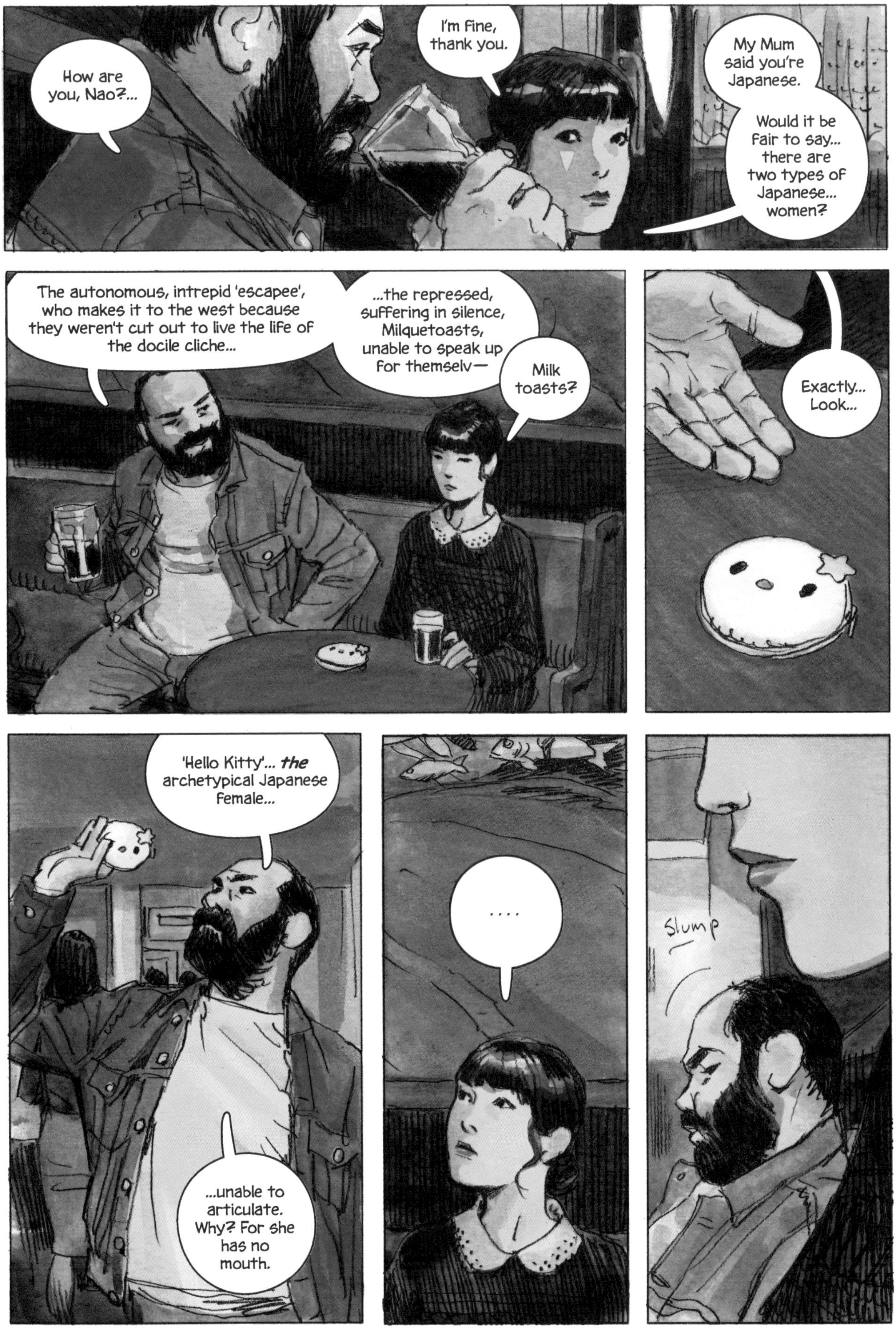
How are you, Nao?...
I'm fine, thank you.
My Mum said you're Japanese.
Would it be fair to say... there are two types of Japanese... women?
The autonomous, intrepid 'escapee', who makes it to the west because they weren't cut out to live the life of the docile cliche...
...the repressed, suffering in silence, Milquetoasts, unable to speak up for themselv—
Milk toasts?
Exactly... Look...
'Hello Kitty'... *the* archetypical Japanese Female...
...unable to articulate. Why? For she has no mouth.
....
Slump

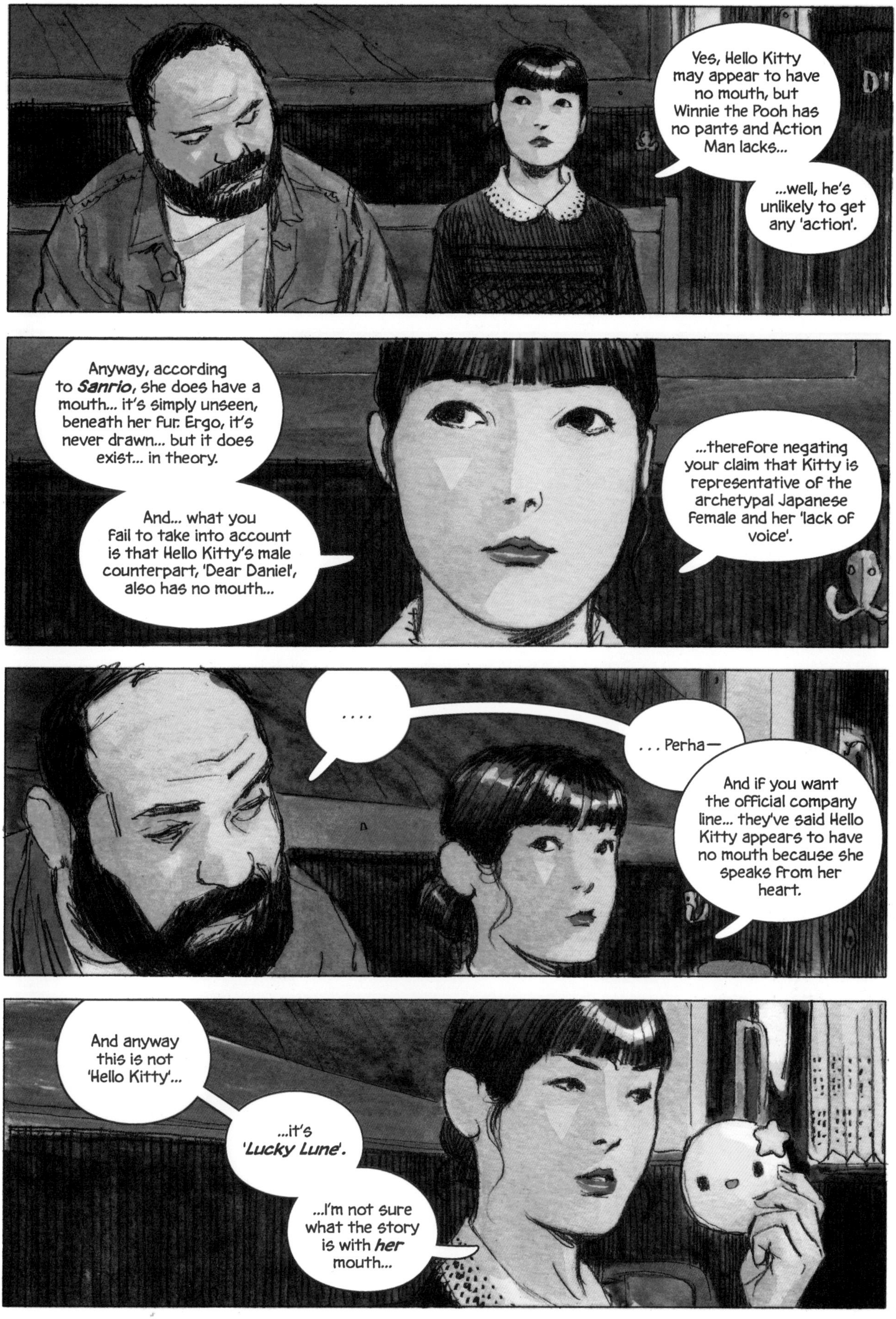
Yes, Hello Kitty may appear to have no mouth, but Winnie the Pooh has no pants and Action Man lacks...
...well, he's unlikely to get any 'action'.
Anyway, according to ***Sanrio***, she does have a mouth... it's simply unseen, beneath her fur. Ergo, it's never drawn... but it does exist... in theory.
And... what you fail to take into account is that Hello Kitty's male counterpart, 'Dear Daniel', also has no mouth...
...therefore negating your claim that Kitty is representative of the archetypal Japanese female and her 'lack of voice'.
....
... Perha—
And if you want the official company line... they've said Hello Kitty appears to have no mouth because she speaks from her heart.
And anyway this is not 'Hello Kitty'...
...it's ***'Lucky Lune'***.
...I'm not sure what the story is with ***her*** mouth...

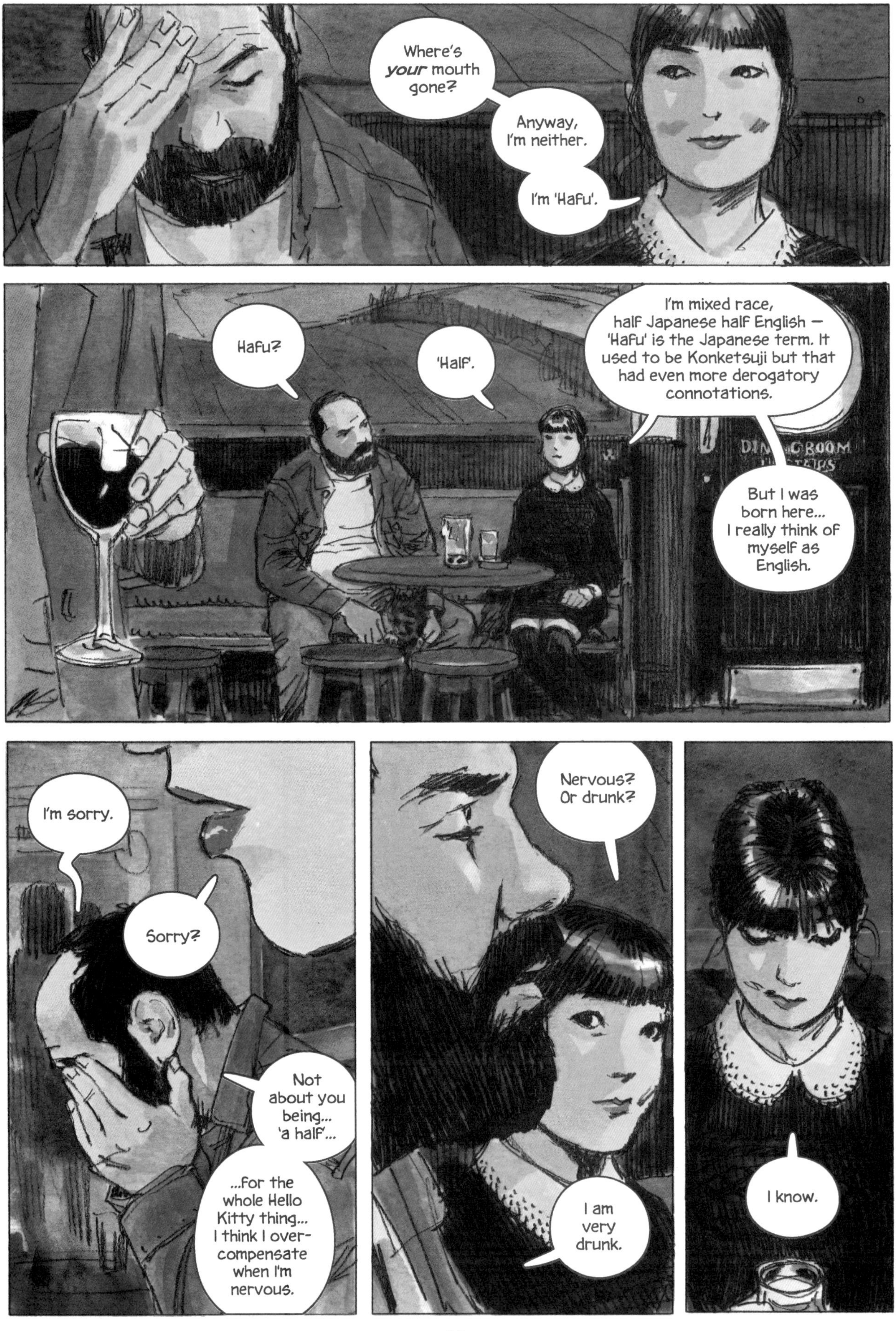

Where's *your* mouth gone?
Anyway, I'm neither.
I'm 'Hafu'.
Hafu?
'Half'.
I'm mixed race, half Japanese half English — 'Hafu' is the Japanese term. It used to be Konketsuji but that had even more derogatory connotations.
But I was born here... I really think of myself as English.
I'm sorry.
Sorry?
Not about you being... 'a half'...
...for the whole Hello Kitty thing... I think I over-compensate when I'm nervous.
Nervous? Or drunk?
I am very drunk.
I know.

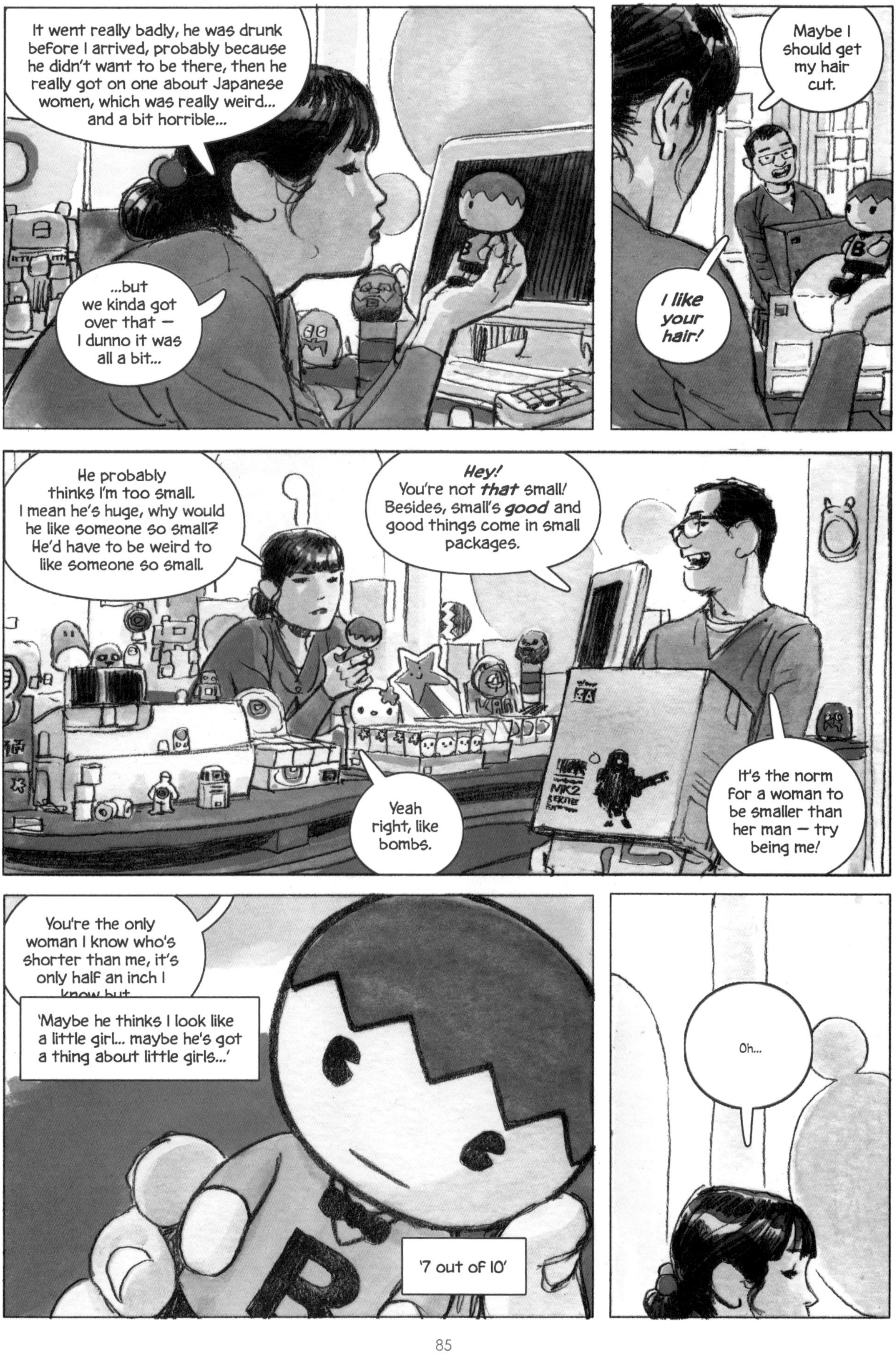

It went really badly, he was drunk before I arrived, probably because he didn't want to be there, then he really got on one about Japanese women, which was really weird... and a bit horrible...
...but we kinda got over that — I dunno it was all a bit...
Maybe I should get my hair cut.
I like your hair!
He probably thinks I'm too small. I mean he's huge, why would he like someone so small? He'd have to be weird to like someone so small.
Hey! You're not *that* small! Besides, small's *good* and good things come in small packages.
Yeah right, like bombs.
It's the norm for a woman to be smaller than her man — try being me!
You're the only woman I know who's shorter than me, it's only half an inch I know but...
'Maybe he thinks I look like a little girl... maybe he's got a thing about little girls...'
'7 out of 10'
Oh...

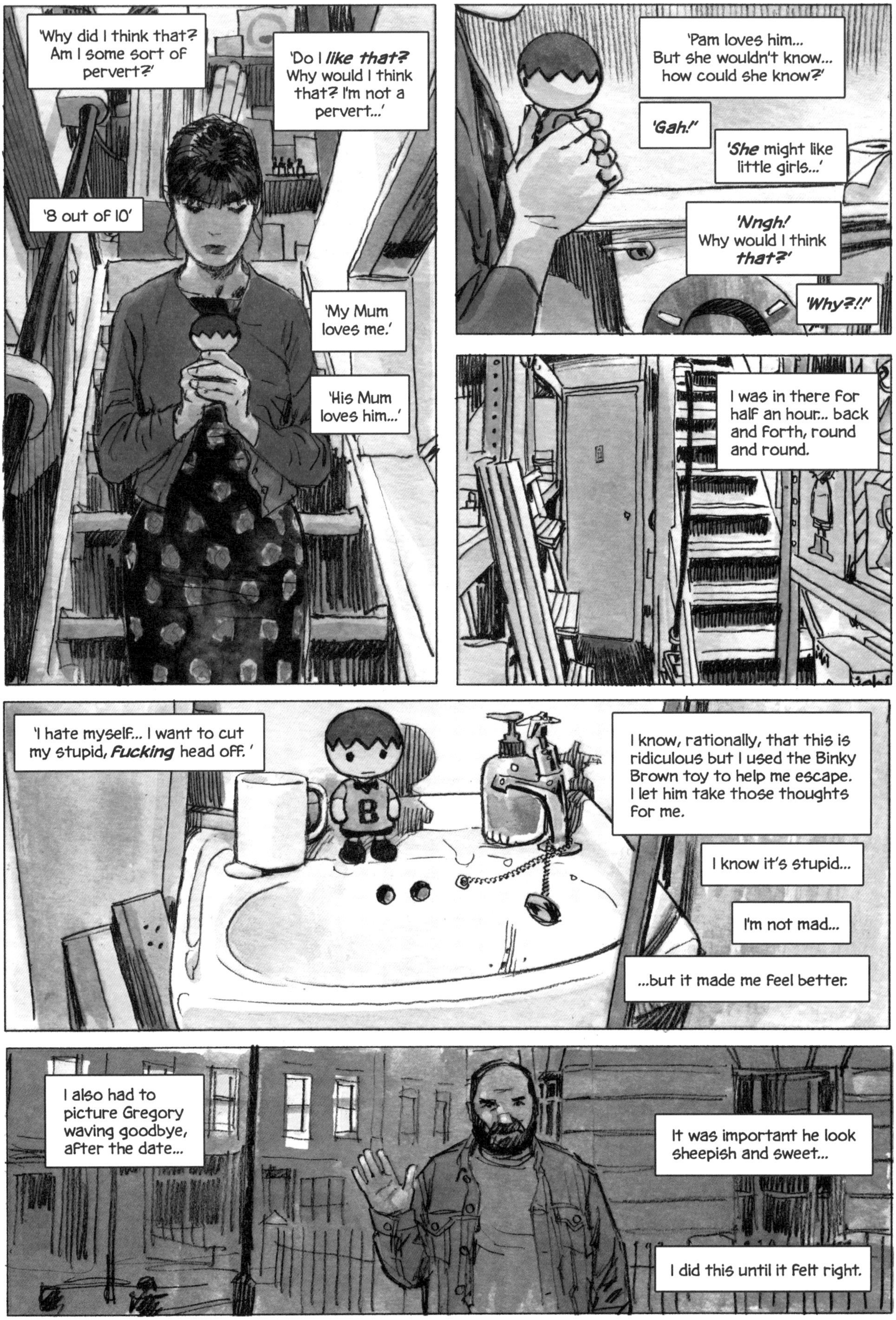

'Why did I think that? Am I some sort of pervert?'
'Do I *like that?* Why would I think that? I'm not a pervert...'
'8 out of 10'
'My Mum loves me.'
'His Mum loves him...'
'Pam loves him... But she wouldn't know... how could she know?'
'Gah!'
'*She* might like little girls...'
'*Nngh!* Why would I think *that?*'
'Why?!!'
I was in there for half an hour... back and forth, round and round.
'I hate myself... I want to cut my stupid, *Fucking* head off.'
I know, rationally, that this is ridiculous but I used the Binky Brown toy to help me escape. I let him take those thoughts for me.
I know it's stupid...
I'm not mad...
...but it made me feel better.
I also had to picture Gregory waving goodbye, after the date...
It was important he look sheepish and sweet...
I did this until it felt right.

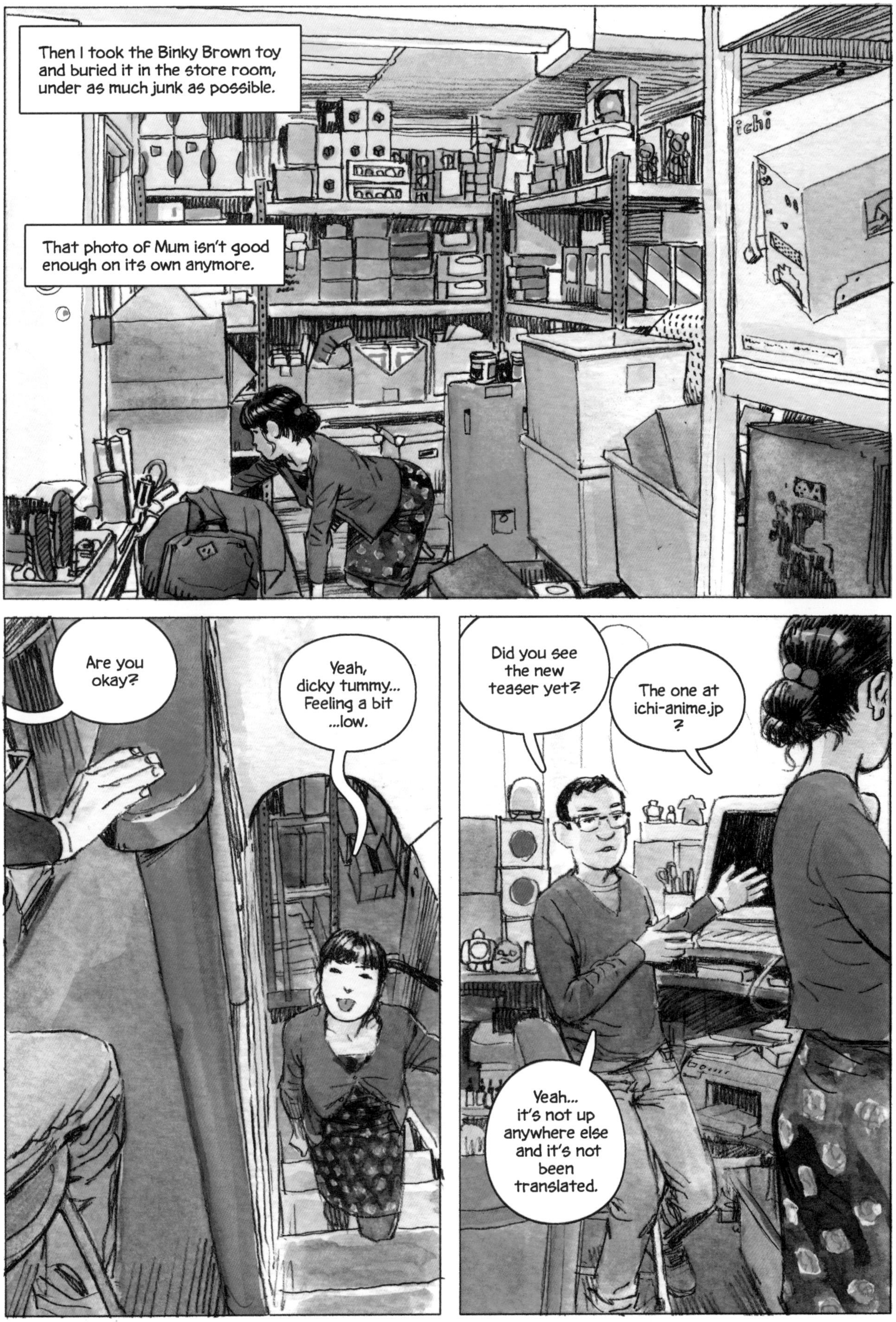
Then I took the Binky Brown toy and buried it in the store room, under as much junk as possible.
That photo of Mum isn't good enough on its own anymore.
ichi
Are you okay?
Yeah, dicky tummy... Feeling a bit ...low.
Did you see the new teaser yet?
The one at ichi-anime.jp ?
Yeah... it's not up anywhere else and it's not been translated.

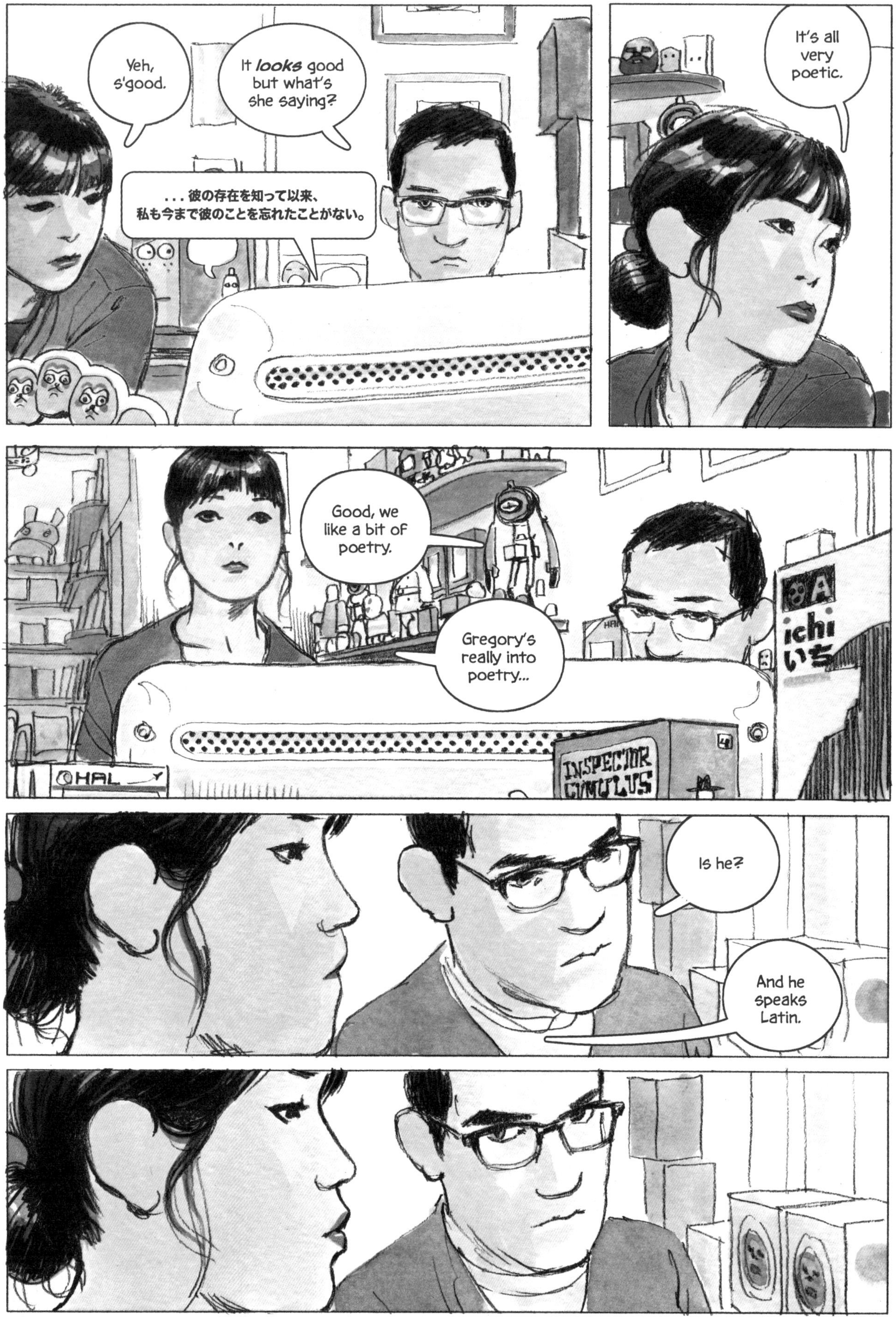
Yeh, s'good.
It *looks* good but what's she saying?
. . . 彼の存在を知って以来、私も今まで彼のことを忘れたことがない。
It's all very poetic.
Good, we like a bit of poetry.
Gregory's really into poetry...
HAL
INSPECTOR CUMULUS
ichi いち
Is he?
And he speaks Latin.

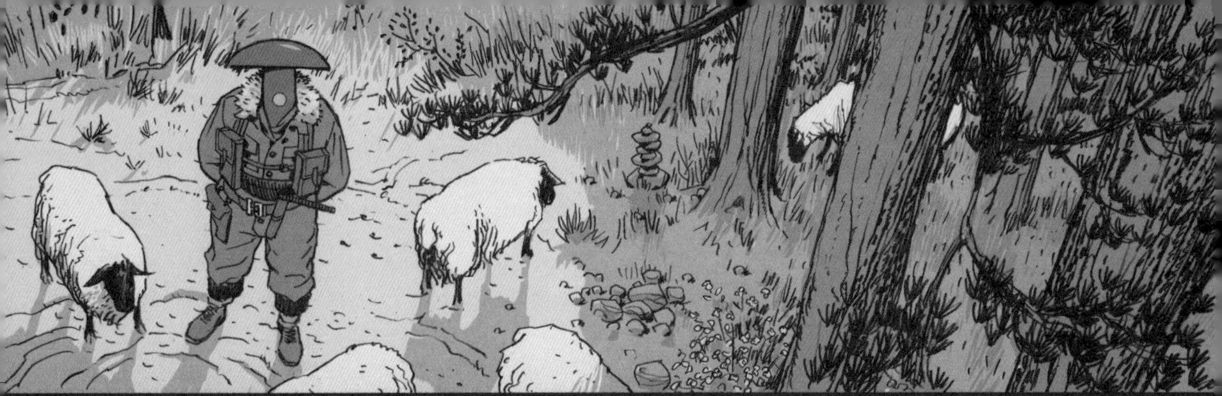

The good boy Pictor continued tending his herd. He was always content to be sitting, perched in his roost. Now it happened that another Captain came driving by with a small company of men. He too had lost his way, unable to find the route back to his fort. He too had heard the comforting music from afar and ordered his sergeant to go see what it was. So the sergeant went to the tree, saw the sheep and looked up to see Pictor sitting in the branches playing a small black music box. "What are you doing up there?" asked the sergeant. "I'm sitting... What can I do for you?" The sergeant asked whether he could guide them out of the woods since they were lost.

Pictor climbed down from the tree with his music box and told the old Captain that he would show him the way only if the Captain agreed to give him his daughter's hand in marriage. This Captain agreed and put it in writing that the boy Pictor was to have what he desired. When that was done Pictor strode ahead of them with his sheep, guiding them on their way.

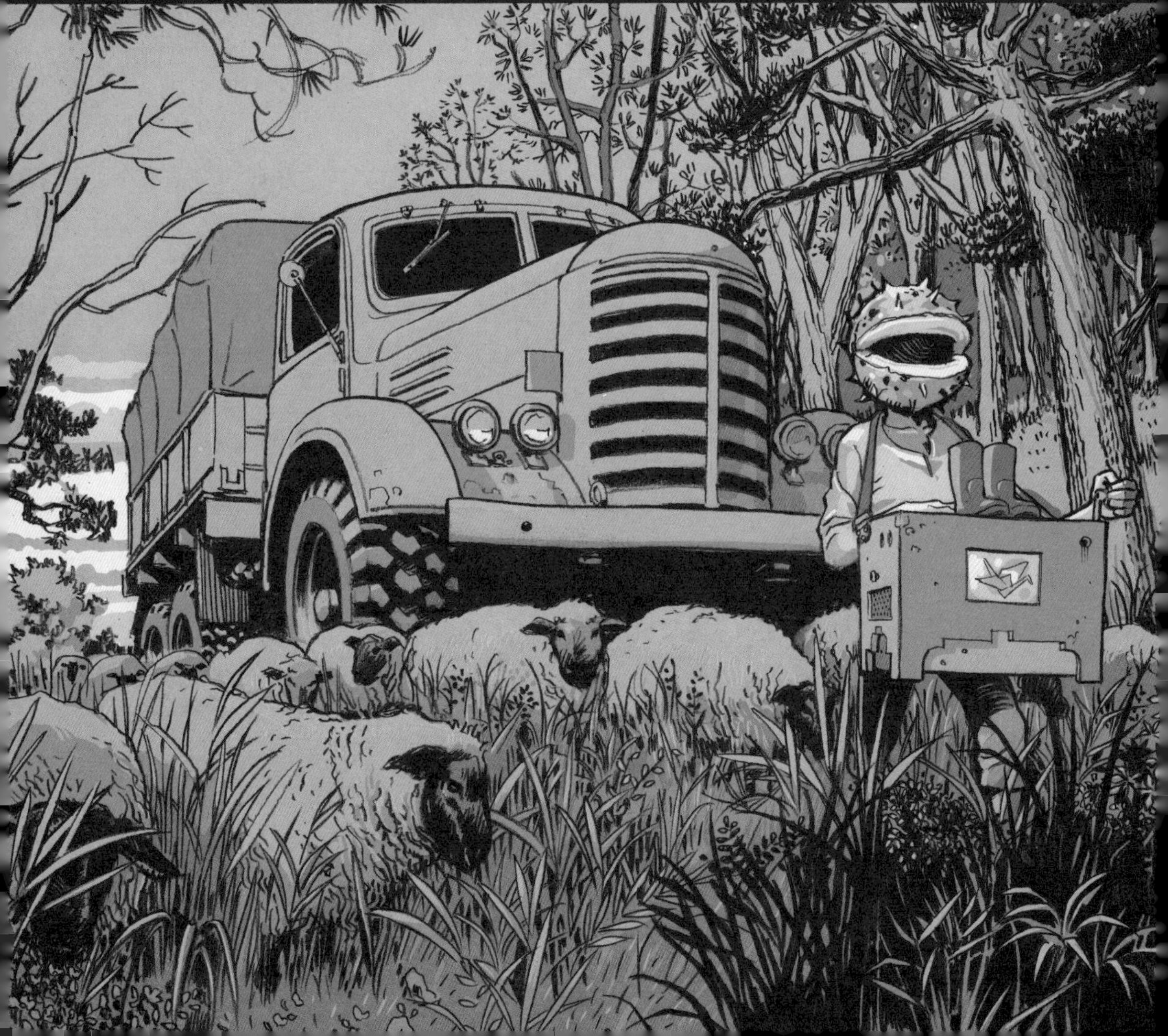

The Captain reached his fort safely, and as he entered the courtyard there was much gladness at his return. His only daughter, who was very beautiful, ran to him and embraced him. He told her he had lost his way and would not have made it back at all had it not been for a strange wood creature — part human, part tree — who had helped him find his way out of the giant woods. In return for this aid, he had promised to give him his daughter's hand in marriage. Now he was very sorry it had happened, especially as she was his only child. However, out of love for her old father, the daughter promised him that she would honour his pledge and go with this Pictor creature whenever he came.

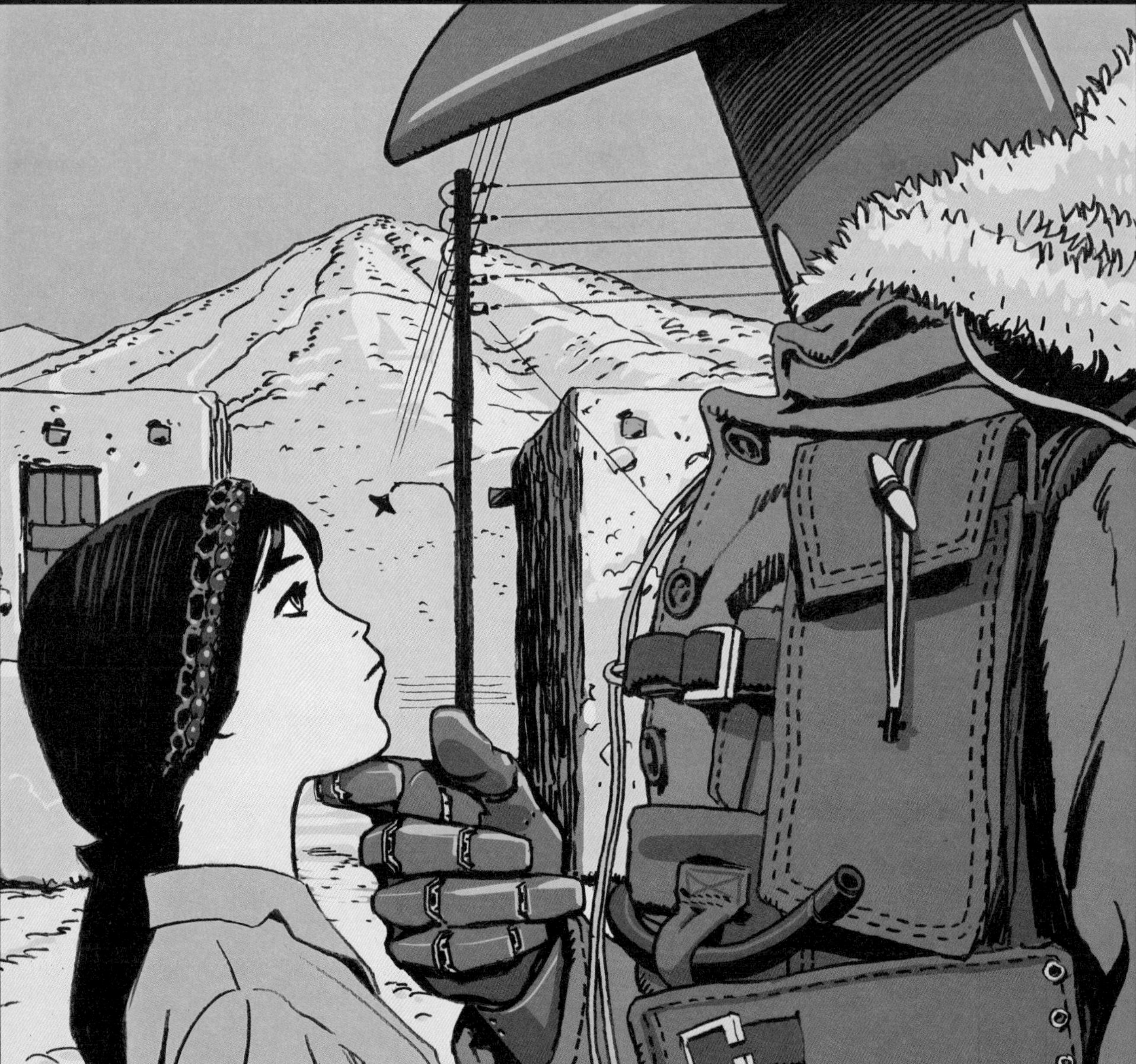

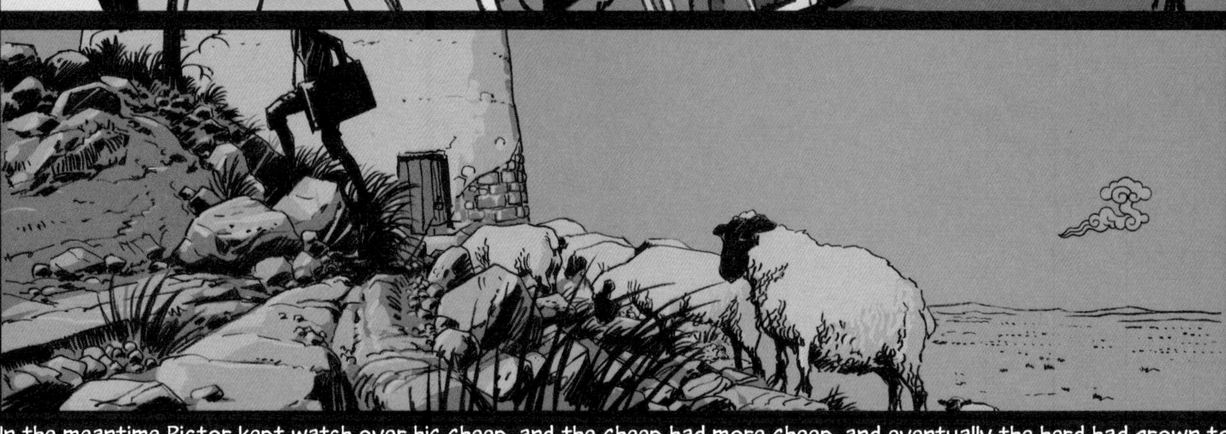

In the meantime Pictor kept watch over his sheep, and the sheep had more sheep, and eventually the herd had grown to be most unwieldy, so Pictor decided it was time to return to his old family home.... The tree was still there, uprooted, still fighting... in fact, it didn't even notice that Pictor had returned...

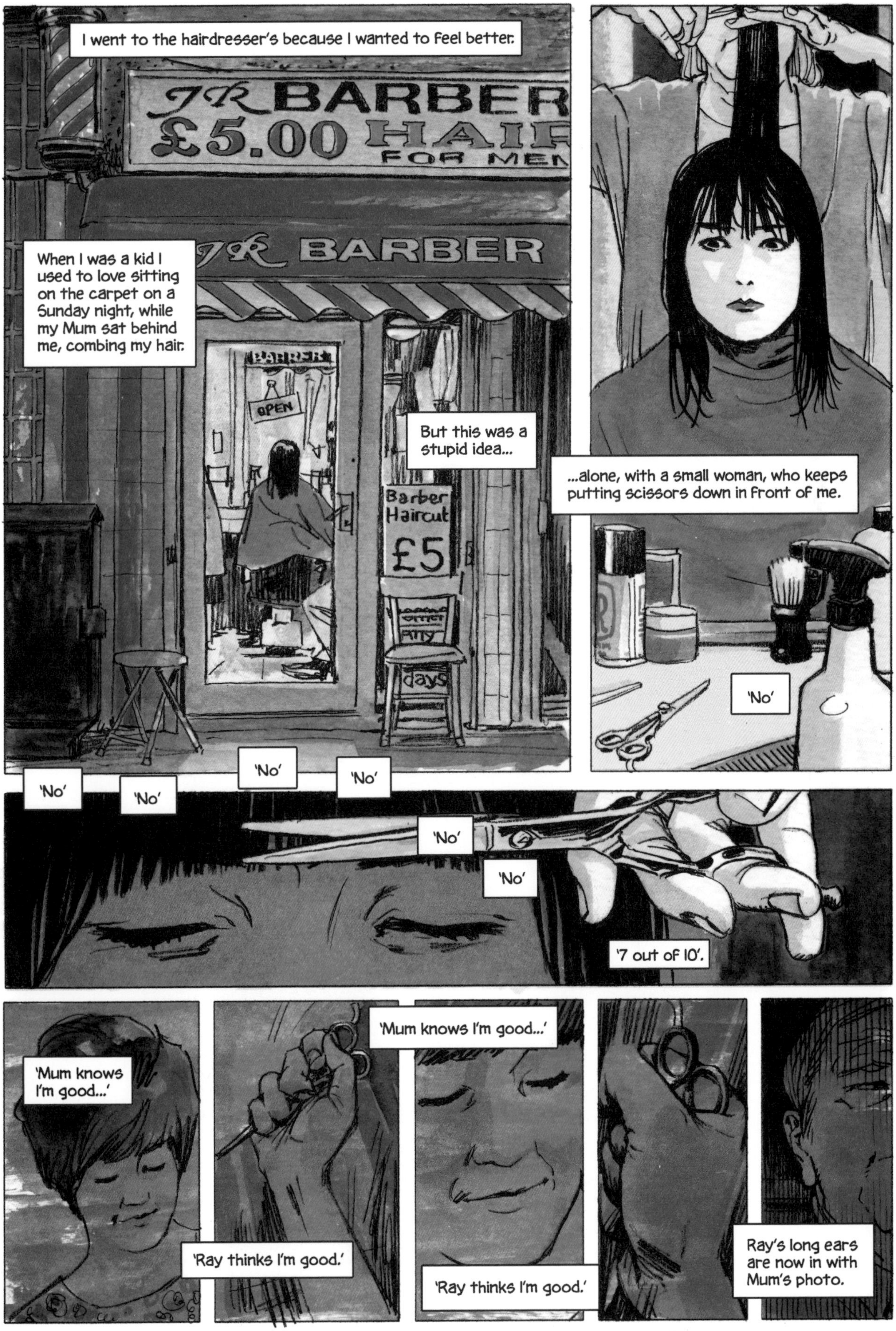
I went to the hairdresser's because I wanted to feel better.
JR BARBER
£5.00 HAIR
FOR MEN
JR BARBER
When I was a kid I used to love sitting on the carpet on a Sunday night, while my Mum sat behind me, combing my hair.
OPEN
But this was a stupid idea...
Barber Haircut £5
...alone, with a small woman, who keeps putting scissors down in front of me.
'No'
'No'
'No'
'No'
'No'
'No'
'No'
'7 out of 10'.
'Mum knows I'm good...'
'Ray thinks I'm good.'
'Mum knows I'm good...'
'Ray thinks I'm good.'
Ray's long ears are now in with Mum's photo.

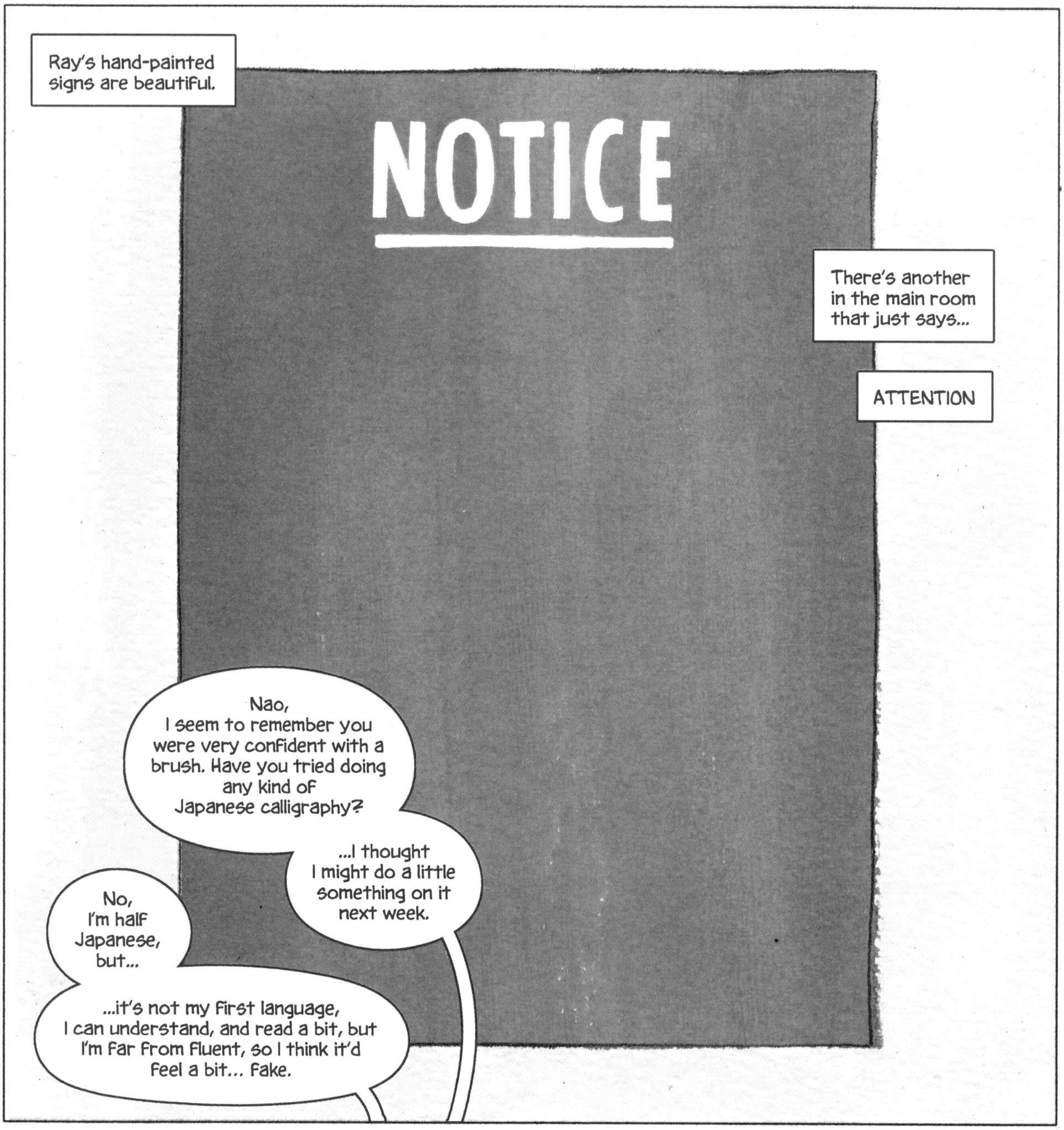
Ray's hand-painted signs are beautiful.
NOTICE
There's another in the main room that just says...
ATTENTION
Nao, I seem to remember you were very confident with a brush. Have you tried doing any kind of Japanese calligraphy?
No, I'm half Japanese, but...
...it's not my first language, I can understand, and read a bit, but I'm far from fluent, so I think it'd feel a bit... fake.
...I thought I might do a little something on it next week.

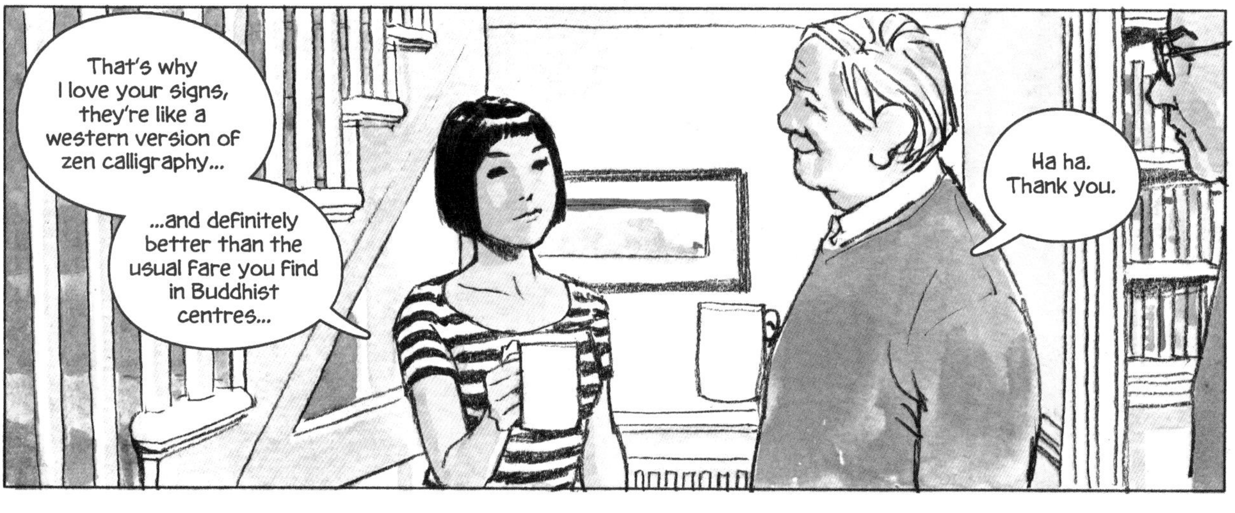
That's why I love your signs, they're like a western version of zen calligraphy...
...and definitely better than the usual fare you find in Buddhist centres...
Ha ha. Thank you.

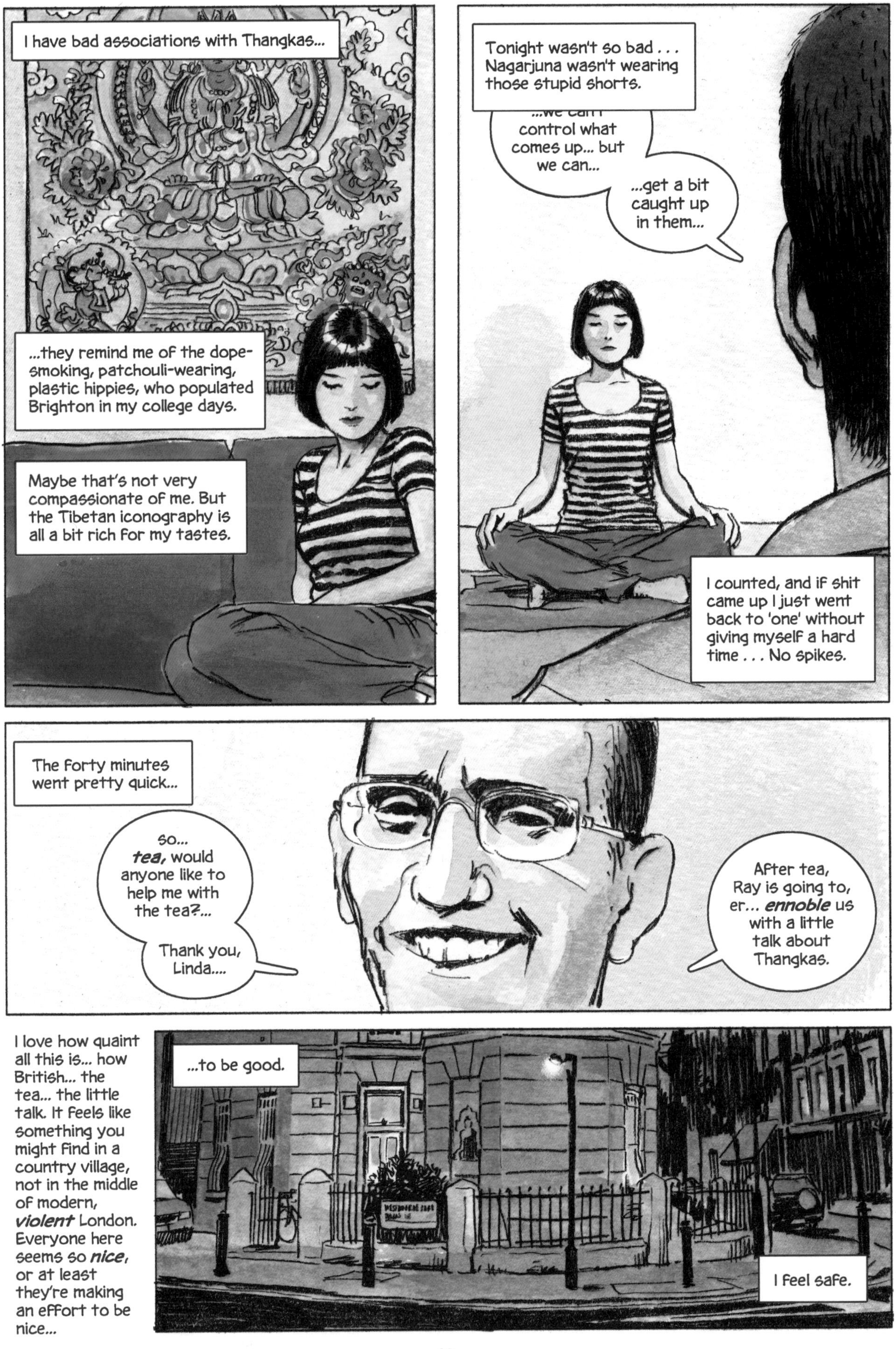
I have bad associations with Thangkas...
...they remind me of the dope-smoking, patchouli-wearing, plastic hippies, who populated Brighton in my college days.
Maybe that's not very compassionate of me. But the Tibetan iconography is all a bit rich for my tastes.
Tonight wasn't so bad . . . Nagarjuna wasn't wearing those stupid shorts.
control what comes up... but we can...
...get a bit caught up in them...
I counted, and if shit came up I just went back to 'one' without giving myself a hard time . . . No spikes.
The forty minutes went pretty quick...
so... *tea,* would anyone like to help me with the tea?...
Thank you, Linda....
After tea, Ray is going to, er... *ennoble* us with a little talk about Thangkas.
I love how quaint all this is... how British... the tea... the little talk. It feels like something you might find in a country village, not in the middle of modern, *violent* London. Everyone here seems so *nice,* or at least they're making an effort to be nice...
...to be good.
I feel safe.

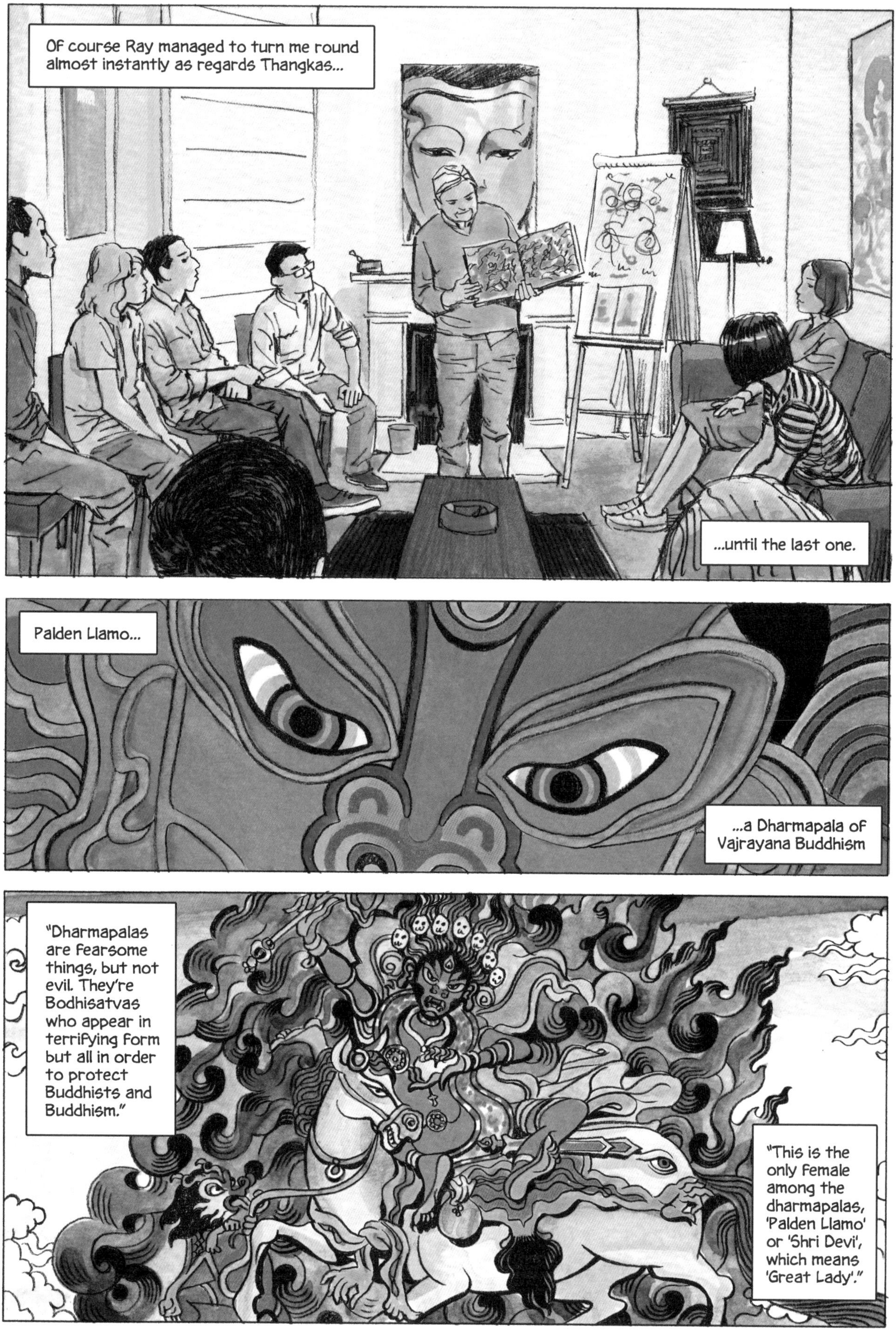
Of course Ray managed to turn me round almost instantly as regards Thangkas...
...until the last one.
Palden Llamo...
...a Dharmapala of Vajrayana Buddhism
"Dharmapalas are fearsome things, but not evil. They're Bodhisatvas who appear in terrifying form but all in order to protect Buddhists and Buddhism."
"This is the only female among the dharmapalas, 'Palden Llamo' or 'Shri Devi', which means 'Great Lady'."

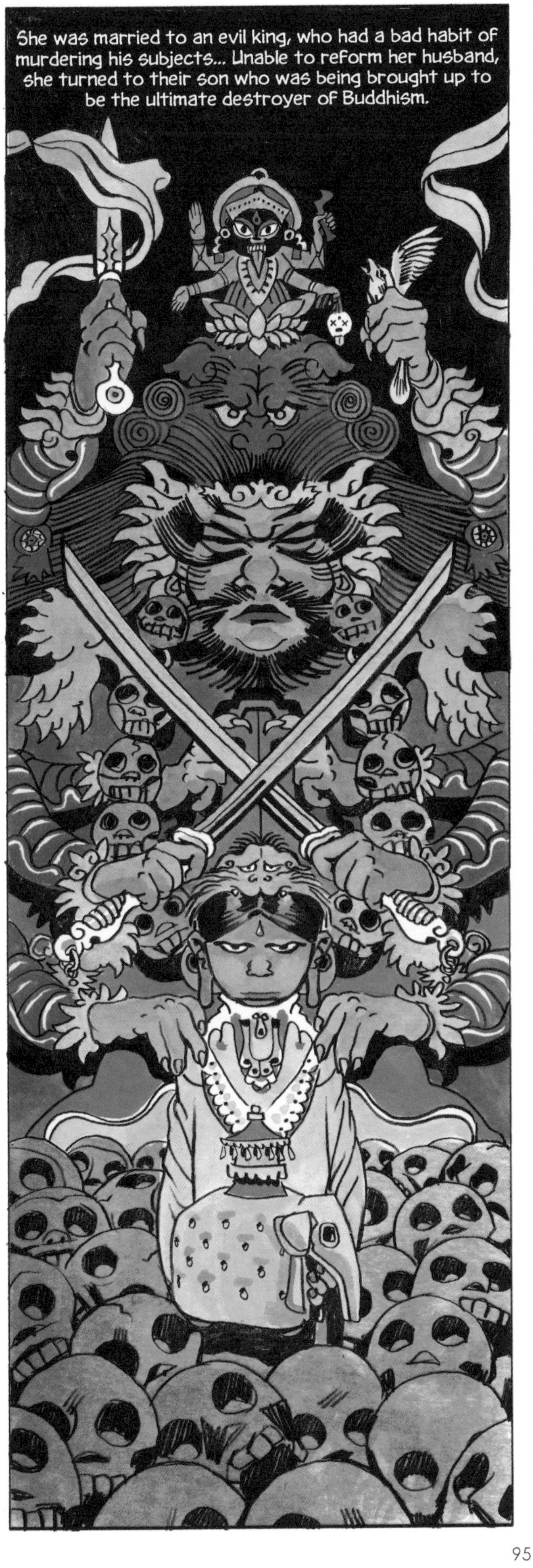
She was married to an evil king, who had a bad habit of murdering his subjects... Unable to reform her husband, she turned to their son who was being brought up to be the ultimate destroyer of Buddhism.

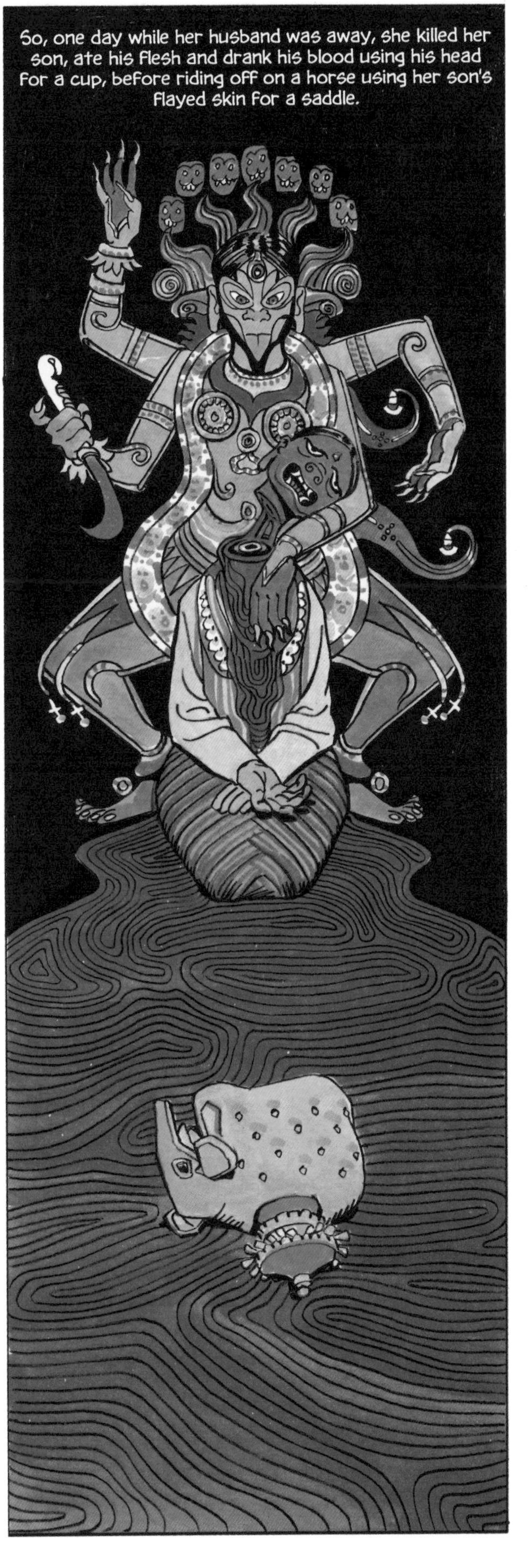
So, one day while her husband was away, she killed her son, ate his flesh and drank his blood using his head for a cup, before riding off on a horse using her son's flayed skin for a saddle.

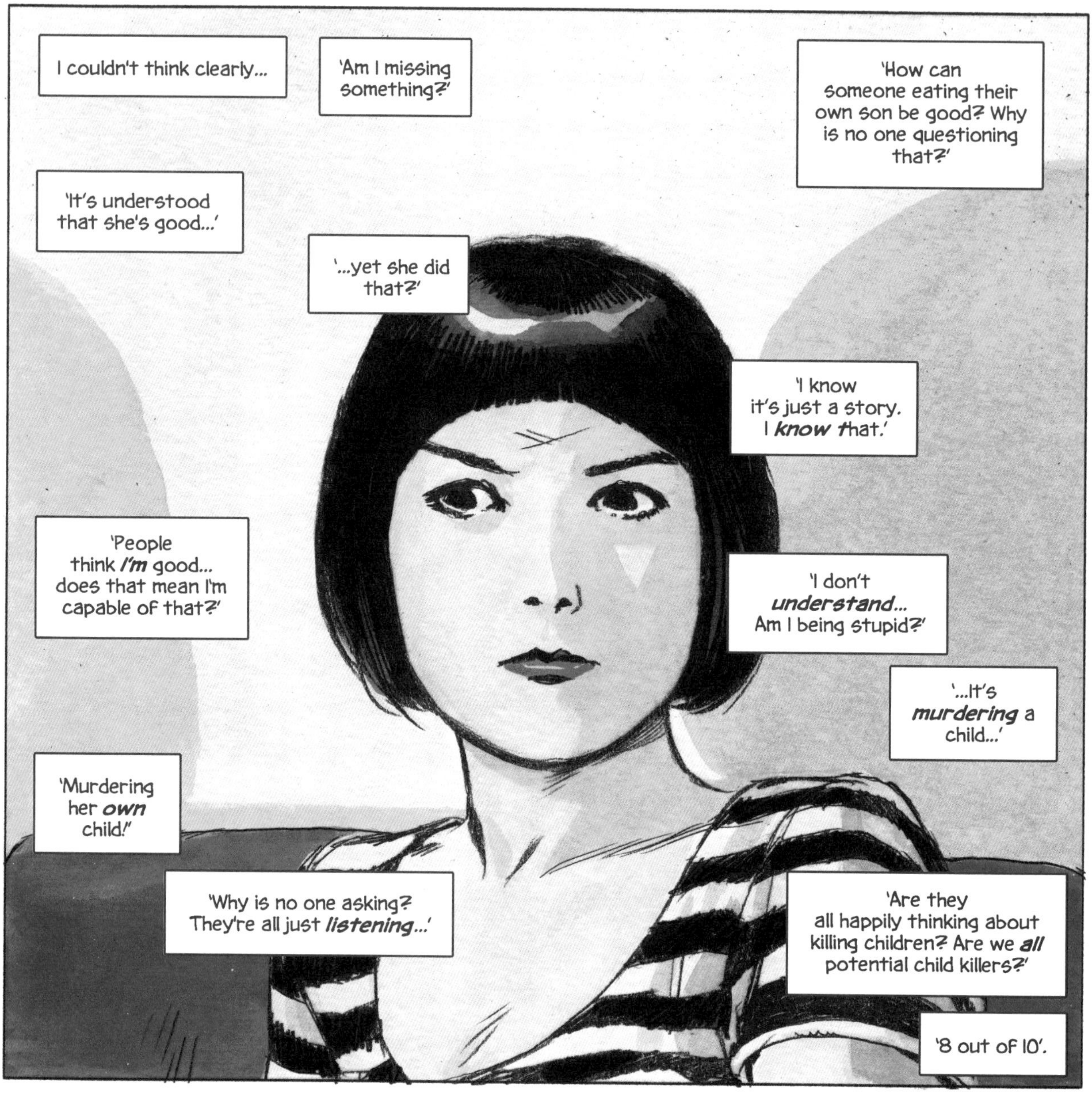
I couldn't think clearly...
'Am I missing something?'
'How can someone eating their own son be good? Why is no one questioning that?'
'It's understood that she's good...'
'...yet she did that?'
'I know it's just a story. I *know* that.'
'People think *I'm* good... does that mean I'm capable of that?'
'I don't *understand*... Am I being stupid?'
'...It's *murdering* a child...'
'Murdering her *own* child!'
'Why is no one asking? They're all just *listening*...'
'Are they all happily thinking about killing children? Are we *all* potential child killers?'
'8 out of 10'.

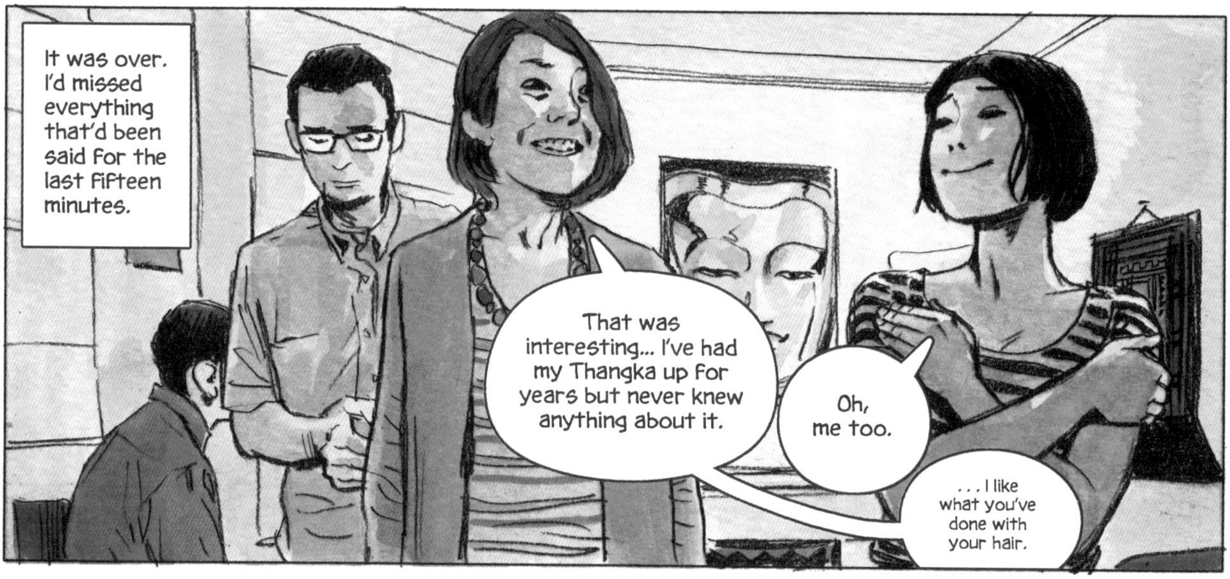
It was over. I'd missed everything that'd been said for the last fifteen minutes.
That was interesting... I've had my Thangka up for years but never knew anything about it.
Oh, me too.
. . . I like what you've done with your hair.

I'd done the dishes already...

...hung the washing out...

...I'd even colour co-ordinated my Tintin books...

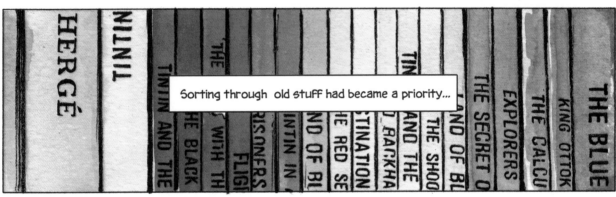

Sorting through old stuff had became a priority...

Anything to avoid *'homework'*.

Weird.

Riiiiiiiiiiiiiiiiiiing... Riiiiiiiiiiiiiiiii-

Gregory?

He was drunk...

...said he'd written a poem about me...

But he'd written it on the back of an invoice sheet, then forgot, and gave it to his next customer...

...and now he can't remember how it went.

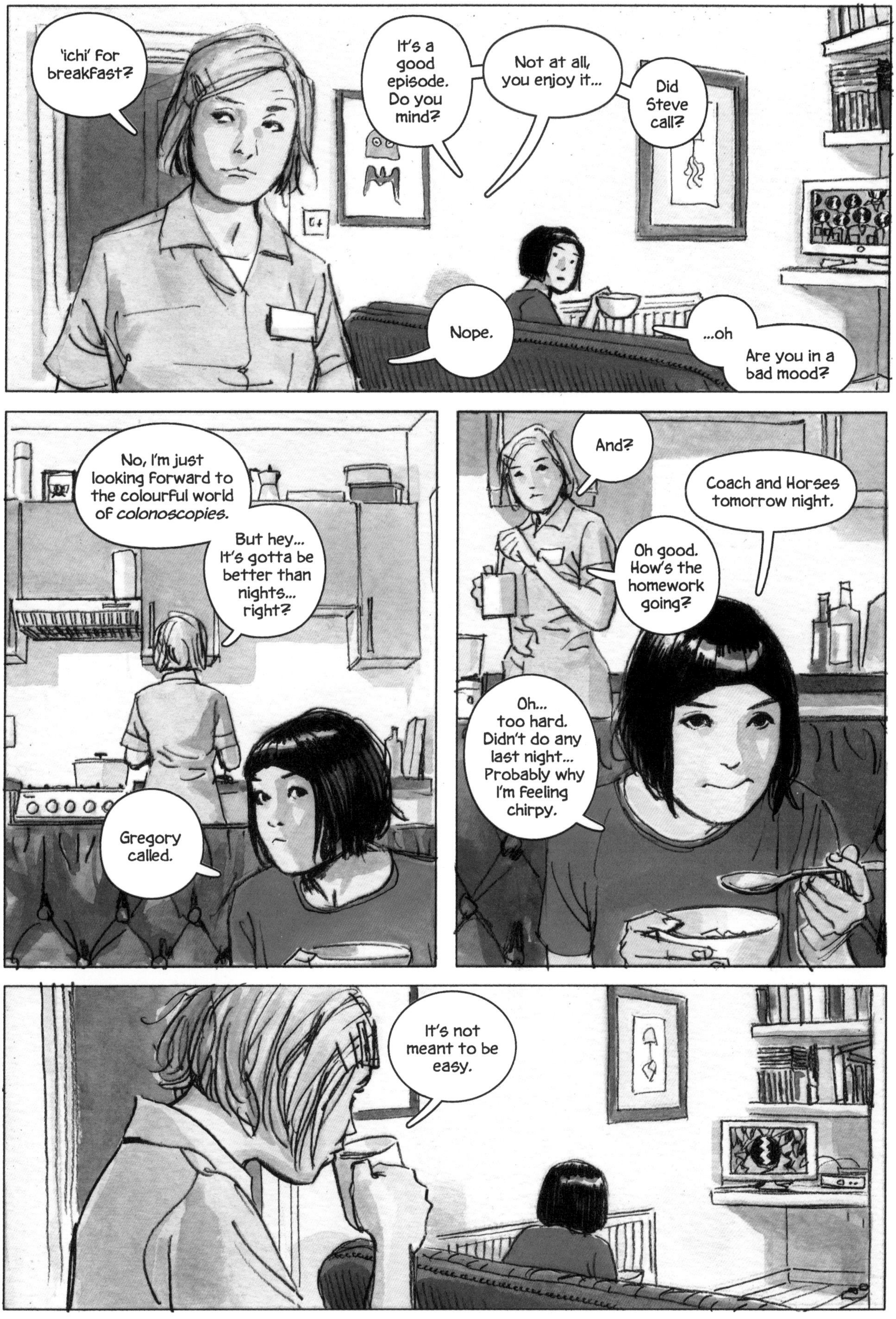
'ichi' for breakfast?
It's a good episode. Do you mind?
Not at all, you enjoy it...
Did Steve call?
Nope.
...oh
Are you in a bad mood?
No, I'm just looking forward to the colourful world of *colonoscopies.*
But hey... It's gotta be better than nights... right?
Gregory called.
And?
Coach and Horses tomorrow night.
Oh good. How's the homework going?
Oh... too hard. Didn't do any last night... Probably why I'm feeling chirpy.
It's not meant to be easy.

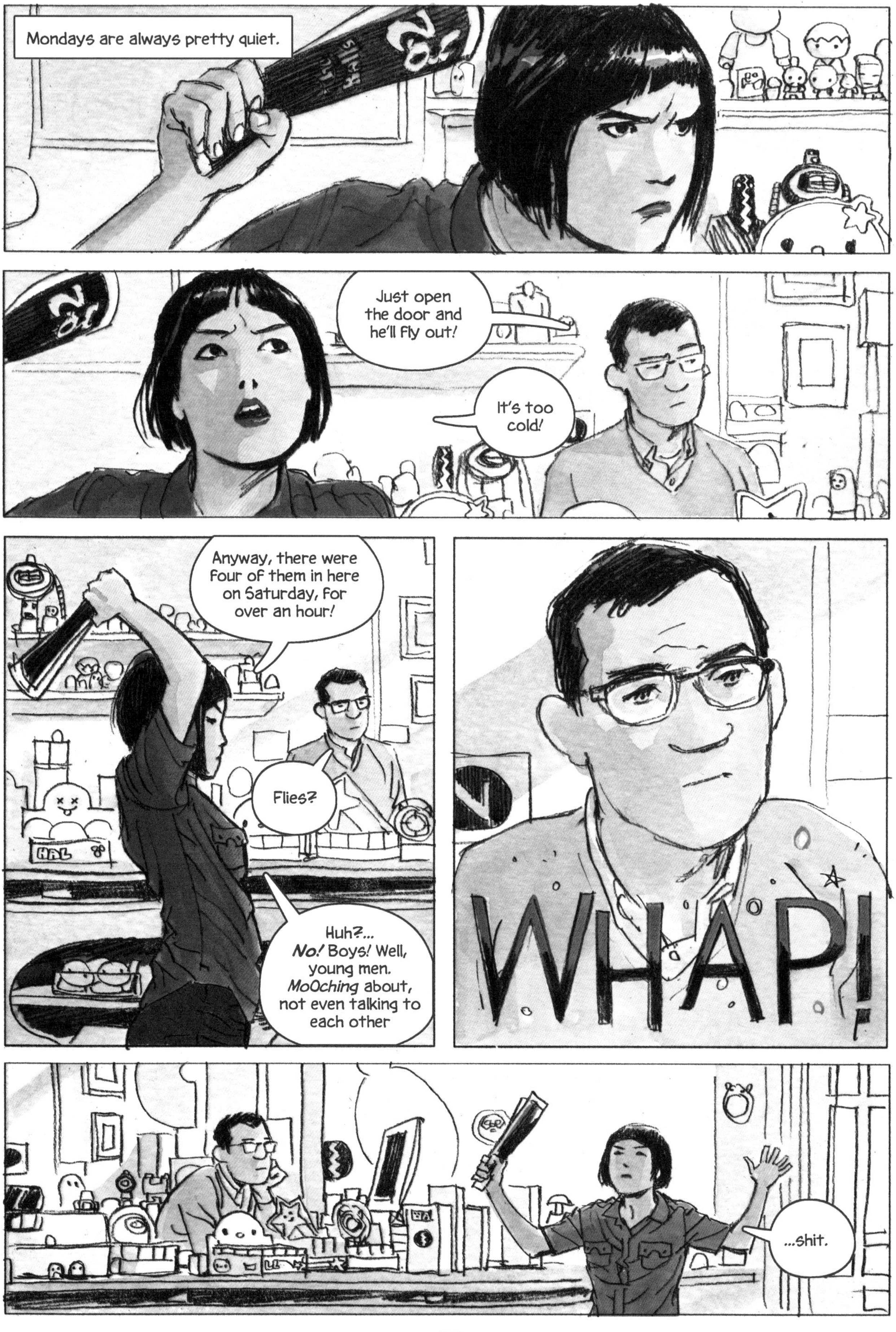
Mondays are always pretty quiet.
Just open the door and he'll fly out!
It's too cold!
Anyway, there were four of them in here on Saturday, for over an hour!
Flies?
Huh?... *No!* Boys! Well, young men. *MoOching* about, not even talking to each other
WHAP!
...shit.

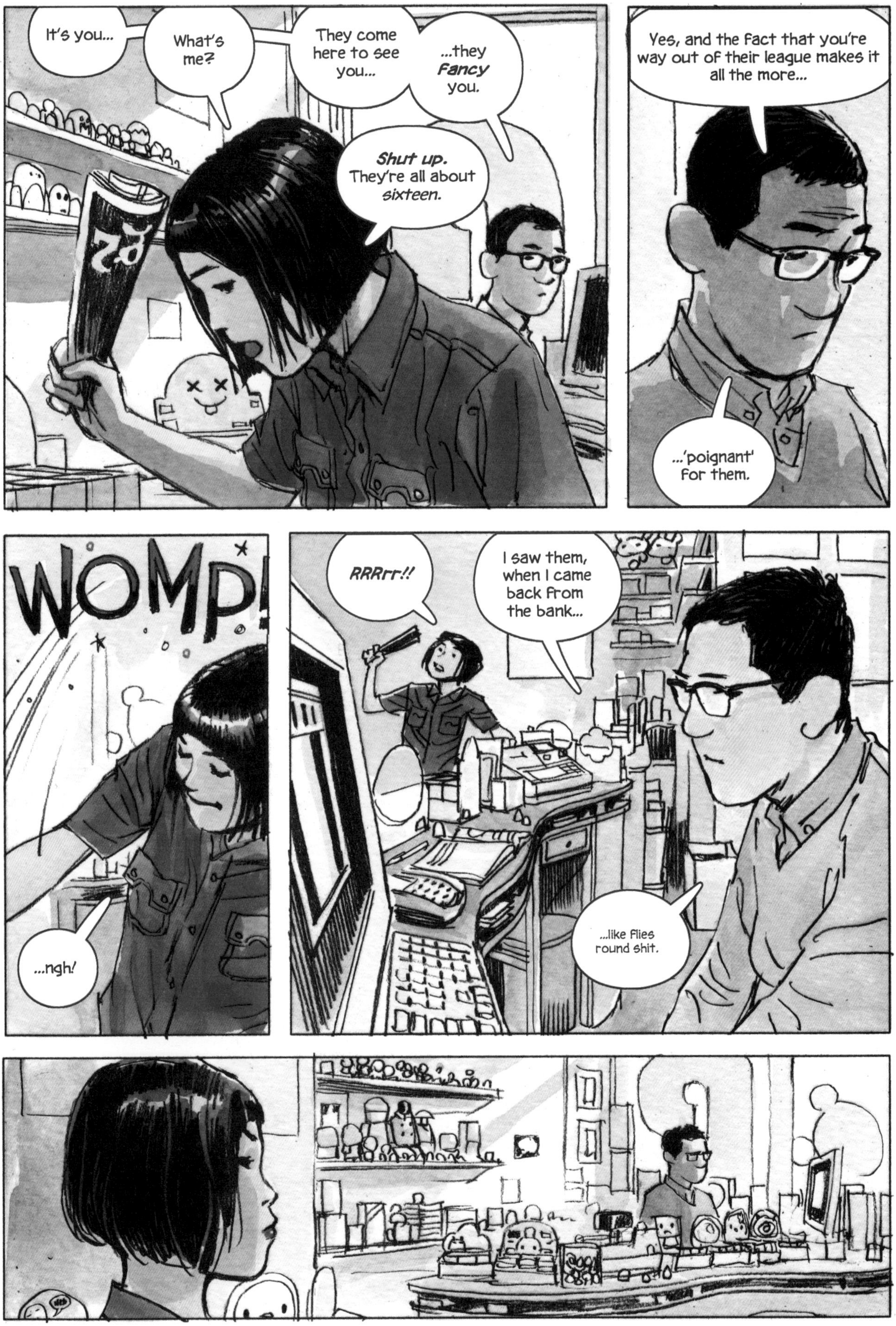
It's you...
What's me?
They come here to see you...
...they *Fancy* you.
Shut up. They're all about *sixteen.*
Yes, and the fact that you're way out of their league makes it all the more...
...'poignant' for them.
WOMP!
...ngh!
RRRrr!!
I saw them, when I came back from the bank...
...like flies round shit.

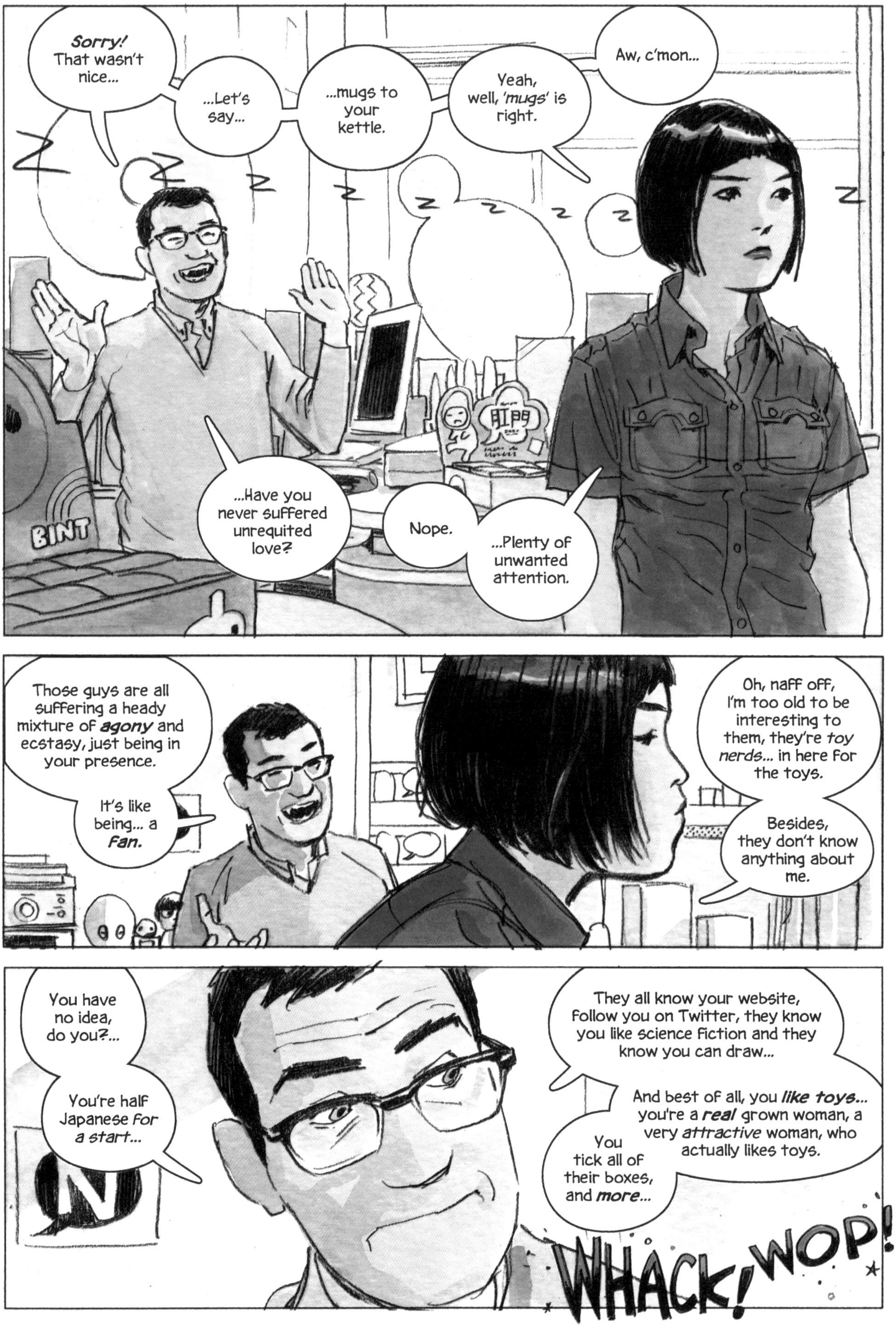

Sorry! That wasn't nice...
...Let's say...
...mugs to your kettle.
Yeah, well, 'mugs' is right.
Aw, c'mon...
...Have you never suffered unrequited love?
Nope.
...Plenty of unwanted attention.
BINT
Those guys are all suffering a heady mixture of agony and ecstasy, just being in your presence.
It's like being... a Fan.
Oh, naff off, I'm too old to be interesting to them, they're toy nerds... in here for the toys.
Besides, they don't know anything about me.
You have no idea, do you?...
You're half Japanese for a start...
They all know your website, follow you on Twitter, they know you like science fiction and they know you can draw...
And best of all, you like toys... you're a real grown woman, a very attractive woman, who actually likes toys.
You tick all of their boxes, and more...
WHACK! WOP!

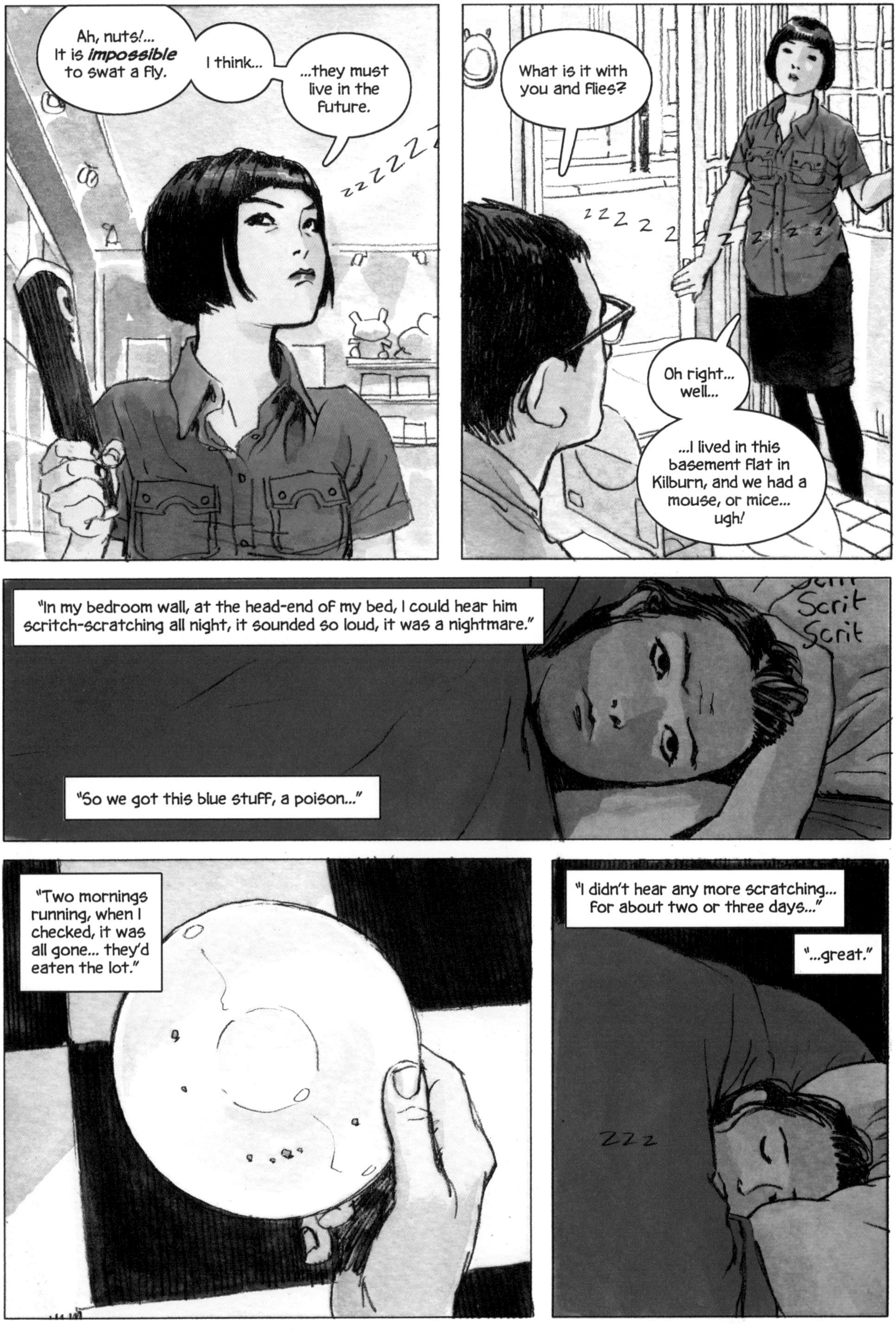
Ah, nuts!... It is ***impossible*** to swat a fly.
I think...
...they must live in the future.
zzzZZZ
What is it with you and flies?
zzZzzZ
Oh right... well...
...I lived in this basement flat in Kilburn, and we had a mouse, or mice... ugh!
"In my bedroom wall, at the head-end of my bed, I could hear him scritch-scratching all night, it sounded so loud, it was a nightmare."
Scrit
Scrit
"So we got this blue stuff, a poison..."
"Two mornings running, when I checked, it was all gone... they'd eaten the lot."
"I didn't hear any more scratching... for about two or three days..."
"...great."
zzz

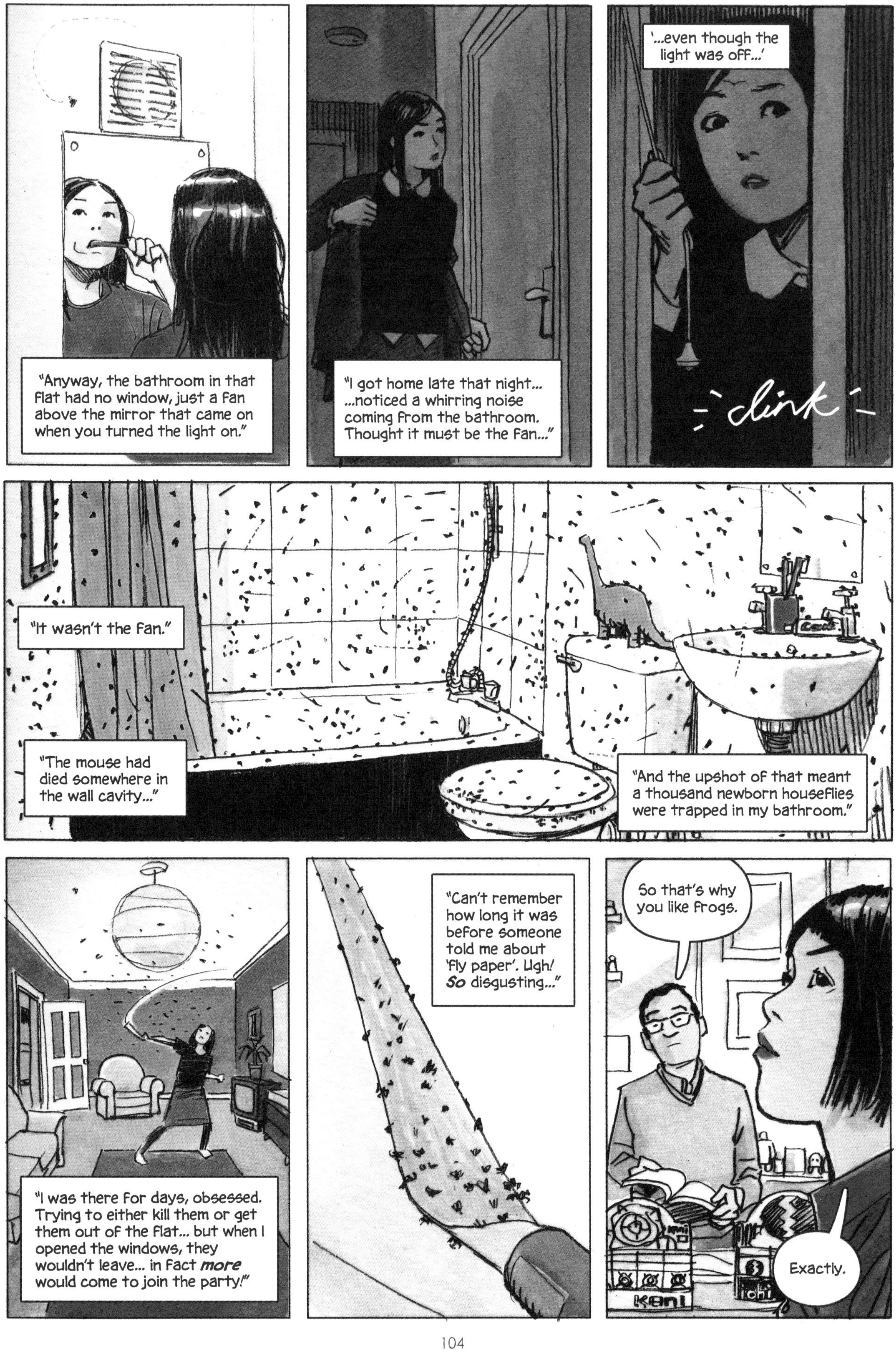
"Anyway, the bathroom in that flat had no window, just a fan above the mirror that came on when you turned the light on."
"I got home late that night... ...noticed a whirring noise coming from the bathroom. Thought it must be the fan..."
'...even though the light was off...'
clink
"It wasn't the fan."
"The mouse had died somewhere in the wall cavity..."
"And the upshot of that meant a thousand newborn houseflies were trapped in my bathroom."
"I was there for days, obsessed. Trying to either kill them or get them out of the flat... but when I opened the windows, they wouldn't leave... in fact *more* would come to join the party!"
"Can't remember how long it was before someone told me about 'fly paper'. Ugh! *So* disgusting..."
So that's why you like frogs.
Exactly.

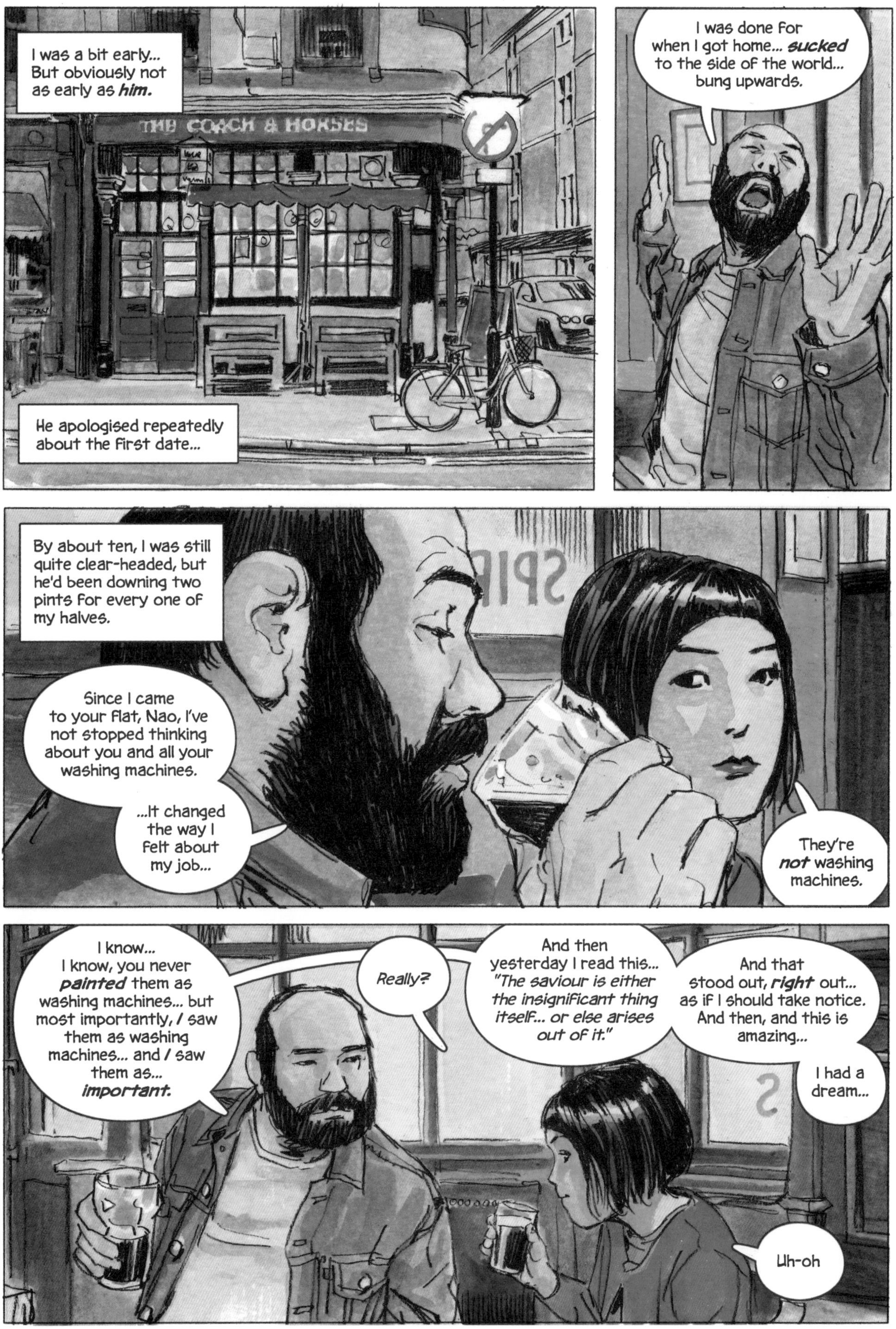
I was a bit early... But obviously not as early as ***him.***
THE COACH & HORSES
He apologised repeatedly about the first date...
I was done for when I got home... ***sucked*** to the side of the world... bung upwards.
By about ten, I was still quite clear-headed, but he'd been downing two pints for every one of my halves.
Since I came to your flat, Nao, I've not stopped thinking about you and all your washing machines.
...It changed the way I felt about my job...
They're ***not*** washing machines.
I know... I know, you never ***painted*** them as washing machines... but most importantly, ***I*** saw them as washing machines... and ***I*** saw them as... ***important.***
Really?
And then yesterday I read this... *"The saviour is either the insignificant thing itself... or else arises out of it."*
And that stood out, ***right*** out... as if I should take notice. And then, and this is amazing...
I had a dream...
Uh-oh

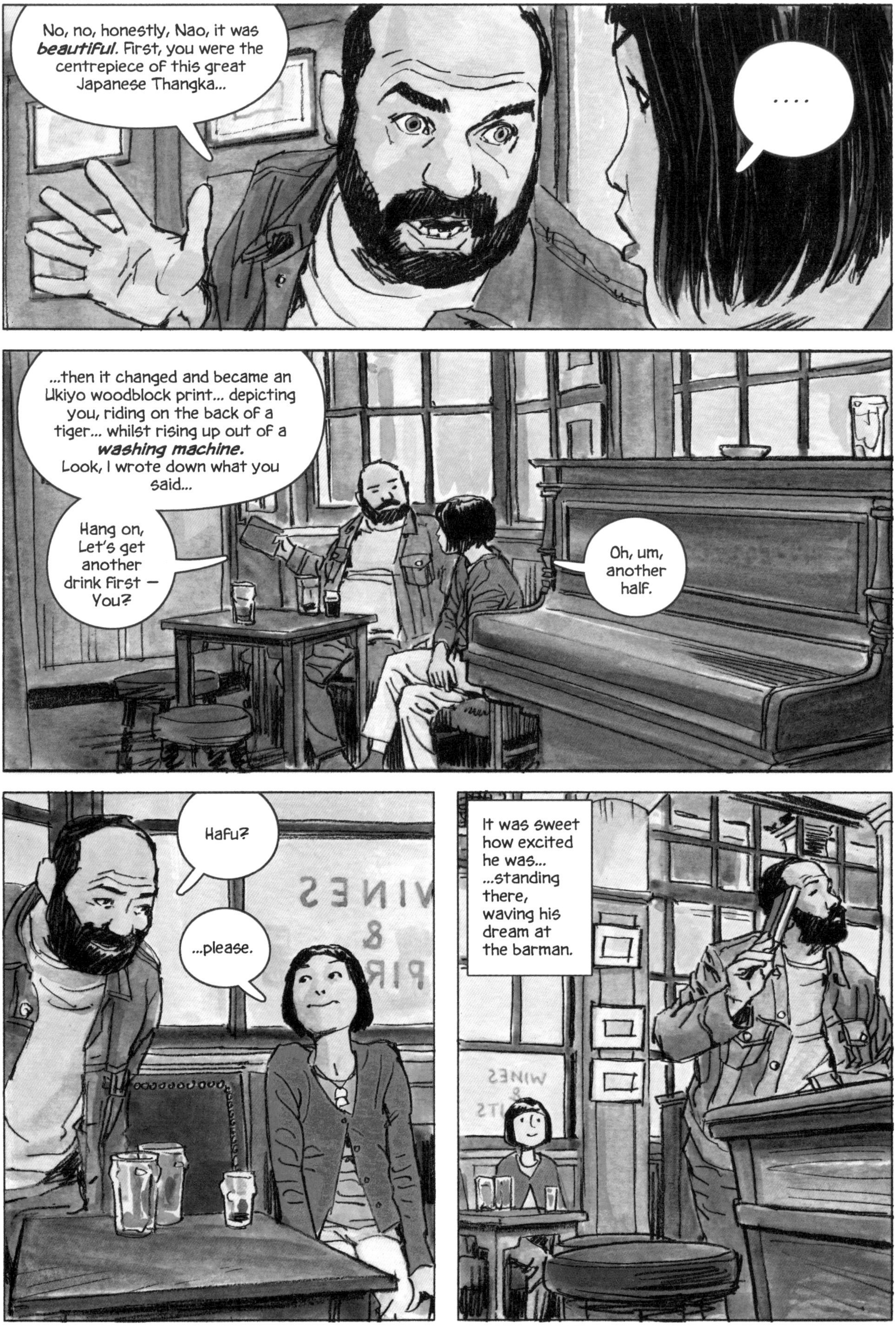

No, no, honestly, Nao, it was **beautiful**. First, you were the centrepiece of this great Japanese Thangka...
....
...then it changed and became an Ukiyo woodblock print... depicting you, riding on the back of a tiger... whilst rising up out of a **washing machine.** Look, I wrote down what you said...
Hang on, Let's get another drink first — You?
Oh, um, another half.
Hafu?
...please.
It was sweet how excited he was... ...standing there, waving his dream at the barman.

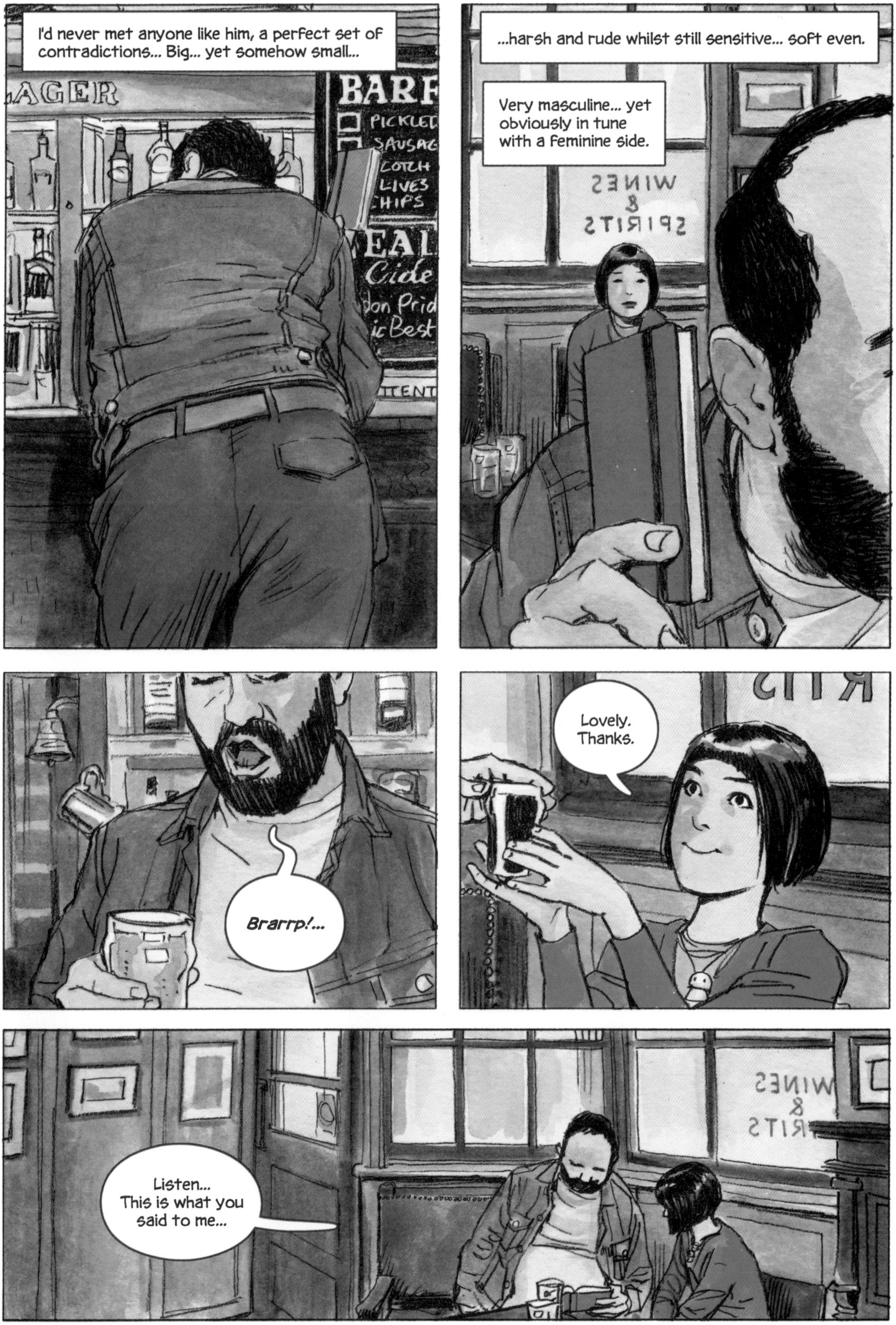
I'd never met anyone like him, a perfect set of contradictions... Big... yet somehow small...
...harsh and rude whilst still sensitive... soft even.
Very masculine... yet obviously in tune with a feminine side.
Brarrp!...
Lovely. Thanks.
Listen... This is what you said to me...

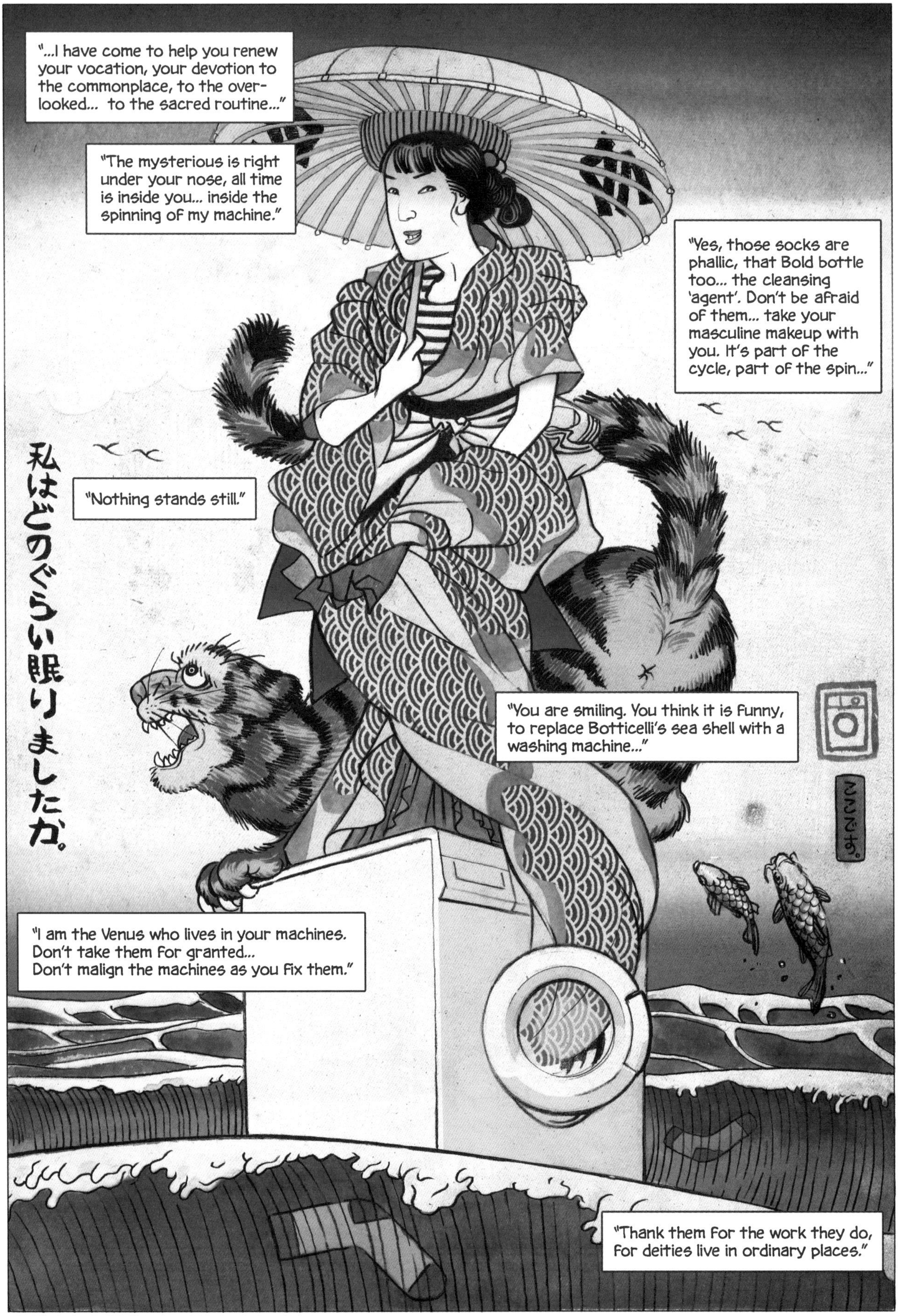
"...I have come to help you renew your vocation, your devotion to the commonplace, to the over-looked... to the sacred routine..."
"The mysterious is right under your nose, all time is inside you... inside the spinning of my machine."
"Yes, those socks are phallic, that Bold bottle too... the cleansing 'agent'. Don't be afraid of them... take your masculine makeup with you. It's part of the cycle, part of the spin..."
私はどのぐらい眠りましたか。
"Nothing stands still."
"You are smiling. You think it is funny, to replace Botticelli's sea shell with a washing machine..."
ここです。
"I am the Venus who lives in your machines. Don't take them for granted... Don't malign the machines as you fix them."
"Thank them for the work they do, for deities live in ordinary places."

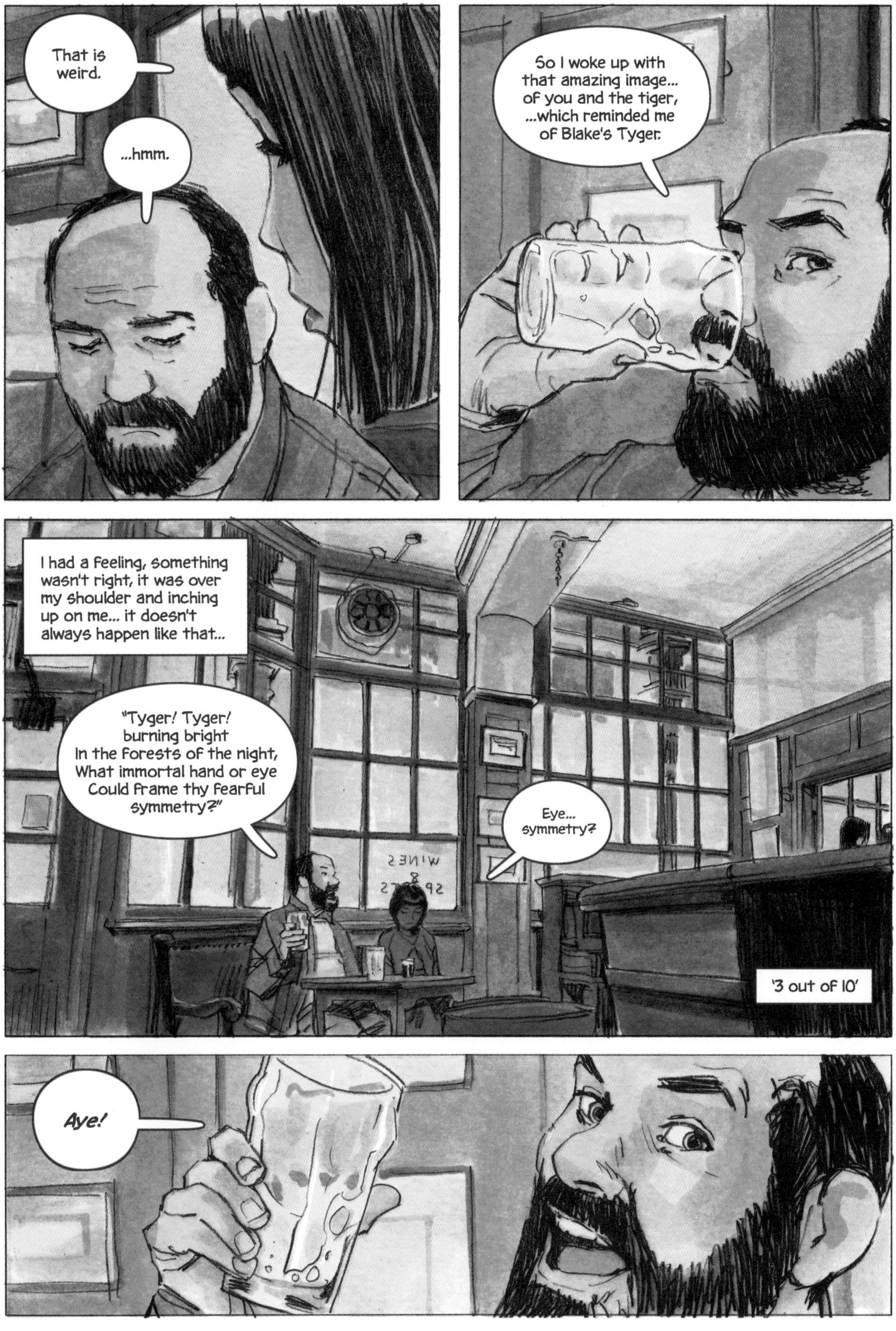
That is weird.
...hmm.
So I woke up with that amazing image... of you and the tiger, ...which reminded me of Blake's Tyger.
I had a feeling, something wasn't right, it was over my shoulder and inching up on me... it doesn't always happen like that...
"Tyger! Tyger! burning bright In the forests of the night, What immortal hand or eye Could frame thy fearful symmetry?"
Eye... symmetry?
'3 out of 10'
Aye!

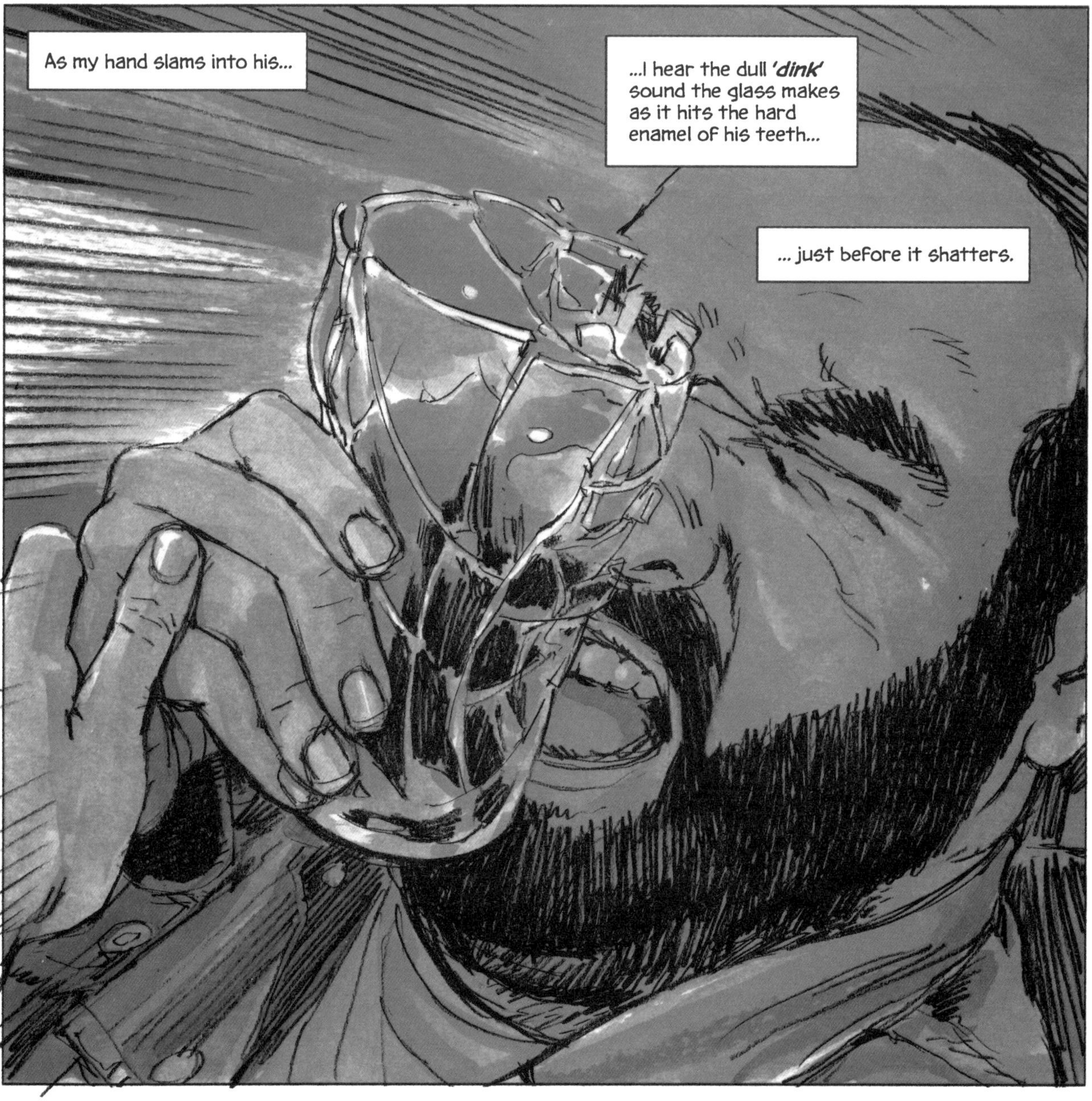
As my hand slams into his...
...I hear the dull *'dink'* sound the glass makes as it hits the hard enamel of his teeth...
... just before it shatters.

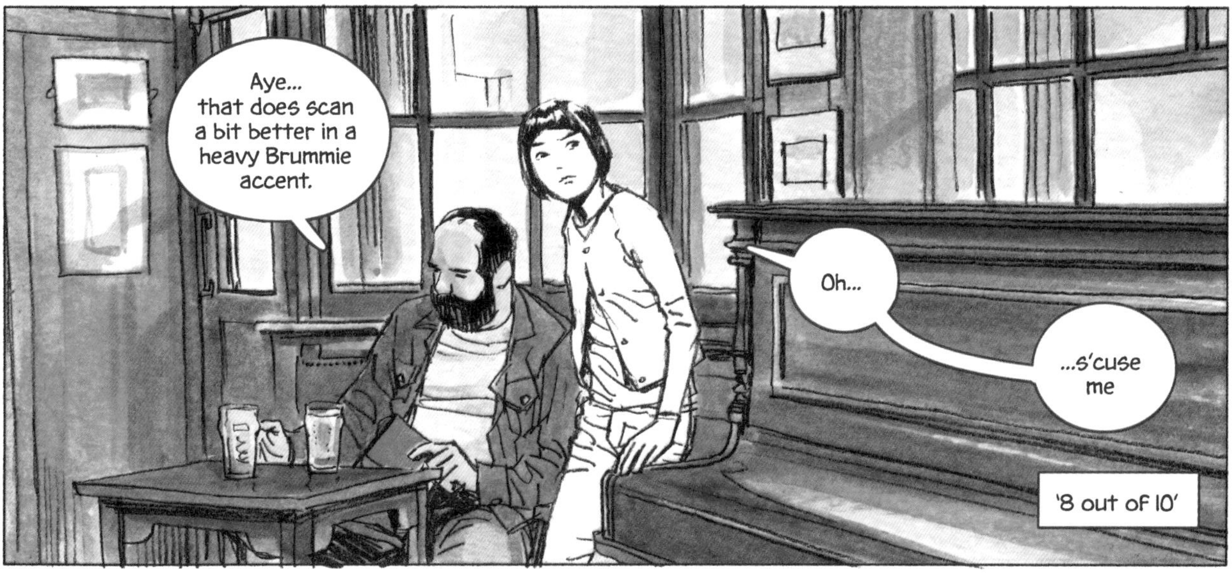
Aye... that does scan a bit better in a heavy Brummie accent.
Oh...
...s'cuse me
'8 out of 10'

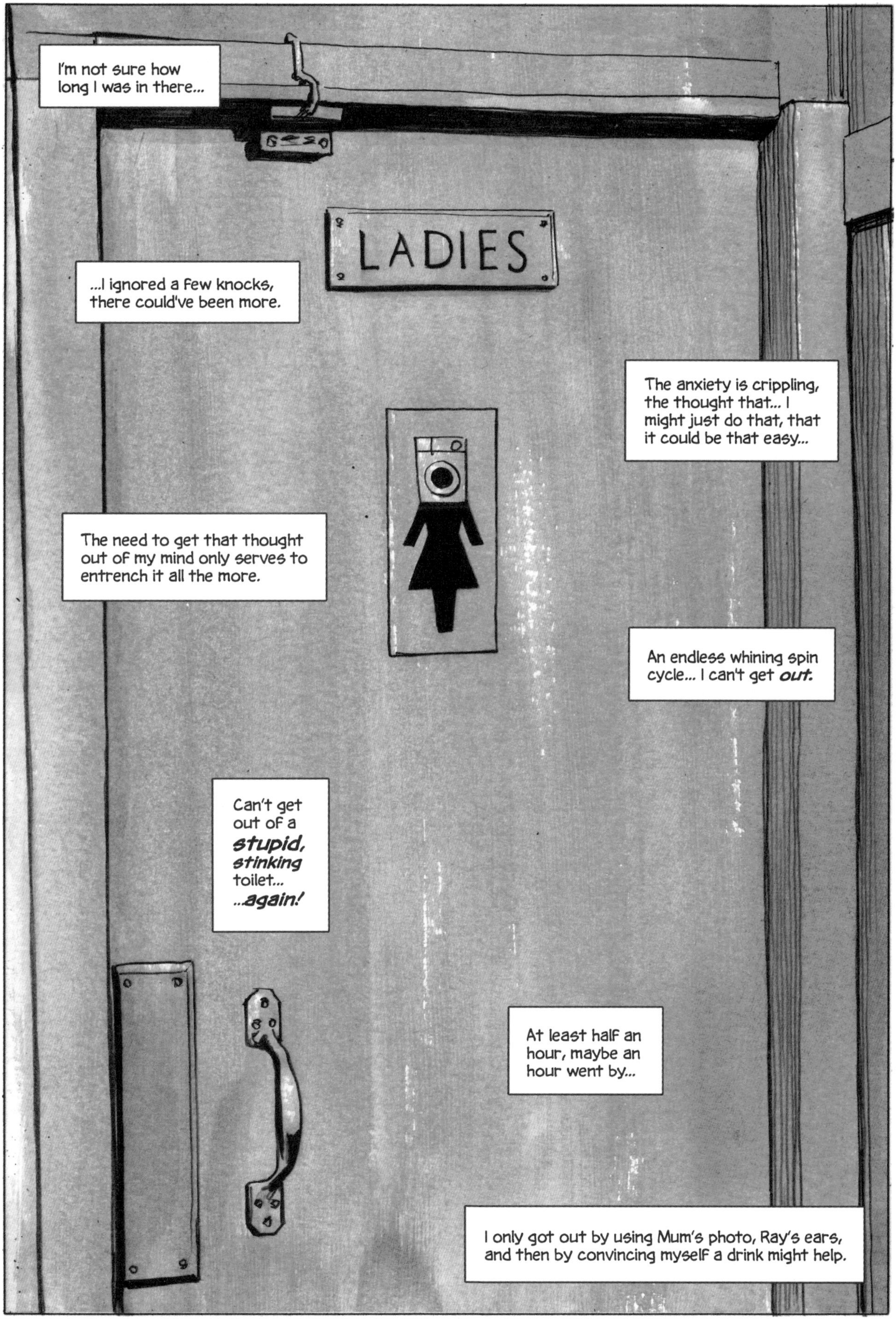
I'm not sure how long I was in there...
LADIES
...I ignored a few knocks, there could've been more.
The anxiety is crippling, the thought that... I might just do that, that it could be that easy...
The need to get that thought out of my mind only serves to entrench it all the more.
An endless whining spin cycle... I can't get *out.*
Can't get out of a ***stupid, stinking*** toilet... ***...again!***
At least half an hour, maybe an hour went by...
I only got out by using Mum's photo, Ray's ears, and then by convincing myself a drink might help.

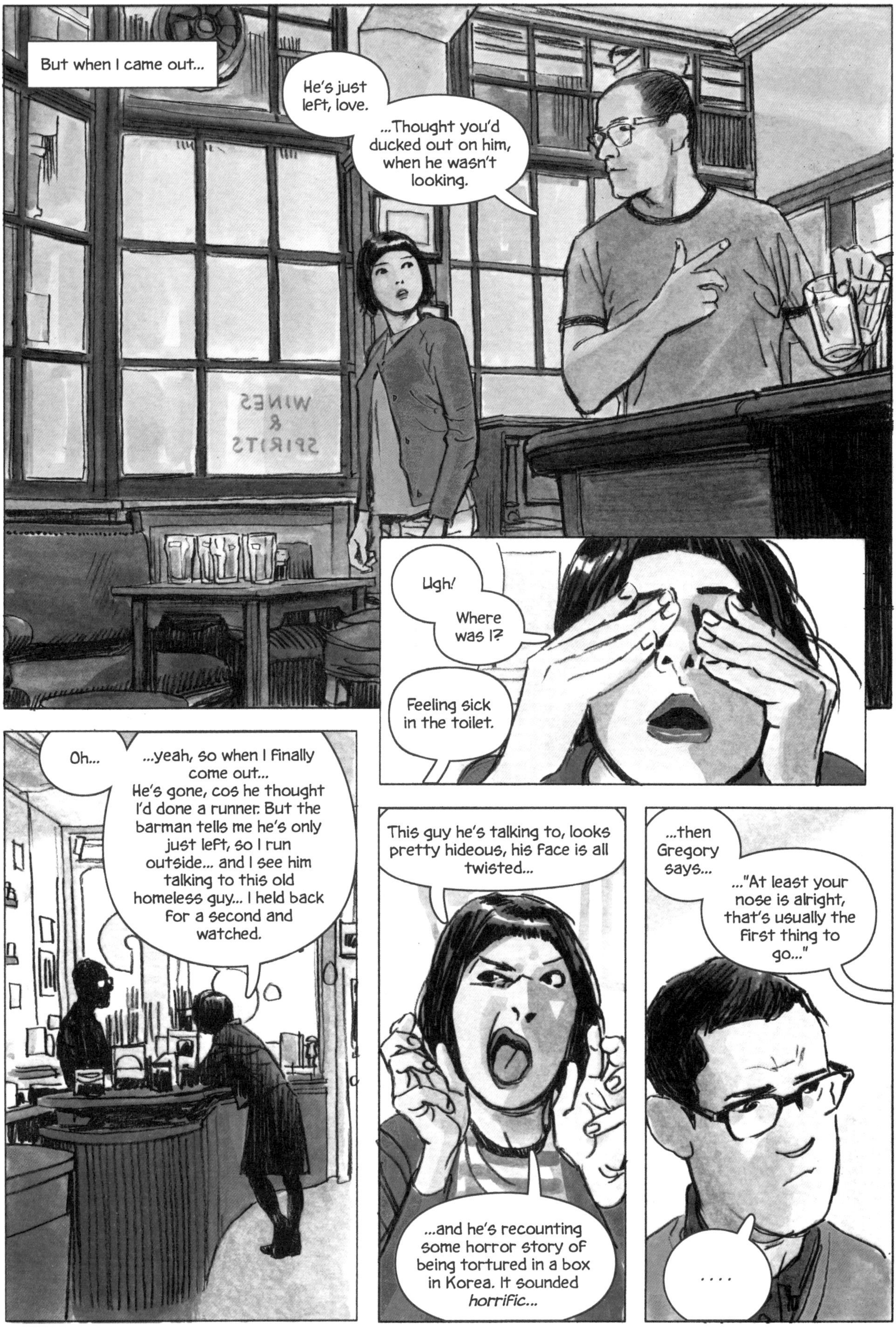
But when I came out...
He's just left, love.
...Thought you'd ducked out on him, when he wasn't looking.
WINES & SPIRITS
Ugh!
Where was I?
Feeling sick in the toilet.
Oh...
...yeah, so when I finally come out...
He's gone, cos he thought I'd done a runner. But the barman tells me he's only just left, so I run outside... and I see him talking to this old homeless guy... I held back for a second and watched.
This guy he's talking to, looks pretty hideous, his face is all twisted...
...and he's recounting some horror story of being tortured in a box in Korea. It sounded *horrific*...
...then Gregory says...
..."At least your nose is alright, that's usually the first thing to go..."
. . . .

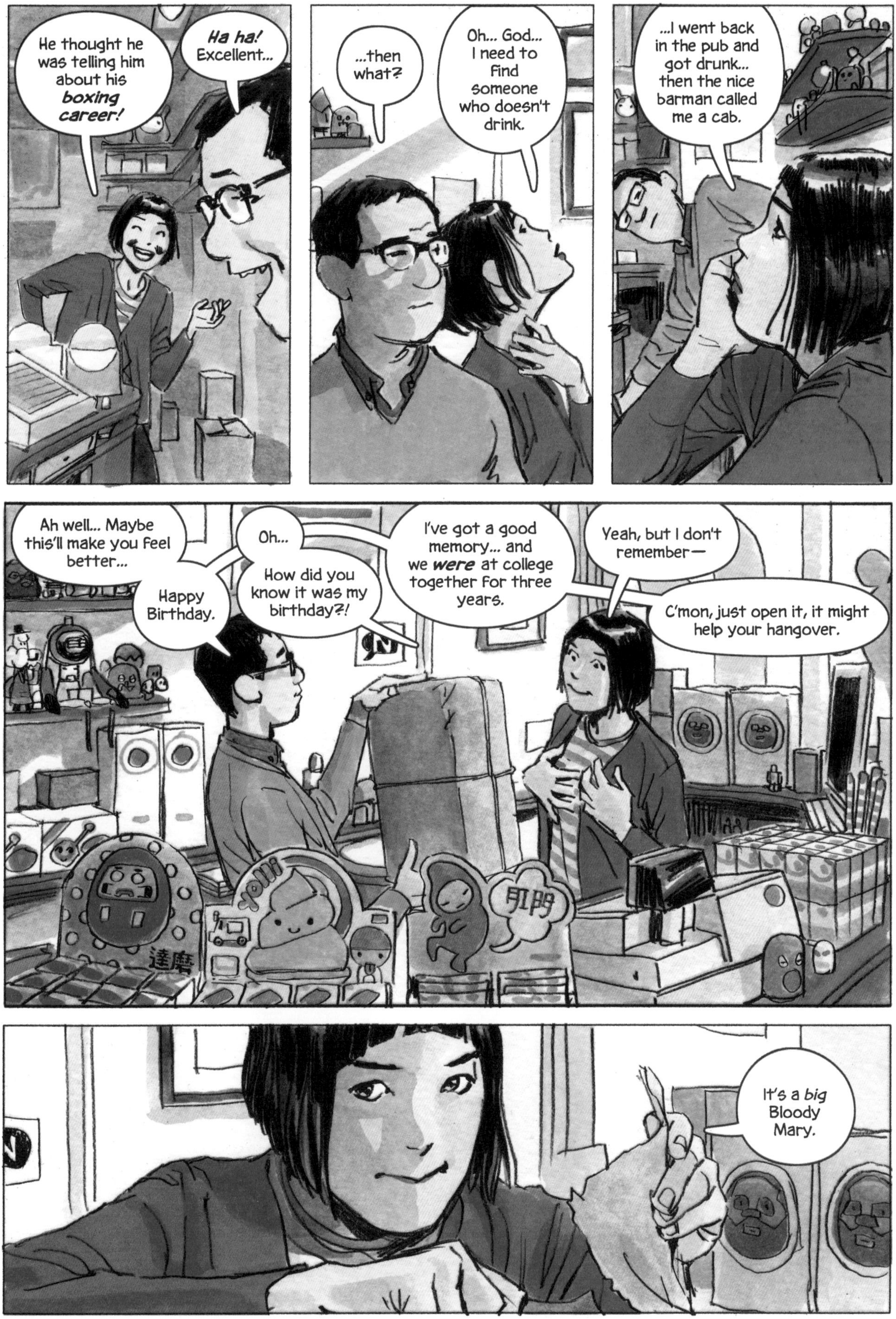
He thought he was telling him about his ***boxing career!***
Ha ha! Excellent...
...then what?
Oh... God... I need to find someone who doesn't drink.
...I went back in the pub and got drunk... then the nice barman called me a cab.
Ah well... Maybe this'll make you feel better...
Happy Birthday.
Oh...
How did you know it was my birthday?!
I've got a good memory... and we ***were*** at college together for three years.
Yeah, but I don't remember—
C'mon, just open it, it might help your hangover.
It's a *big* Bloody Mary.

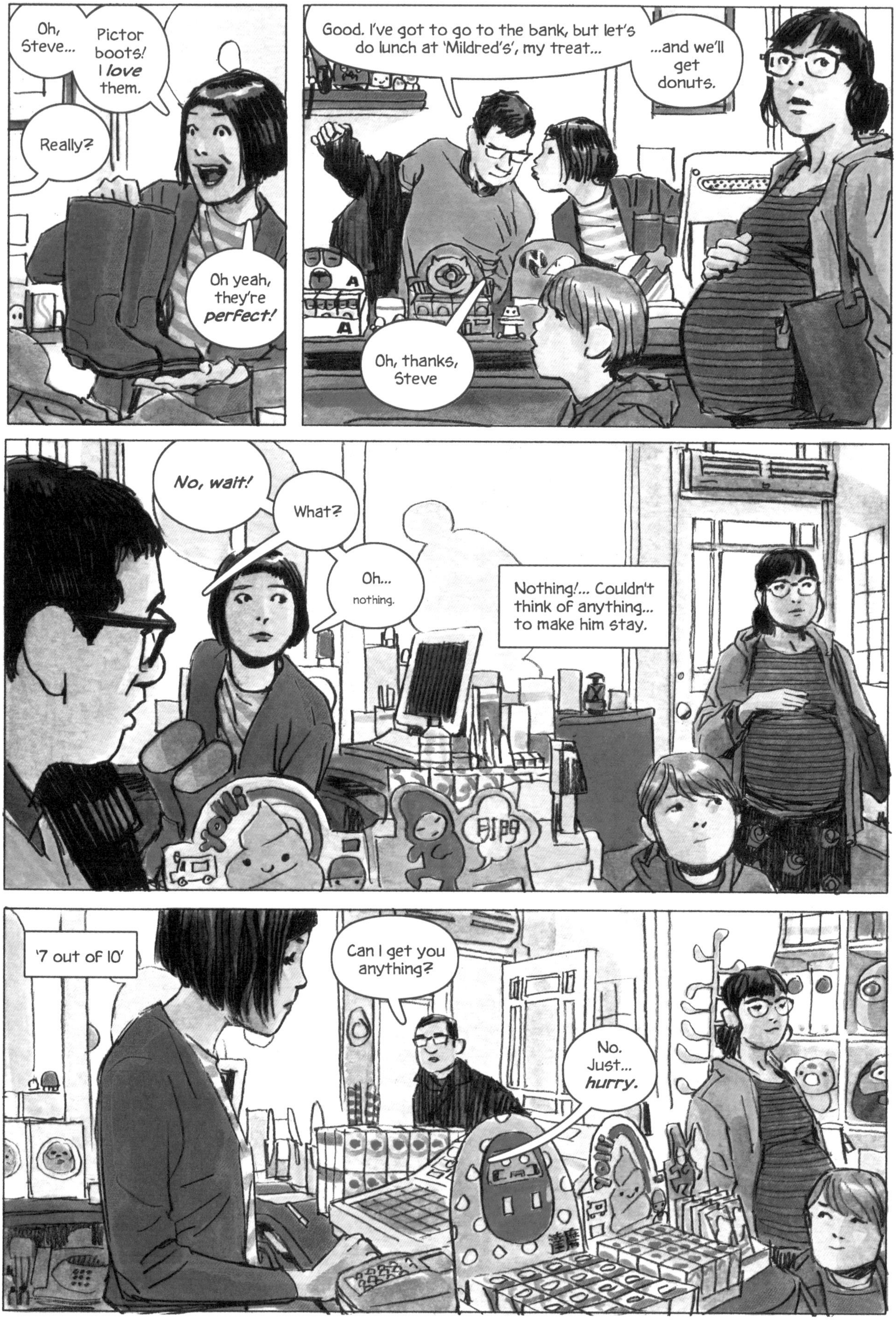

Oh, Steve...
Pictor boots! I *love* them.
Really?
Oh yeah, they're ***perfect!***
Good. I've got to go to the bank, but let's do lunch at 'Mildred's', my treat...
...and we'll get donuts.
Oh, thanks, Steve
No, wait!
What?
Oh... nothing.
Nothing!... Couldn't think of anything... to make him stay.
yolli
'7 out of 10'
Can I get you anything?
No. Just... ***hurry.***
yolli

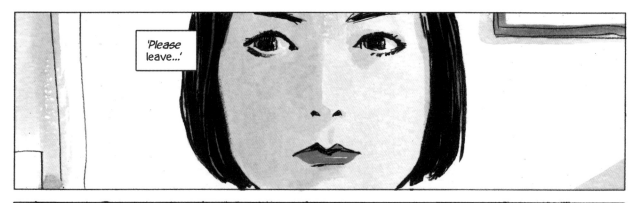

'Please leave...'

'Why now? *Why did he have to go now?* I should've just told him to stay... *Idiot!*'

'...Pens!'

'8 out of 10.'

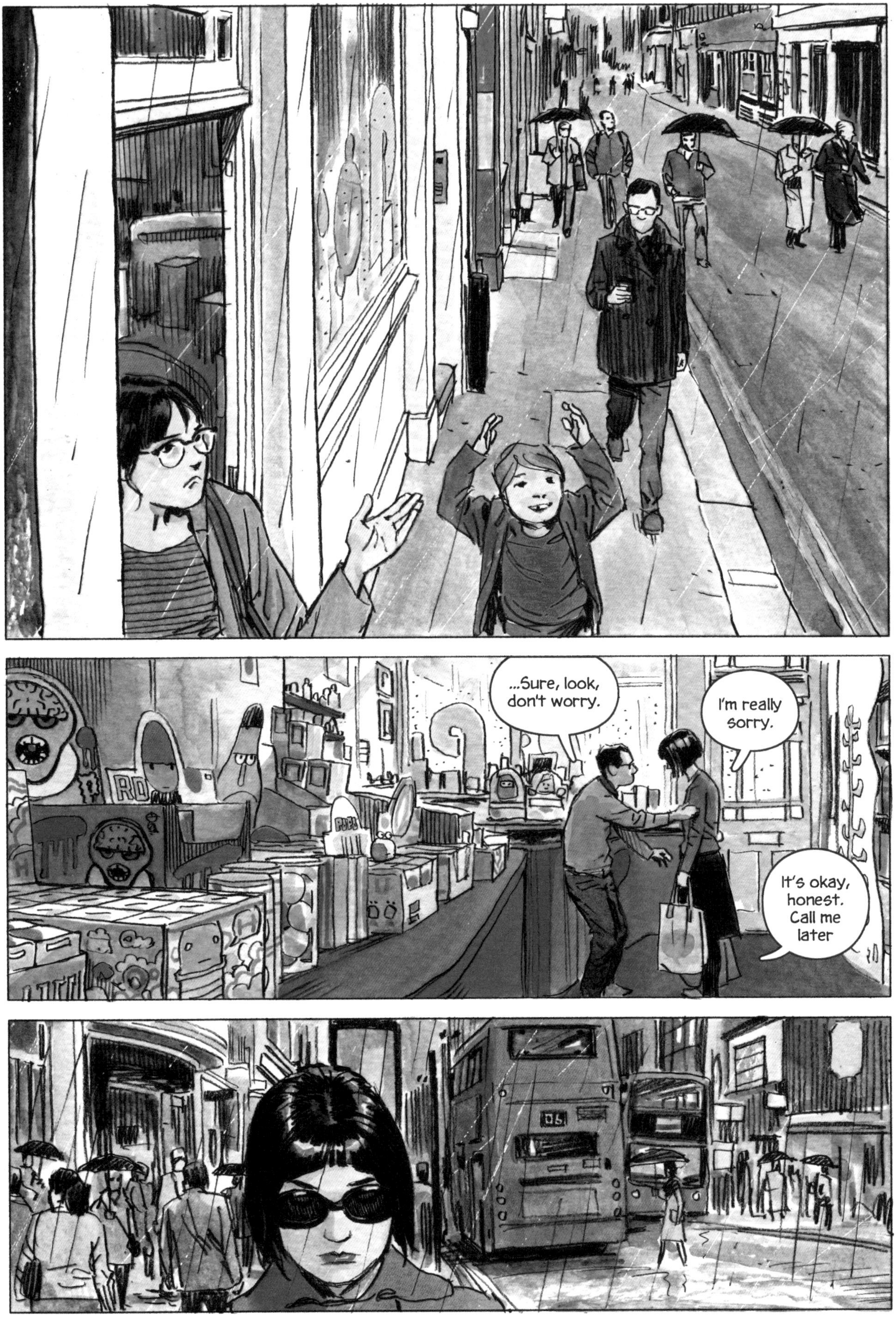
...Sure, look, don't worry.
I'm really sorry.
It's okay, honest. Call me later

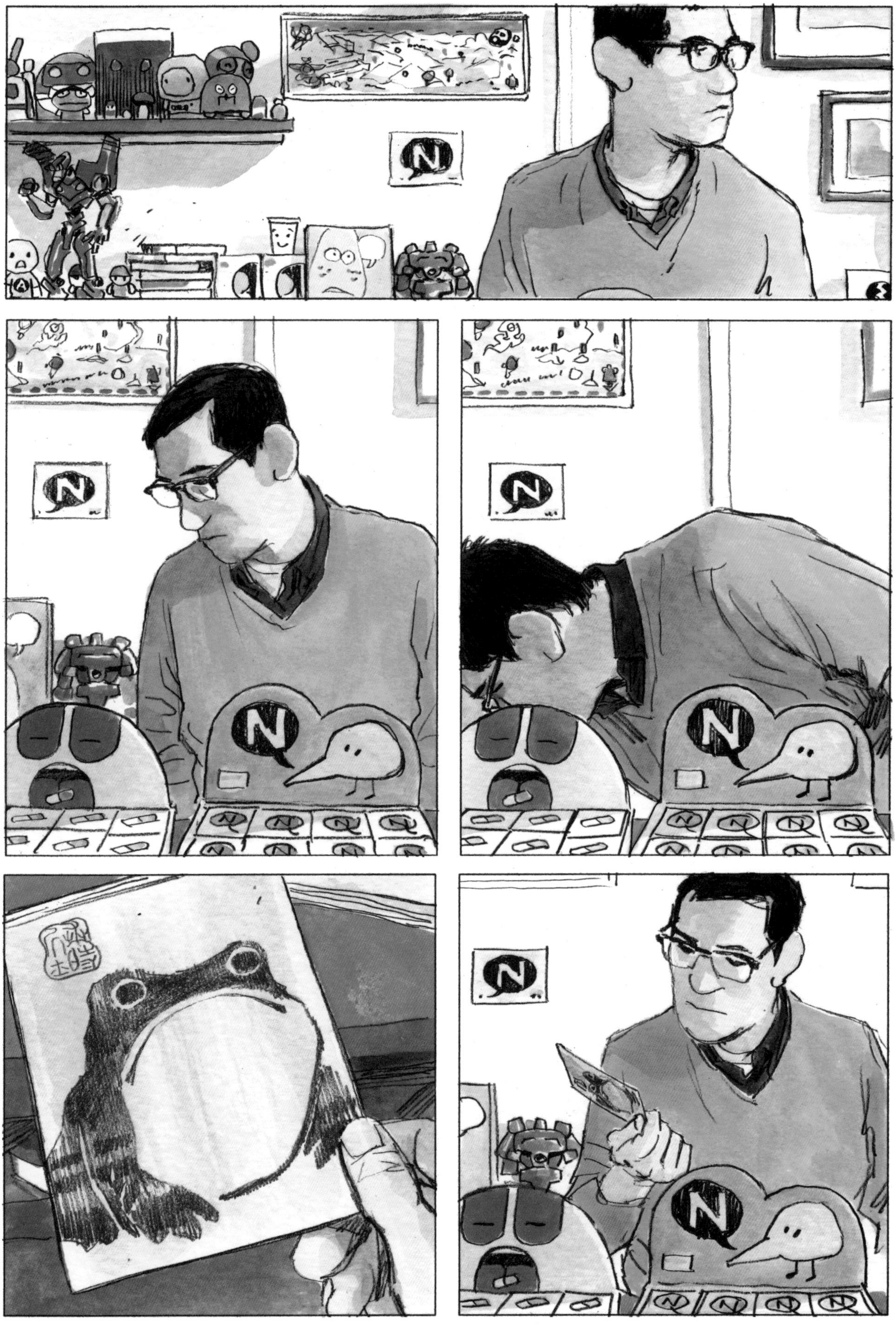

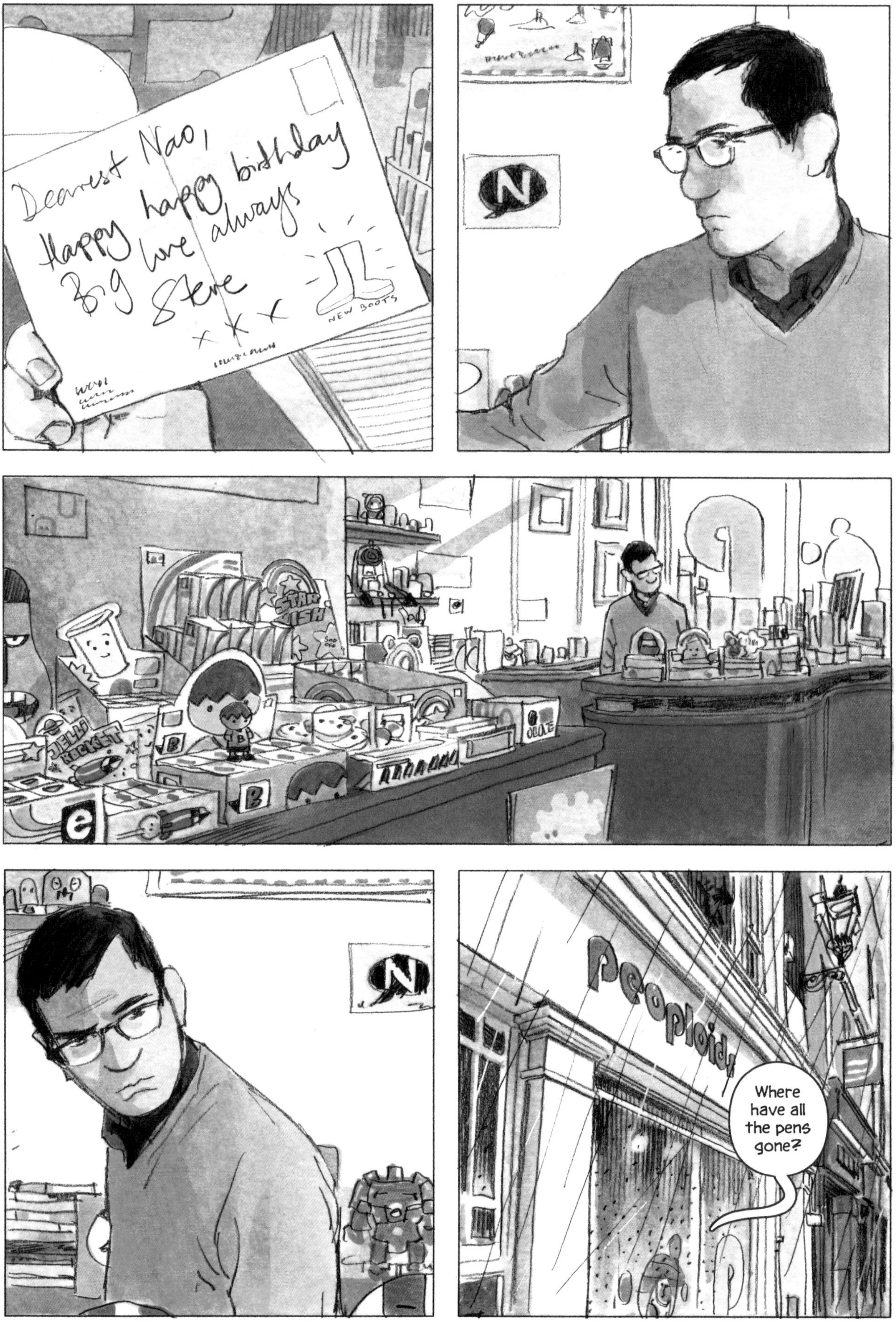
Dearest Nao,
Happy happy birthday
Big love always
Steve
x x x
NEW BOOTS
Peoploids
Where have all the pens gone?

...It just so happened that the 'League' were passing through that day, conscripting young men for the war. Pictor was made to go with them, but not until he'd settled his beloved herd in the old family home. The League did not care that Pictor was part man, part tree, and dressed him in a uniform like all the other cadets.

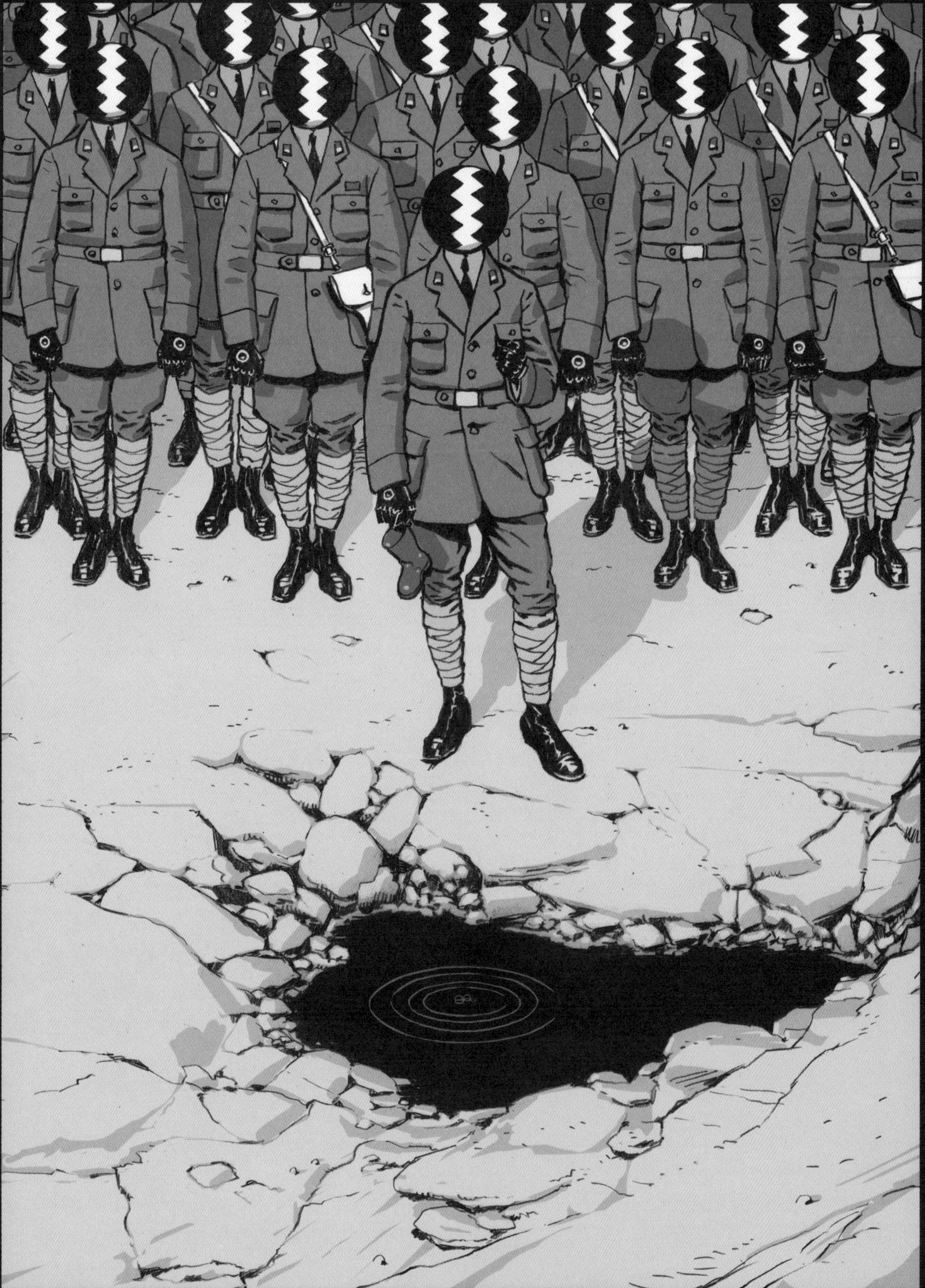

They taught him to pilot flying machines, and to fly alongside the godbots, bombarding the enemy from the sky. He became a good pilot, flying many sorties... Until one unfortunate night, he came under fierce attack from a 'Tyger Mot'. Peppered with holes he limped home... Pictor himself had been shot.

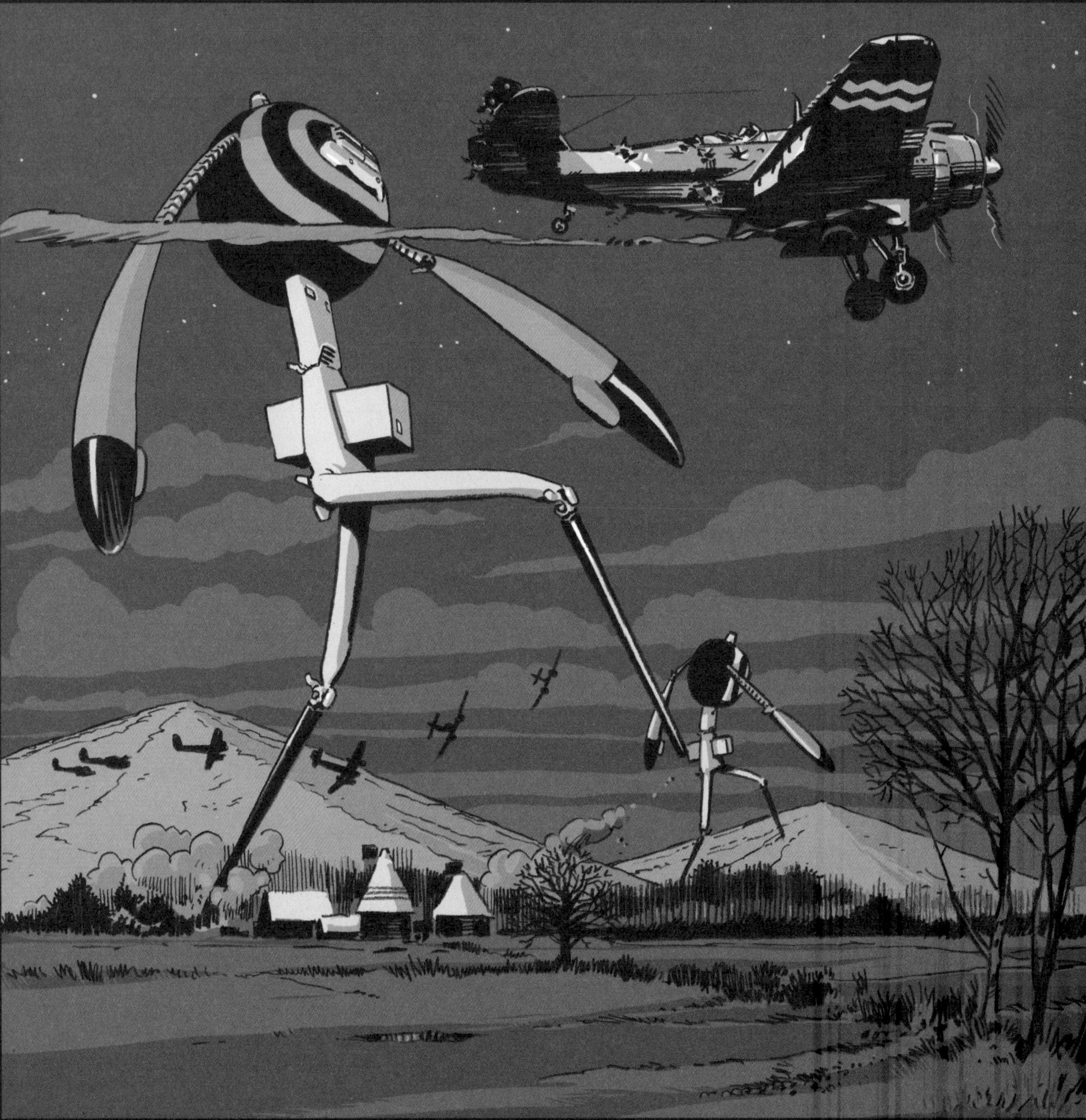

It was only after he was wounded and could no longer fly that he found himself serving the great offensive on the ground. For more than a year he fought along the Eastern Front... and killed many men who stood before him.

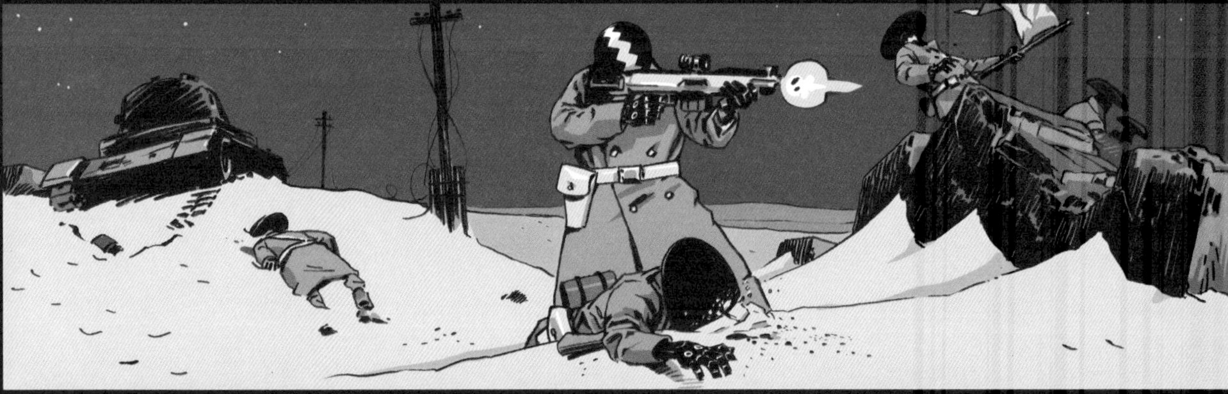

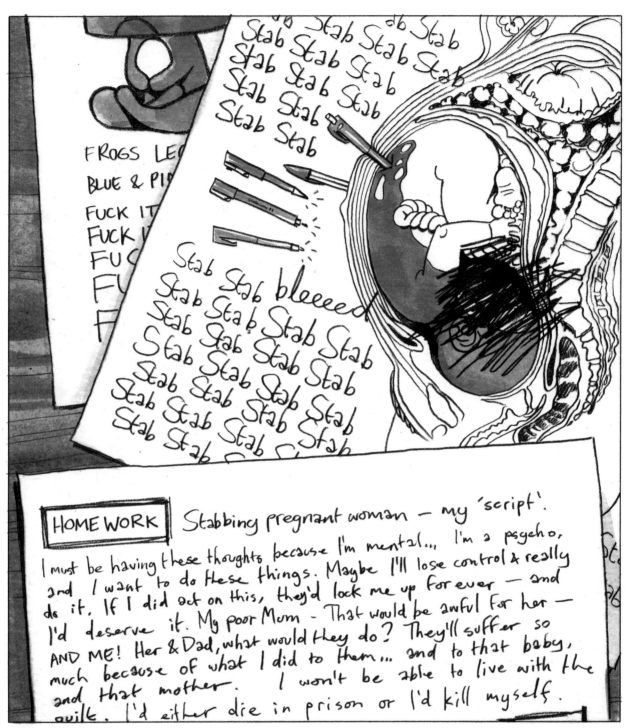

FROGS LEG[...]

BLUE & PI[...]

FUCK IT[...]

FUCK [...]

FU[...]

F[...]

Stab Stab db Stab
Stab Stab Stab Stab
Stab Stab Stab
Stab Stab Stab
Stab Stab Stab
Stab Stab

Stab Stab bleeeed[...]
Stab Stab Stab Stab
Stab Stab Stab Stab
Stab Stab Stab Stab
Stab Stab Stab Stab
Stab Stab Stab Stab
Stab Stab Stab Stab
Stab Stab Stab Stab

| HOME WORK | Stabbing pregnant woman — my 'script'.

I must be having these thoughts because I'm mental... I'm a psycho, and I want to do these things. Maybe I'll lose control & really do it. If I did act on this, they'd lock me up forever — and I'd deserve it. My poor Mom - That would be awful for her — AND ME! Her & Dad, what would they do? They'll suffer so much because of what I did to them... and to that baby, and that mother.   I won't be able to live with the guilt. I'd either die in prison or I'd kill myself.

Did you see I put traps down?

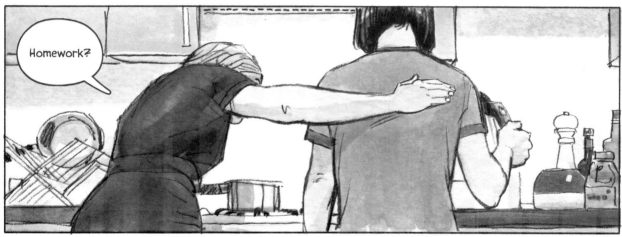

Homework?

You're doing so well.

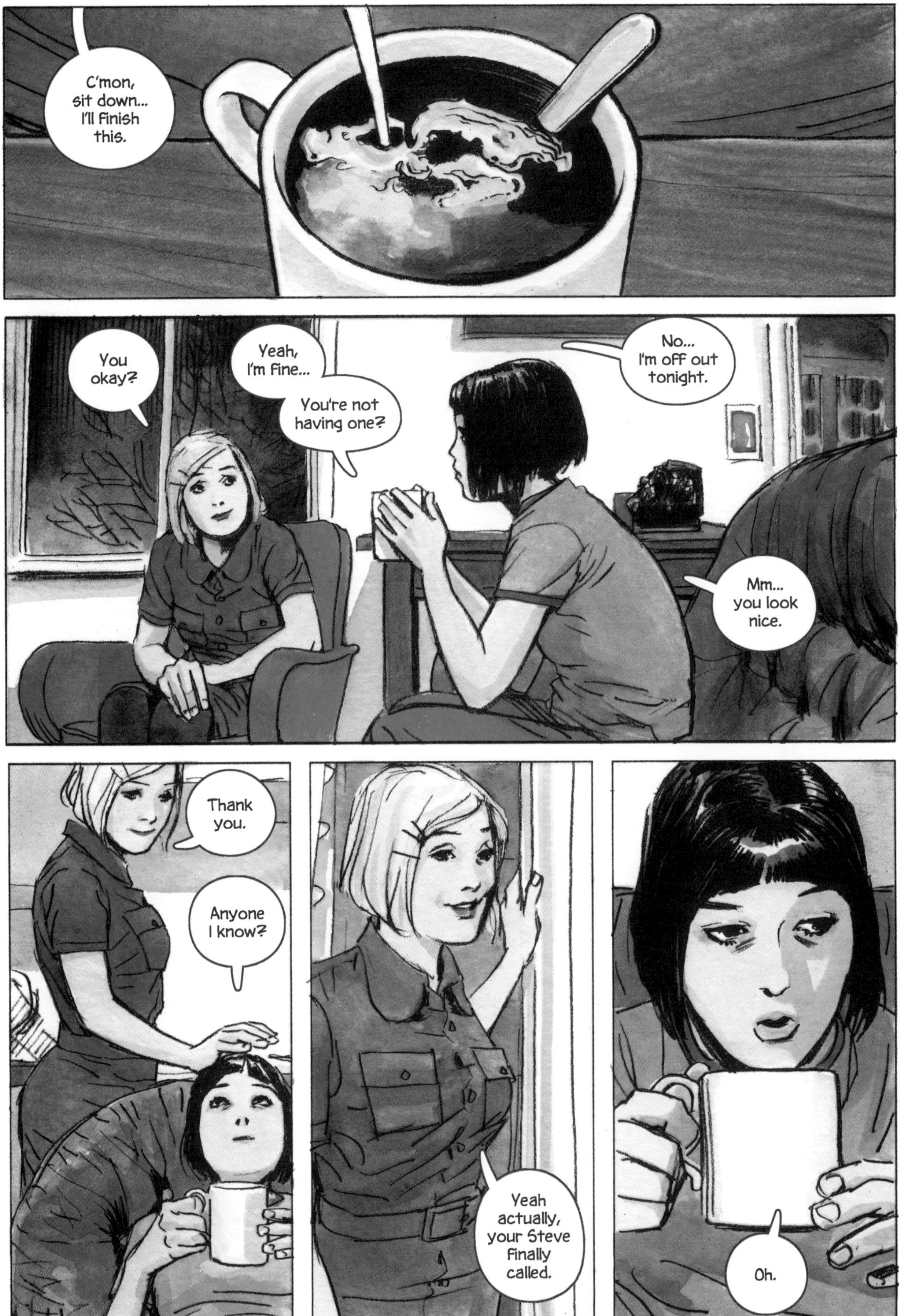
C'mon, sit down... I'll finish this.
You okay?
Yeah, I'm fine...
You're not having one?
No... I'm off out tonight.
Mm... you look nice.
Thank you.
Anyone I know?
Yeah actually, your Steve finally called.
Oh.

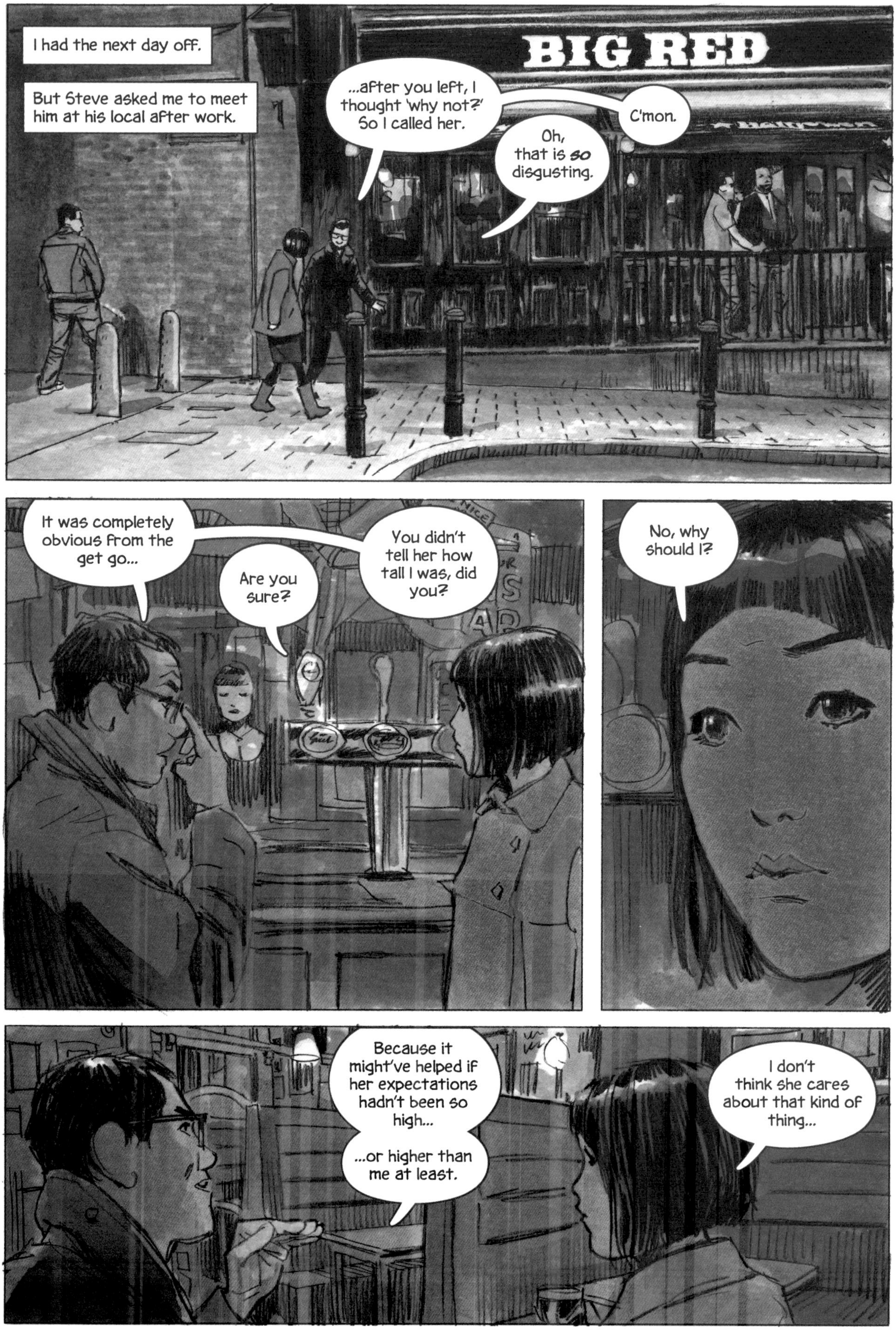
I had the next day off.
But Steve asked me to meet him at his local after work.
BIG RED
...after you left, I thought 'why not?' So I called her.
C'mon.
Oh, that is *so* disgusting.
It was completely obvious from the get go...
You didn't tell her how tall I was, did you?
Are you sure?
No, why should I?
Because it might've helped if her expectations hadn't been so high...
...or higher than me at least.
I don't think she cares about that kind of thing...

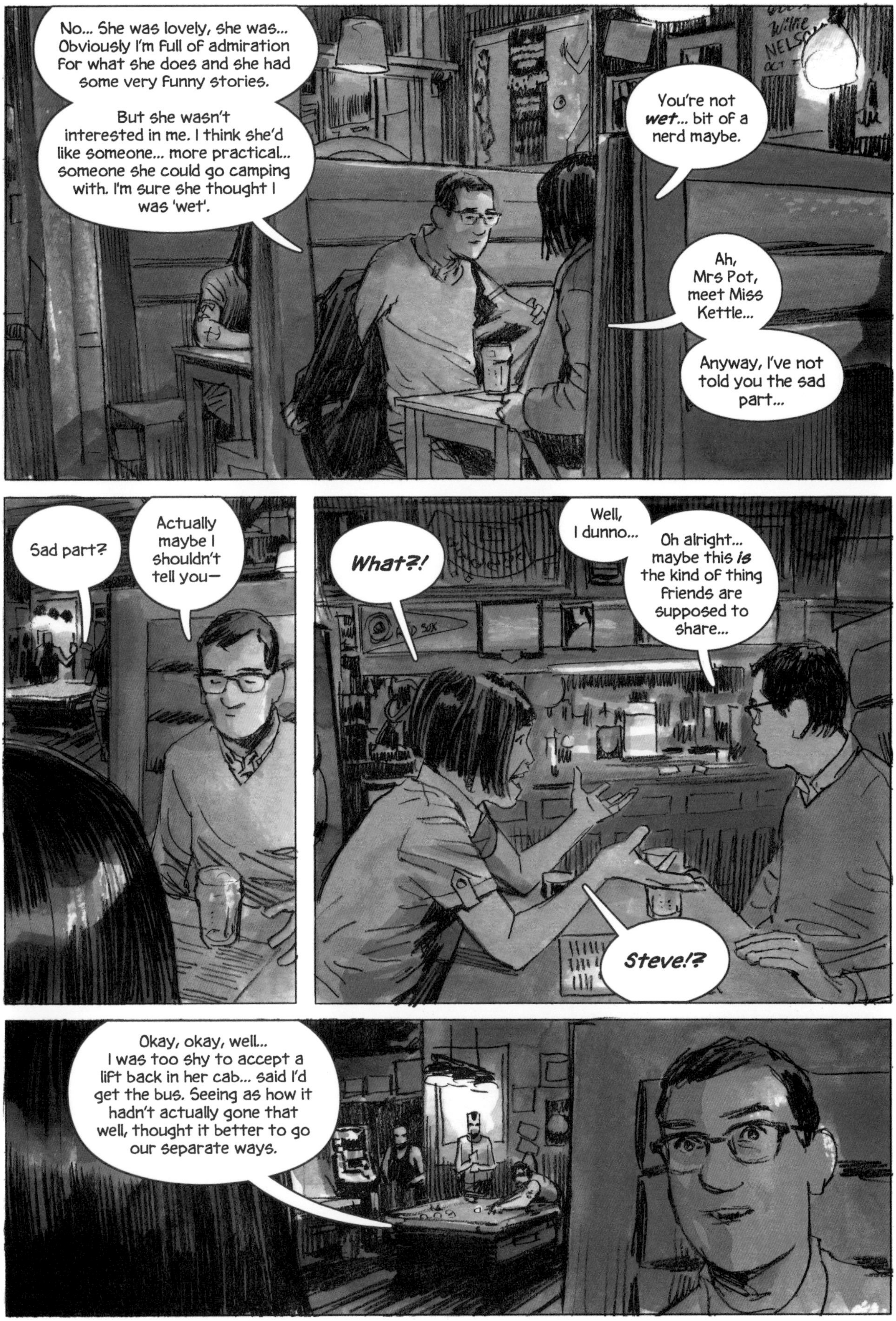
No... She was lovely, she was... Obviously I'm full of admiration for what she does and she had some very funny stories.
But she wasn't interested in me. I think she'd like someone... more practical... someone she could go camping with. I'm sure she thought I was 'wet'.
You're not **wet**... bit of a nerd maybe.
Ah, Mrs Pot, meet Miss Kettle...
Anyway, I've not told you the sad part...
Sad part?
Actually maybe I shouldn't tell you—
What?!
Well, I dunno...
Oh alright... maybe this *is* the kind of thing friends are supposed to share...
Steve!?
Okay, okay, well... I was too shy to accept a lift back in her cab... said I'd get the bus. Seeing as how it hadn't actually gone that well, thought it better to go our separate ways.

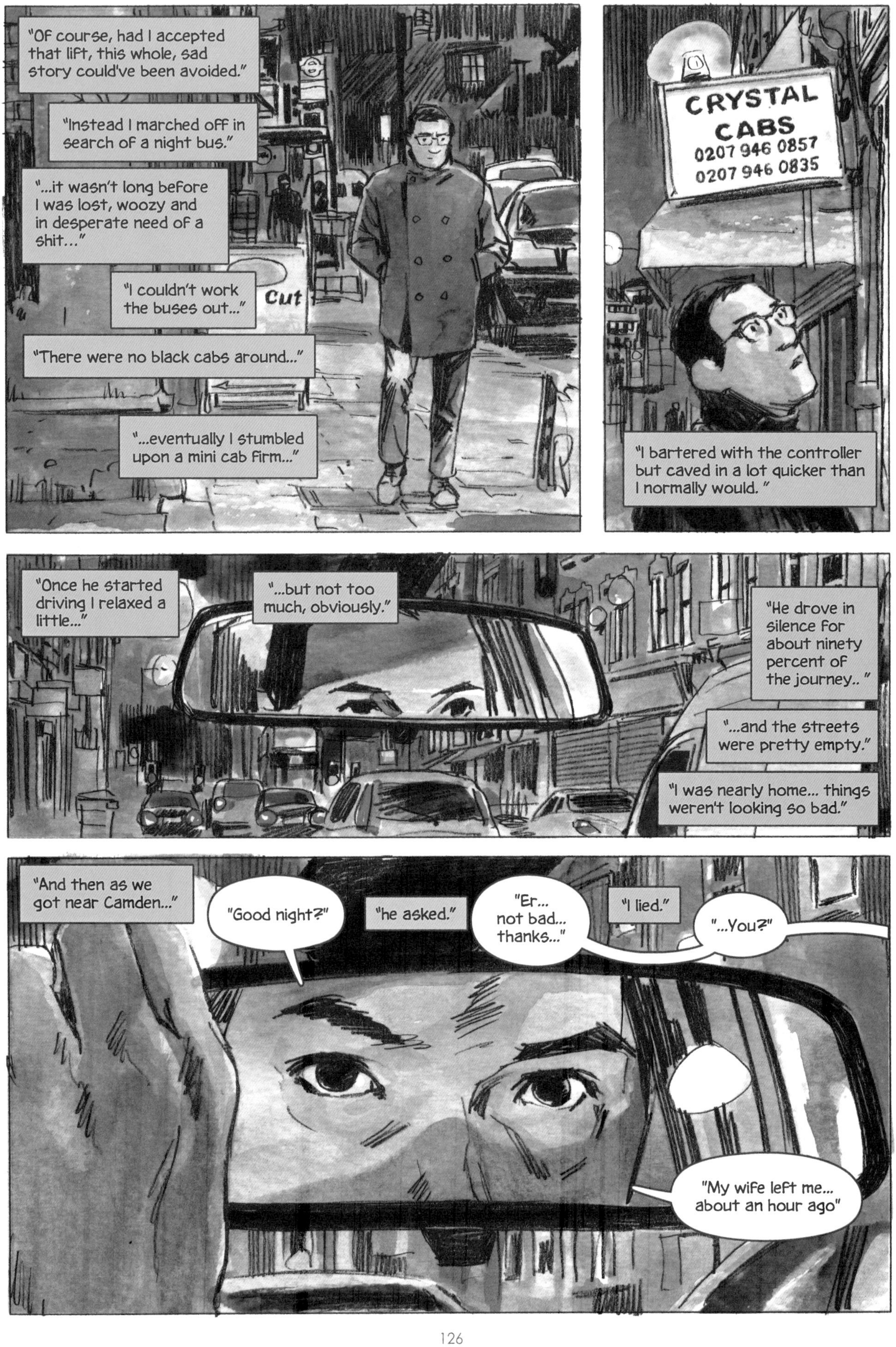
"Of course, had I accepted that lift, this whole, sad story could've been avoided."
"Instead I marched off in search of a night bus."
"...it wasn't long before I was lost, woozy and in desperate need of a shit..."
"I couldn't work the buses out..."
"There were no black cabs around..."
"...eventually I stumbled upon a mini cab firm..."
CRYSTAL CABS 0207 946 0857 0207 946 0835
"I bartered with the controller but caved in a lot quicker than I normally would."
"Once he started driving I relaxed a little..."
"...but not too much, obviously."
"He drove in silence for about ninety percent of the journey.."
"...and the streets were pretty empty."
"I was nearly home... things weren't looking so bad."
"And then as we got near Camden..."
"Good night?"
"he asked."
"Er... not bad... thanks..."
"I lied."
"...You?"
"My wife left me... about an hour ago"

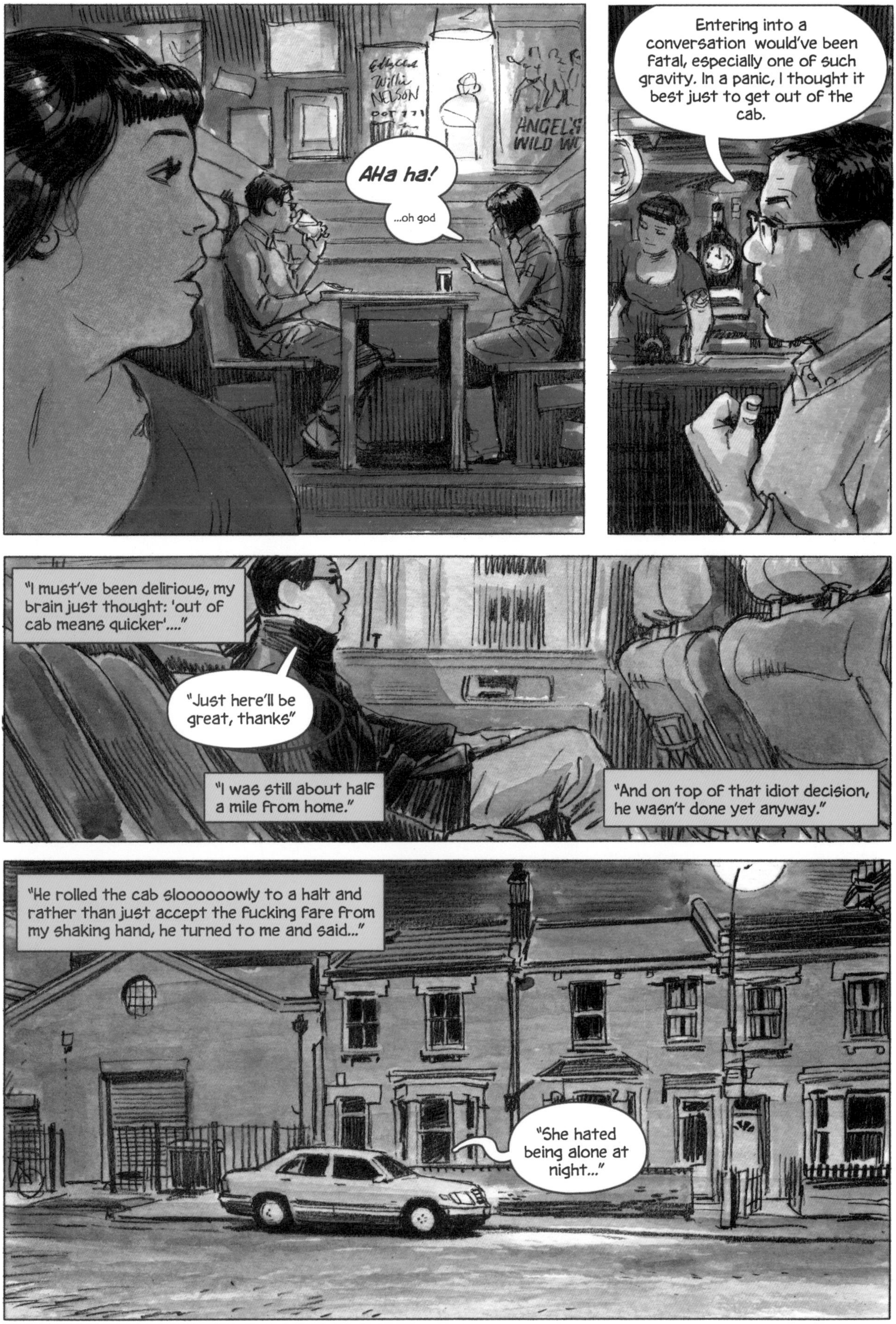
Willie
NELSON
ANGEL'S
AHa ha!
...oh god
Entering into a conversation would've been fatal, especially one of such gravity. In a panic, I thought it best just to get out of the cab.
"I must've been delirious, my brain just thought: 'out of cab means quicker'...."
"Just here'll be great, thanks"
"I was still about half a mile from home."
"And on top of that idiot decision, he wasn't done yet anyway."
"He rolled the cab slooooowly to a halt and rather than just accept the fucking fare from my shaking hand, he turned to me and said..."
"She hated being alone at night..."

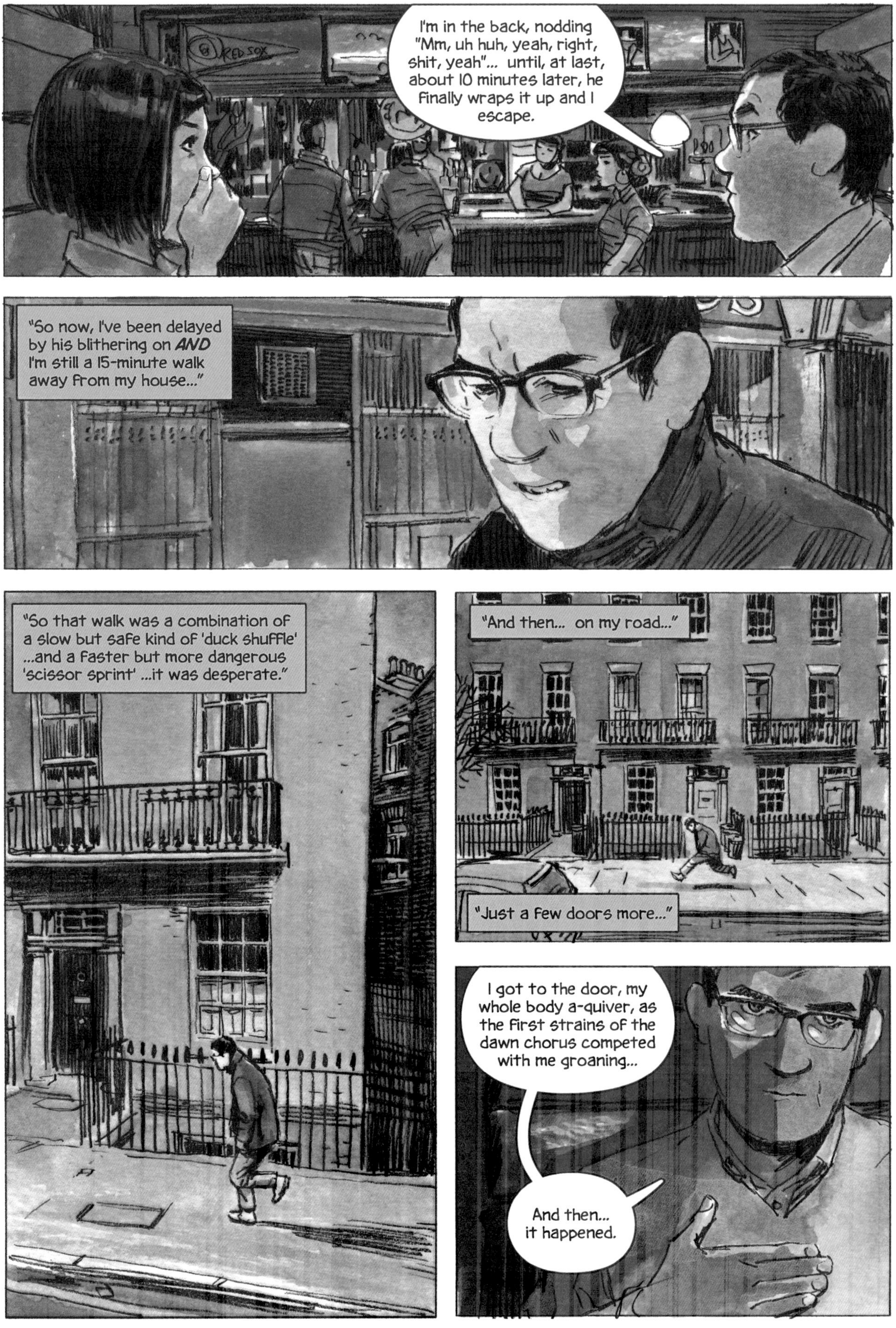
I'm in the back, nodding "Mm, uh huh, yeah, right, shit, yeah"... until, at last, about 10 minutes later, he finally wraps it up and I escape.
RED SOX
"So now, I've been delayed by his blithering on ***AND*** I'm still a 15-minute walk away from my house..."
"So that walk was a combination of a slow but safe kind of 'duck shuffle' ...and a faster but more dangerous 'scissor sprint' ...it was desperate."
"And then... on my road..."
"Just a few doors more..."
I got to the door, my whole body a-quiver, as the first strains of the dawn chorus competed with me groaning...
And then... it happened.

"My body was shaking so violently from the effort it took *not* to do, what it so *wanted* to do..."

"...I couldn't find my keys for all the *convulsing*."

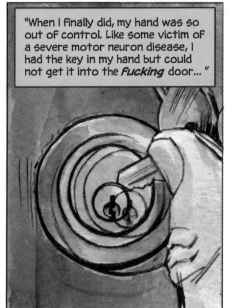

"When I finally did, my hand was so out of control. Like some victim of a severe motor neuron disease, I had the key in my hand but could not get it into the *fucking* door..."

Then I started crying.

And then I shat myself.

Ha Ha! Urrgh! Steve! AHa ha!!

oooh, god... it were...

...*mammoth*...

...*terrifying*.

...oh god... please *stop* Ha ha!

And the saddest thing is, Nao... as I capitulated to this 'movement'...

I decided I'd... *enjoy* it. I looked up to the moon... and just...

...let go.

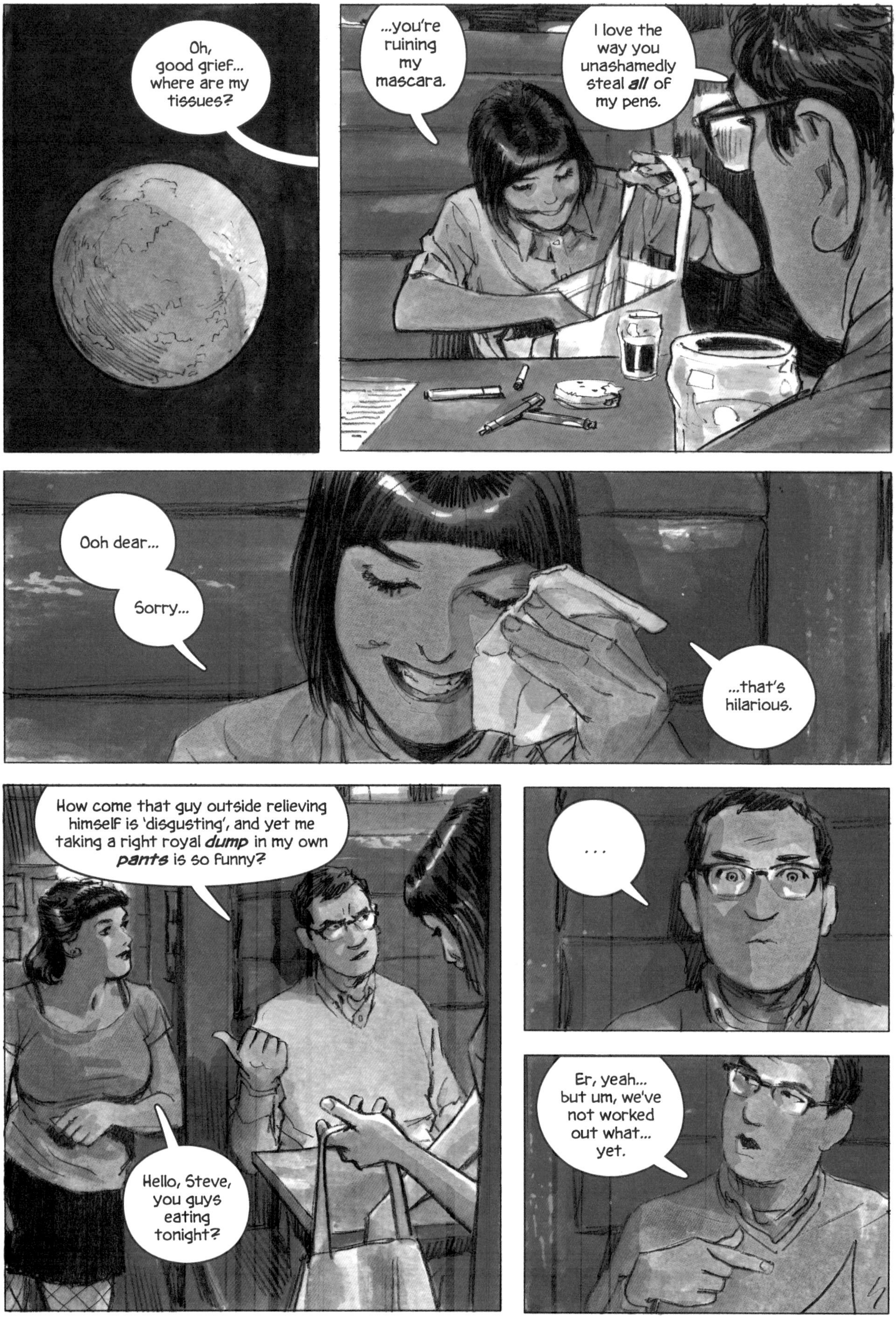
Oh, good grief... where are my tissues?
...you're ruining my mascara.
I love the way you unashamedly steal *all* of my pens.
Ooh dear...
Sorry...
...that's hilarious.
How come that guy outside relieving himself is 'disgusting', and yet me taking a right royal *dump* in my own *pants* is so funny?
Hello, Steve, you guys eating tonight?
. . .
Er, yeah... but um, we've not worked out what... yet.

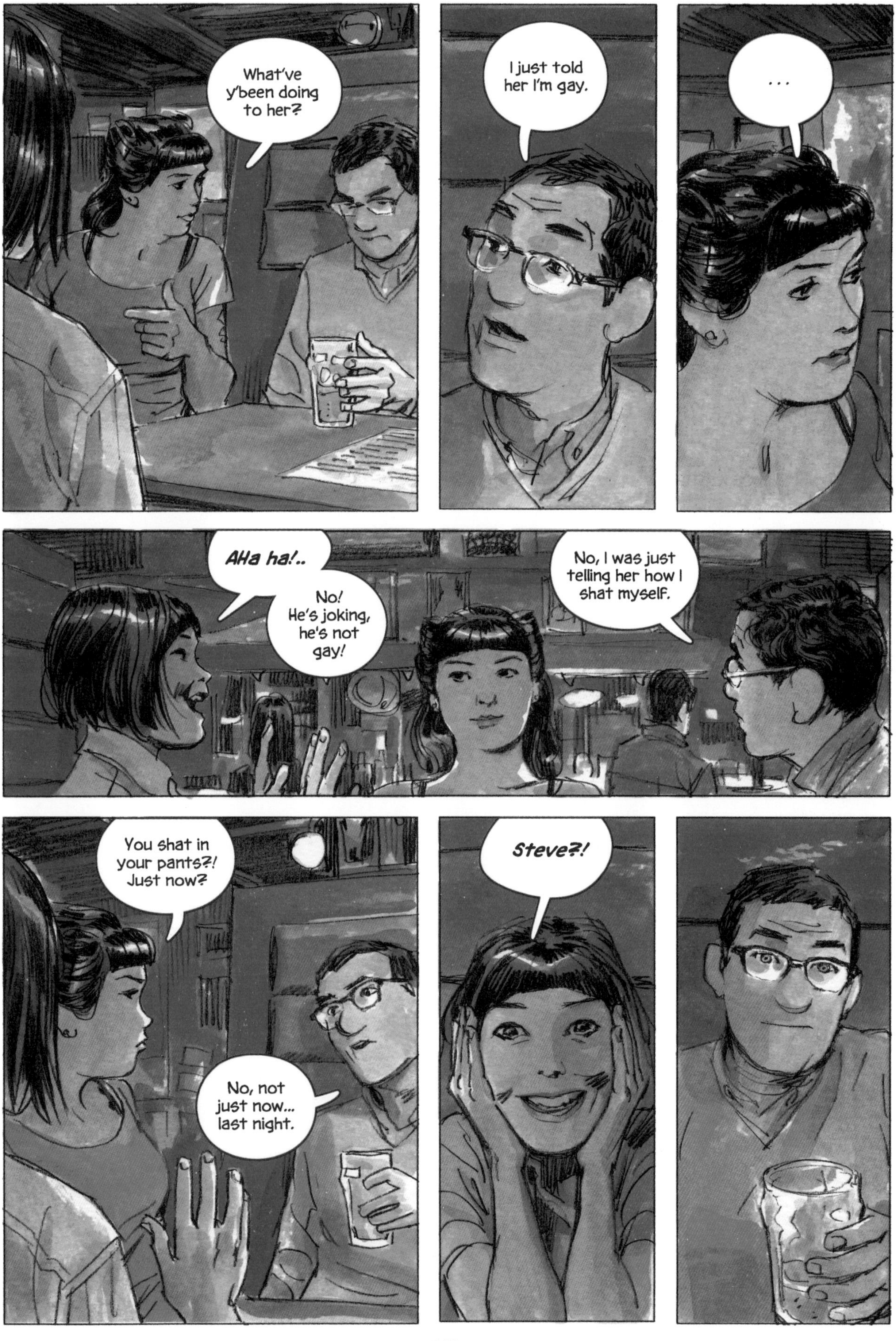
What've y'been doing to her?
I just told her I'm gay.
...
AHa ha!..
No! He's joking, he's not gay!
No, I was just telling her how I shat myself.
You shat in your pants?! Just now?
No, not just now... last night.
Steve?!

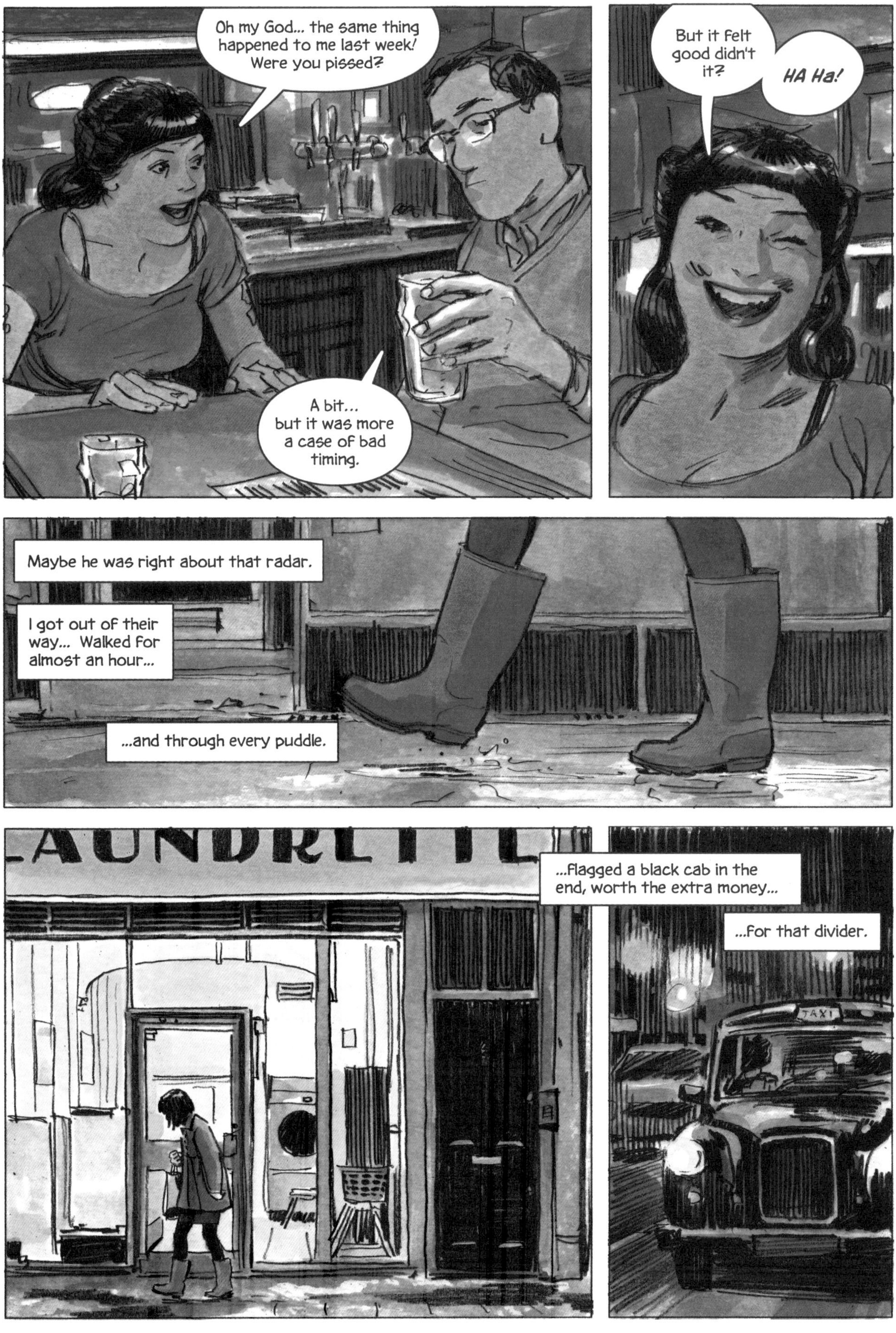
Oh my God... the same thing happened to me last week! Were you pissed?
A bit... but it was more a case of bad timing.
But it felt good didn't it?
HA Ha!
Maybe he was right about that radar.
I got out of their way... Walked for almost an hour...
...and through every puddle.
LAUNDRETTE
...flagged a black cab in the end, worth the extra money...
...for that divider.
TAXI

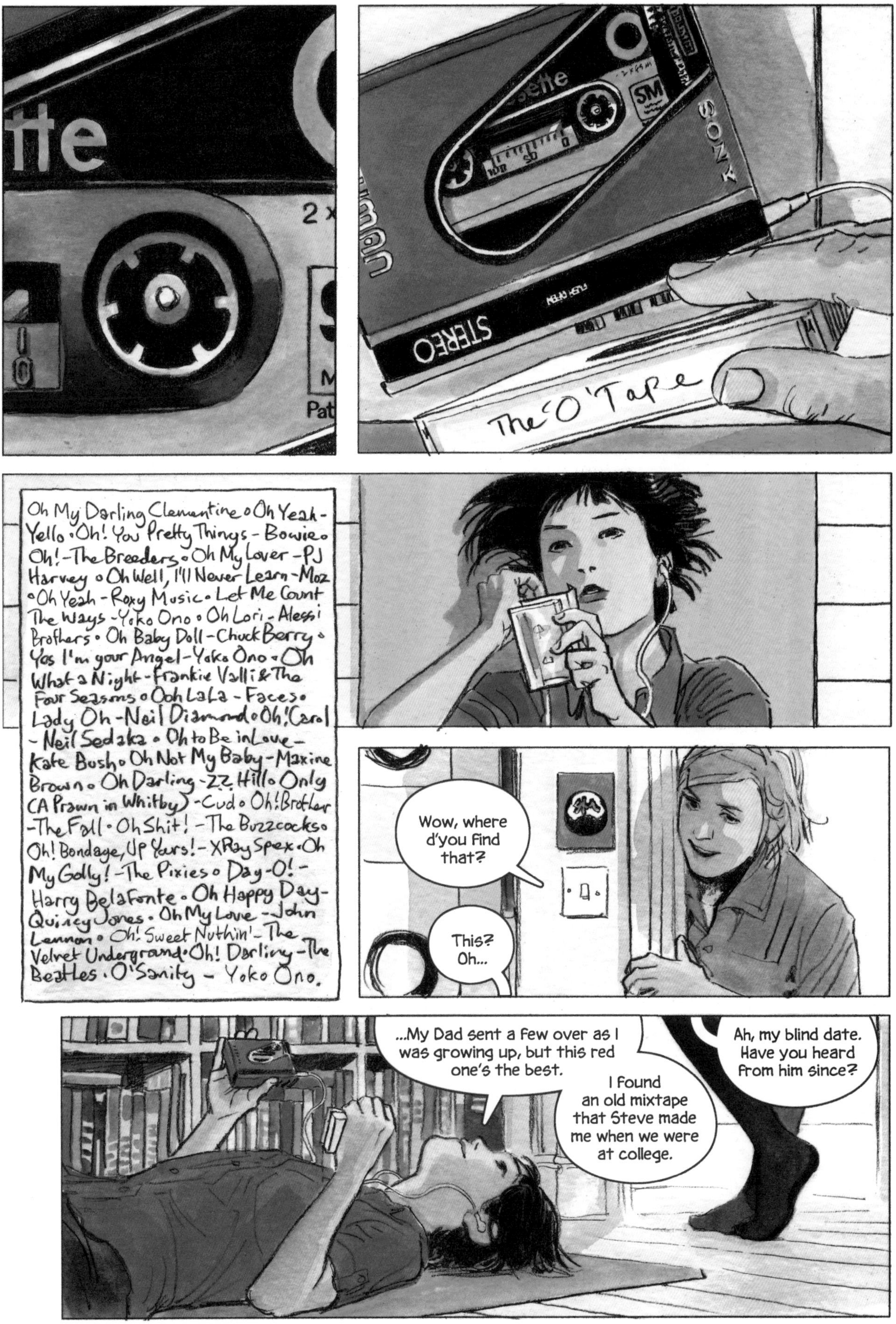
The 'O' Tape
Oh My Darling Clementine • Oh Yeah - Yello • Oh! You Pretty Things - Bowie • Oh! - The Breeders • Oh My Lover - PJ Harvey • Oh Well, I'll Never Learn - Moz • Oh Yeah - Roxy Music • Let Me Count The Ways - Yoko Ono • Oh Lori - Alessi Brothers • Oh Baby Doll - Chuck Berry • Yes I'm your Angel - Yoko Ono • Oh What a Night - Frankie Valli & The Four Seasons • Ooh La La - Faces • Lady Oh - Neil Diamond • Oh! Carol - Neil Sedaka • Oh to Be in Love - Kate Bush • Oh Not My Baby - Maxine Brown • Oh Darling - Z.Z. Hill • Only (A Prawn in Whitby) - Cud • Oh! Brother - The Fall • Oh Shit! - The Buzzcocks • Oh! Bondage, Up Yours! - X Ray Spex • Oh My Golly! - The Pixies • Day-O! - Harry Belafonte • Oh Happy Day - Quincy Jones • Oh My Love - John Lennon • Oh! Sweet Nuthin' - The Velvet Underground • Oh! Darling - The Beatles • O'Sanity - Yoko Ono.
Wow, where d'you find that?
This? Oh...
...My Dad sent a few over as I was growing up, but this red one's the best.
I found an old mixtape that Steve made me when we were at college.
Ah, my blind date. Have you heard from him since?

Yeah, I saw him tonight.

What did he say?

That you thought he was too short.

Ah, well... I suppose I did... ...but I didn't *say* that.

He said you'd prefer some *'camper'*.

Someone camper?

No, someone who likes *camping*.

Really?

...

Did you ever have a thing with him?

Me and Steve? Oh... ...no.

I love him... he's always made me laugh but nothing ever happened.

He's no good at talking to girls he likes...

I'm sure he sees us as more of a 'brother-sister' thing...

Tea?

No thanks.

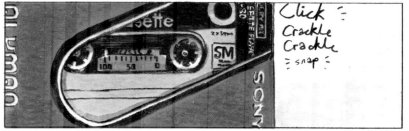

Click
Crackle
Crackle
: snap :

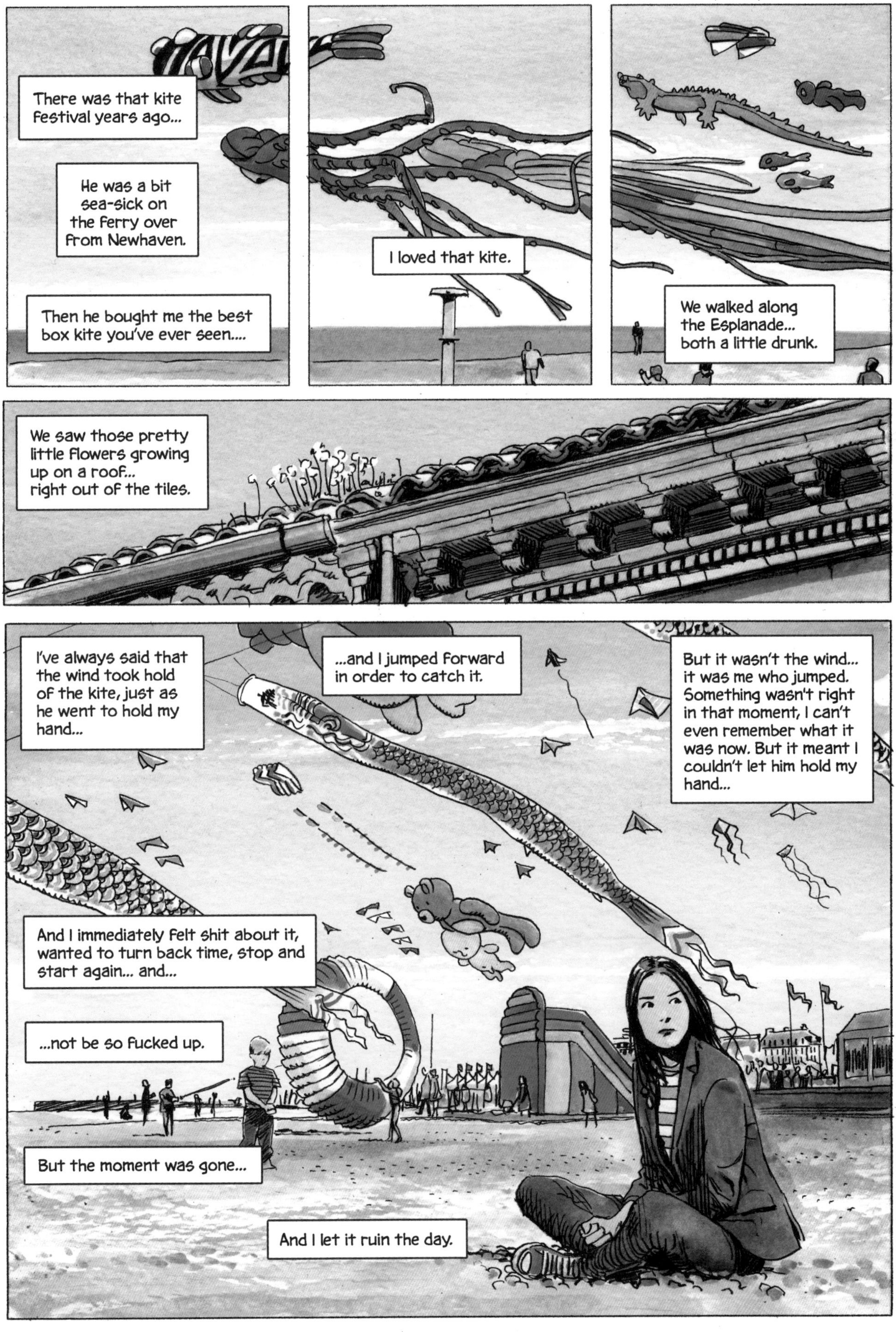
There was that kite festival years ago...
He was a bit sea-sick on the ferry over from Newhaven.
Then he bought me the best box kite you've ever seen....
I loved that kite.
We walked along the Esplanade... both a little drunk.
We saw those pretty little flowers growing up on a roof... right out of the tiles.
I've always said that the wind took hold of the kite, just as he went to hold my hand...
...and I jumped forward in order to catch it.
But it wasn't the wind... it was me who jumped. Something wasn't right in that moment, I can't even remember what it was now. But it meant I couldn't let him hold my hand...
And I immediately felt shit about it, wanted to turn back time, stop and start again... and...
...not be so fucked up.
But the moment was gone...
And I let it ruin the day.

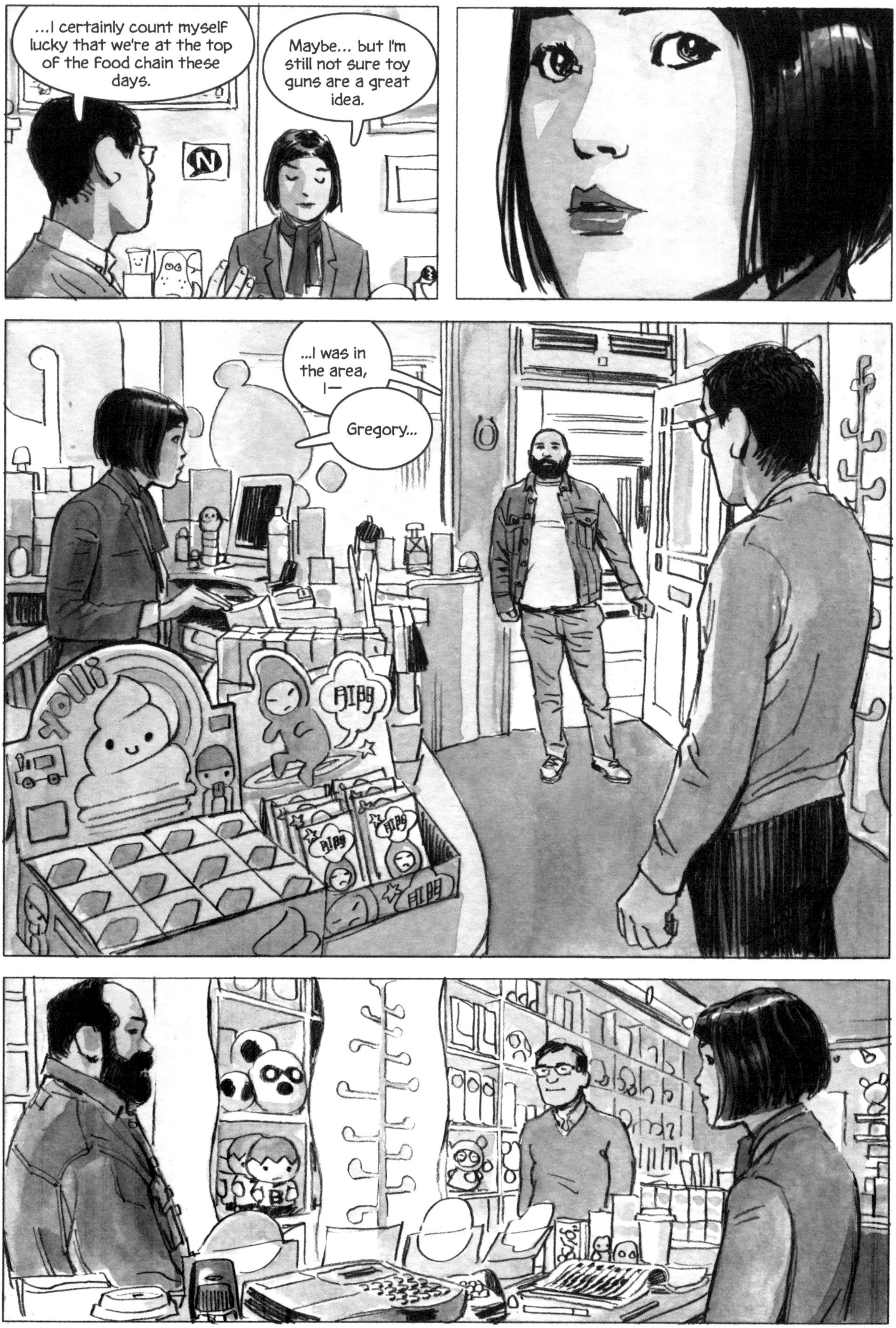
...I certainly count myself lucky that we're at the top of the food chain these days.
Maybe... but I'm still not sure toy guns are a great idea.
...I was in the area, I—
Gregory...

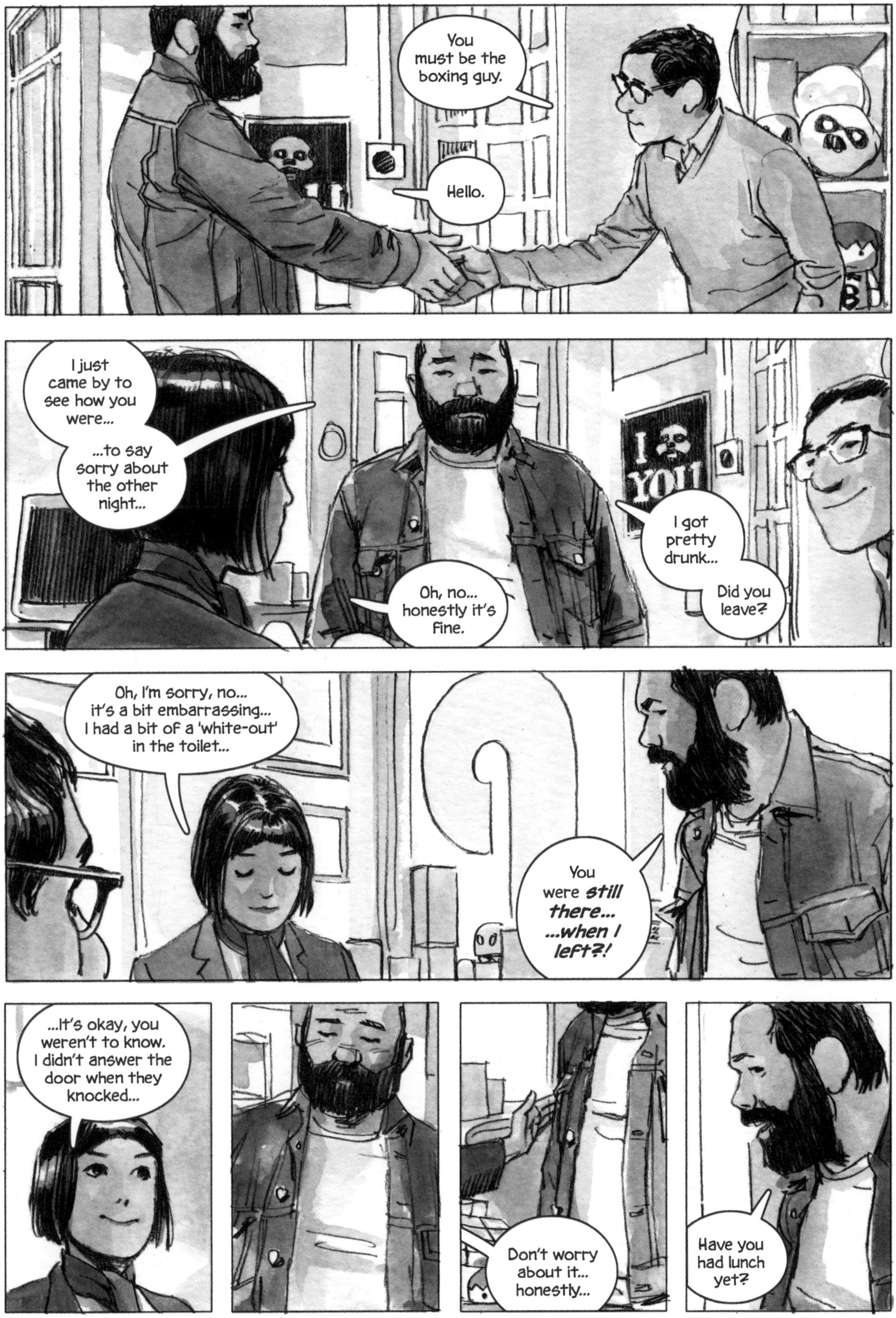
You must be the boxing guy.
Hello.
I just came by to see how you were...
...to say sorry about the other night...
I got pretty drunk...
Did you leave?
Oh, no... honestly it's fine.
Oh, I'm sorry, no... it's a bit embarrassing... I had a bit of a 'white-out' in the toilet...
You were ***still there...*** ***...when I left?!***
...It's okay, you weren't to know. I didn't answer the door when they knocked...
Don't worry about it... honestly...
Have you had lunch yet?

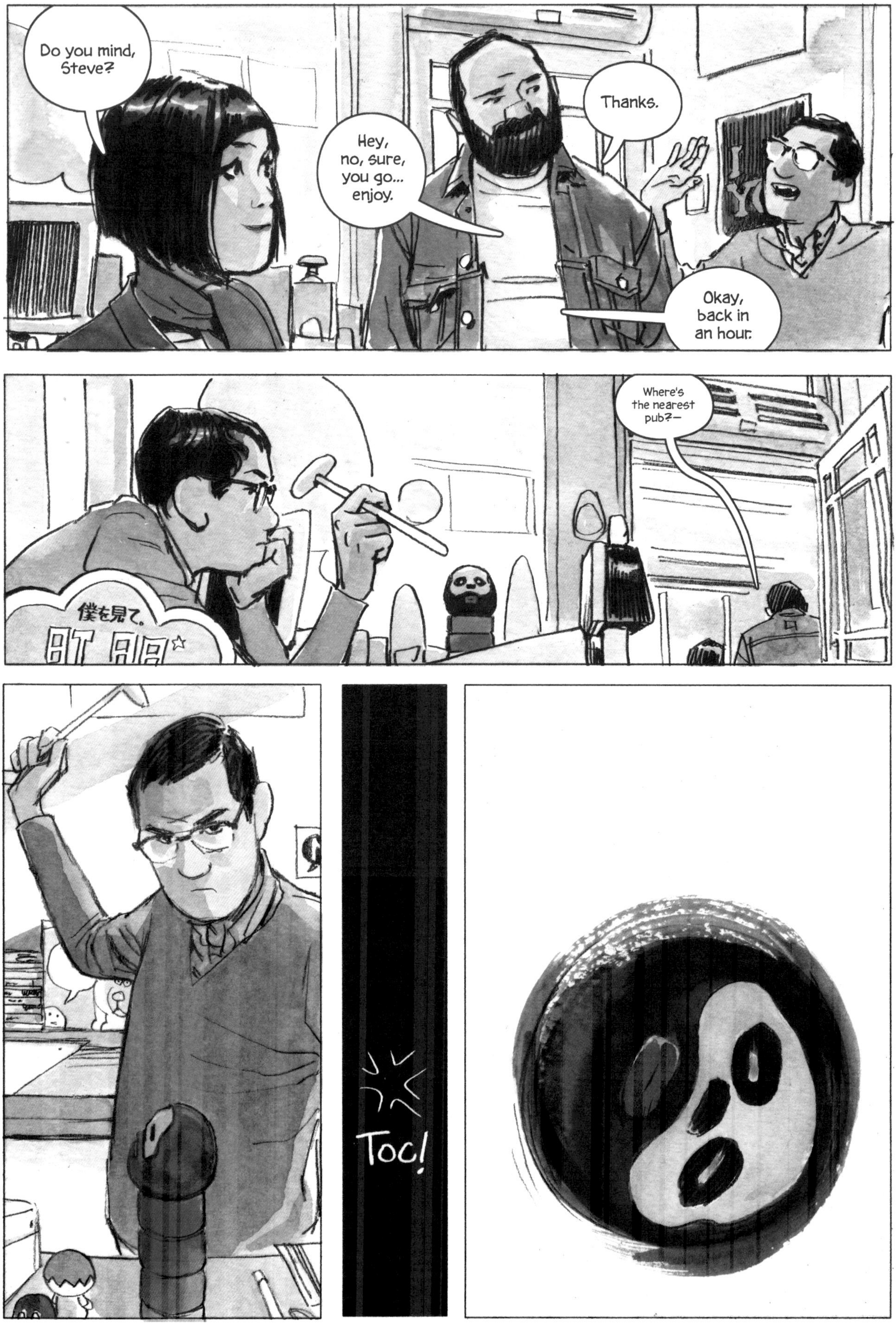
Do you mind, Steve?
Hey, no, sure, you go... enjoy.
Thanks.
Okay, back in an hour.
Where's the nearest pub?—
僕を見て。
Toc!

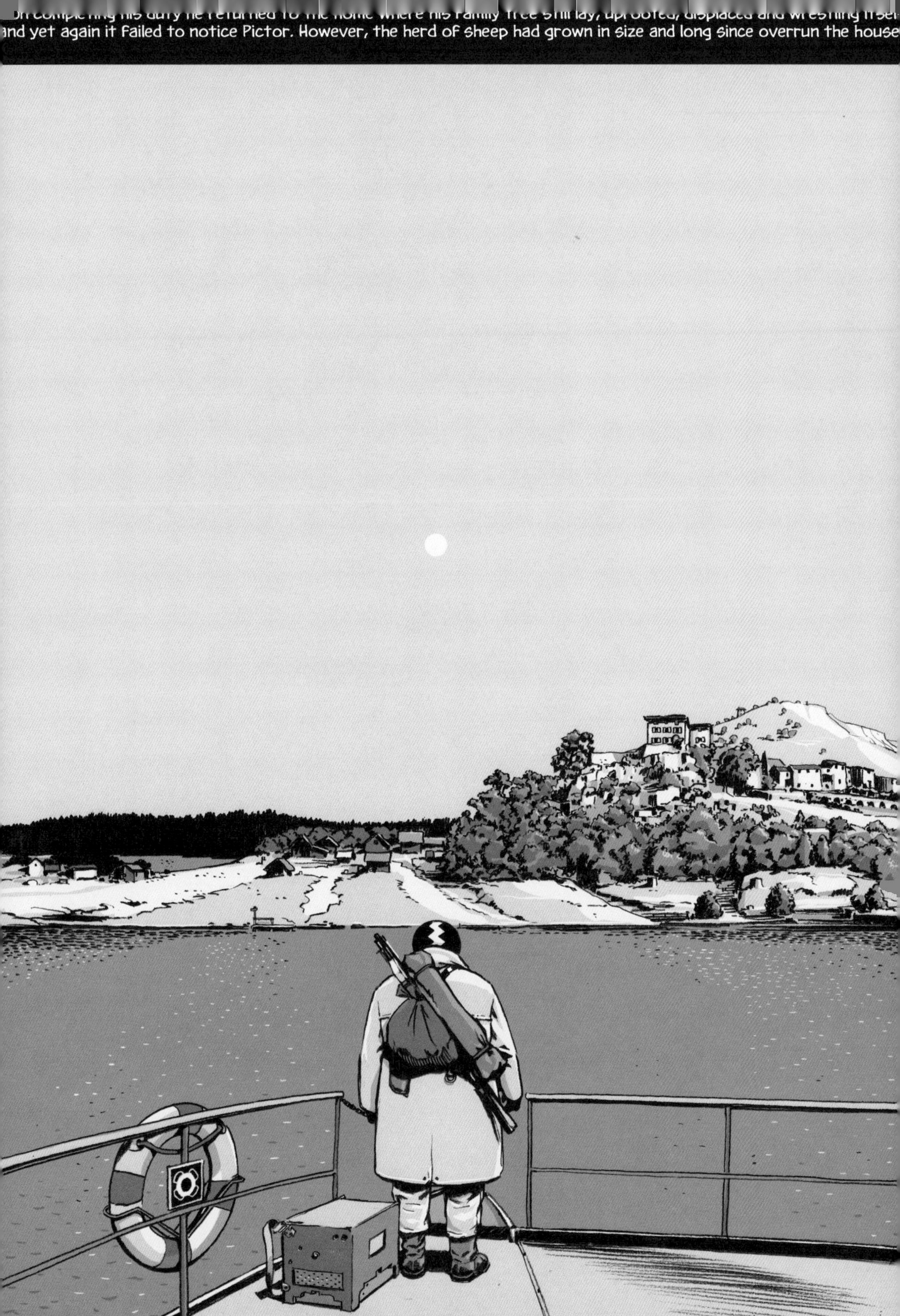
On completing his duty he returned to the home where his family tree still lay, uprooted, displaced and wrestling itself
and yet again it failed to notice Pictor. However, the herd of sheep had grown in size and long since overrun the house

Pictor drove the herd out onto the mead and the slaughtering began. There was such cleaving and chopping that the commotion could be heard for miles around. Pictor worked until both arms ached, and a great wave of red ran away from where he stood. He then set out for the first Captain's garrison.

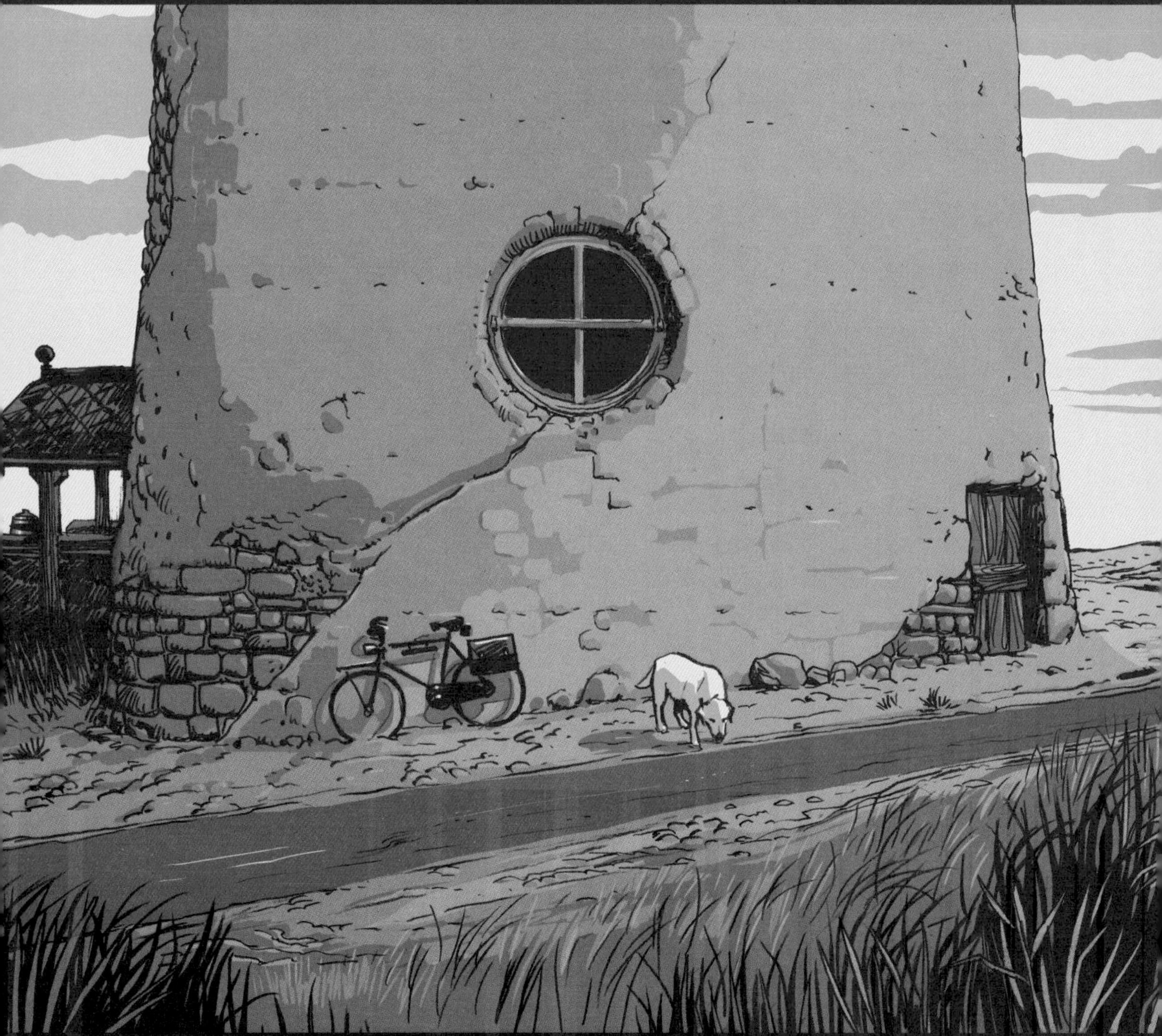

The Captain's guards had been given orders not to let Pictor enter... so he was turned away at the gates, only to circle the grounds from a distance until nightfall. Under the cover of darkness Pictor scaled the giant hardwood that stretched over the barricades and stole into the Captain's chamber as he slept.

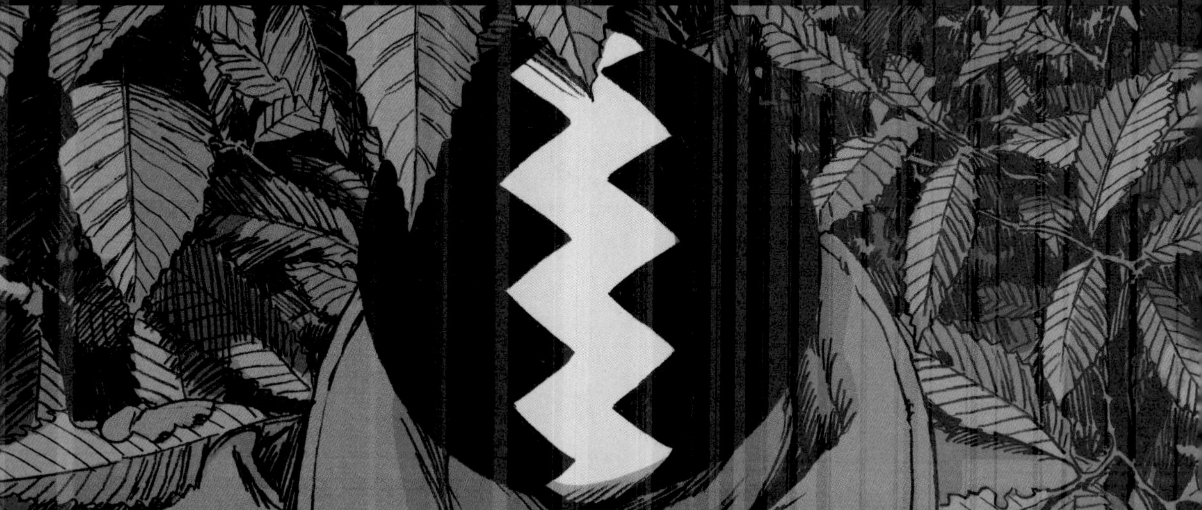

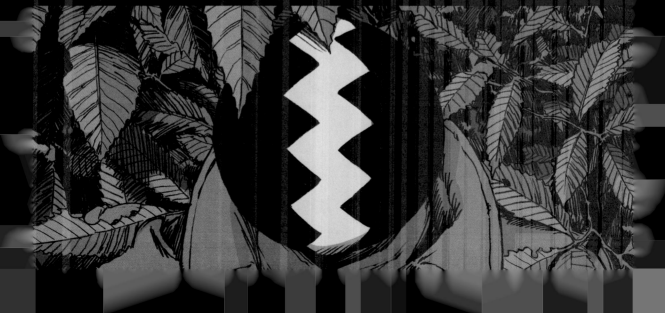

Holding a gun to his head he demanded the Captain keep his word, otherwise he would take his life and his daughter's as well.

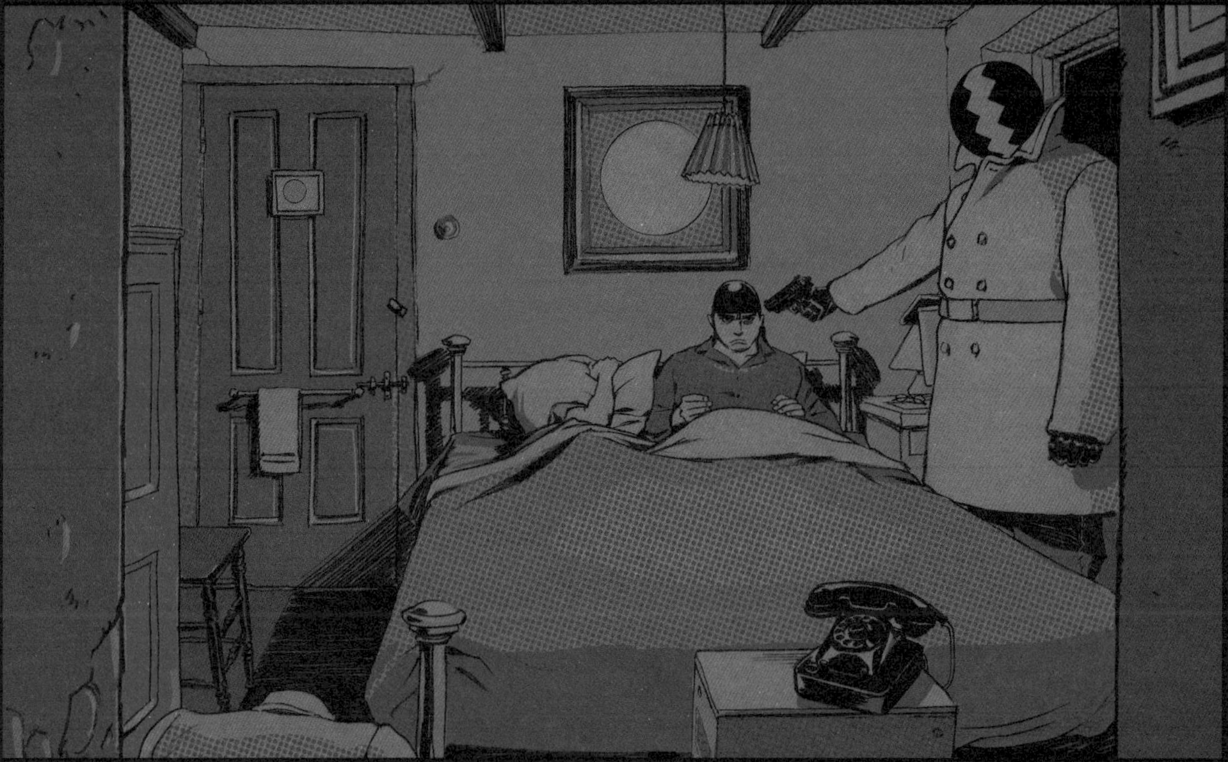

Then the Captain commanded his daughter to go with Pictor in order to save their lives. So she dressed herself in white as her father ordered a hardtop be packed with all his worth... for the Captain feared that was the last he would ever see of his only daughter... But events were to turn elseways.

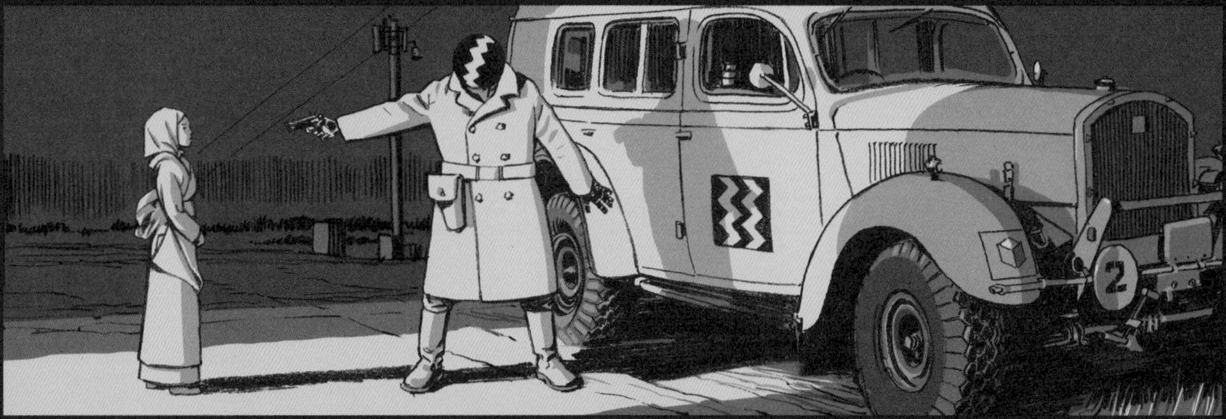

When they had only gone a little way, Pictor took off her milky clothes and stuck her with his barbs until she was veiled in blood. "Go back home. I don't want you..." said Pictor. Then he sent her away... and her wounds only healed when she was able to forgive him.

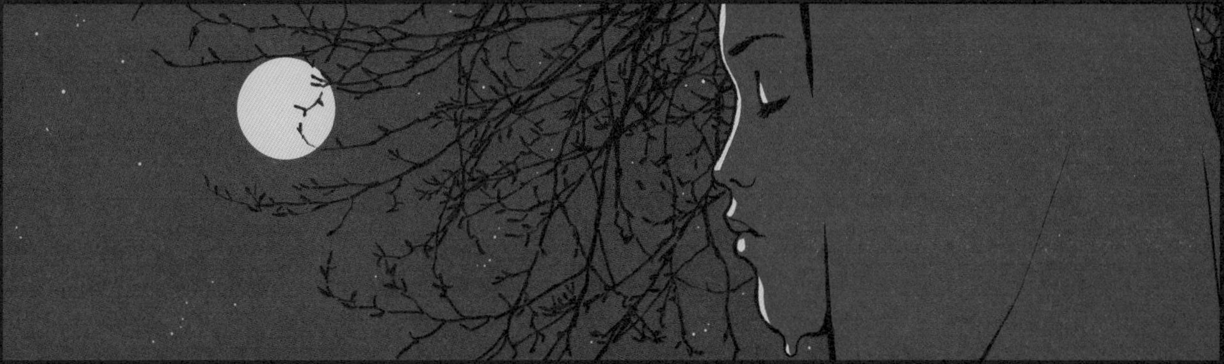

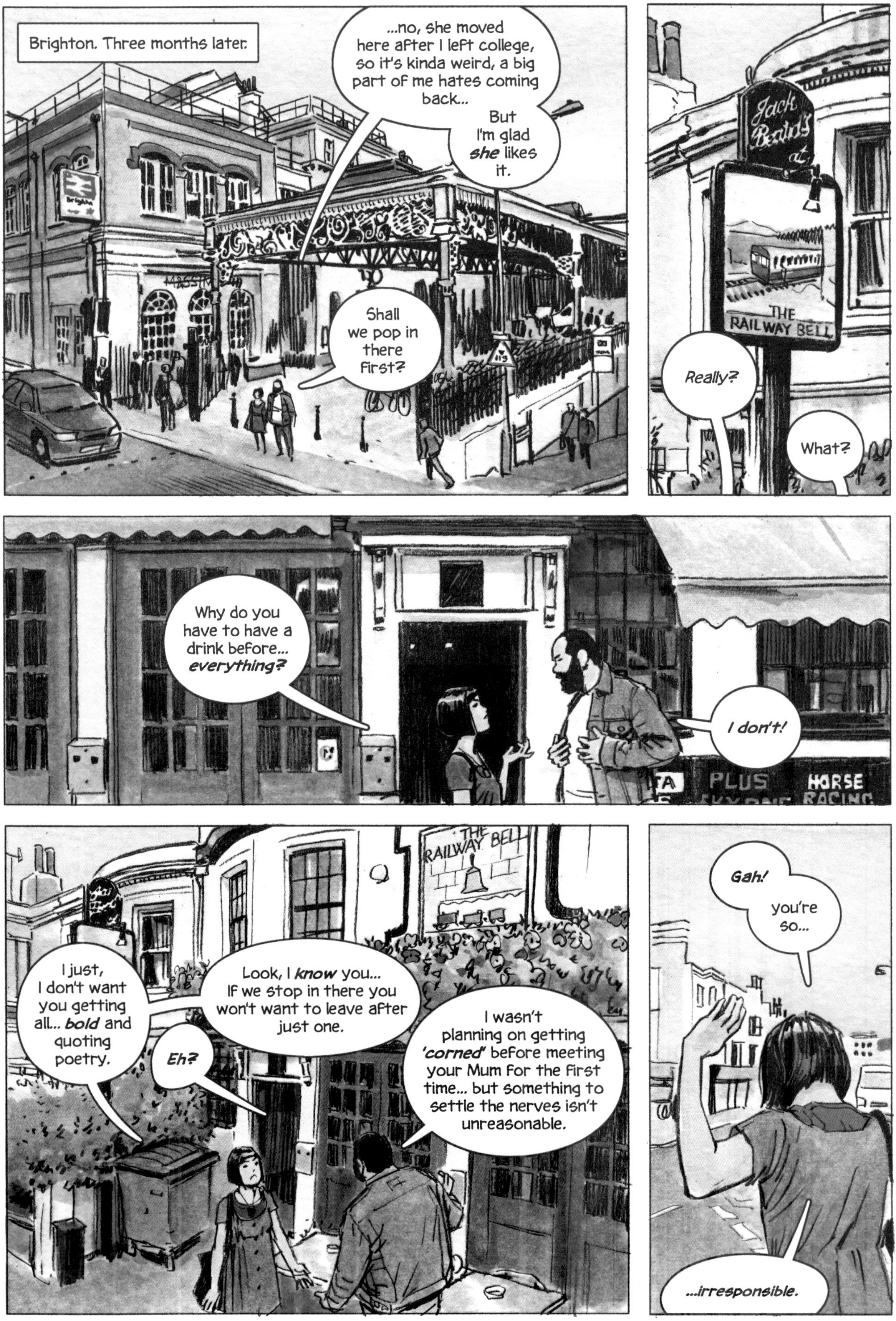
Brighton. Three months later.
...no, she moved here after I left college, so it's kinda weird, a big part of me hates coming back...
But I'm glad *she* likes it.
Shall we pop in there first?
Jack Baird's at
THE RAILWAY BELL
Really?
What?
Why do you have to have a drink before... *everything?*
I don't!
PLUS
HORSE RACING
THE RAILWAY BELL
I just, I don't want you getting all... *bold* and quoting poetry.
Look, I *know* you... If we stop in there you won't want to leave after just one.
Eh?
I wasn't planning on getting *'corned'* before meeting your Mum for the first time... but something to settle the nerves isn't unreasonable.
Gah!
you're so...
...irresponsible.

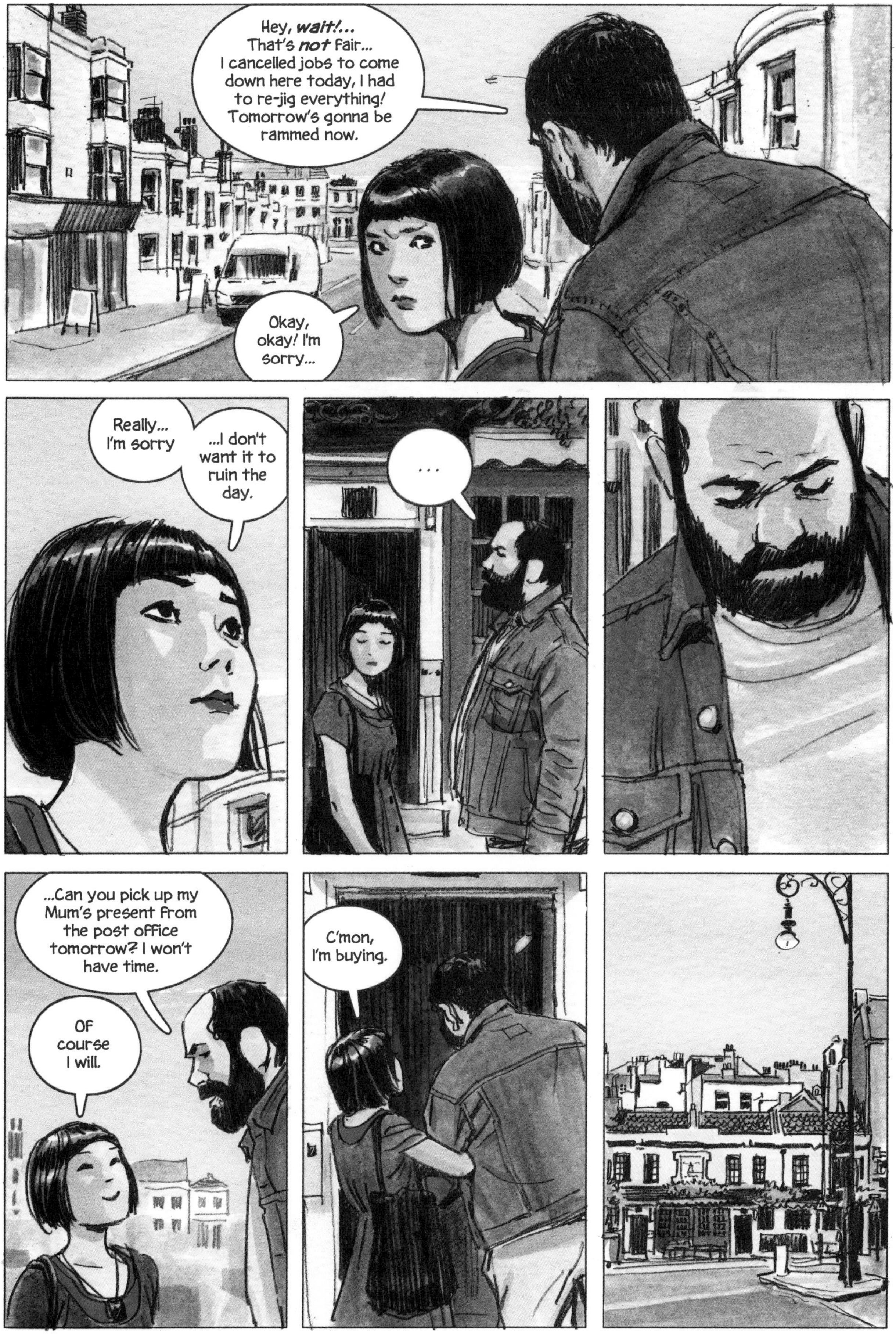
Hey, *wait!...* That's *not* fair... I cancelled jobs to come down here today, I had to re-jig everything! Tomorrow's gonna be rammed now.
Okay, okay! I'm sorry...
Really... I'm sorry
...I don't want it to ruin the day.
...
...Can you pick up my Mum's present from the post office tomorrow? I won't have time.
Of course I will.
C'mon, I'm buying.

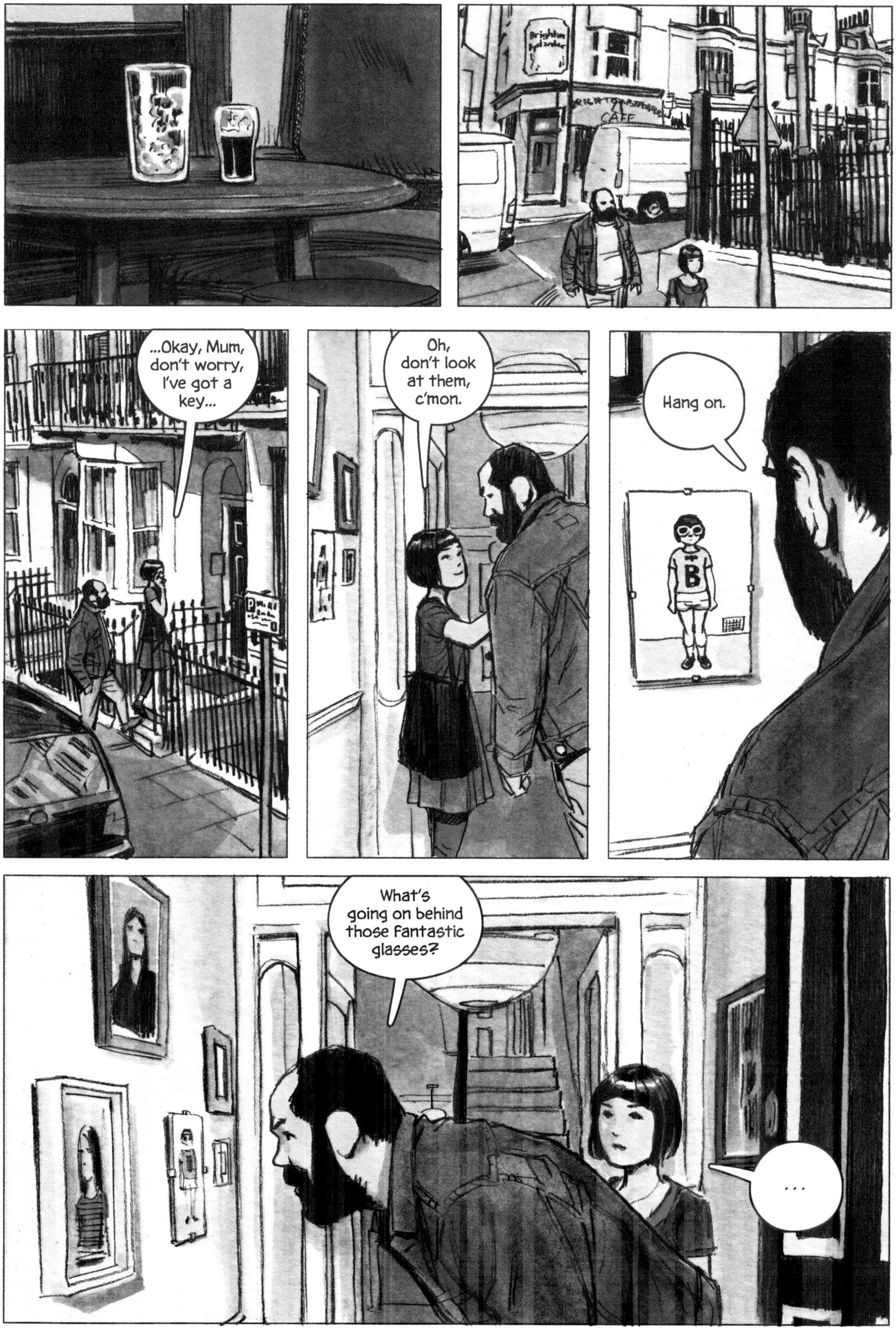

...Okay, Mum, don't worry, I've got a key...
Oh, don't look at them, c'mon.
Hang on.
What's going on behind those fantastic glasses?
...

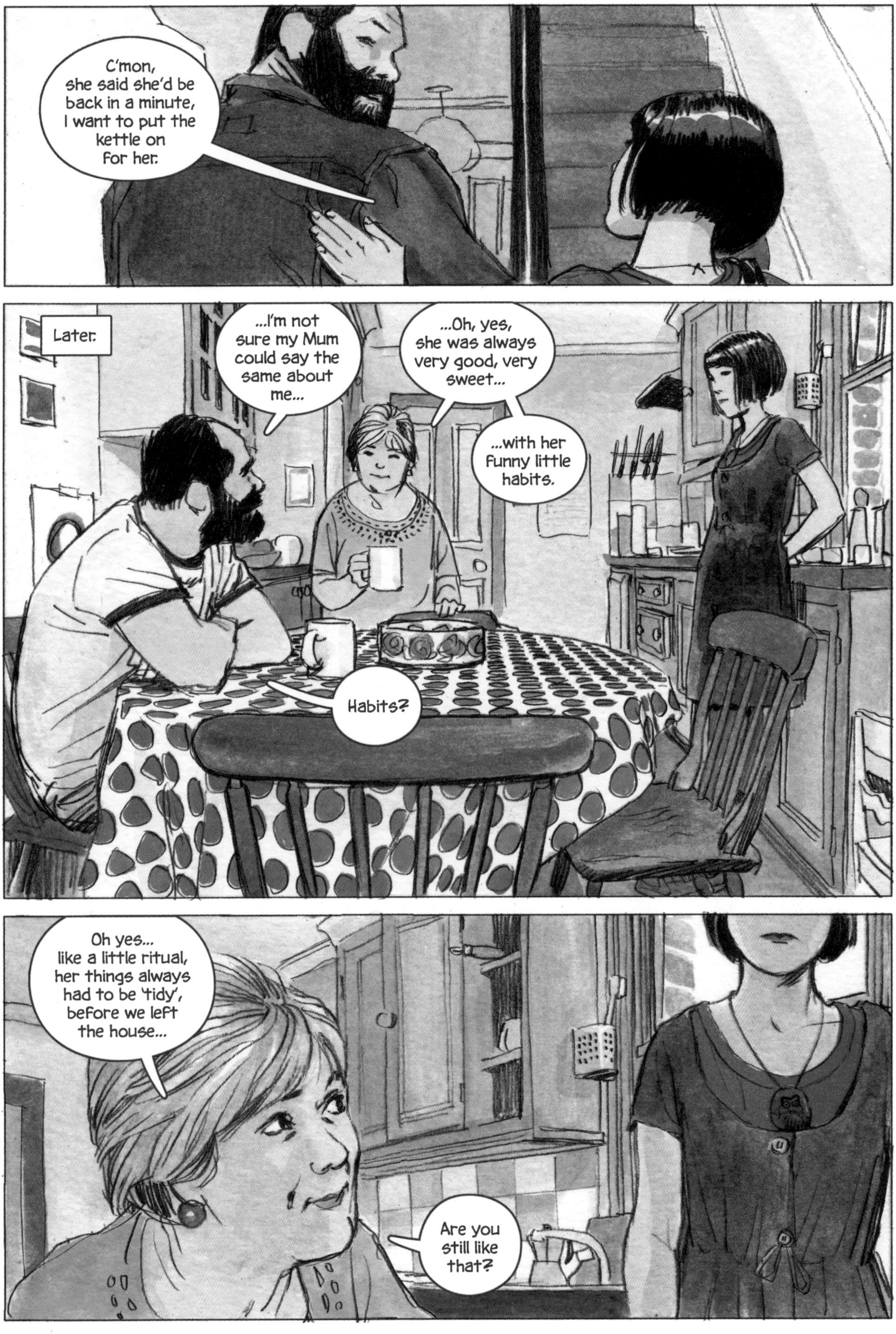
C'mon, she said she'd be back in a minute, I want to put the kettle on for her.
Later.
...I'm not sure my Mum could say the same about me...
...Oh, yes, she was always very good, very sweet...
...with her funny little habits.
Habits?
Oh yes... like a little ritual, her things always had to be 'tidy', before we left the house...
Are you still like that?

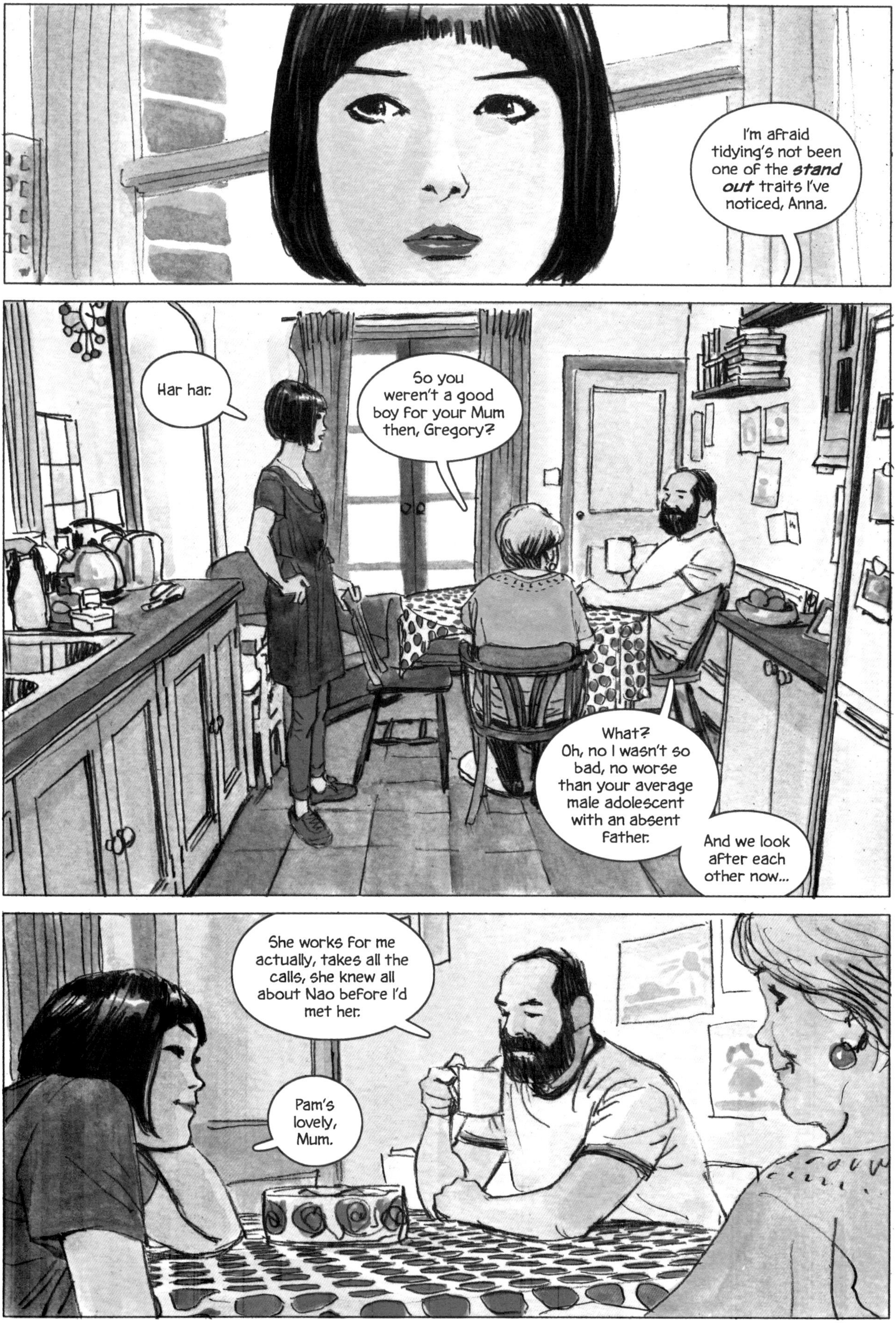
I'm afraid tidying's not been one of the ***stand out*** traits I've noticed, Anna.
Har har.
So you weren't a good boy for your Mum then, Gregory?
What? Oh, no I wasn't so bad, no worse than your average male adolescent with an absent father.
And we look after each other now...
She works for me actually, takes all the calls, she knew all about Nao before I'd met her.
Pam's lovely, Mum.

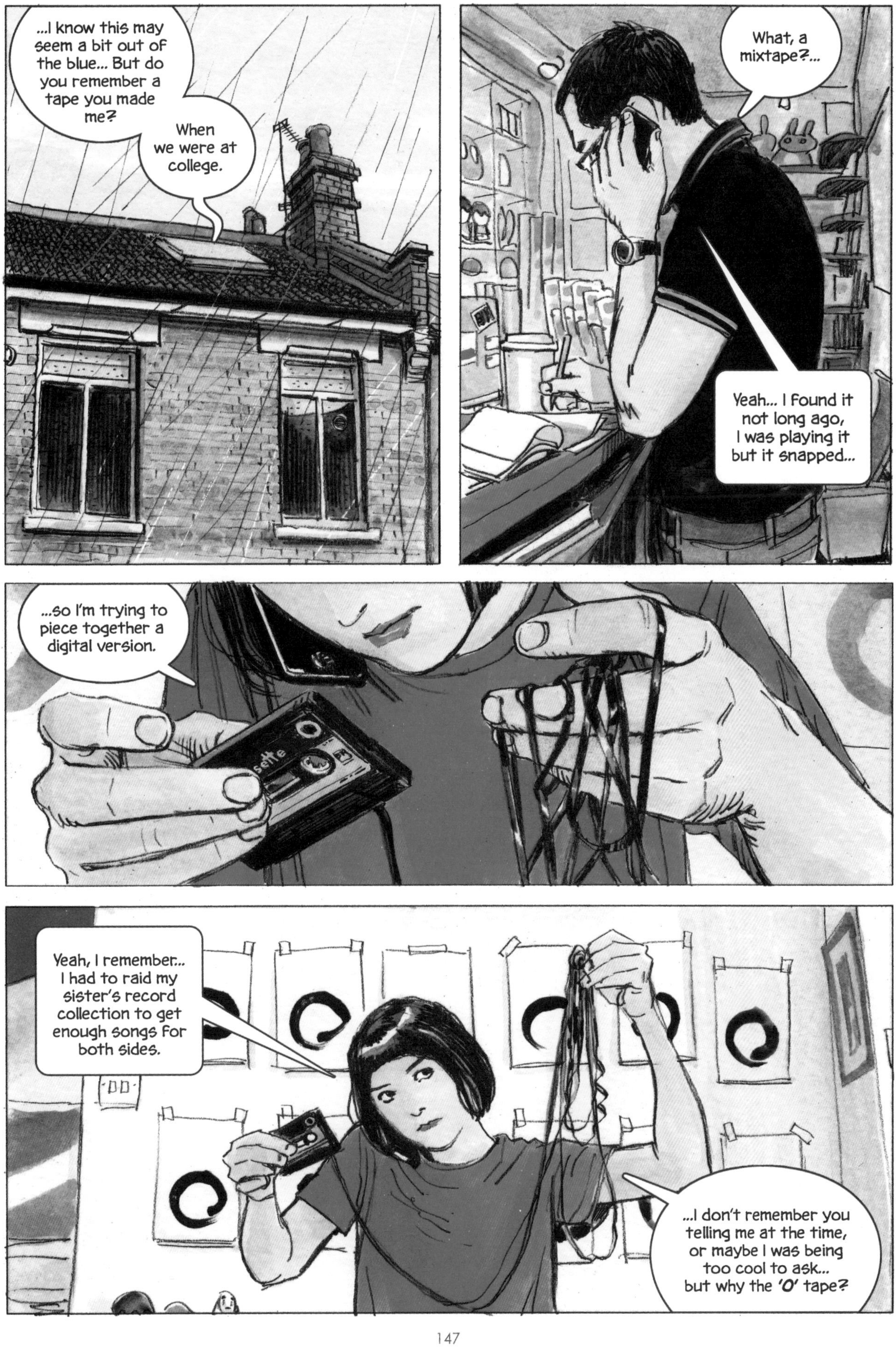
...I know this may seem a bit out of the blue... But do you remember a tape you made me?
When we were at college.
What, a mixtape?...
Yeah... I found it not long ago, I was playing it but it snapped...
...so I'm trying to piece together a digital version.
Yeah, I remember... I had to raid my sister's record collection to get enough songs for both sides.
...I don't remember you telling me at the time, or maybe I was being too cool to ask... but why the 'O' tape?

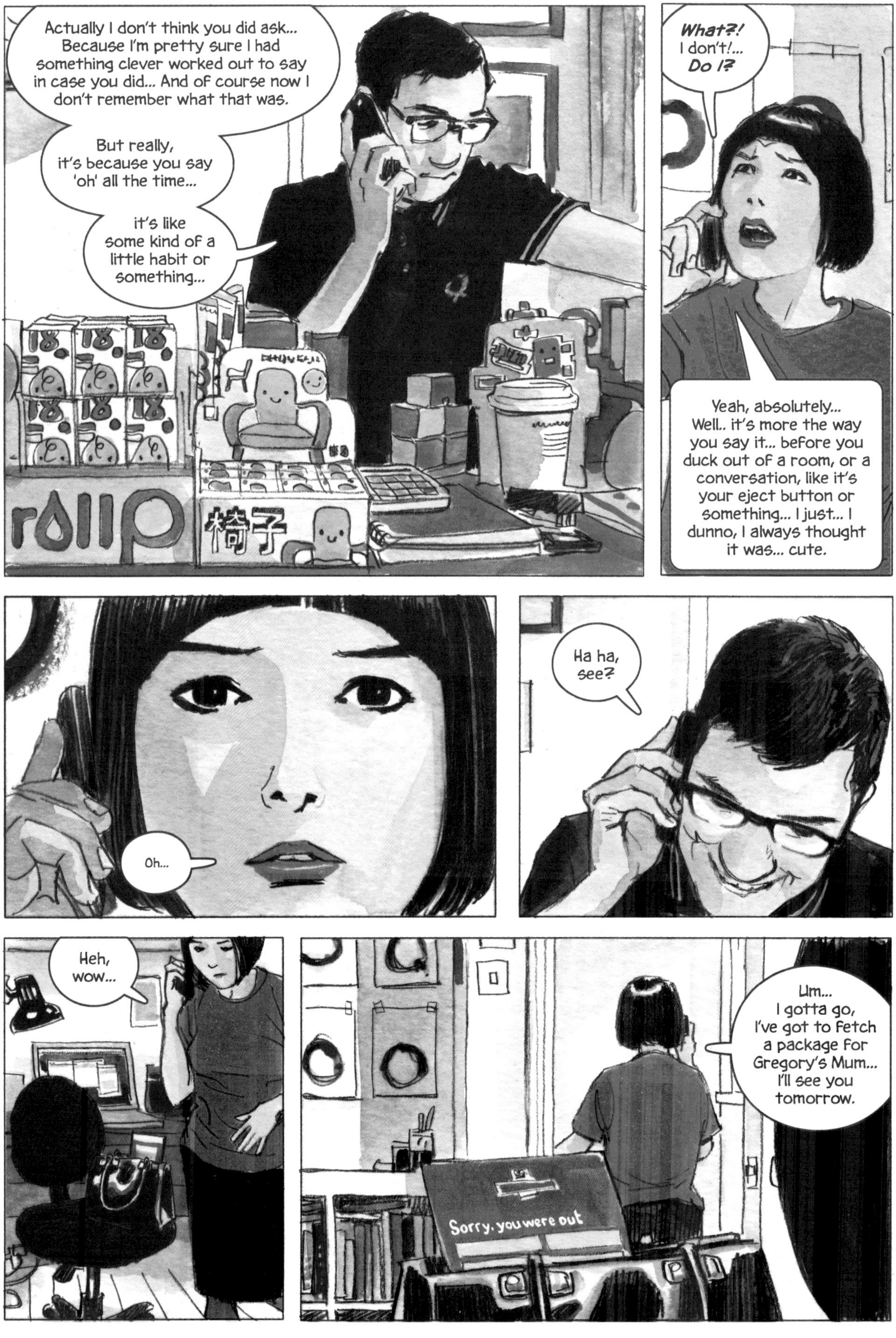
Actually I don't think you did ask... Because I'm pretty sure I had something clever worked out to say in case you did... And of course now I don't remember what that was.
But really, it's because you say 'oh' all the time...
it's like some kind of a little habit or something...
rollp
椅子
What?! I don't!... Do I?
Yeah, absolutely... Well.. it's more the way you say it... before you duck out of a room, or a conversation, like it's your eject button or something... I just... I dunno, I always thought it was... cute.
Oh...
Ha ha, see?
Heh, wow...
Um... I gotta go, I've got to fetch a package for Gregory's Mum... I'll see you tomorrow.
Sorry, you were out

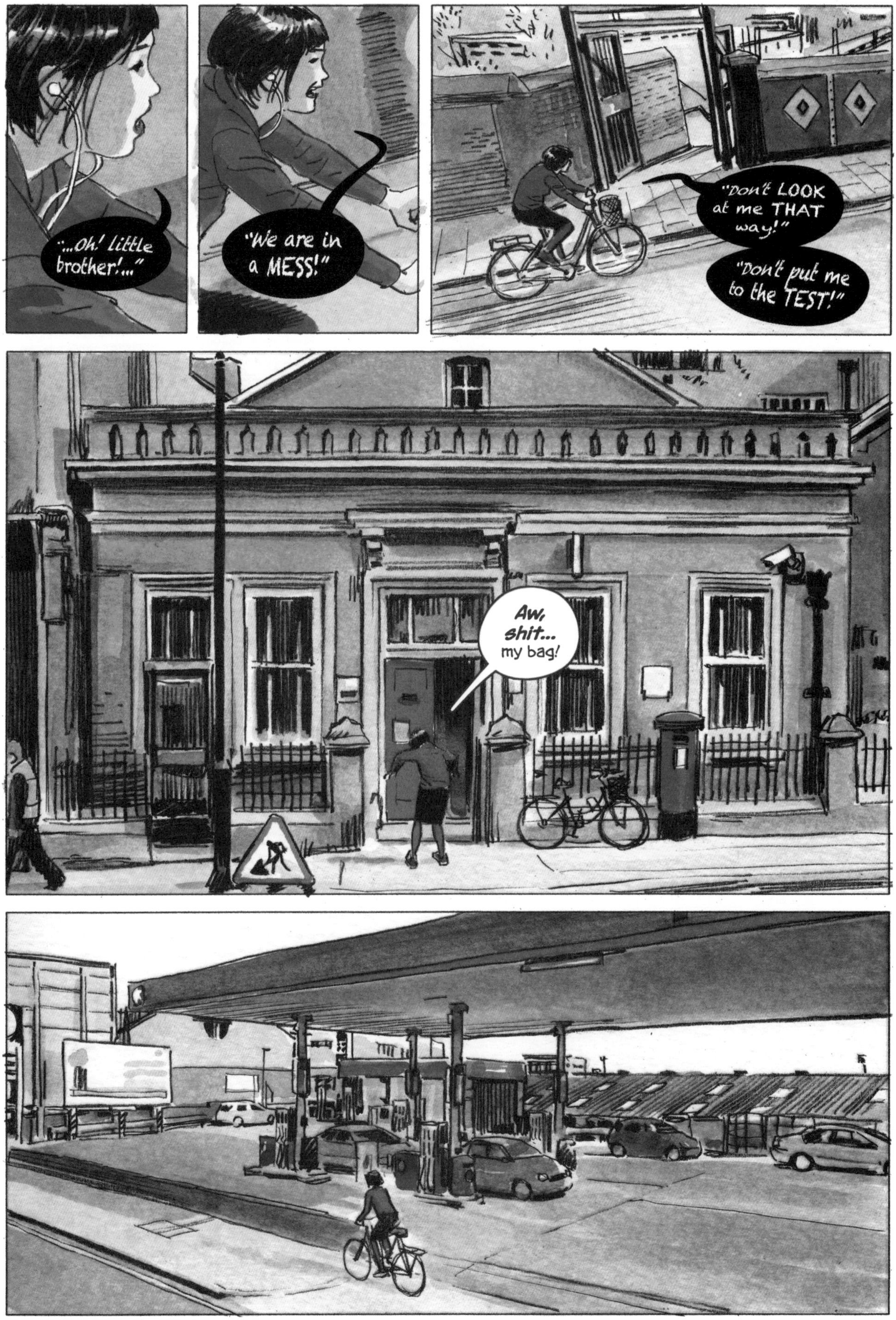
"...Oh! little brother!..."
"We are in a MESS!"
"Don't LOOK at me THAT way!"
"Don't put me to the TEST!"
Aw, shit... my bag!

. . .

No calls?...
He always
calls after
lunch...

'Something must've
happened to him...'

slide to unlock

That's how
easily it
can start.

'...an accident... he's been killed.'

'Murdered...'

'...I'll be questioned.'

'... *Fuck!*'

'I'd be a suspect...'

'7 out of 10'

'*Fuck*... they'd think it was *me*.'

'Where have I been?'

'No one's seen me.'

'7 out of 10'

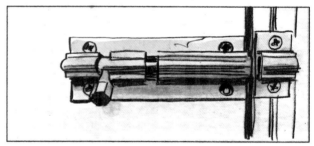

'I'd be a suspect...'

'8 out of 10'

'Where have I been?'

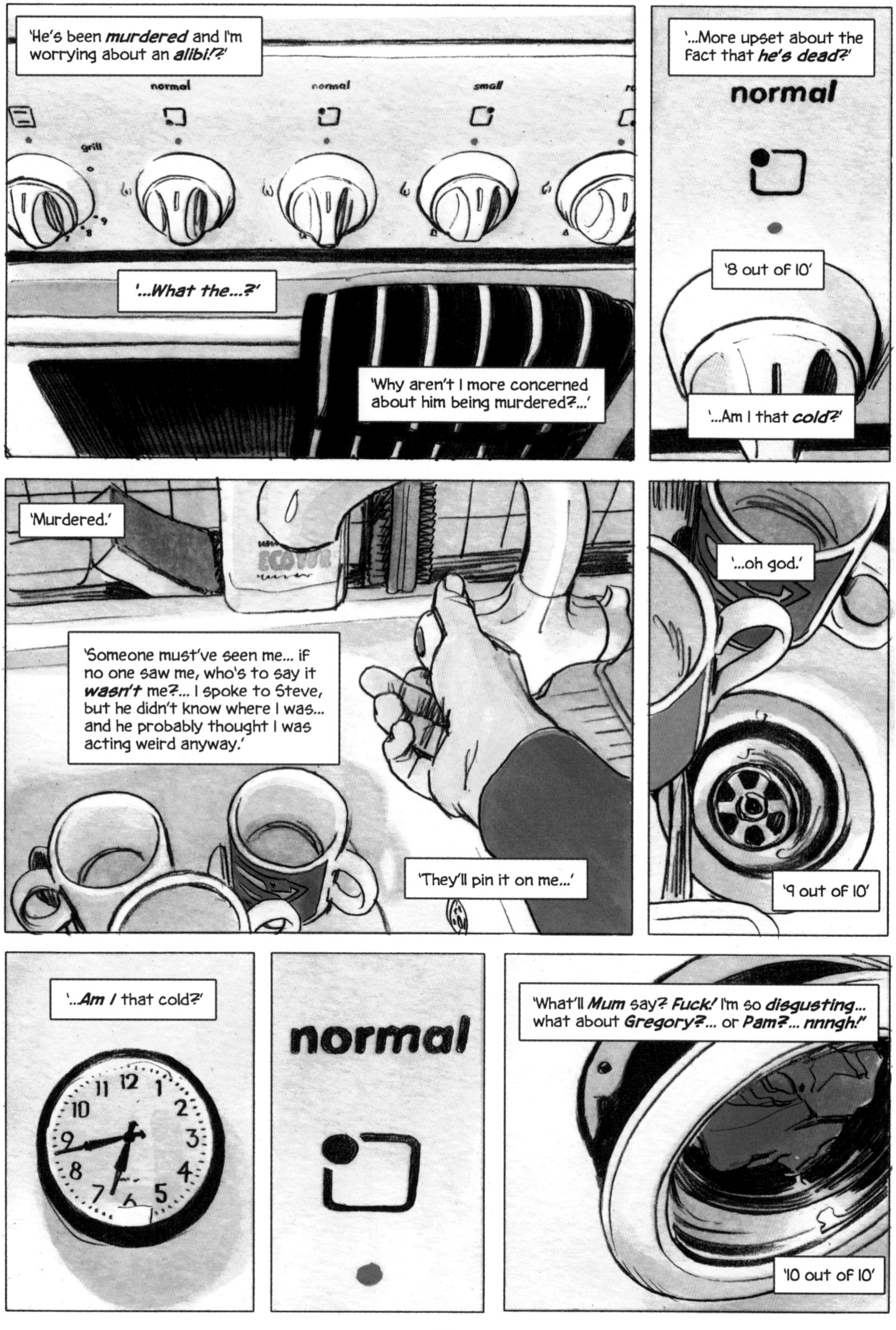
'He's been *murdered* and I'm worrying about an *alibi!?*'
normal
normal
small
grill
'...What the...?'
'Why aren't I more concerned about him being murdered?...'
'...More upset about the fact that *he's dead?*'
normal
'8 out of 10'
'...Am I that *cold?*'
'Murdered.'
ECOVER
'Someone must've seen me... if no one saw me, who's to say it *wasn't* me?... I spoke to Steve, but he didn't know where I was... and he probably thought I was acting weird anyway.'
'They'll pin it on me...'
'...oh god.'
'9 out of 10'
'...*Am I* that cold?'
normal
'What'll *Mum* say? *Fuck!* I'm so *disgusting*... what about *Gregory?*... or *Pam?*... *nnngh!*'
'10 out of 10'

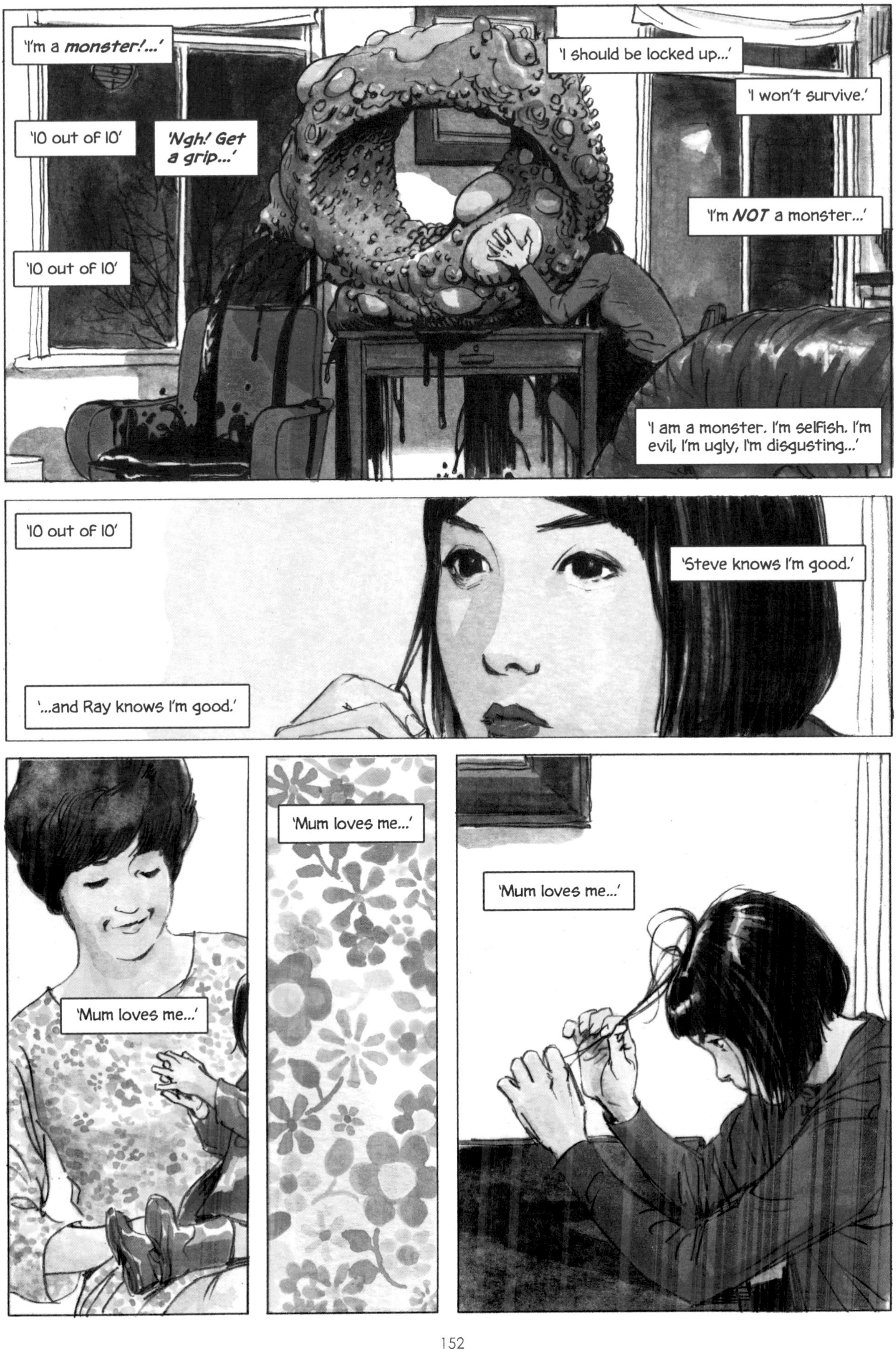
'I'm a ***monster!...***'
'I should be locked up...'
'I won't survive.'
'10 out of 10'
'Ngh! Get a grip...'
'I'm ***NOT*** a monster...'
'10 out of 10'
'I am a monster. I'm selfish. I'm evil, I'm ugly, I'm disgusting...'
'10 out of 10'
'Steve knows I'm good.'
'...and Ray knows I'm good.'
'Mum loves me...'
'Mum loves me...'
'Mum loves me...'

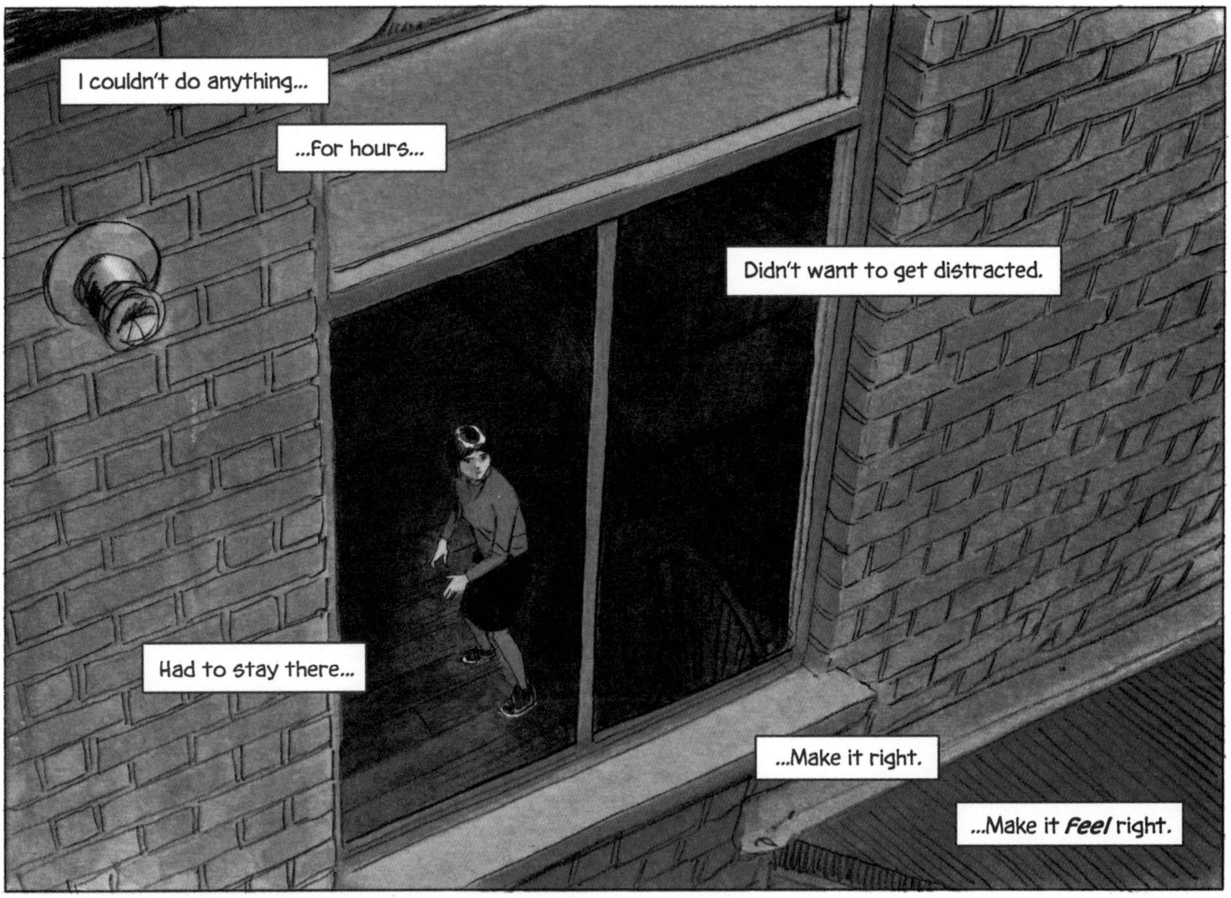
I couldn't do anything...
...for hours...
Didn't want to get distracted.
Had to stay there...
...Make it right.
...Make it *Feel* right.

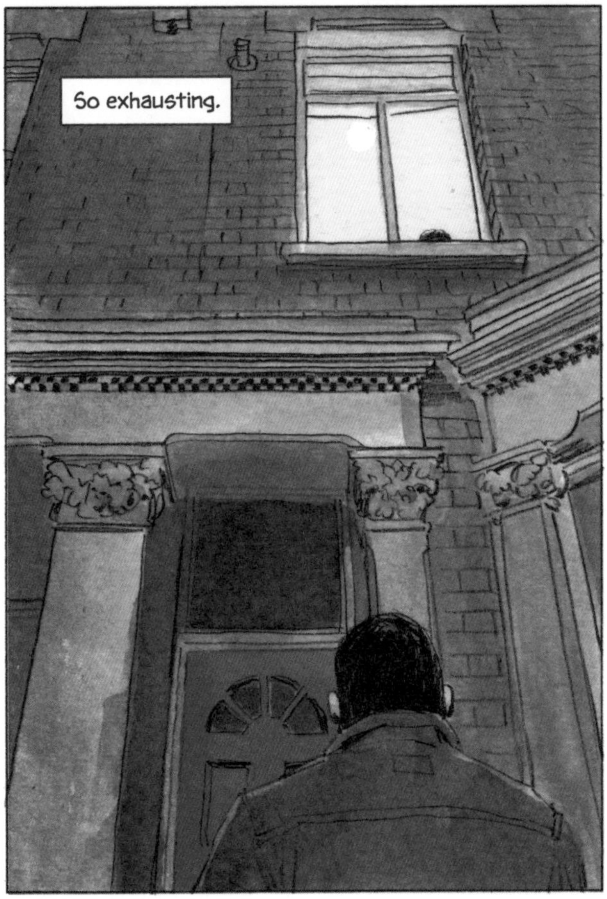
So exhausting.

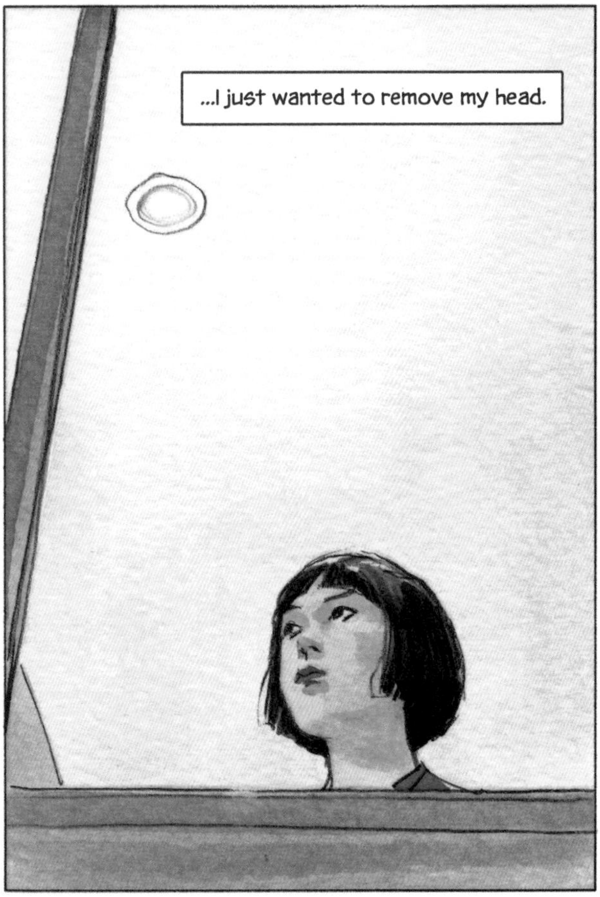
...I just wanted to remove my head.

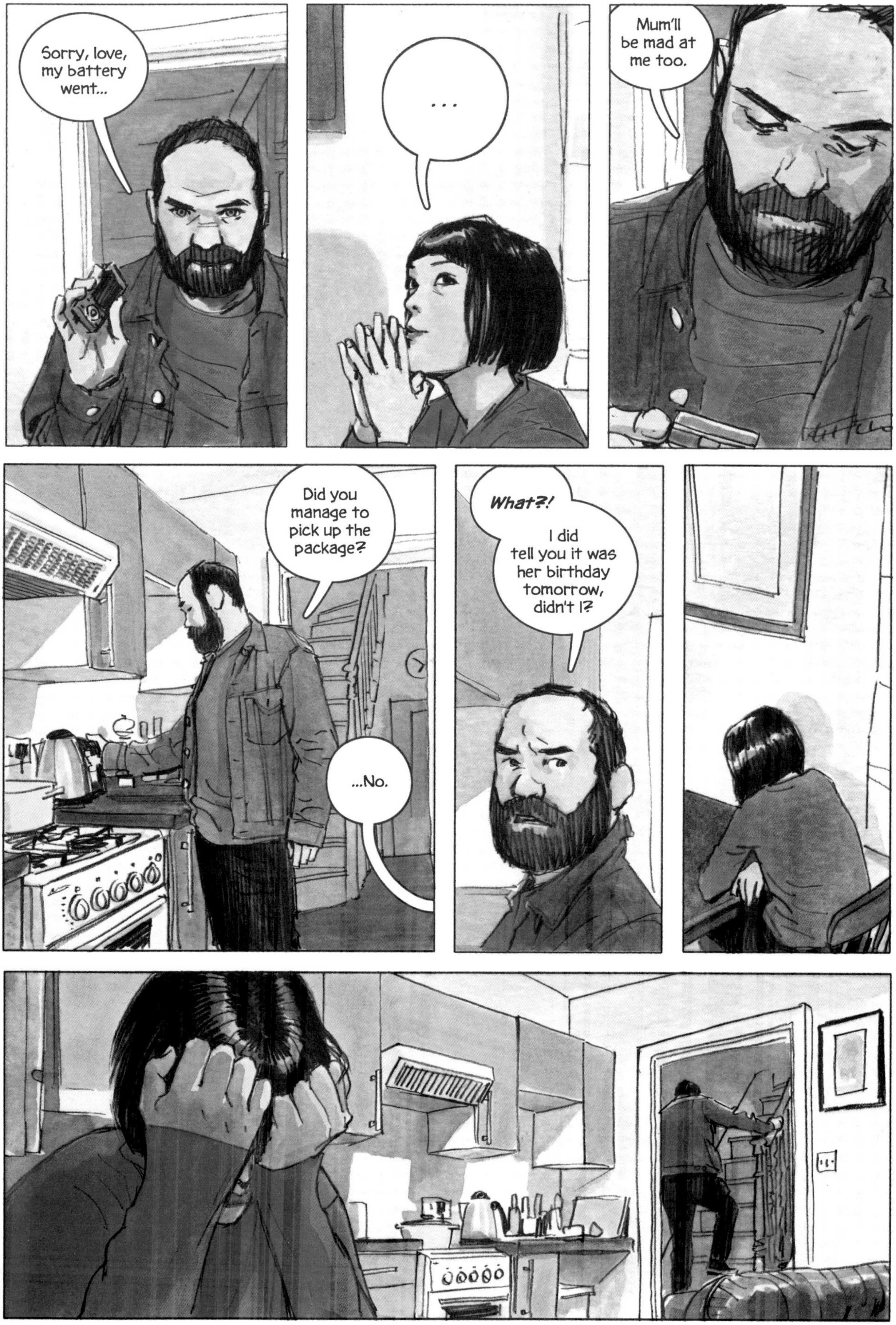
Sorry, love, my battery went...
. . .
Mum'll be mad at me too.
Did you manage to pick up the package?
...No.
What?!
I did tell you it was her birthday tomorrow, didn't I?

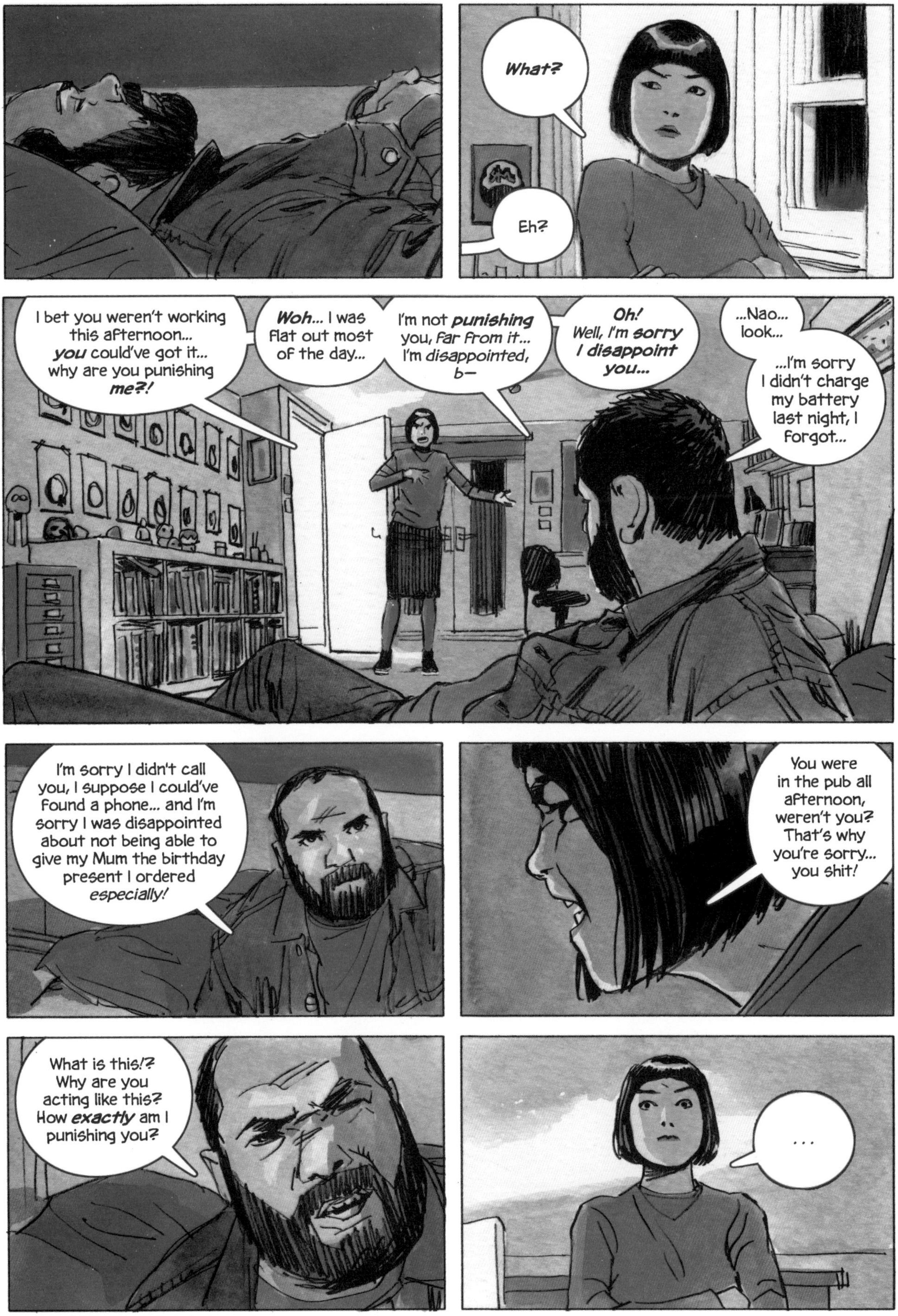
What?
Eh?
I bet you weren't working this afternoon... you could've got it... why are you punishing me?!
Woh... I was flat out most of the day...
I'm not punishing you, far from it... I'm disappointed, b—
Oh! Well, I'm sorry I disappoint you...
...Nao... look...
...I'm sorry I didn't charge my battery last night, I forgot...
I'm sorry I didn't call you, I suppose I could've found a phone... and I'm sorry I was disappointed about not being able to give my Mum the birthday present I ordered especially!
You were in the pub all afternoon, weren't you? That's why you're sorry... you shit!
What is this!? Why are you acting like this? How exactly am I punishing you?
...

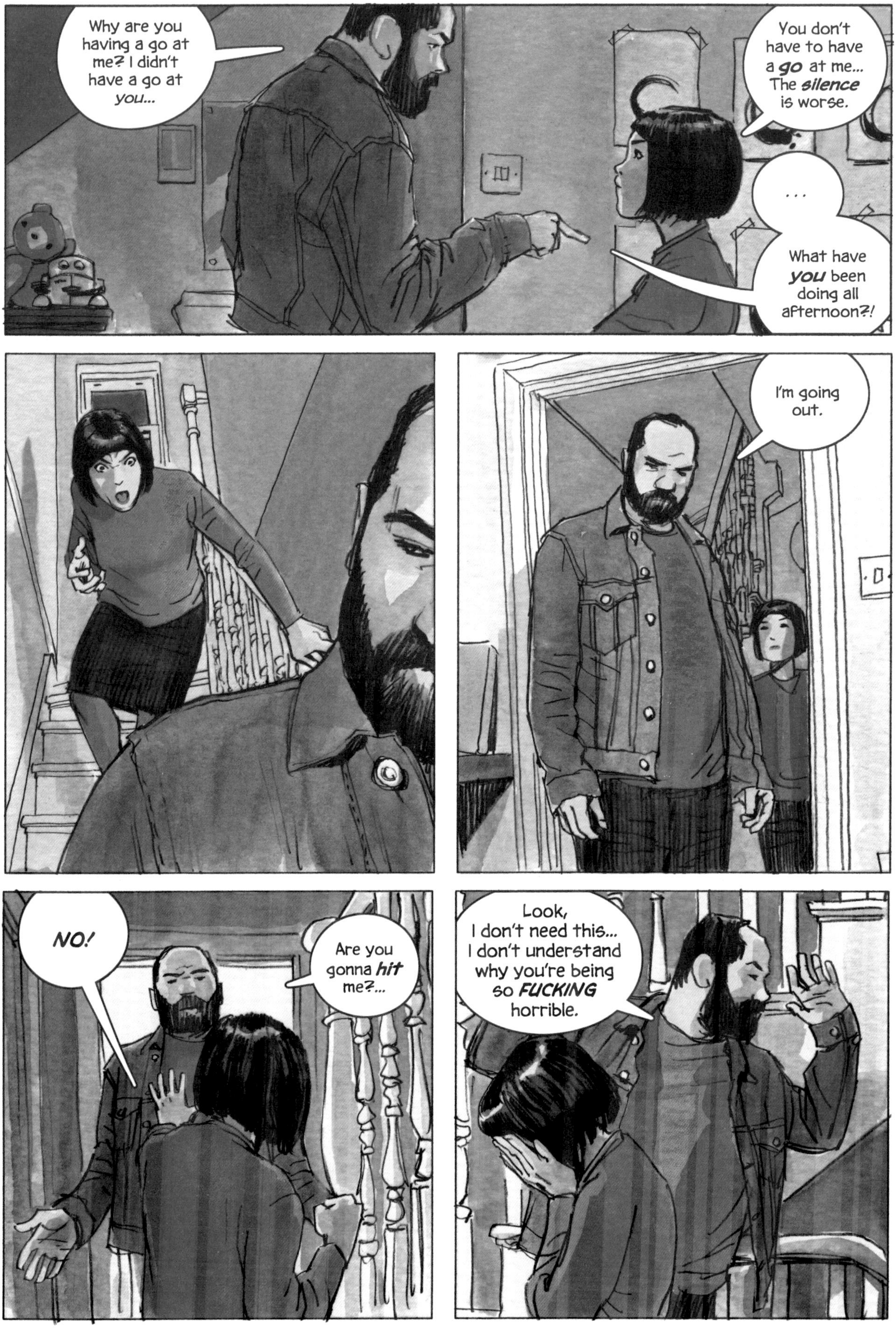

Why are you having a go at me?! I didn't have a go at *you*...
You don't have to have a ***go*** at me... The ***silence*** is worse.
...
What have ***you*** been doing all afternoon?!
I'm going out.
NO!
Are you gonna ***hit*** me?...
Look, I don't need this... I don't understand why you're being so ***FUCKING*** horrible.

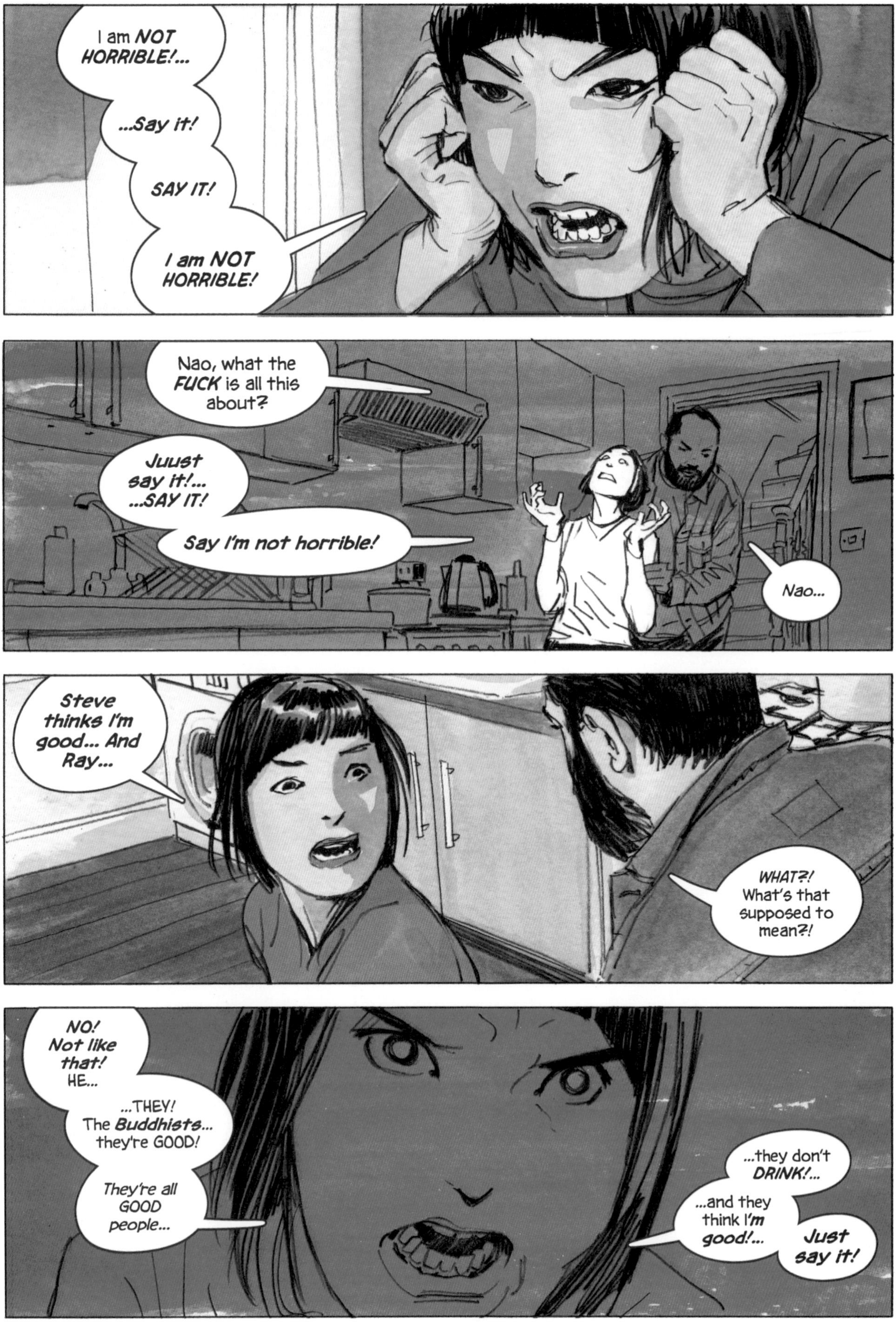
I am NOT HORRIBLE!...
...Say it!
SAY IT!
I am NOT HORRIBLE!
Nao, what the FUCK is all this about?
Juust say it!... ...SAY IT!
Say I'm not horrible!
Nao...
Steve thinks I'm good... And Ray...
WHAT?! What's that supposed to mean?!
NO! Not like that! HE...
...THEY! The Buddhists... they're GOOD!
They're all GOOD people...
...they don't DRINK!...
...and they think I'm good!...
Just say it!

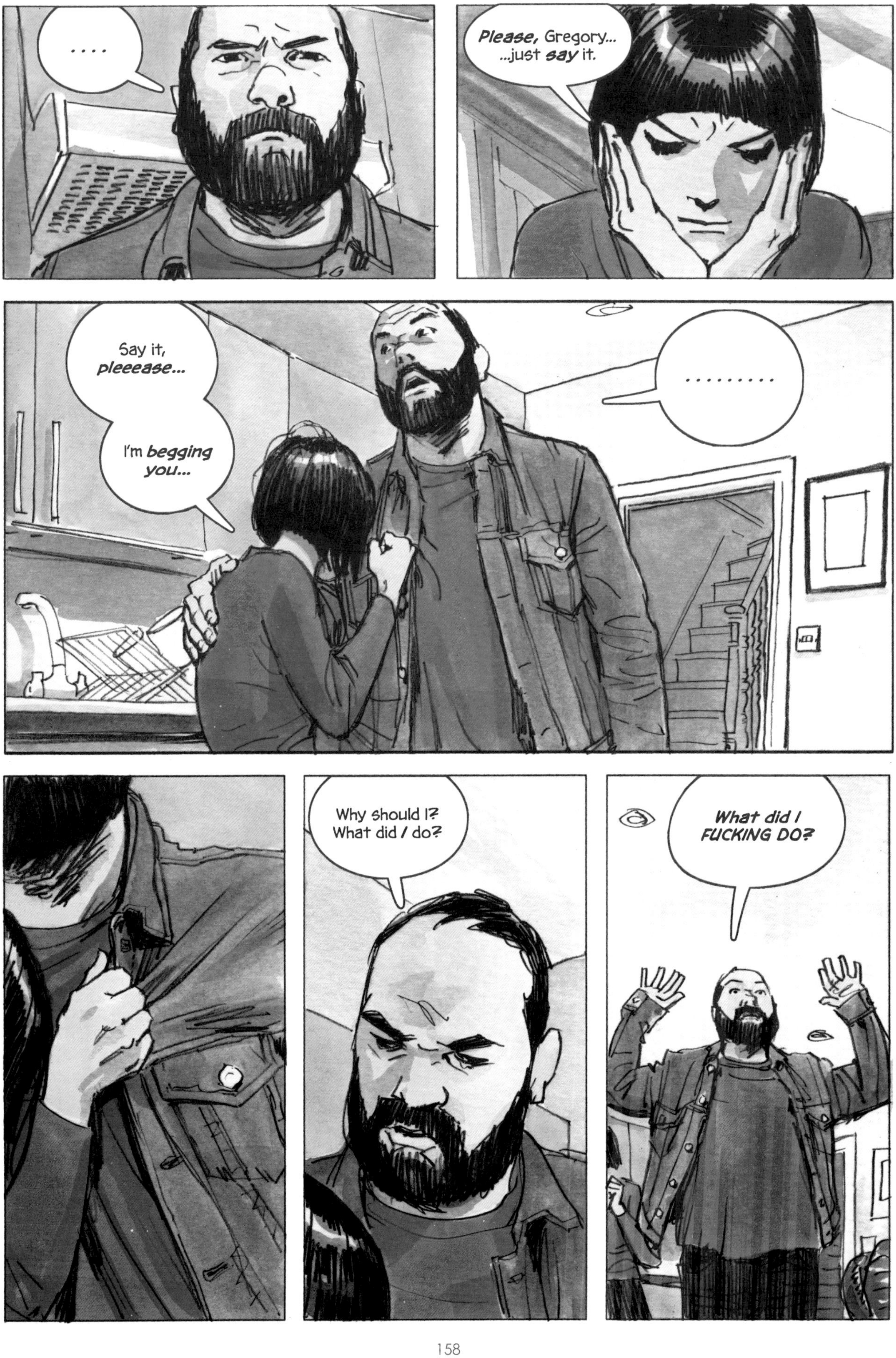
. . . .
Please, Gregory... ...just *say* it.
Say it, *pleeease...*
I'm *begging you...*
. . . .
Why should I? What did *I* do?
What did I FUCKING DO?

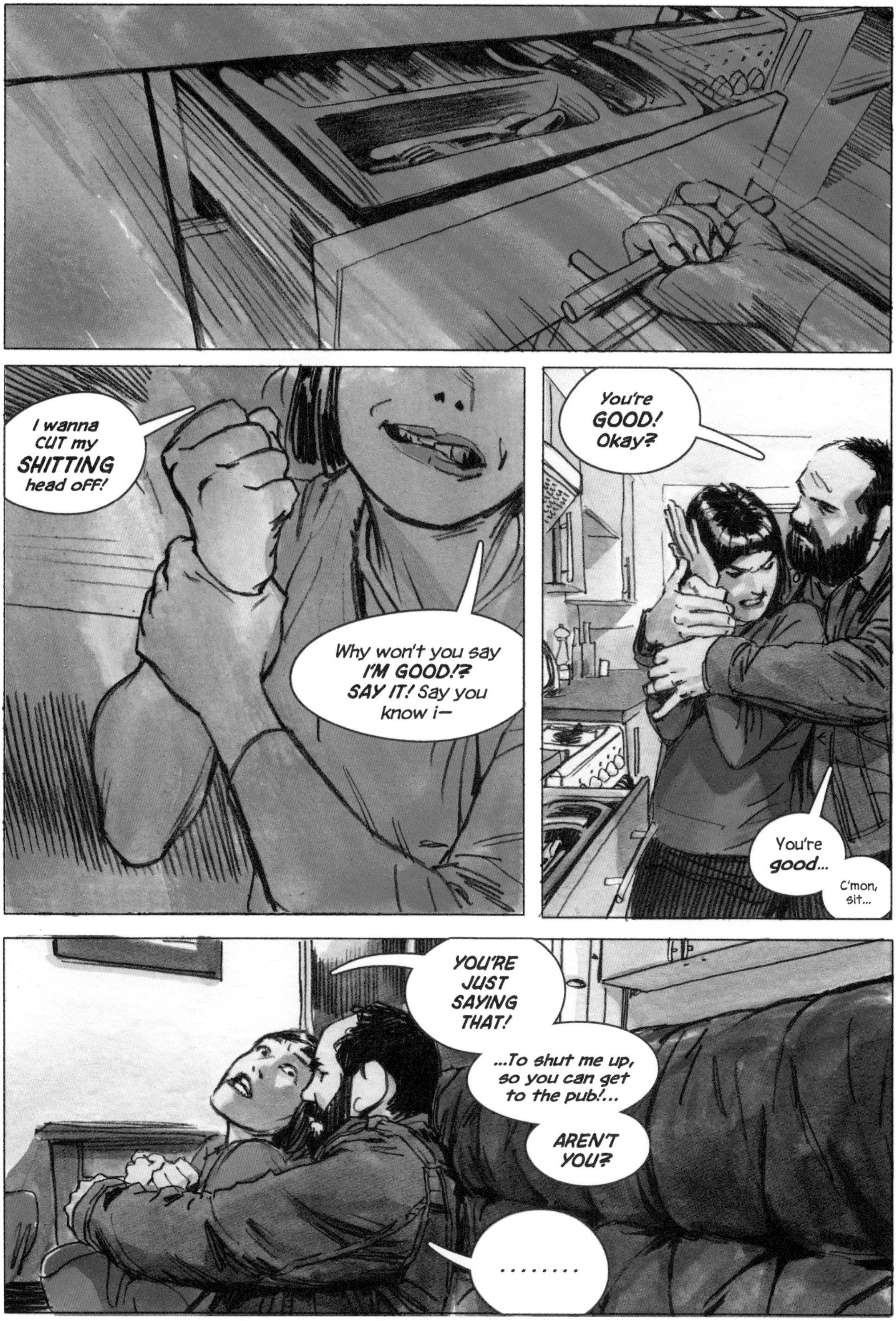
I wanna CUT my SHITTING head off!
Why won't you say I'M GOOD!? SAY IT! Say you know i—
You're GOOD! Okay?
You're good...
C'mon, sit...
YOU'RE JUST SAYING THAT!
...To shut me up, so you can get to the pub!...
AREN'T YOU?
....

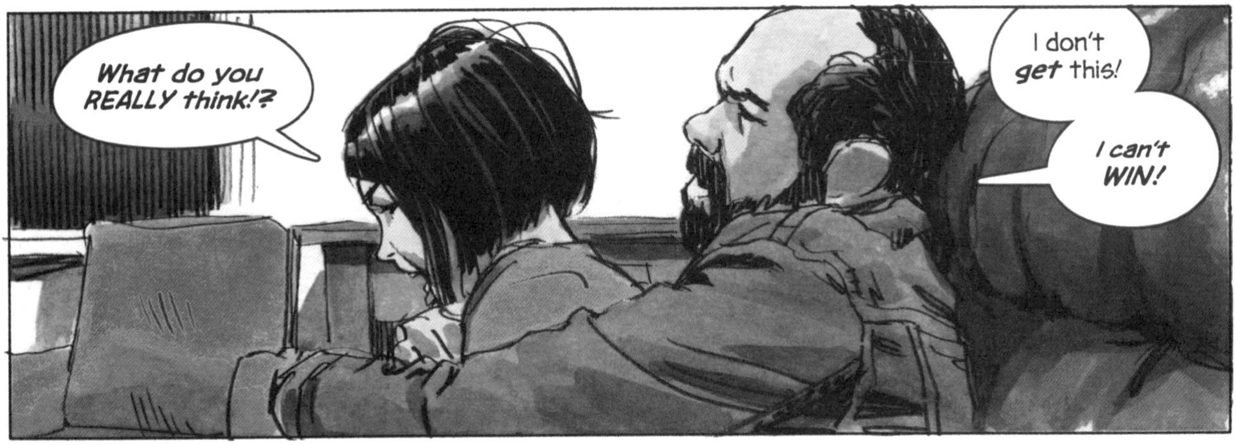
What do you REALLY think!?
I don't get this!
I can't WIN!

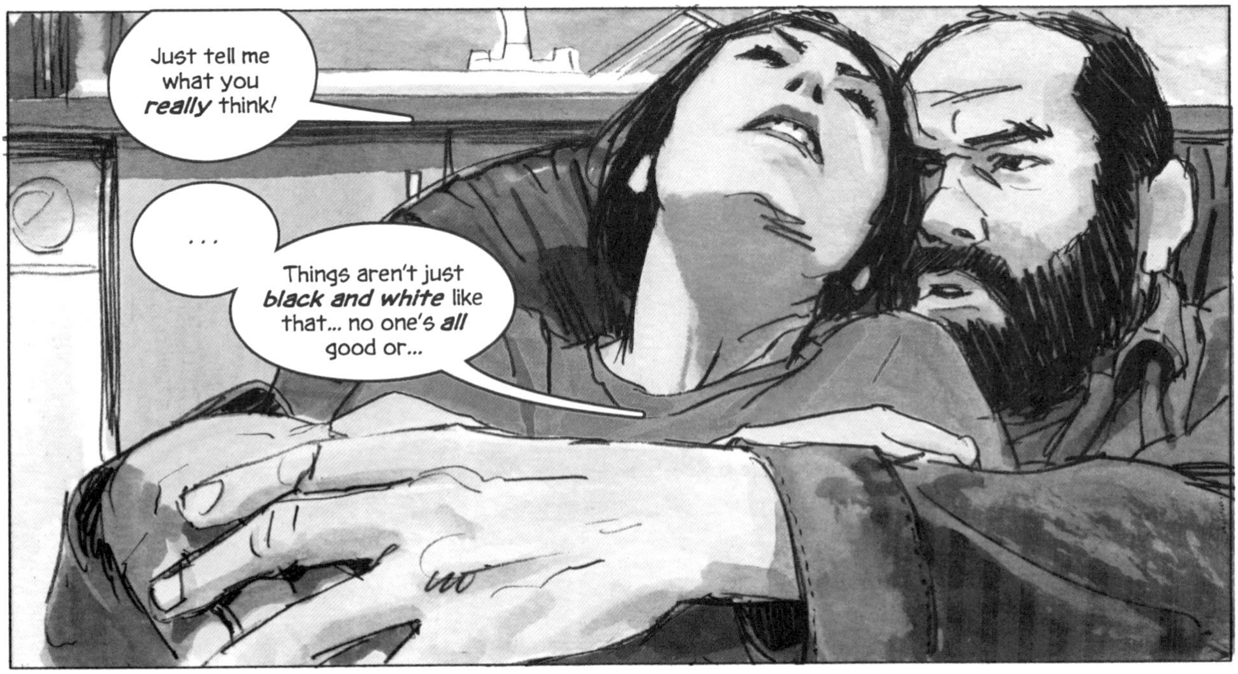
Just tell me what you really think!
...
Things aren't just black and white like that... no one's all good or...

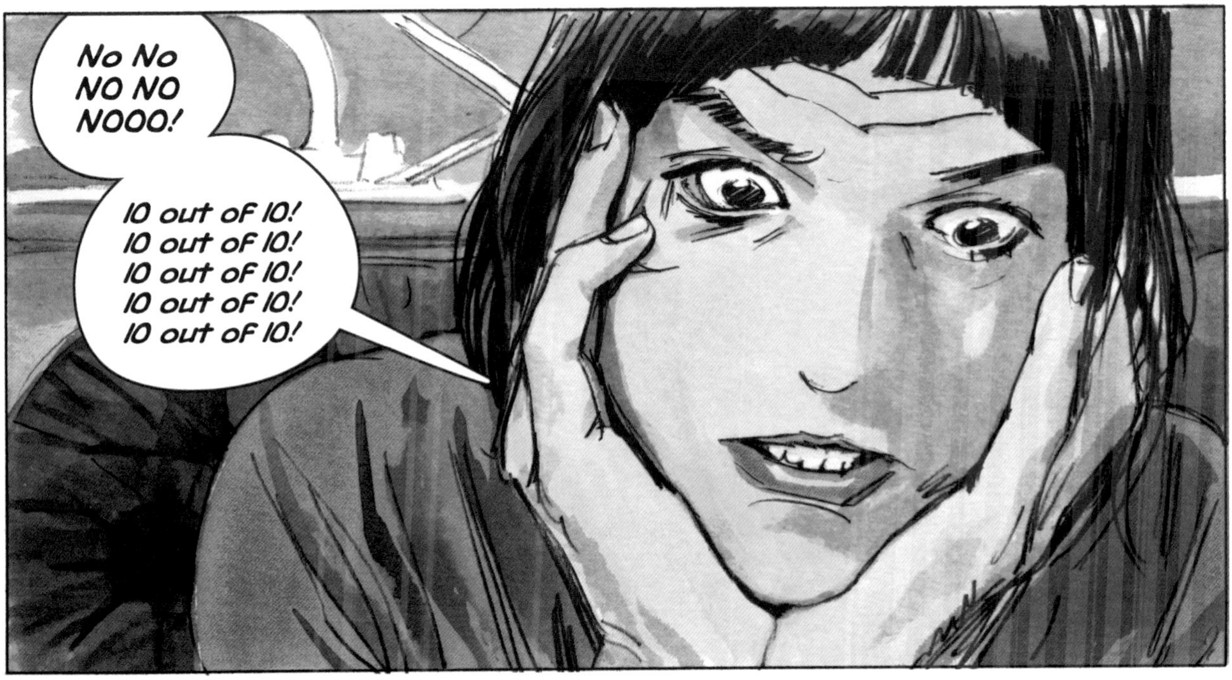
No No NO NO NOOO!
10 out of 10!
10 out of 10!
10 out of 10!
10 out of 10!
10 out of 10!

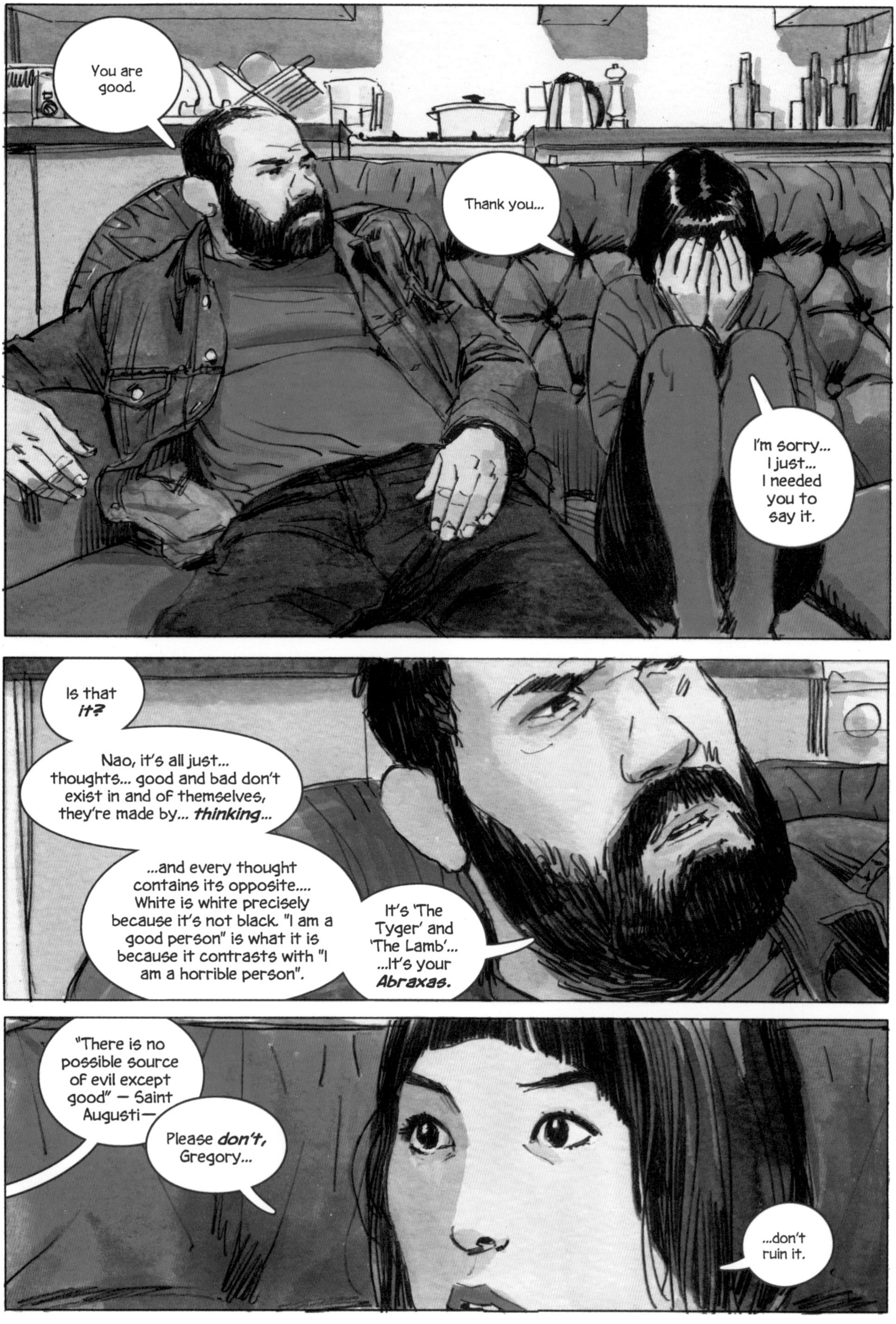
You are good.
Thank you...
I'm sorry... I just... I needed you to say it.
Is that *it?*
Nao, it's all just... thoughts... good and bad don't exist in and of themselves, they're made by... *thinking*...
...and every thought contains its opposite.... White is white precisely because it's not black. "I am a good person" is what it is because it contrasts with "I am a horrible person".
It's 'The Tyger' and 'The Lamb'... ...It's your *Abraxas.*
"There is no possible source of evil except good" — Saint Augusti—
Please *don't,* Gregory...
...don't ruin it.

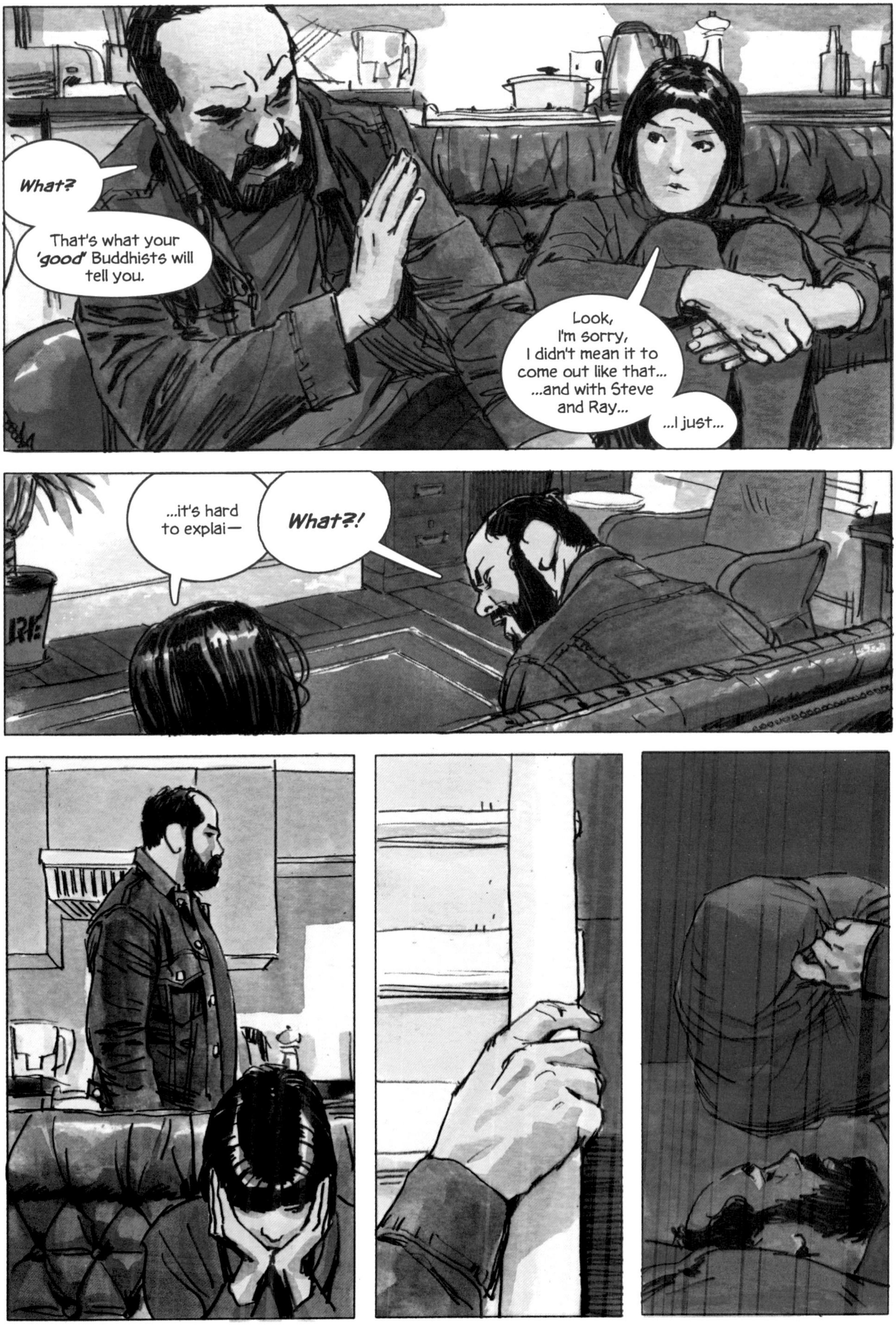
What?
That's what your 'good' Buddhists will tell you.
Look, I'm sorry, I didn't mean it to come out like that... ...and with Steve and Ray...
...I just...
...it's hard to explai—
What?!

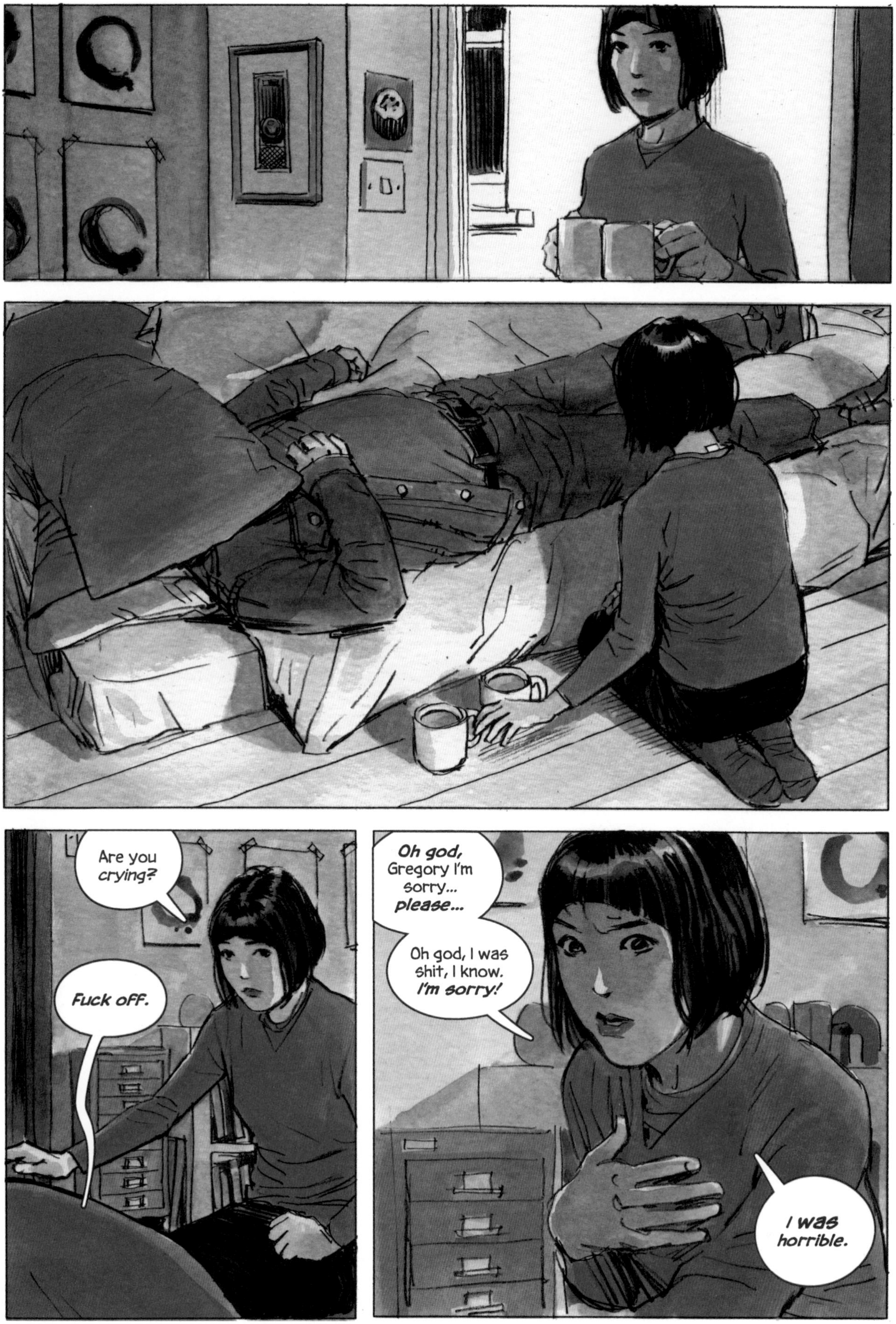
Are you *crying?*
Fuck off.
Oh god, Gregory I'm sorry... ***please...***
Oh god, I was shit, I know. ***I'm sorry!***
I was horrible.

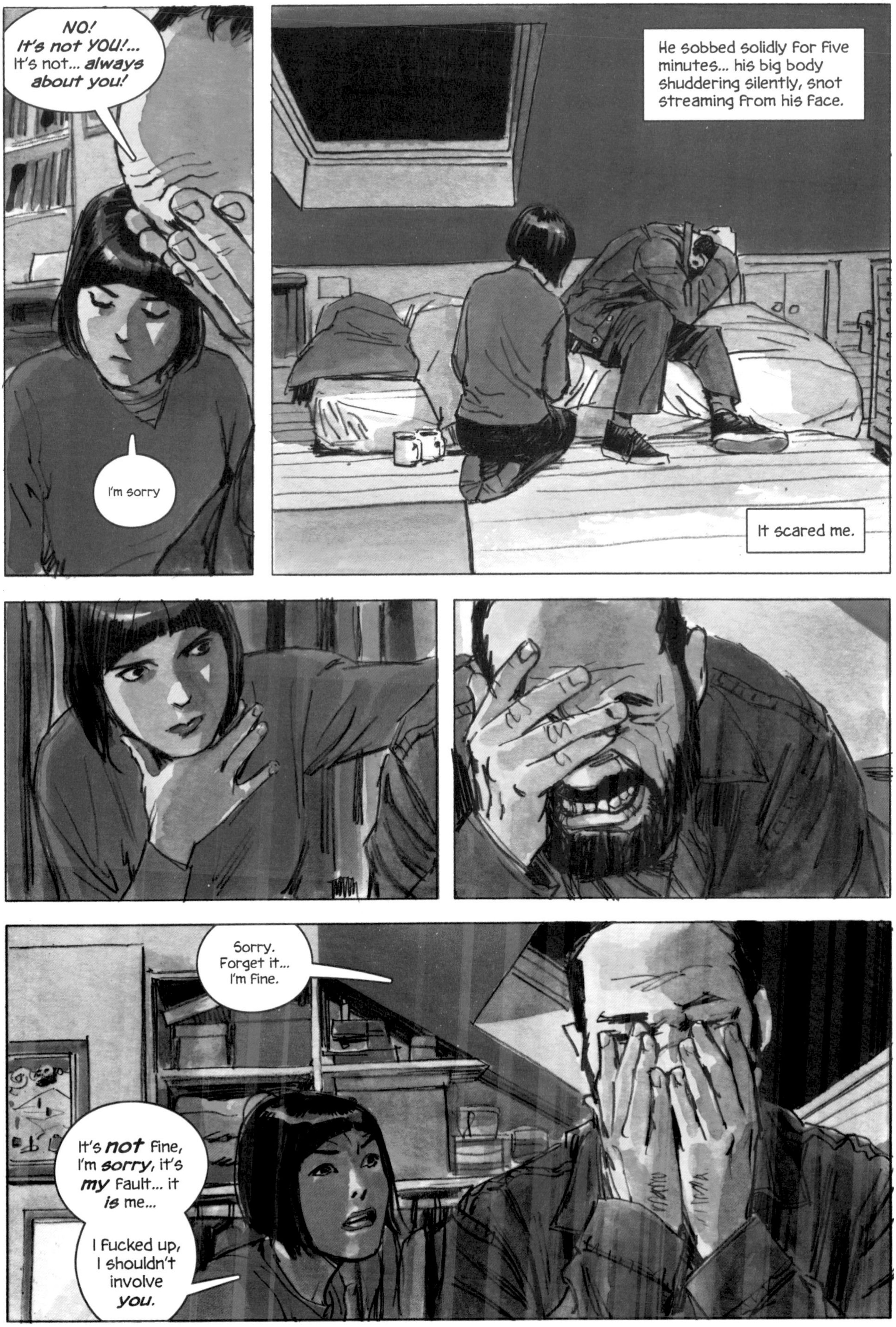
NO! It's not YOU!... It's not... always about you!
I'm sorry
He sobbed solidly for five minutes... his big body shuddering silently, snot streaming from his face.
It scared me.
Sorry. Forget it... I'm fine.
It's not fine, I'm sorry, it's my fault... it is me...
I fucked up, I shouldn't involve you.

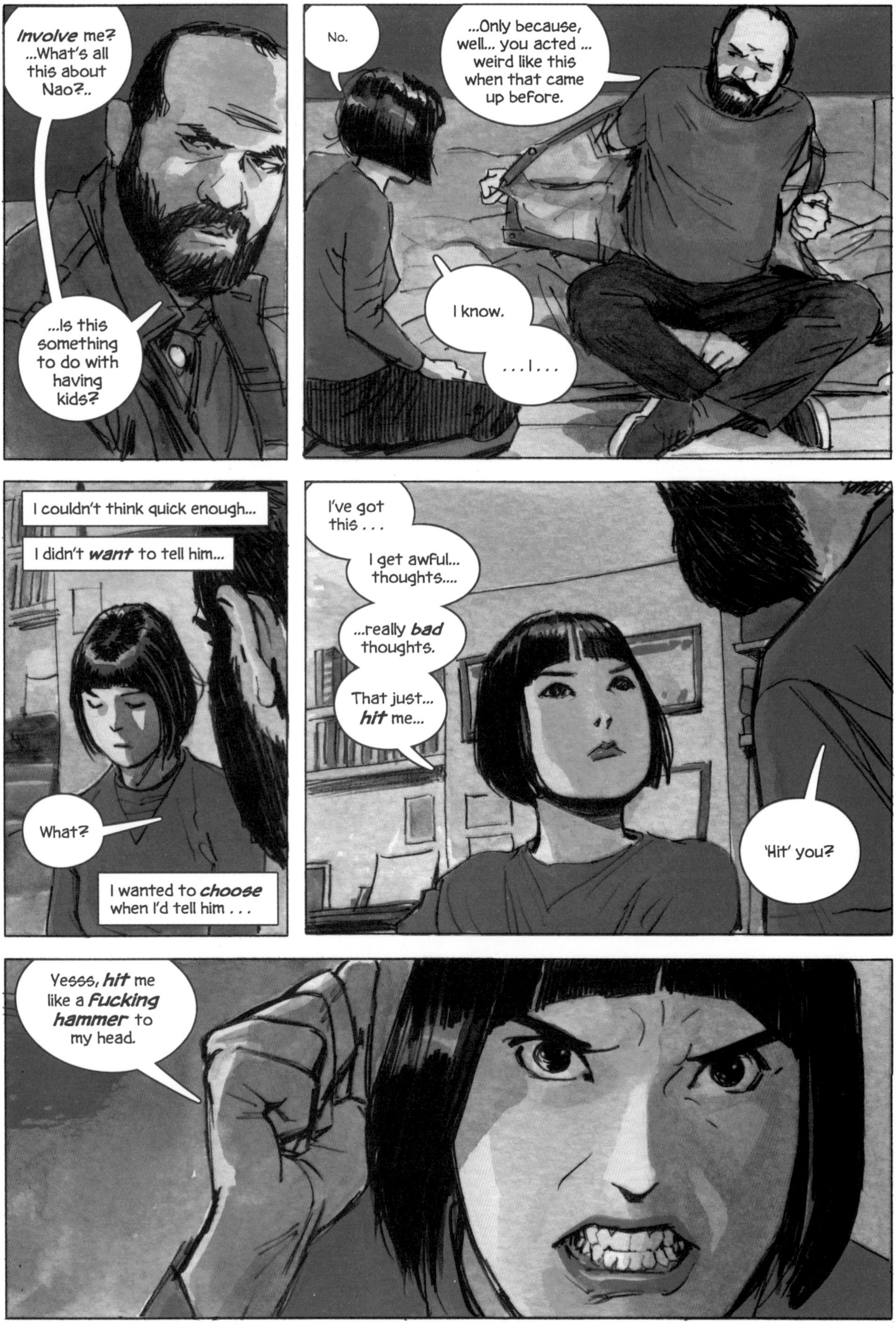
Involve me? ...What's all this about Nao?..
...Is this something to do with having kids?
No.
...Only because, well... you acted ... weird like this when that came up before.
I know.
. . . I . . .
I couldn't think quick enough...
I didn't want to tell him...
What?
I wanted to choose when I'd tell him . . .
I've got this . . .
I get awful... thoughts....
...really bad thoughts.
That just... hit me...
'Hit' you?
Yesss, hit me like a fucking hammer to my head.

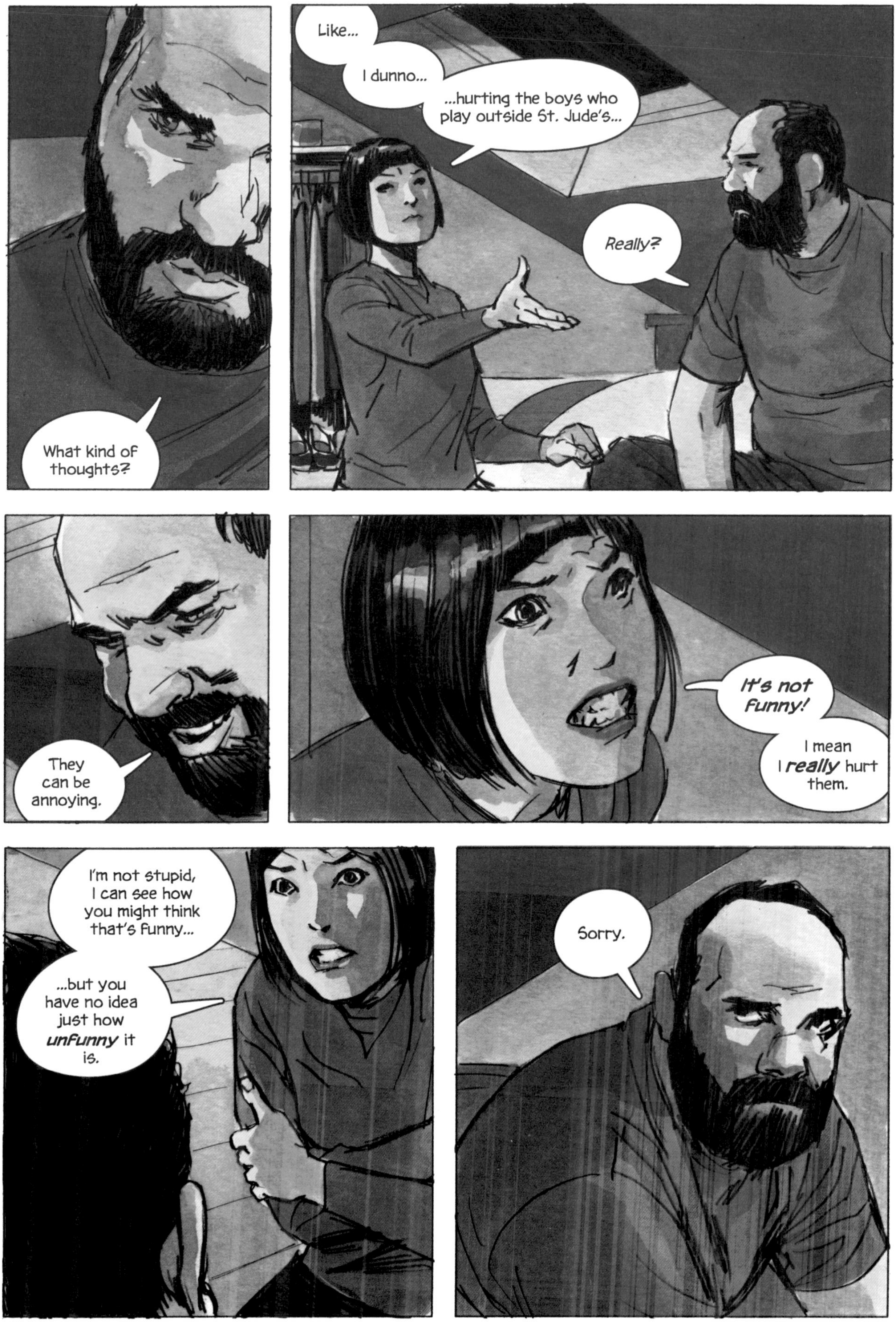
What kind of thoughts?
Like...
I dunno...
...hurting the boys who play outside St. Jude's...
Really?
They can be annoying.
It's not funny!
I mean I really hurt them.
I'm not stupid, I can see how you might think that's funny...
...but you have no idea just how unfunny it is.
Sorry.

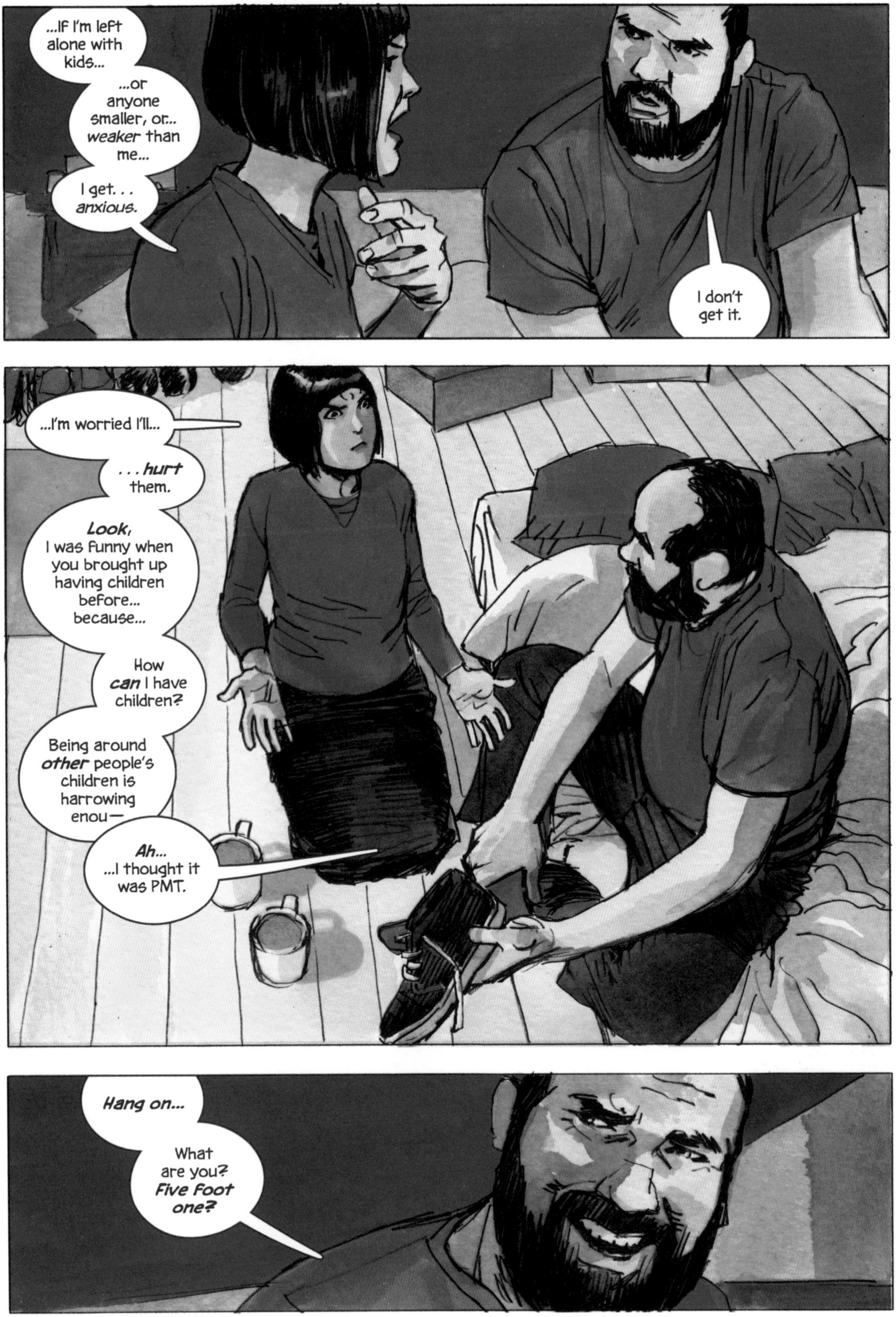
...If I'm left alone with kids...
...or anyone smaller, or... weaker than me...
I get. . . anxious.
I don't get it.
...I'm worried I'll...
. . . hurt them.
Look, I was funny when you brought up having children before... because...
How can I have children?
Being around other people's children is harrowing enou—
Ah... ...I thought it was PMT.
Hang on...
What are you? Five foot one?

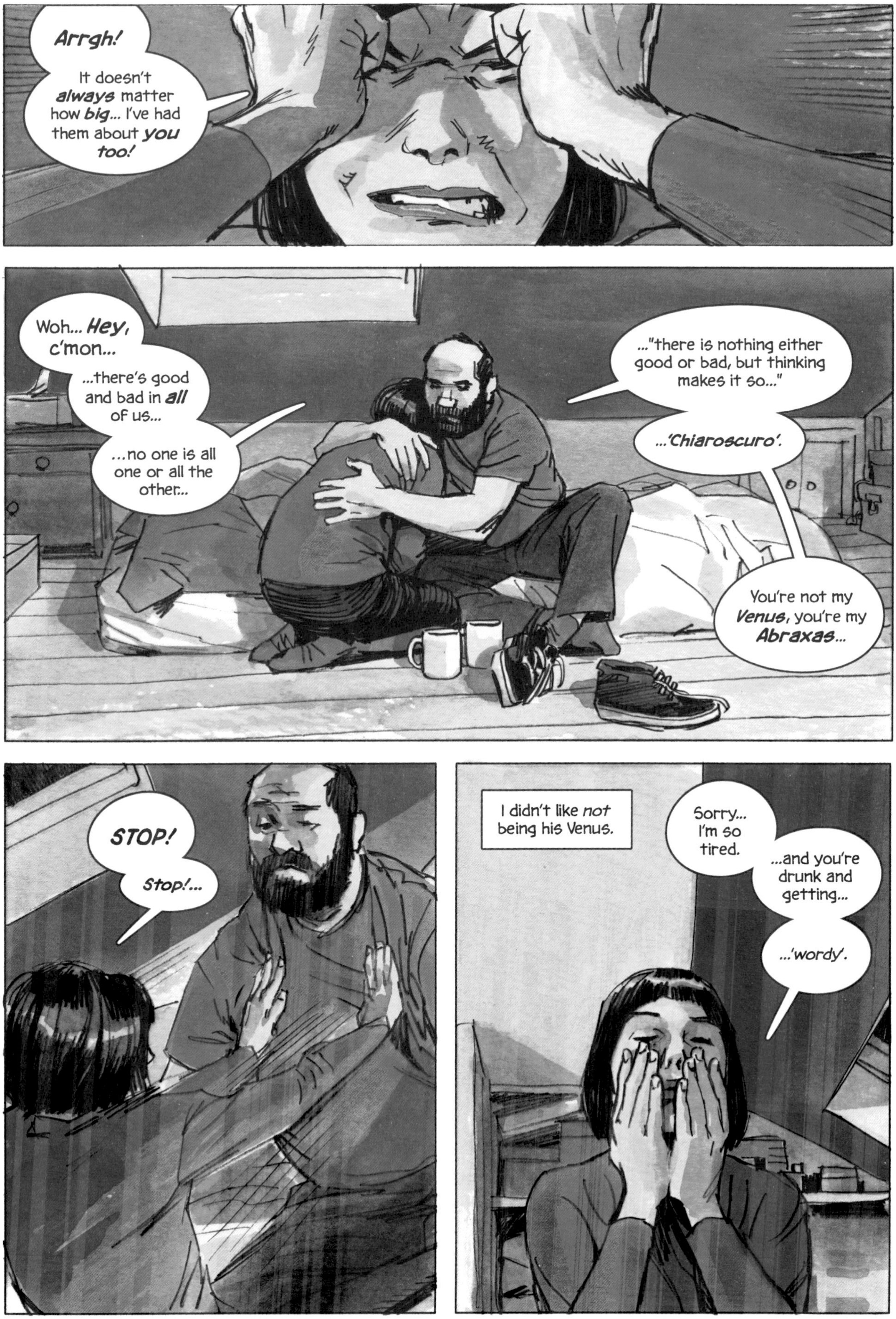
Arrgh!
It doesn't always matter how big... I've had them about you too!
Woh... Hey, c'mon...
...there's good and bad in all of us...
...no one is all one or all the other...
..."there is nothing either good or bad, but thinking makes it so..."
...'Chiaroscuro'.
You're not my Venus, you're my Abraxas...
STOP!
Stop!...
I didn't like not being his Venus.
Sorry... I'm so tired.
...and you're drunk and getting...
...'wordy'.

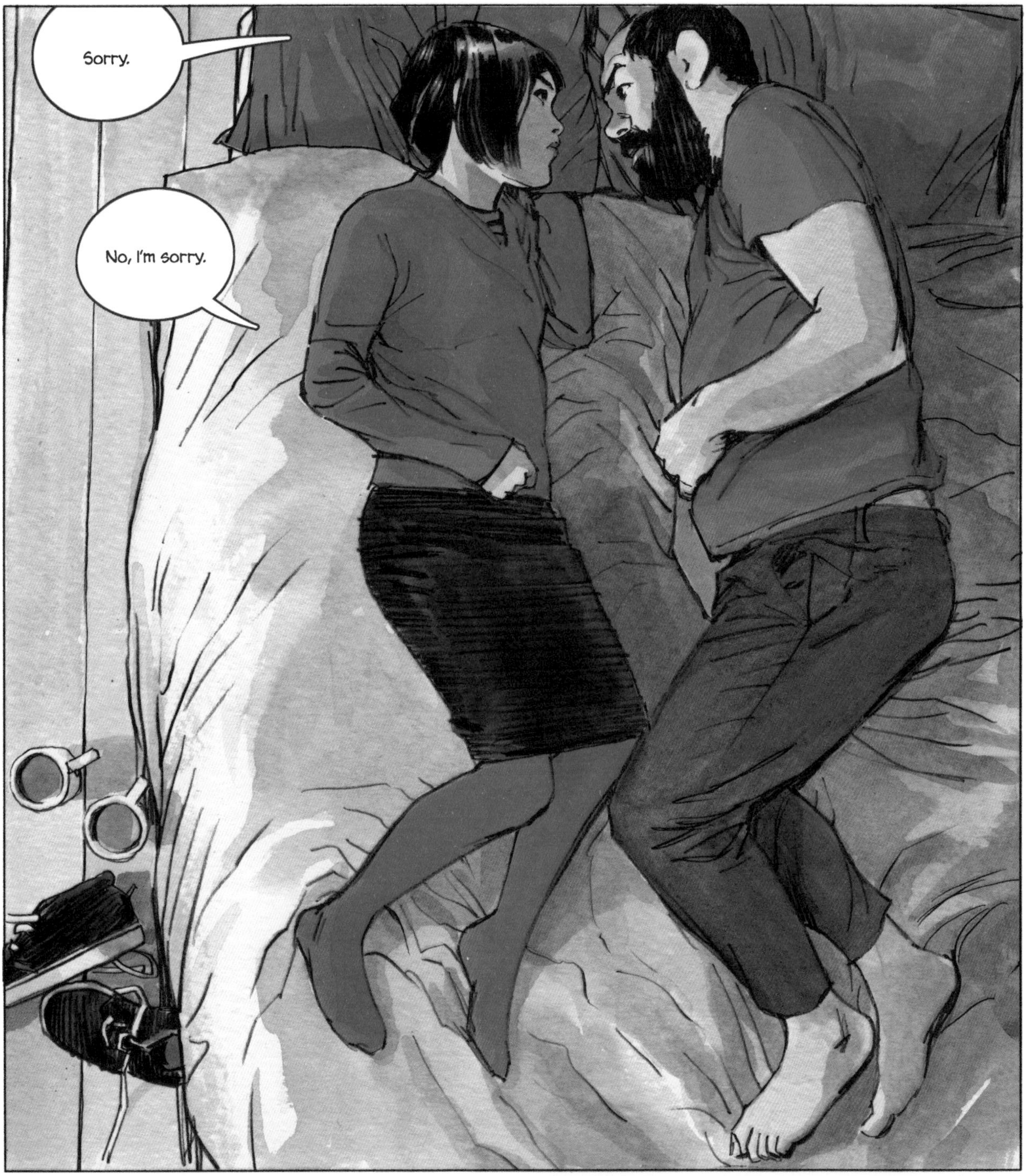
Sorry.
No, I'm sorry.

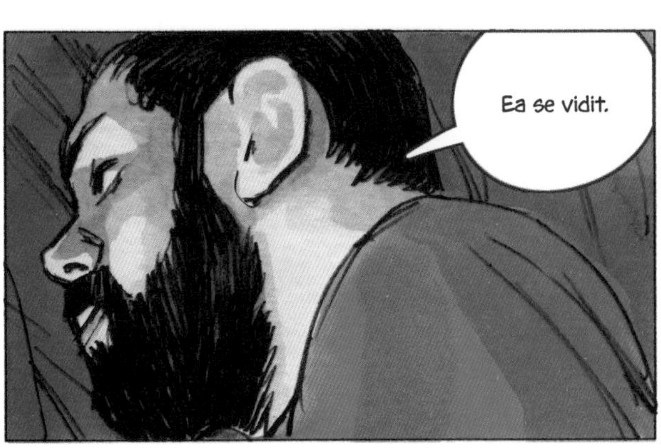
Ea se vidit.

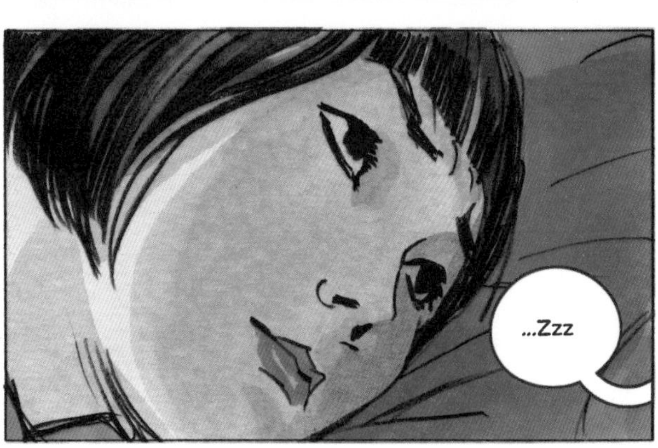
...Zzz

...Meanwhile Pictor continued on until he found the fort which belonged to the other Captain he had led from the giant woods. However, this Captain had ordered his men to present arms and greet him by calling, "May all Nothing prolong his life!" After which they were to escort him to the Captain's quarters.

When the Captain's daughter saw him she was startled and a little frightened because he looked so strange. Yet she had promised her father and there was nothing to be done about it. And so she duly welcomed Pictor, and they were married.

After the formalities Pictor led her to the Captain's table and they ate and drank into the evening. When it came time to retire, the daughter was quite afraid of his barbs, but Pictor said not to be afraid, for he had no intention of harming her.

Then he asked the Captain to have two men stationed at her bedroom door, and two more to assist him. When the Moon was in mid heaven he would undress and hand his uniform to the two men who would take it to his quarters and lay it out on his bed.

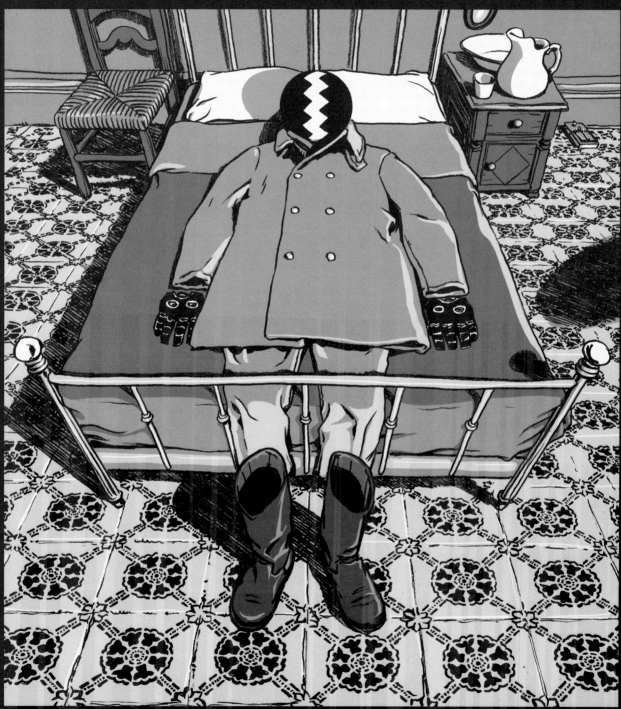

Then one would stand guard at the door while the other would follow him out to the shore. There he would stand safeguard as Pictor sits and sets fire to his head. When the head was almost entirely consumed, the soldier was to chop it off but not with his sword, he must instead use a reed. Then he must bury what was left of the head in the sand and return with the body.

Pictor undressed and walked to the sands with his ward. Meanwhile the other soldier lay Pictor's uniform on his bed and placed his boots upon the floor, and on his signal, the soldier by the shore struck a match and lit Pictor's head and watched over it, warmed, as smoke rolled up from where he stood. As the flames licked their way towards Pictor's neck, the soldier, who was prepared, brought down the reed in one swift flawless arc. Then, following the orders precisely he buried the head, just as the tide came in. "Thank you," said Pictor before the soldier returned to the fort with his body slung over his shoulder.

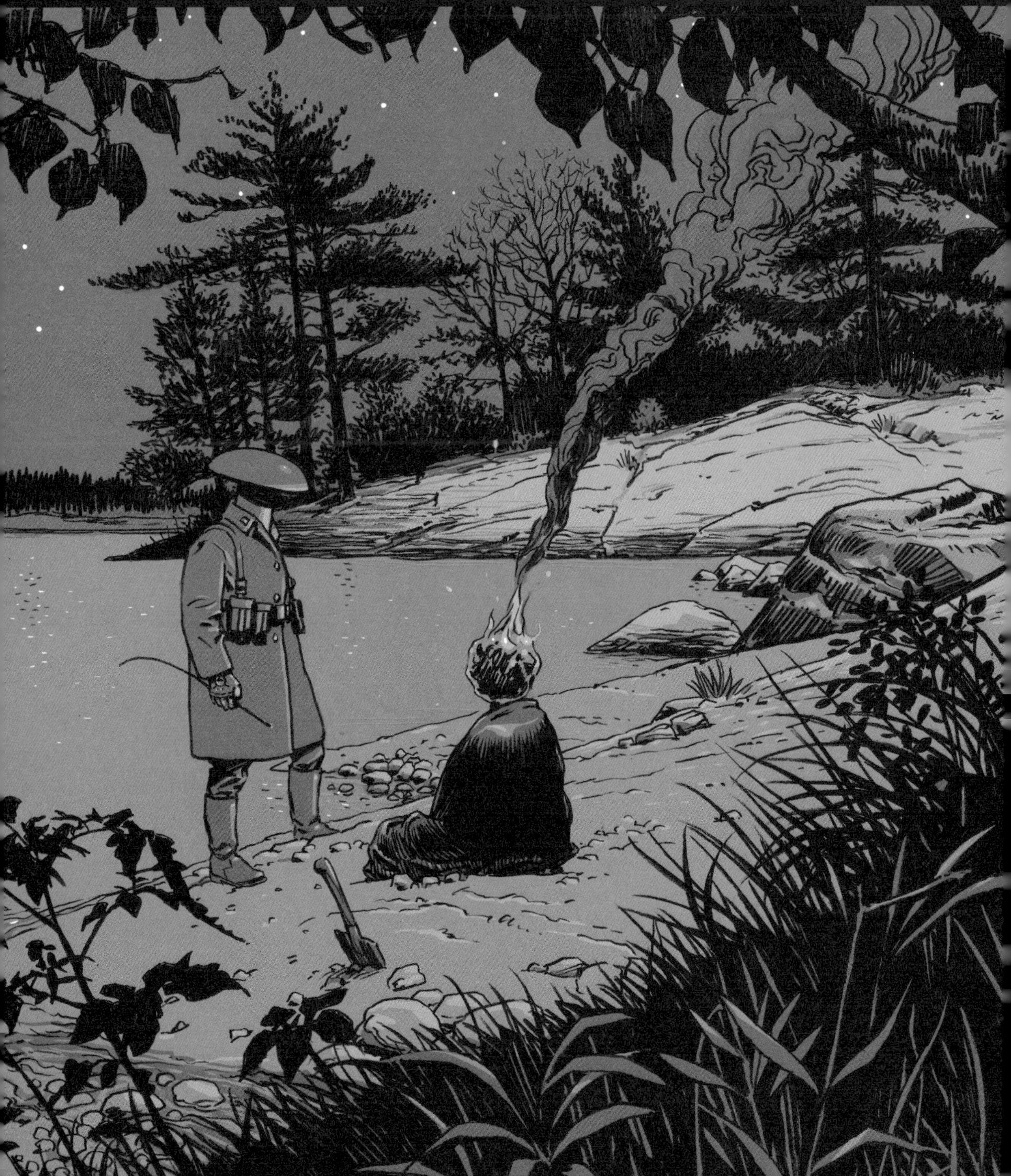

With the Eastern sky leading the dawn chorus, the Captain's daughter woke. Pictor now lay dressed on his bed, his head back in place, but his face pitch black and burnt. The Captain's daughter took up her role and gently applied a balm. Then they both slept deep and long, for all of a day and all of a night, and the following morning his face was pink and warm and the daughter thought him most handsome, as handsome as he was good, and promptly she fell in love.

Pictor awoke in a joyful mood and the marriage was performed again, properly with Pictor as a man. The Captain offered him a commanding role at the blockhouse but Pictor politely refused and set out for his old home, new bride at his side.

Upon returning he found his uprooted family tree to be still. The barbs had fallen and the glossy brown buckeyes lay scattered all around.

Pictor took his axe to the tree, he chopped until both arms ached, but never made a sound. He burned his uniform and boots, then bore his bride across the sill to start his life anew.

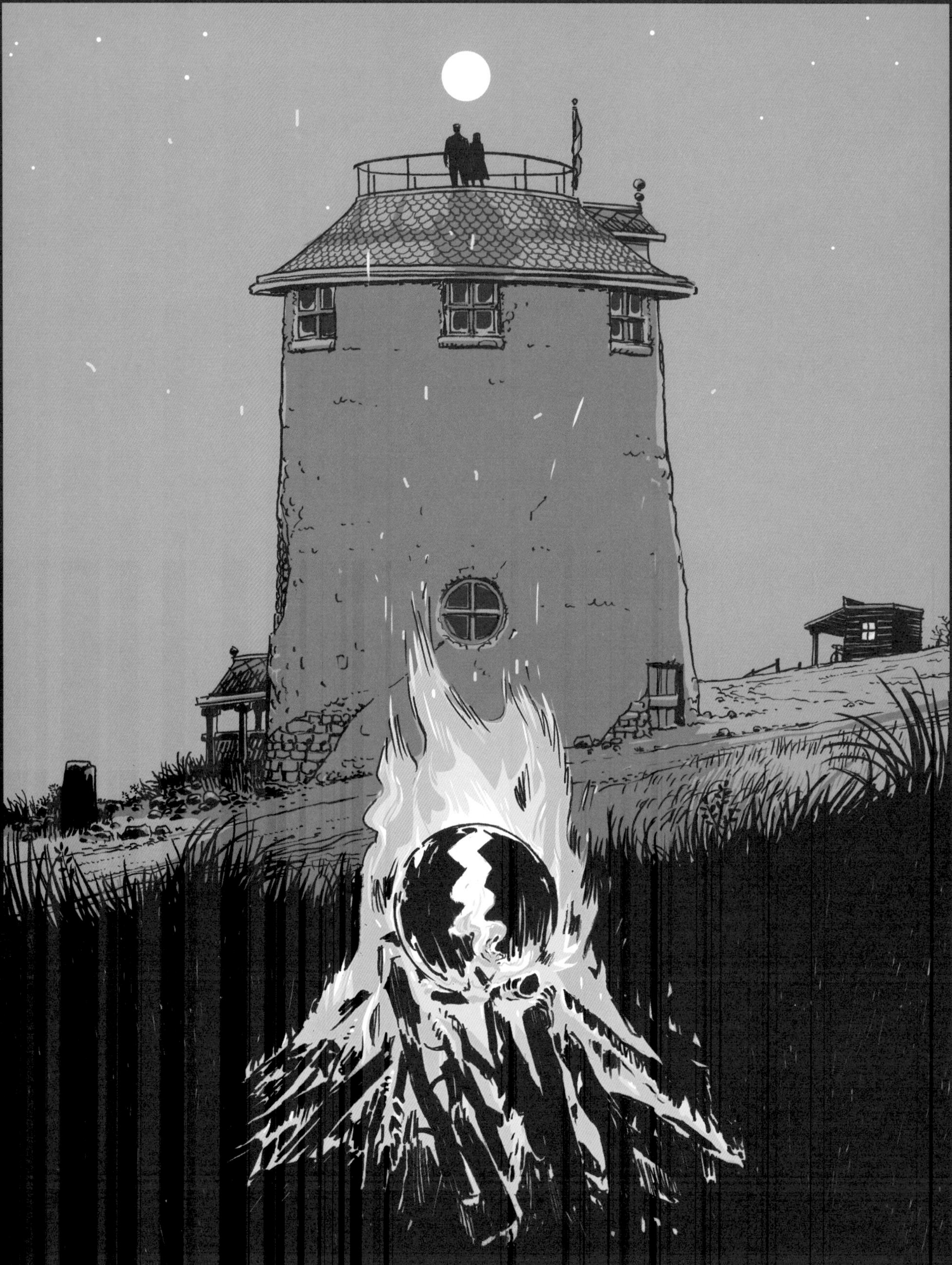

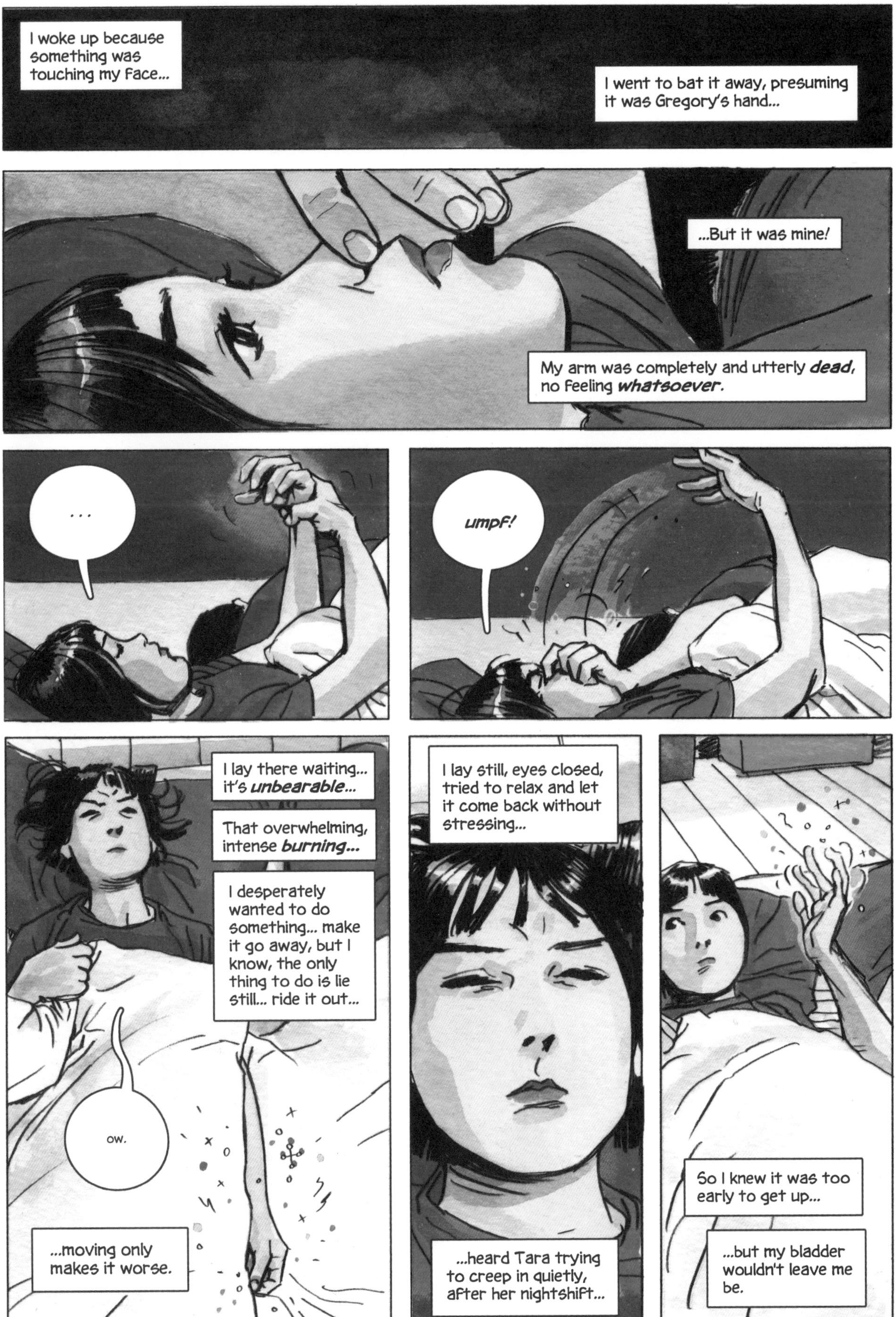
I woke up because something was touching my face...
I went to bat it away, presuming it was Gregory's hand...
...But it was mine!
My arm was completely and utterly *dead*, no feeling *whatsoever*.
...
umpf!
I lay there waiting... it's *unbearable*...
That overwhelming, intense *burning*...
I desperately wanted to do something... make it go away, but I know, the only thing to do is lie still... ride it out...
ow.
...moving only makes it worse.
I lay still, eyes closed, tried to relax and let it come back without stressing...
...heard Tara trying to creep in quietly, after her nightshift...
So I knew it was too early to get up...
...but my bladder wouldn't leave me be.

Neither would the neighbour's cat

Hey Voodoo, what're you doing here?

The flat was still... it felt *empty*...

I felt empty... not in an unpleasant way...

As if there was just...

...room to move.

I put the kettle on.

tic
tic
tic

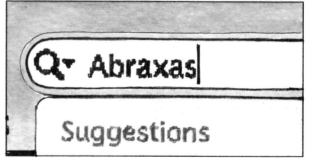

Abraxas

Suggestions

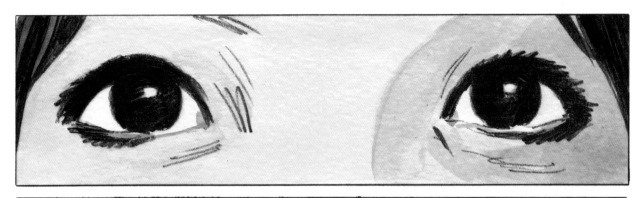

CLAC!

Tea.

...Sorry about last night... I... it's hard...

What?... What's funny?

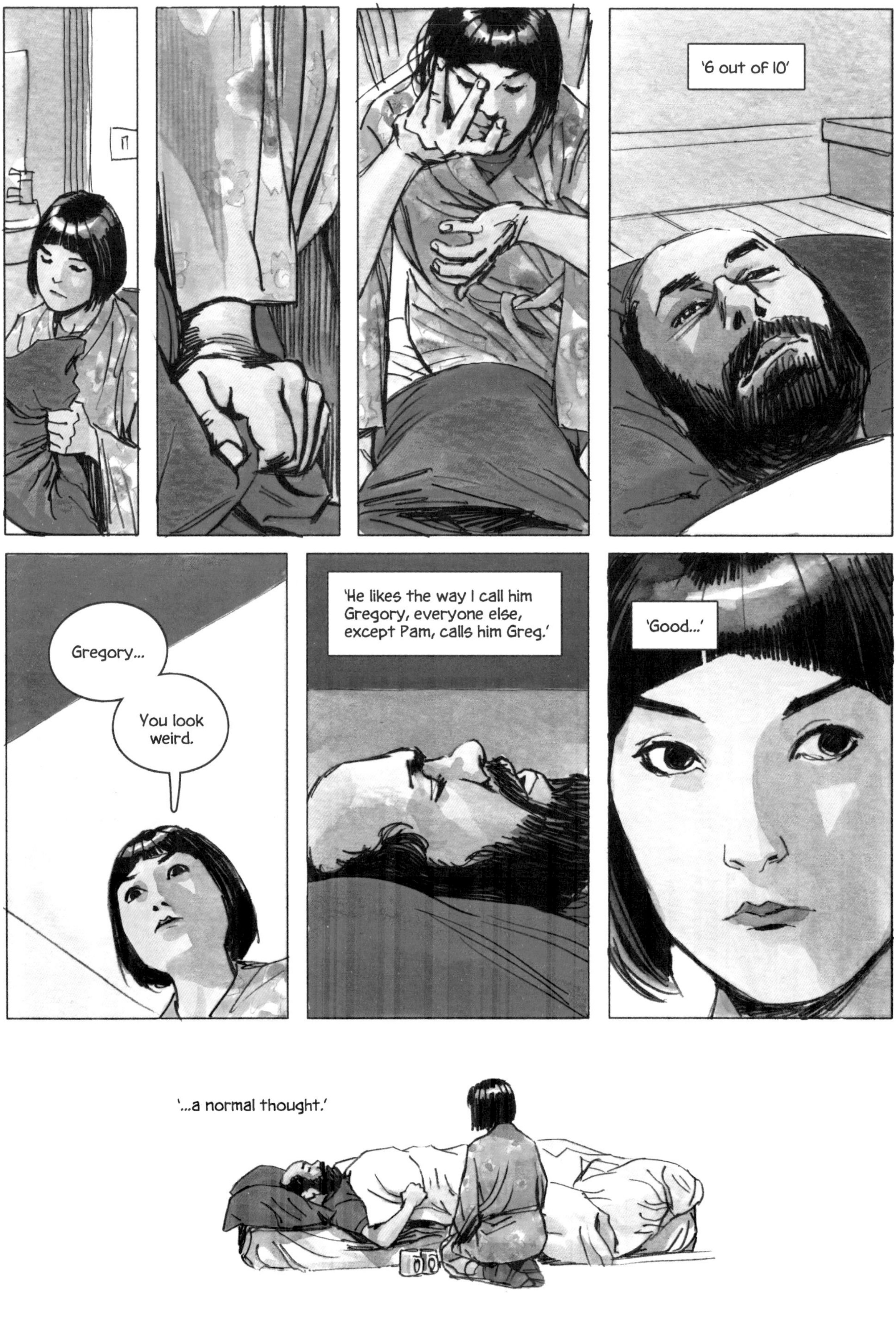
'6 out of 10'
Gregory...
You look weird.
'He likes the way I call him Gregory, everyone else, except Pam, calls him Greg.'
'Good...'
'...a normal thought.'

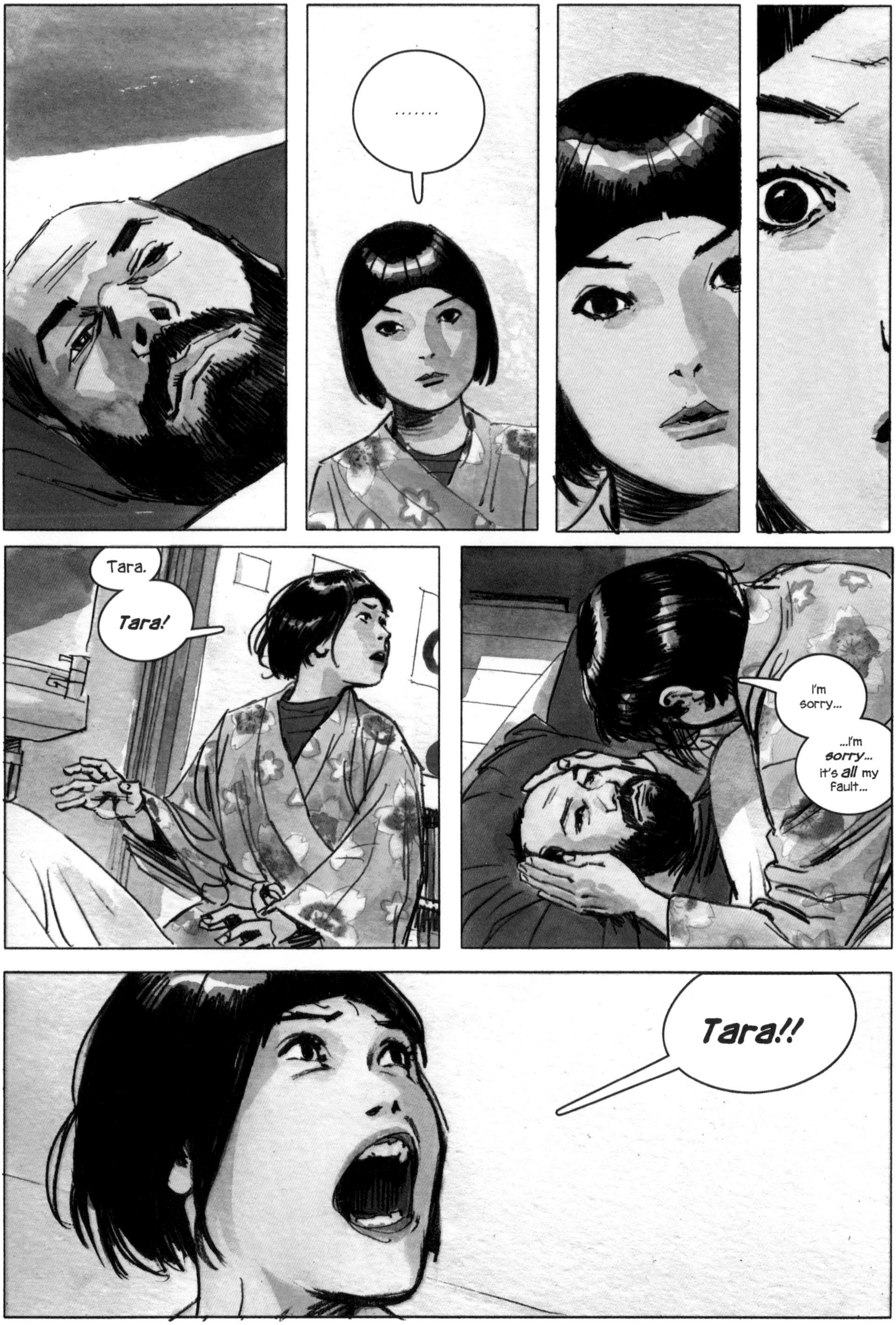

....
Tara.
Tara!
I'm sorry...
...I'm sorry... it's all my fault...
Tara!!

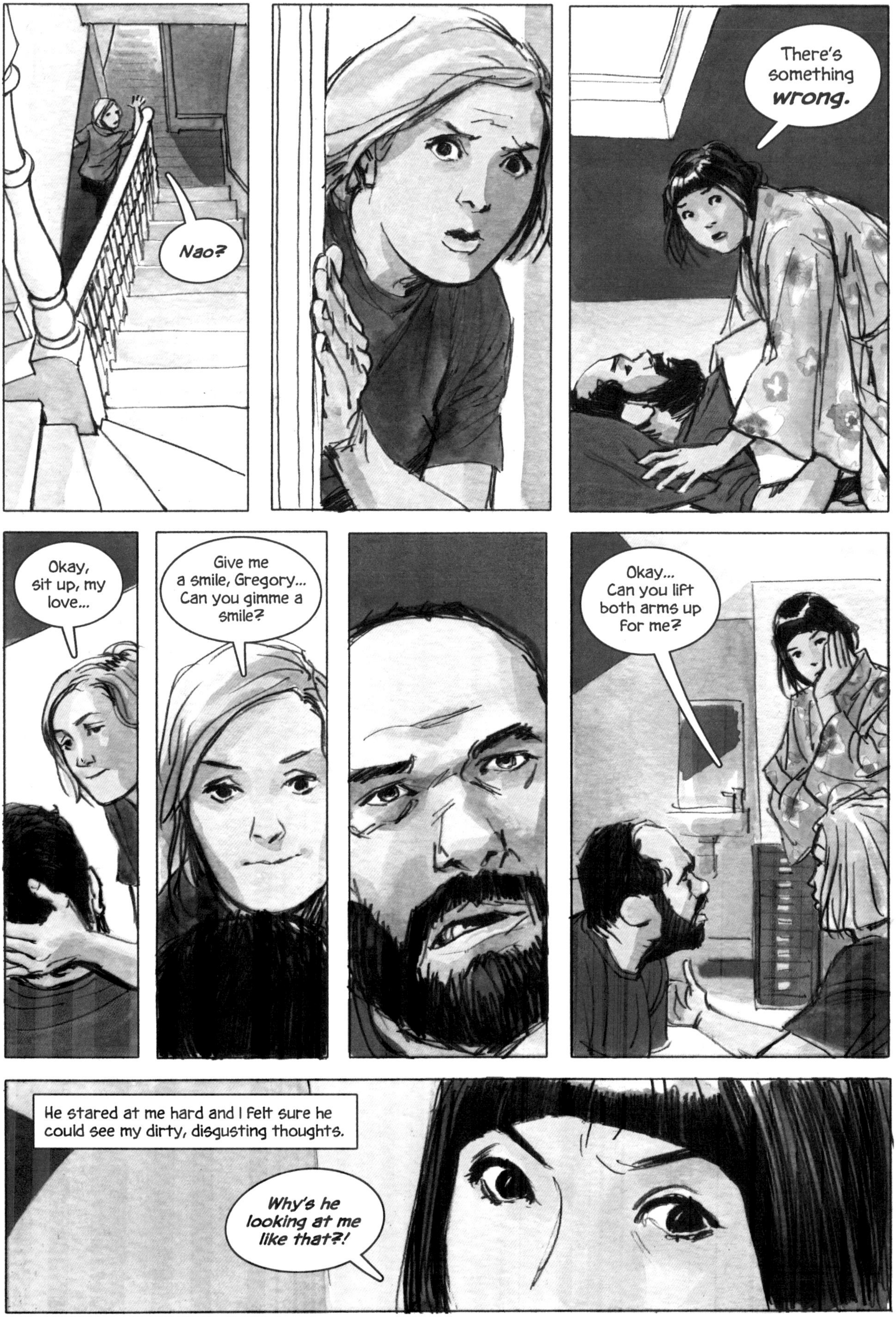
Nao?
There's something wrong.
Okay, sit up, my love...
Give me a smile, Gregory... Can you gimme a smile?
Okay... Can you lift both arms up for me?
He stared at me hard and I felt sure he could see my dirty, disgusting thoughts.
Why's he looking at me like that?!

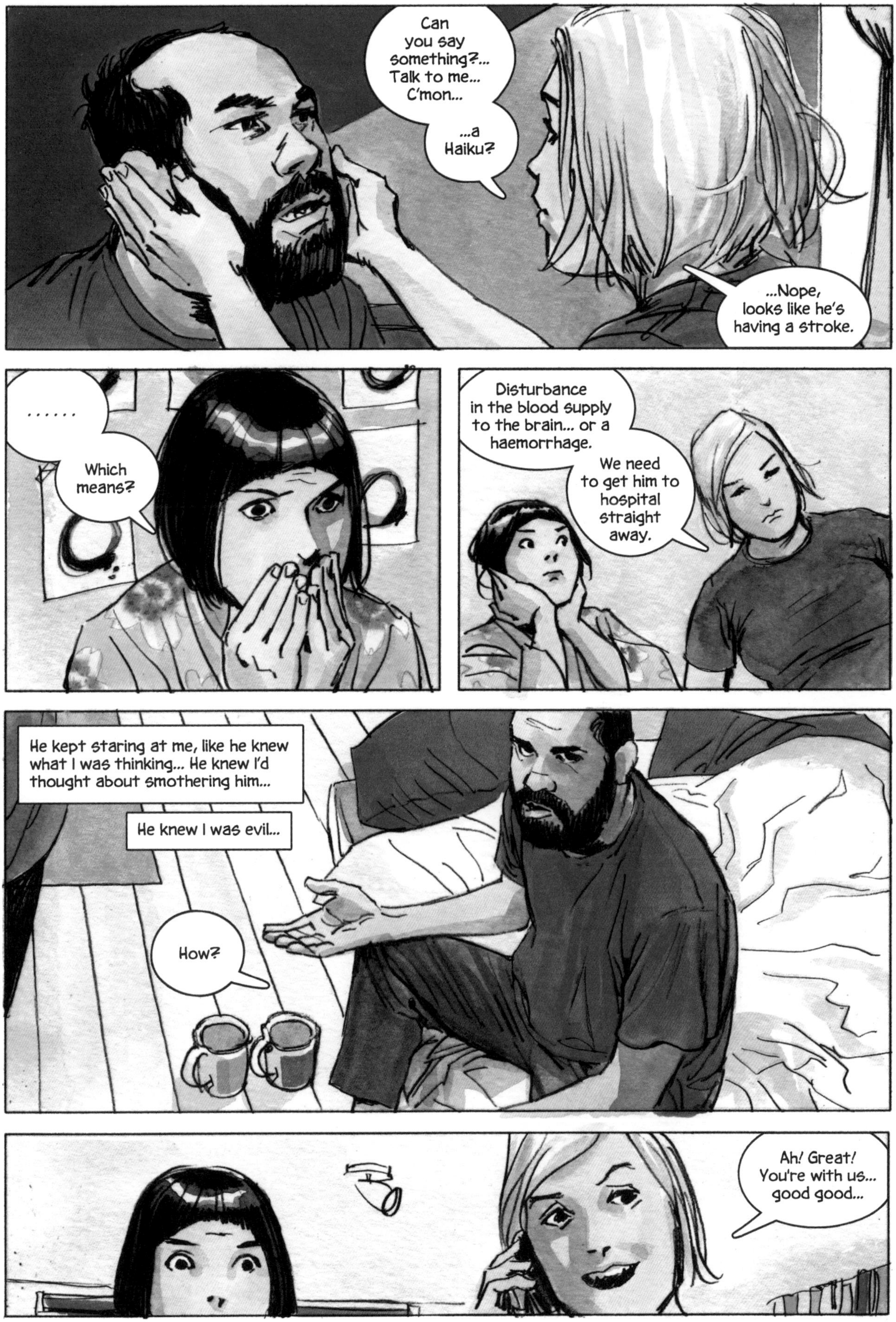
Can you say something?... Talk to me... C'mon...
...a Haiku?
...Nope, looks like he's having a stroke.
......
Which means?
Disturbance in the blood supply to the brain... or a haemorrhage.
We need to get him to hospital straight away.
He kept staring at me, like he knew what I was thinking... He knew I'd thought about smothering him...
He knew I was evil...
How?
Ah! Great! You're with us... good good...

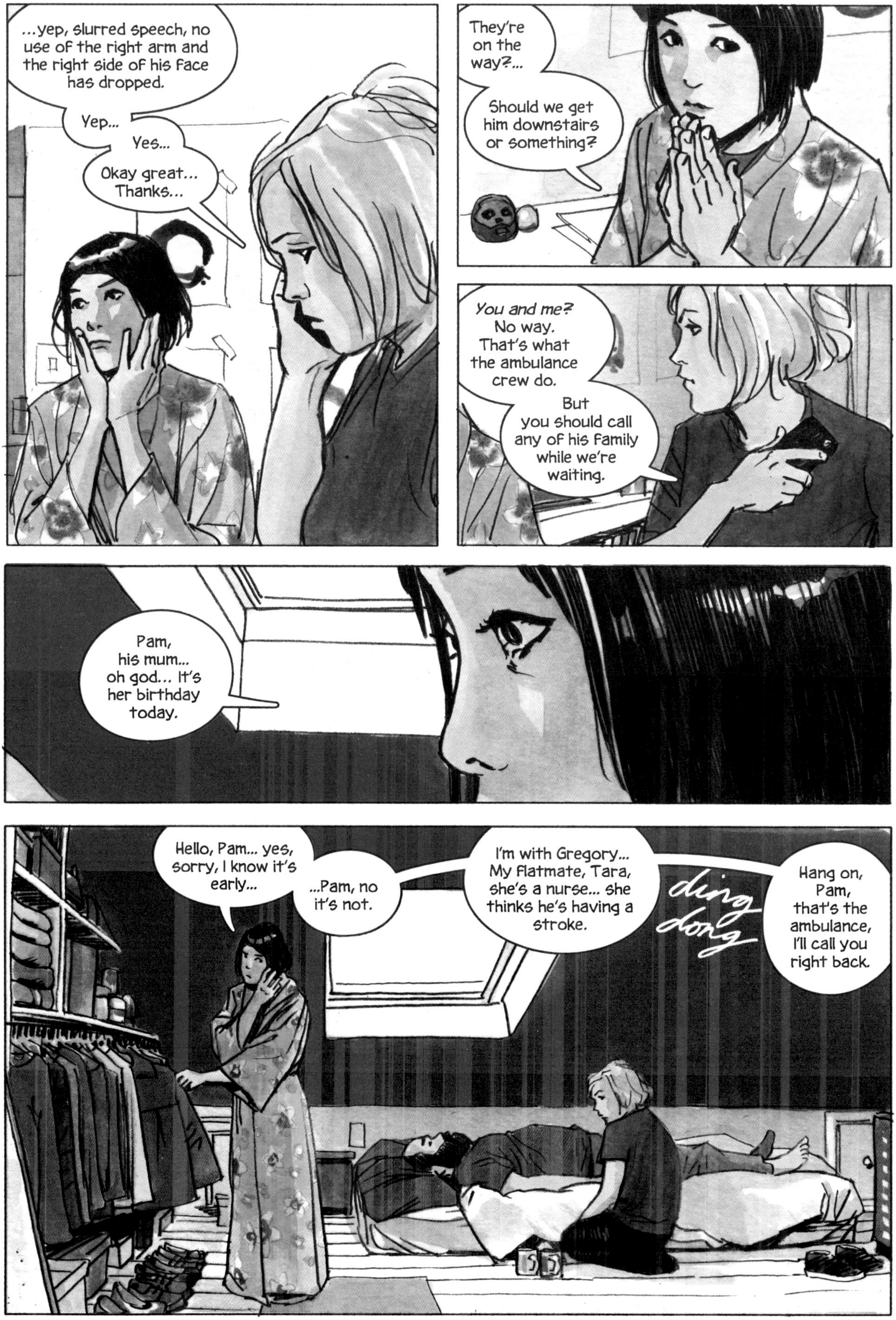

...yep, slurred speech, no use of the right arm and the right side of his face has dropped.
Yep...
Yes...
Okay great... Thanks...
They're on the way?...
Should we get him downstairs or something?
You and me? No way. That's what the ambulance crew do.
But you should call any of his family while we're waiting.
Pam, his mum... oh god... It's her birthday today.
Hello, Pam... yes, sorry, I know it's early...
...Pam, no it's not.
I'm with Gregory... My flatmate, Tara, she's a nurse... she thinks he's having a stroke.
ding dong
Hang on, Pam, that's the ambulance, I'll call you right back.

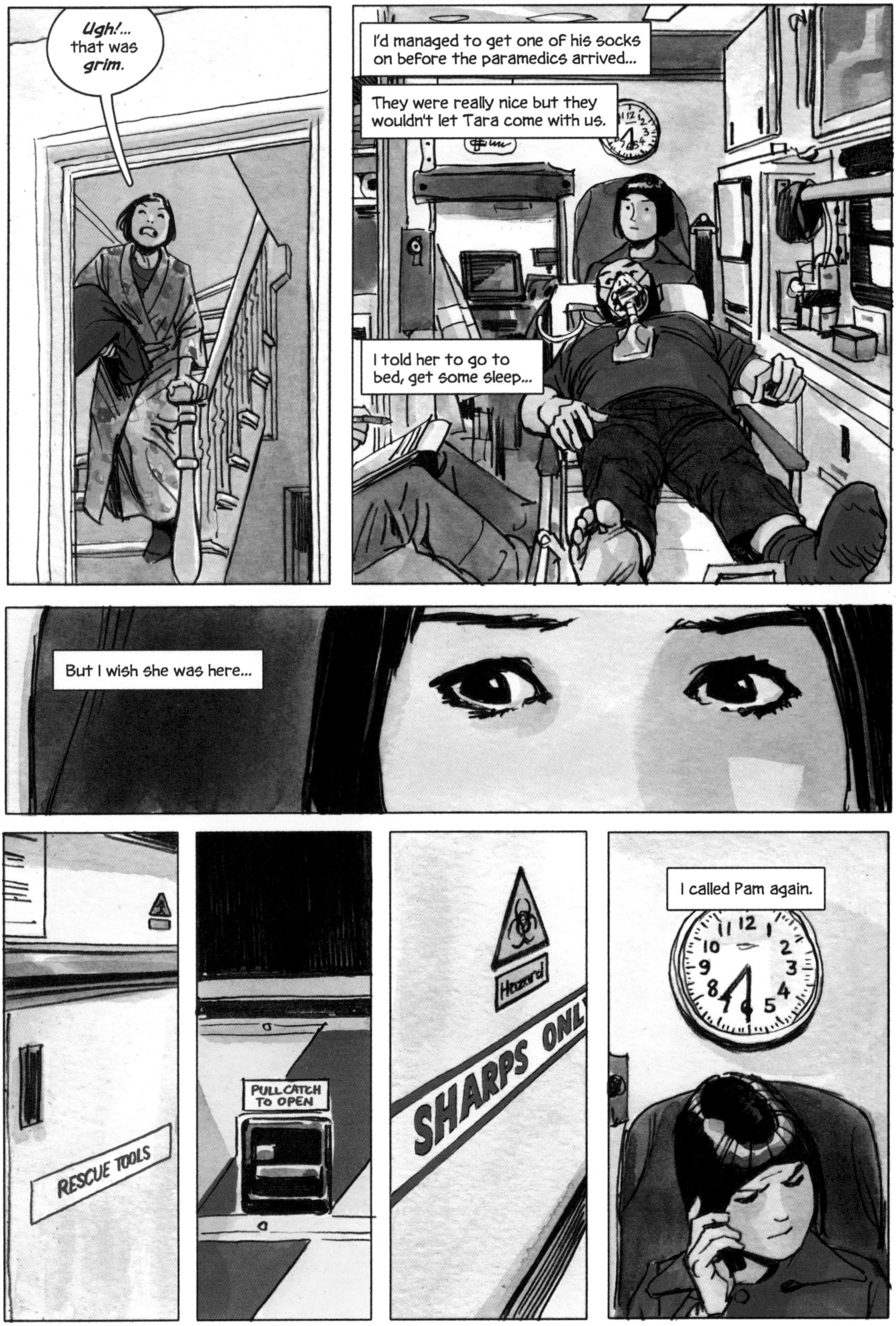
Ugh!... that was *grim.*
I'd managed to get one of his socks on before the paramedics arrived...
They were really nice but they wouldn't let Tara come with us.
I told her to go to bed, get some sleep...
But I wish she was here...
RESCUE TOOLS
PULL CATCH TO OPEN
Hazard
SHARPS ONLY
I called Pam again.

I'd been snapped out of that first spike, and managed to suppress 'the whispers' in the ambulance...

...but the feeling of being followed wouldn't go away.

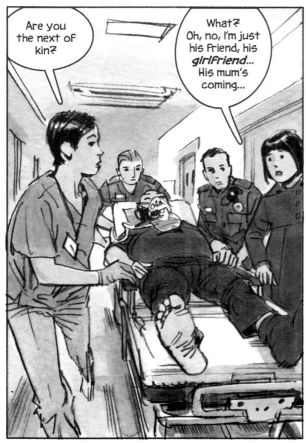

Are you the next of kin?

What? Oh, no, I'm just his friend, his *girlfriend*... His mum's coming...

I think we were left alone for just two seconds... I couldn't speak... I just wanted to *leave* my body...

...it all finally caught up with me...

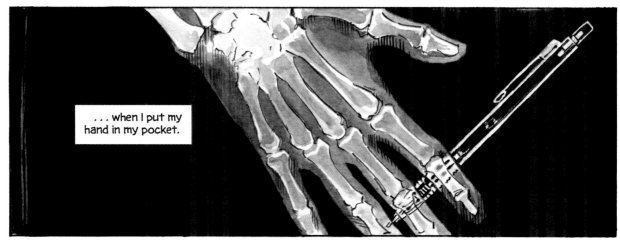

. . . when I put my hand in my pocket.

'8 out of 10'
Stab Stab Stab Stab Stab Stab Stab Stab Stab Stab Stab Stab Stab Stab Stab Stab
'...I'm shit. I'm evil. I'm fucking cold...'
'...heartless.'
...I couldn't stay.
Hello, I'm one of the doctors, Dr. Duk.
.....
'9 out of 10'

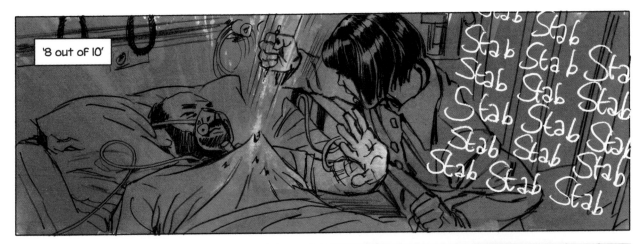

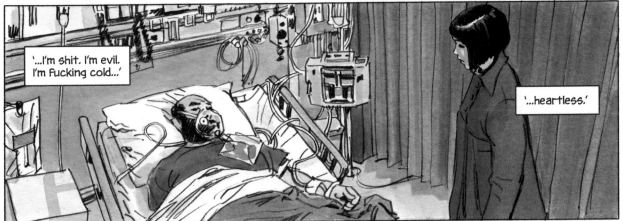

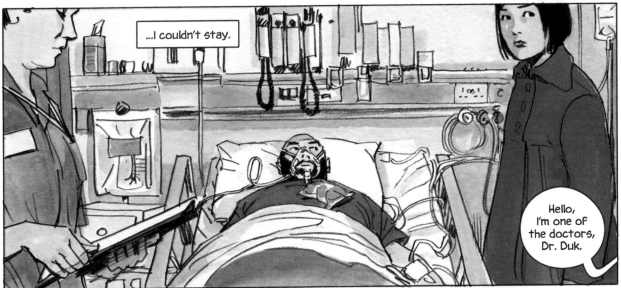

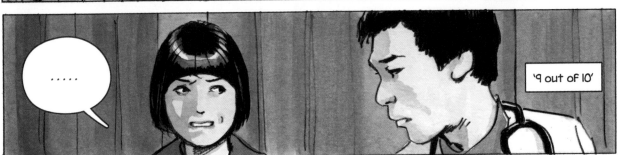

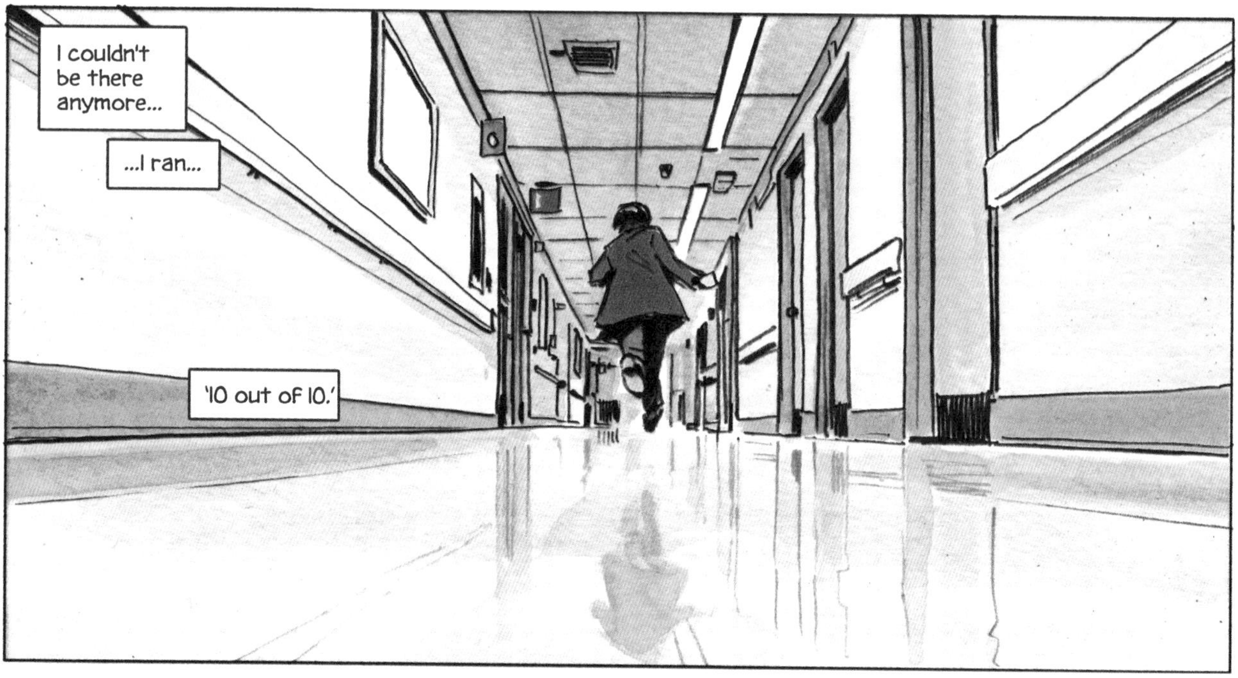
I couldn't be there anymore...
...I ran...
'10 out of 10.'

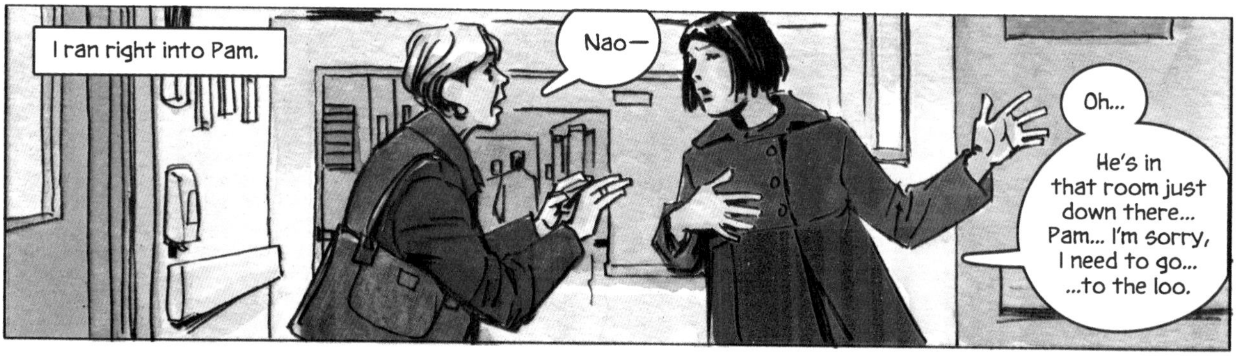
I ran right into Pam.
Nao—
Oh...
He's in that room just down there... Pam... I'm sorry, I need to go... ...to the loo.

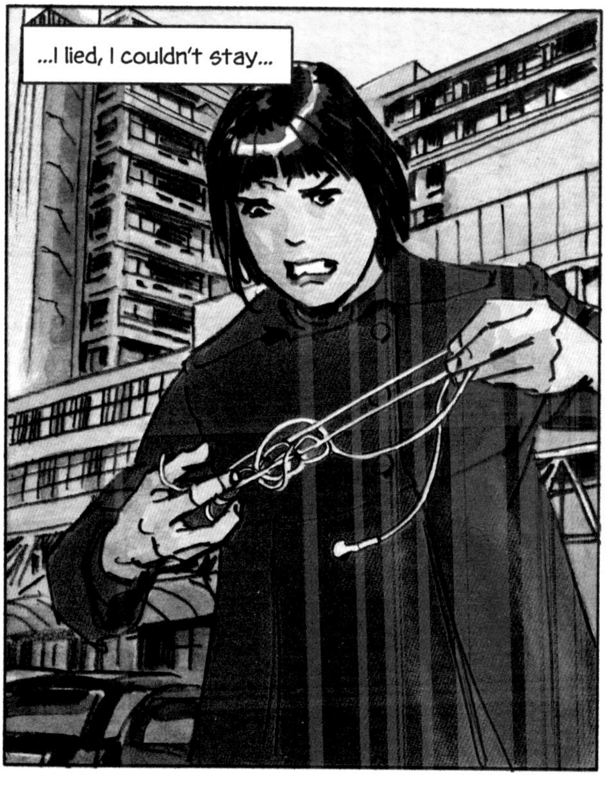
...I lied, I couldn't stay...

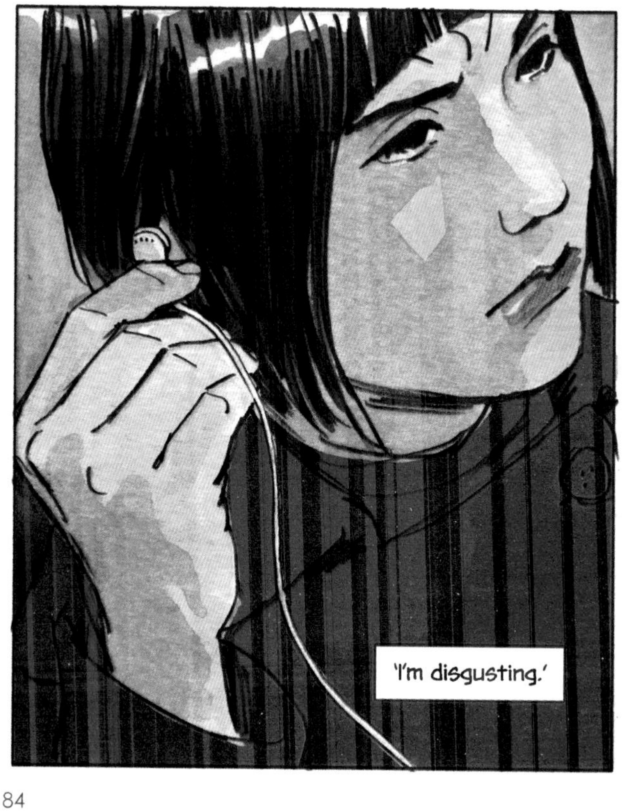
'I'm disgusting.'

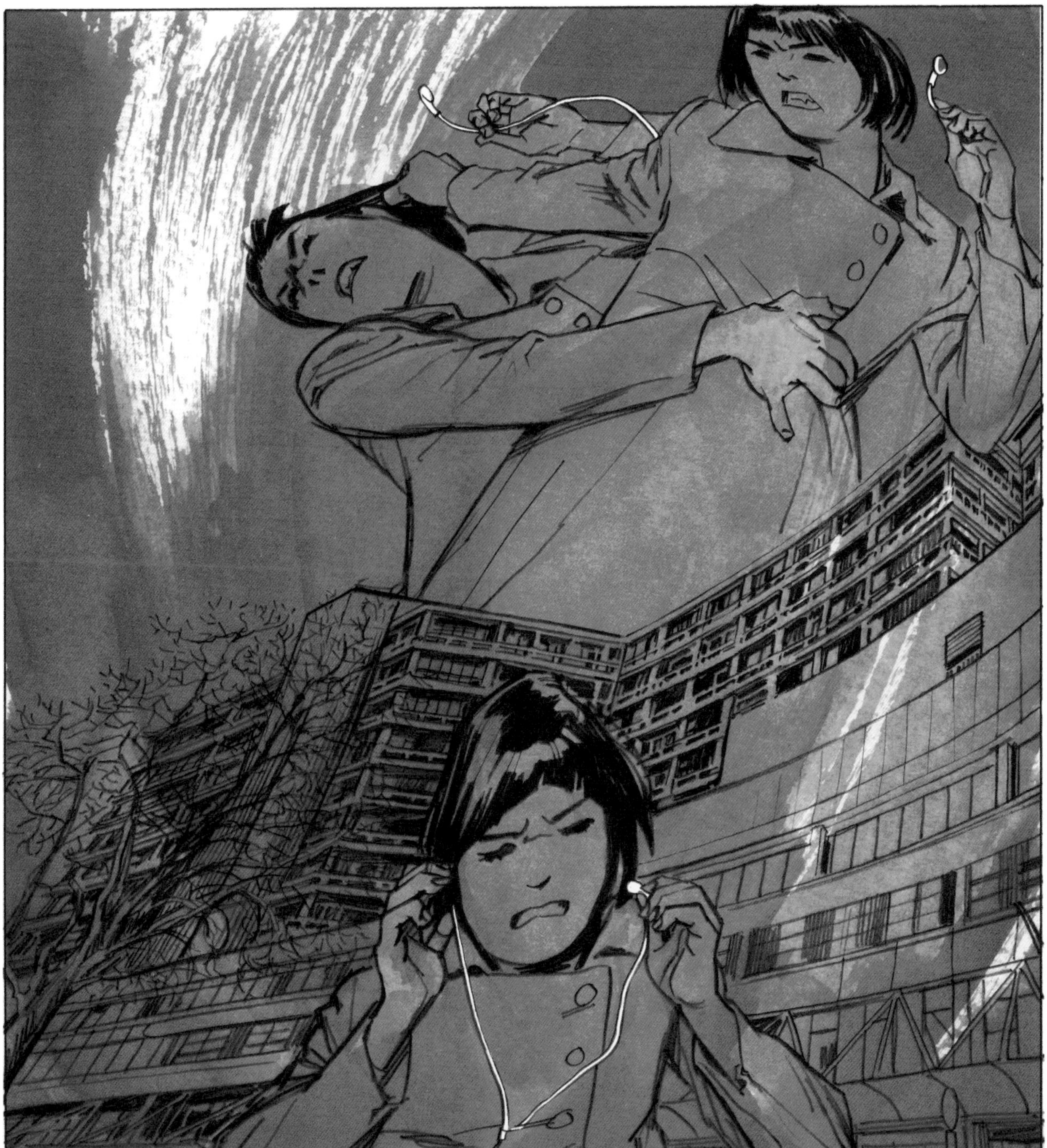

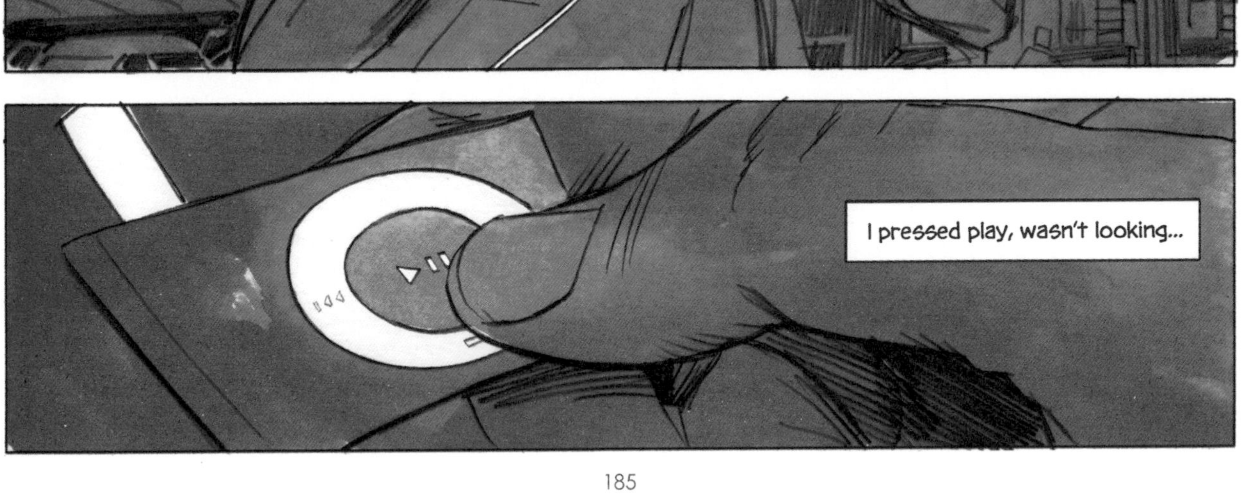
I pressed play, wasn't looking...

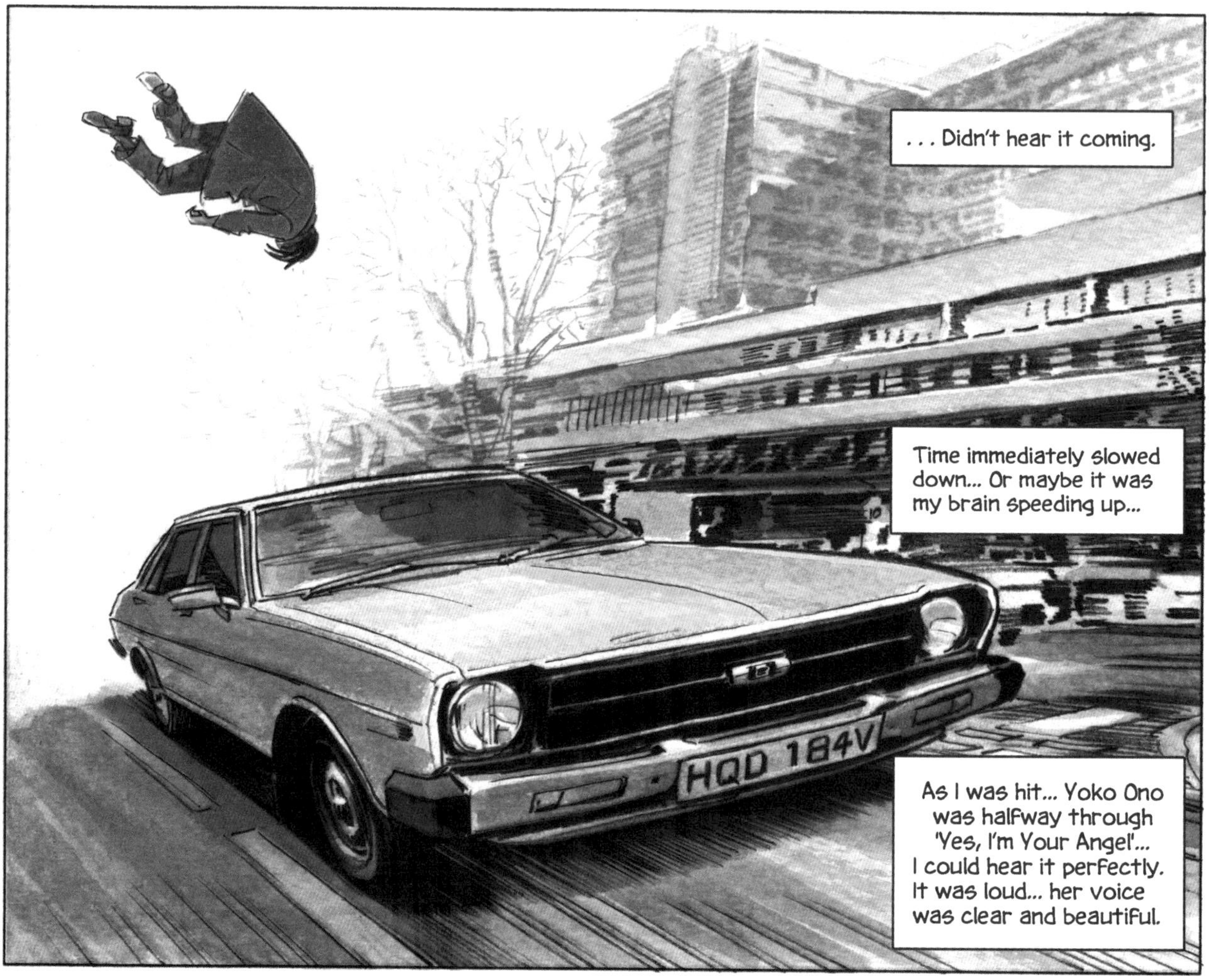
. . . Didn't hear it coming.
Time immediately slowed down... Or maybe it was my brain speeding up...
HQD 184V
As I was hit... Yoko Ono was halfway through 'Yes, I'm Your Angel'... I could hear it perfectly. It was loud... her voice was clear and beautiful.

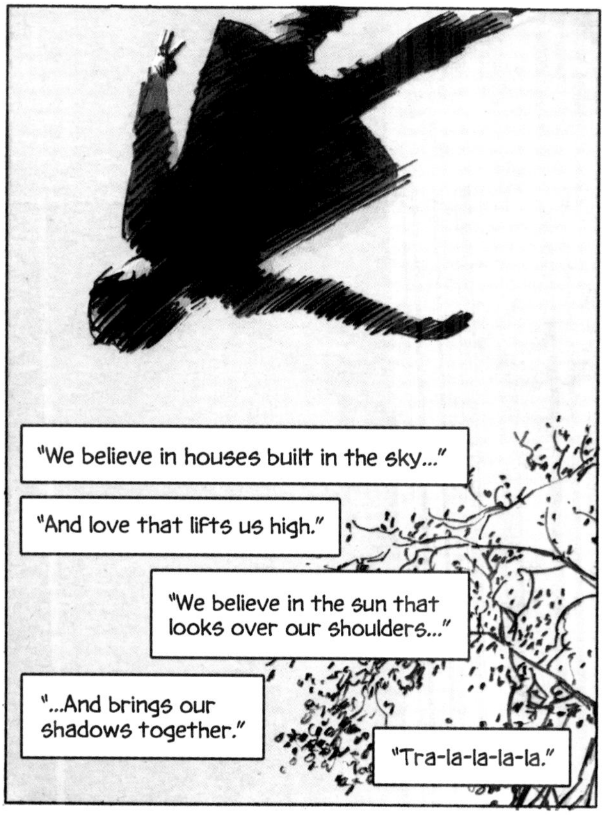
"We believe in houses built in the sky..."
"And love that lifts us high."
"We believe in the sun that looks over our shoulders..."
"...And brings our shadows together."
"Tra-la-la-la-la."

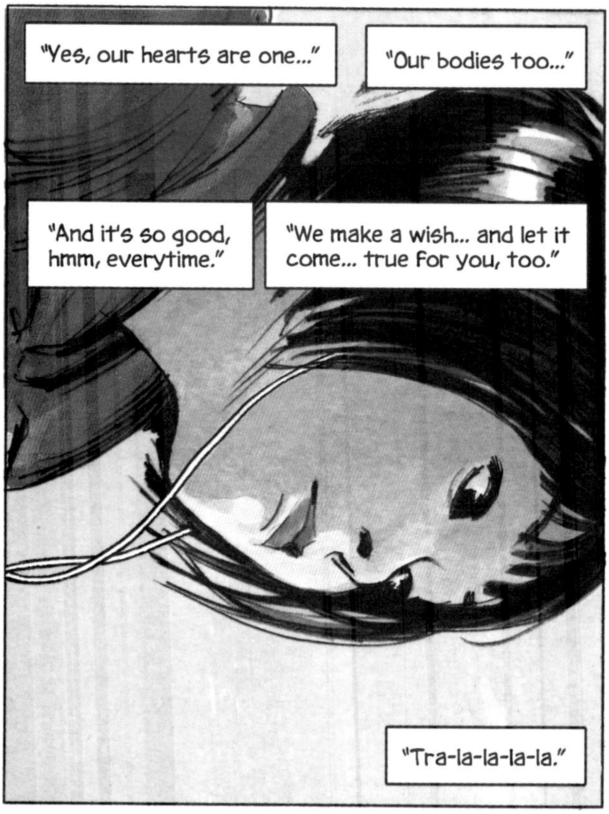
"Yes, our hearts are one..."
"Our bodies too..."
"And it's so good, hmm, everytime."
"We make a wish... and let it come... true for you, too."
"Tra-la-la-la-la."

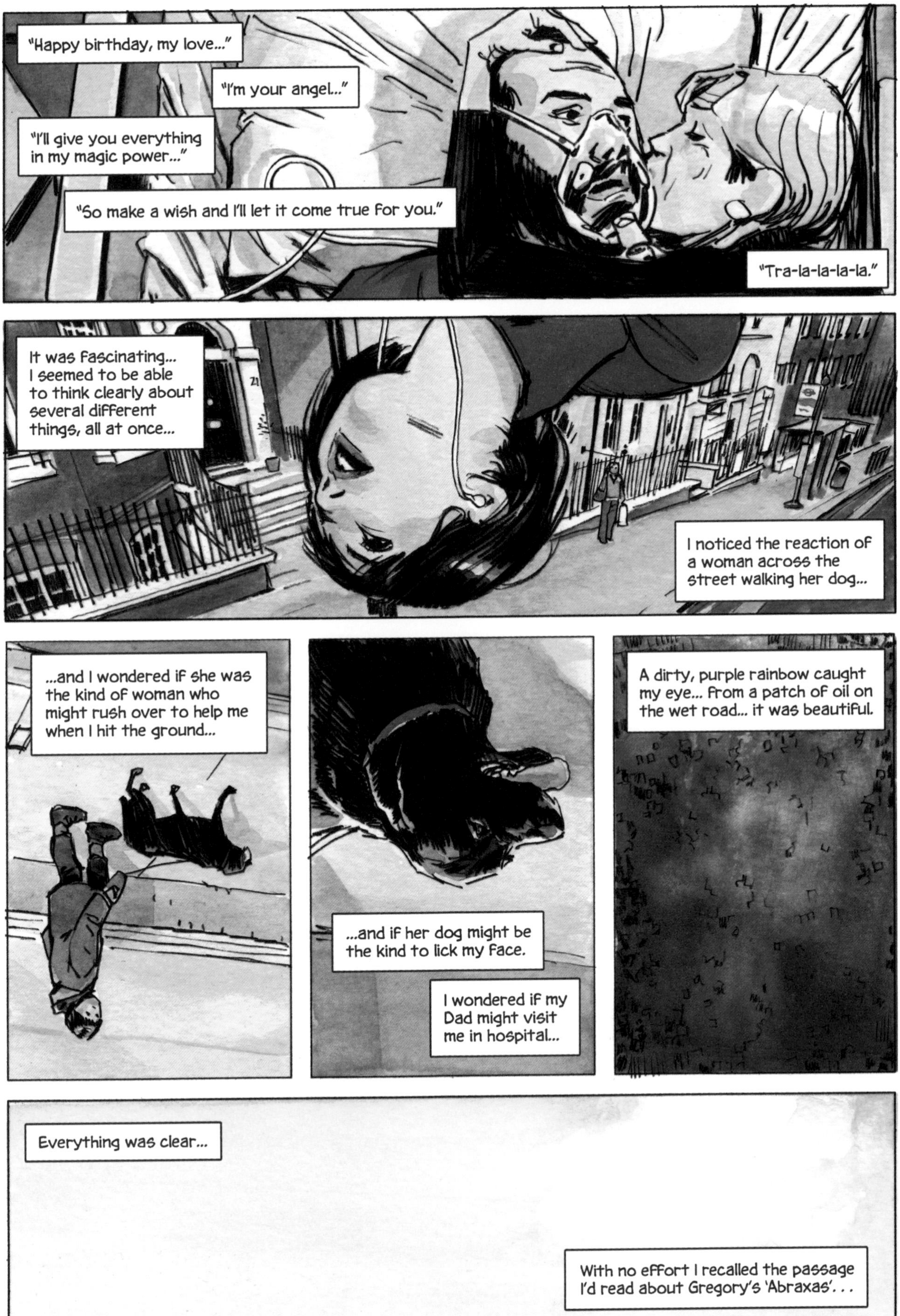
"Happy birthday, my love..."
"I'm your angel..."
"I'll give you everything in my magic power..."
"So make a wish and I'll let it come true for you."
"Tra-la-la-la-la."
It was fascinating... I seemed to be able to think clearly about several different things, all at once...
21
I noticed the reaction of a woman across the street walking her dog...
...and I wondered if she was the kind of woman who might rush over to help me when I hit the ground...
...and if her dog might be the kind to lick my face.
I wondered if my Dad might visit me in hospital...
A dirty, purple rainbow caught my eye... from a patch of oil on the wet road... it was beautiful.
Everything was clear...
With no effort I recalled the passage I'd read about Gregory's 'Abraxas'. . .

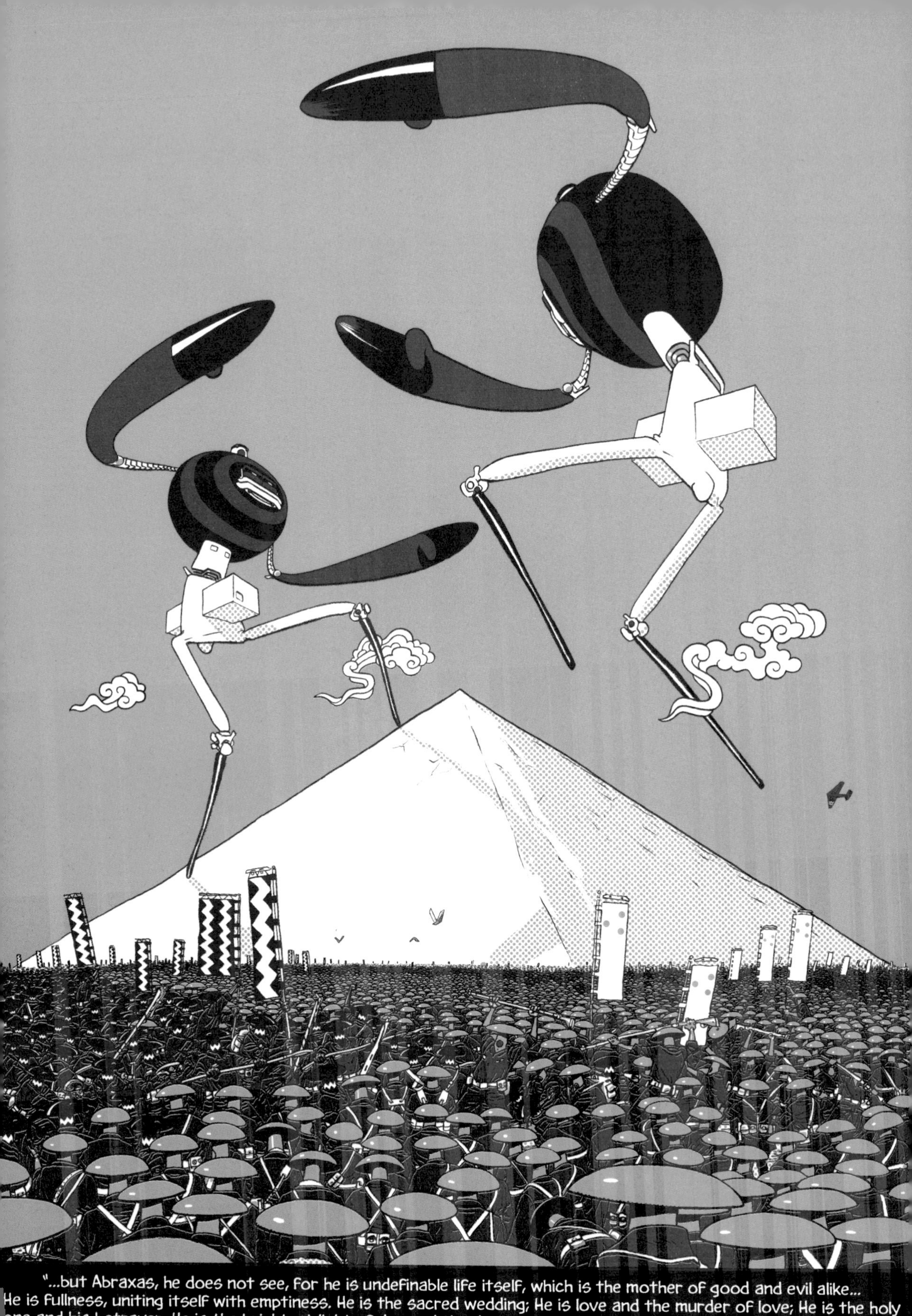
"...but Abraxas, he does not see, for he is undefinable life itself, which is the mother of good and evil alike... He is fullness, uniting itself with emptiness. He is the sacred wedding; He is love and the murder of love; He is the holy one and his betrayer. He is the brightest light of day and the deepest night of madness. To see him means blindness; to know him is sickness; to worship him is death; to fear him is wisdom; not to resist him means liberation."

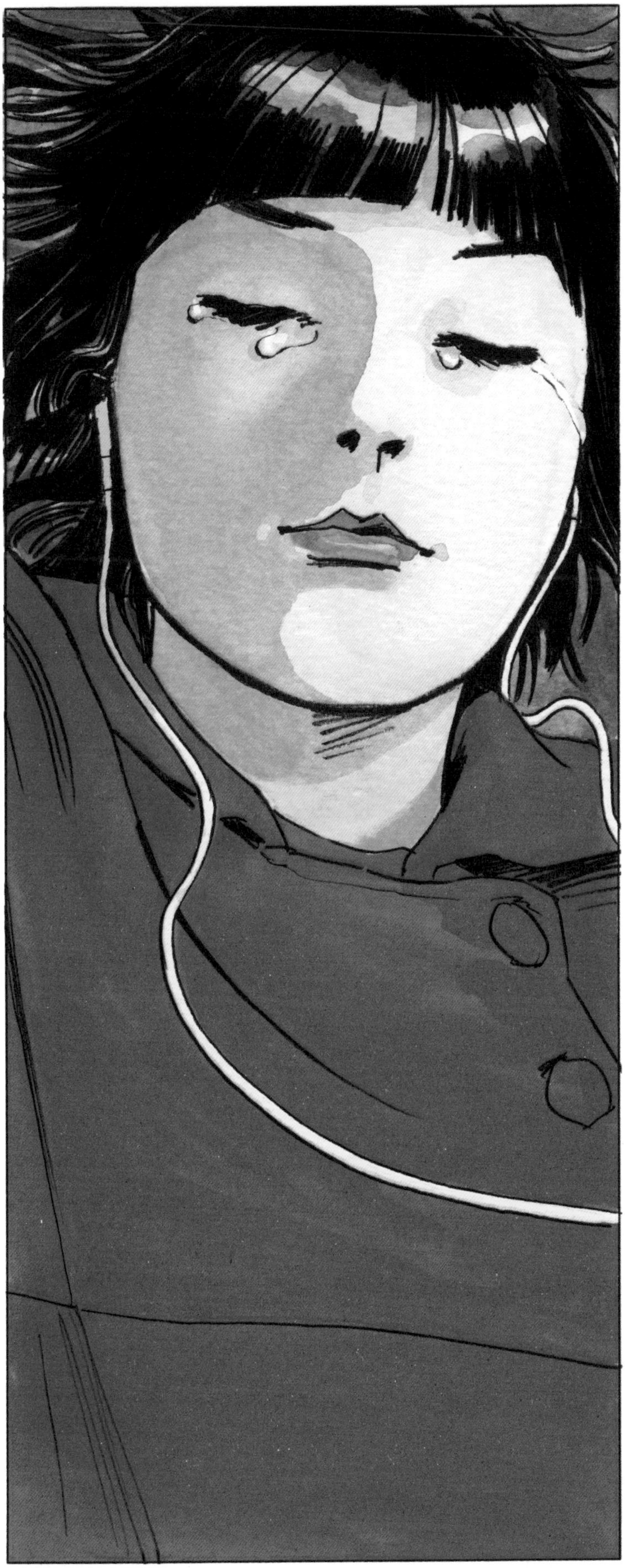

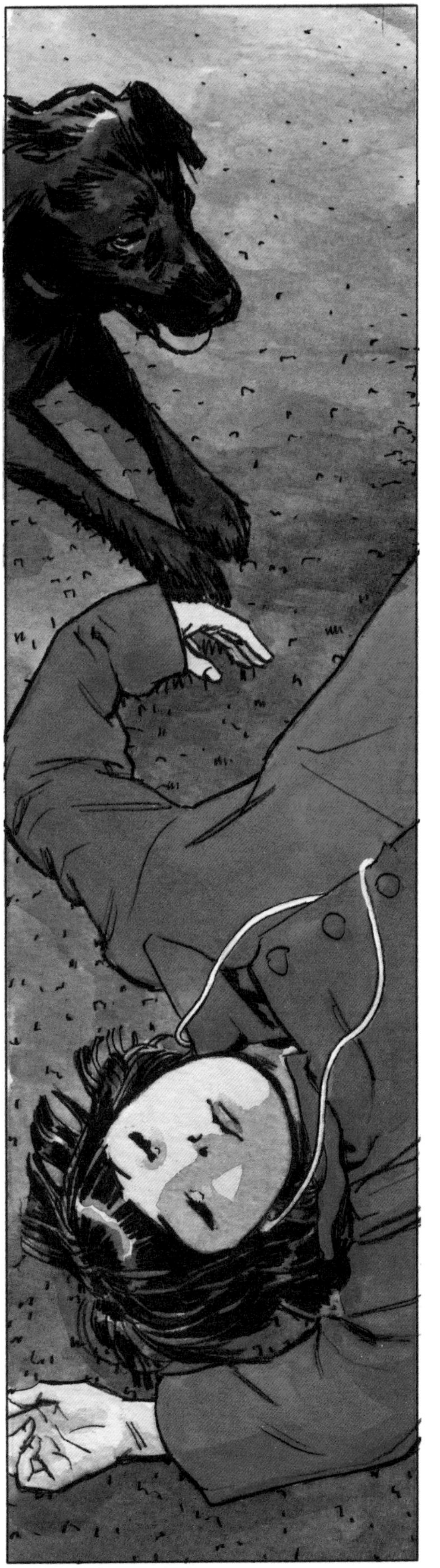

On the day Pictor's
first son was born
the Nothing came...
and, disguised as his
music box...

...this is what it sang.

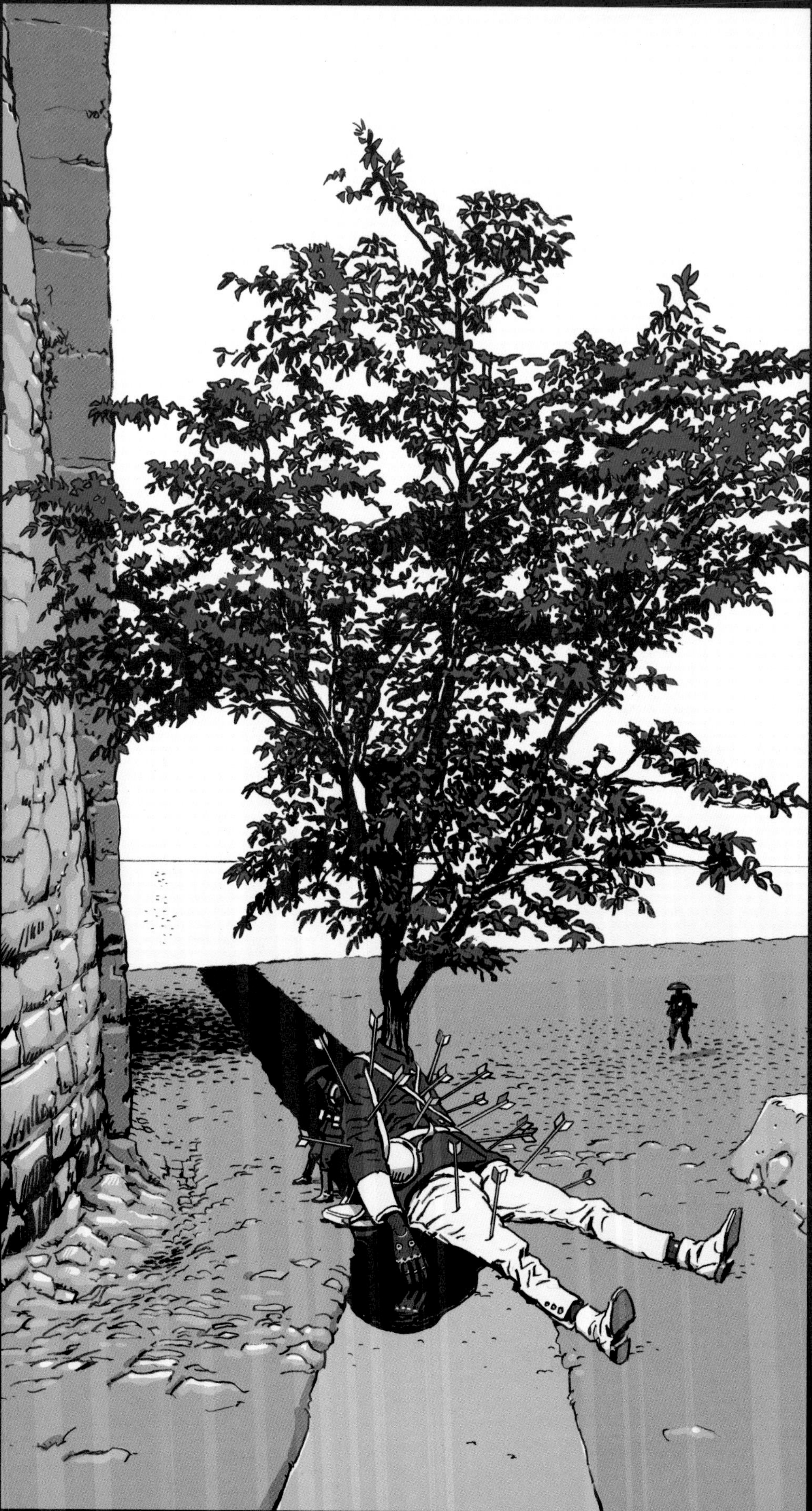

"Black and white or
brown,
I was once a soldier,
Til the enemy shot me
down.

Brown or black and
white,
I then became all
Nothing,
And day was wed with
night.

As I lay there dying,
I branched up towards
the sky,
I had no need of
witness,
For I did not truly die."

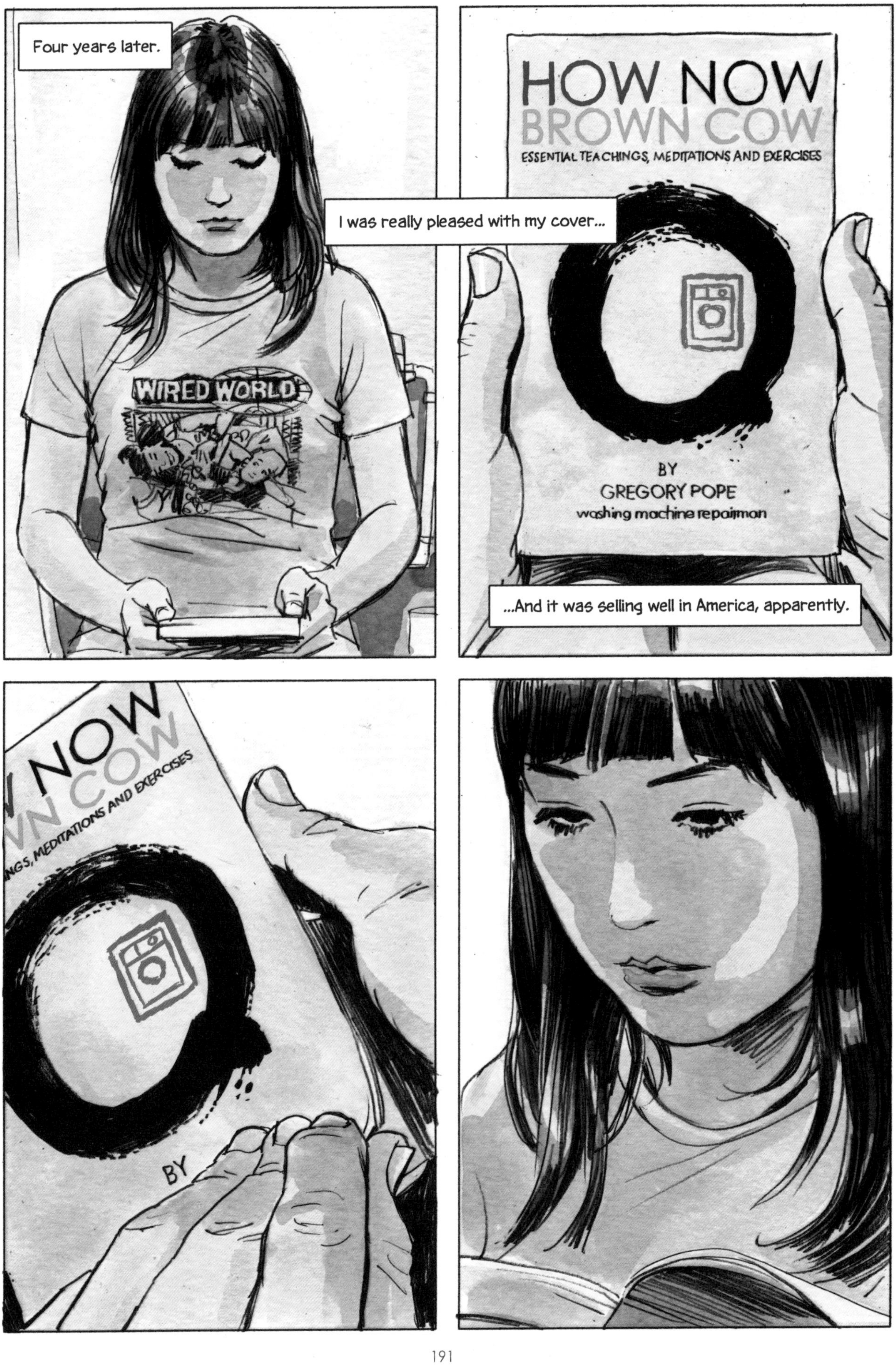
Four years later.
WIRED WORLD
I was really pleased with my cover...
HOW NOW
BROWN COW
ESSENTIAL TEACHINGS, MEDITATIONS AND EXERCISES
BY
GREGORY POPE
washing machine repairman
...And it was selling well in America, apparently.
BY

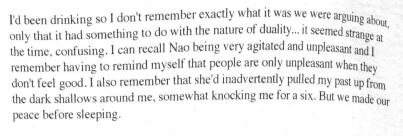

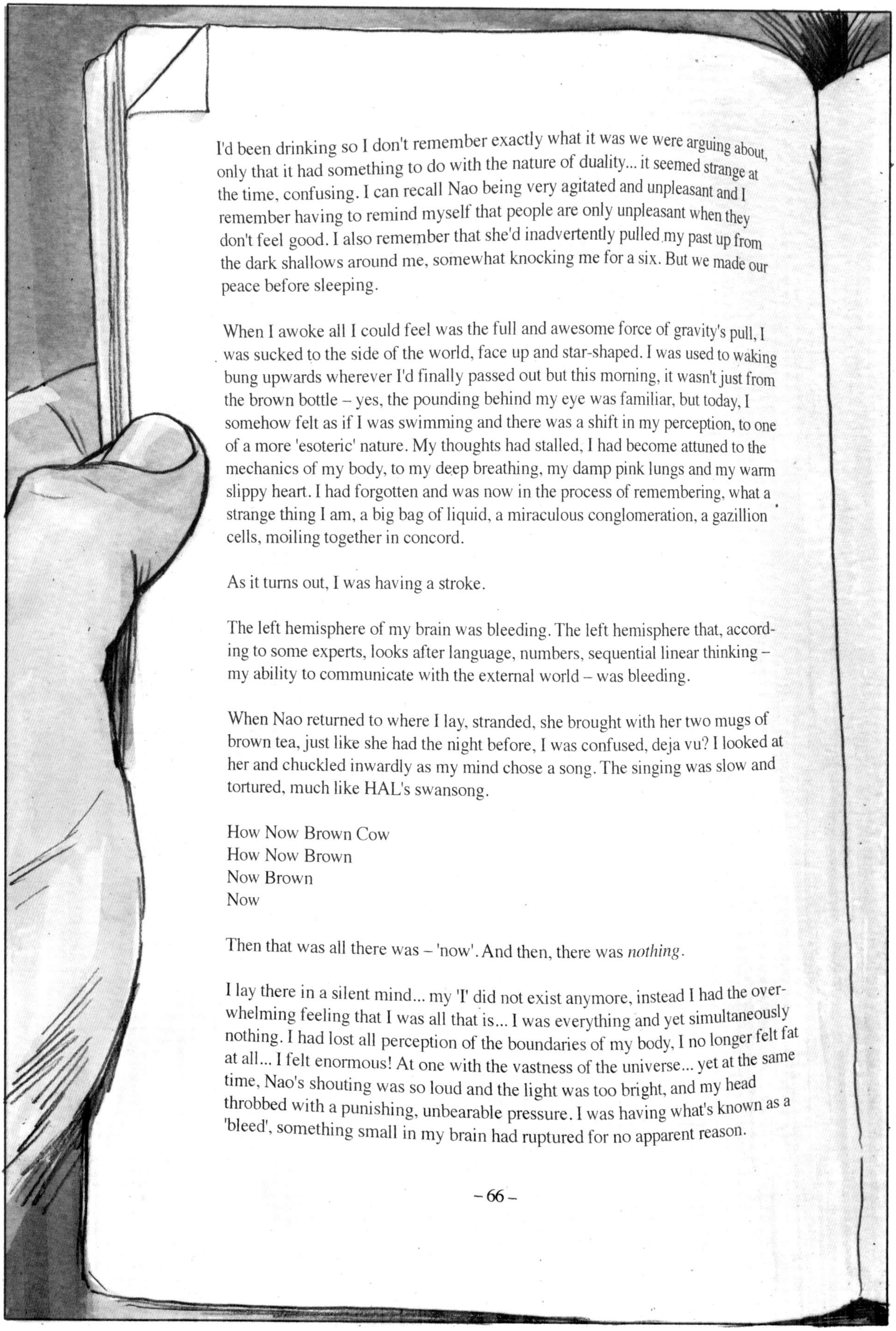

I'd been drinking so I don't remember exactly what it was we were arguing about, only that it had something to do with the nature of duality... it seemed strange at the time, confusing. I can recall Nao being very agitated and unpleasant and I remember having to remind myself that people are only unpleasant when they don't feel good. I also remember that she'd inadvertently pulled my past up from the dark shallows around me, somewhat knocking me for a six. But we made our peace before sleeping.

When I awoke all I could feel was the full and awesome force of gravity's pull, I was sucked to the side of the world, face up and star-shaped. I was used to waking bung upwards wherever I'd finally passed out but this morning, it wasn't just from the brown bottle – yes, the pounding behind my eye was familiar, but today, I somehow felt as if I was swimming and there was a shift in my perception, to one of a more 'esoteric' nature. My thoughts had stalled, I had become attuned to the mechanics of my body, to my deep breathing, my damp pink lungs and my warm slippy heart. I had forgotten and was now in the process of remembering, what a strange thing I am, a big bag of liquid, a miraculous conglomeration, a gazillion cells, moiling together in concord.

As it turns out, I was having a stroke.

The left hemisphere of my brain was bleeding. The left hemisphere that, according to some experts, looks after language, numbers, sequential linear thinking – my ability to communicate with the external world – was bleeding.

When Nao returned to where I lay, stranded, she brought with her two mugs of brown tea, just like she had the night before, I was confused, deja vu? I looked at her and chuckled inwardly as my mind chose a song. The singing was slow and tortured, much like HAL's swansong.

How Now Brown Cow
How Now Brown
Now Brown
Now

Then that was all there was – 'now'. And then, there was *nothing*.

I lay there in a silent mind... my 'I' did not exist anymore, instead I had the overwhelming feeling that I was all that is... I was everything and yet simultaneously nothing. I had lost all perception of the boundaries of my body, I no longer felt fat at all... I felt enormous! At one with the vastness of the universe... yet at the same time, Nao's shouting was so loud and the light was too bright, and my head throbbed with a punishing, unbearable pressure. I was having what's known as a 'bleed', something small in my brain had ruptured for no apparent reason.

– 66 –

192

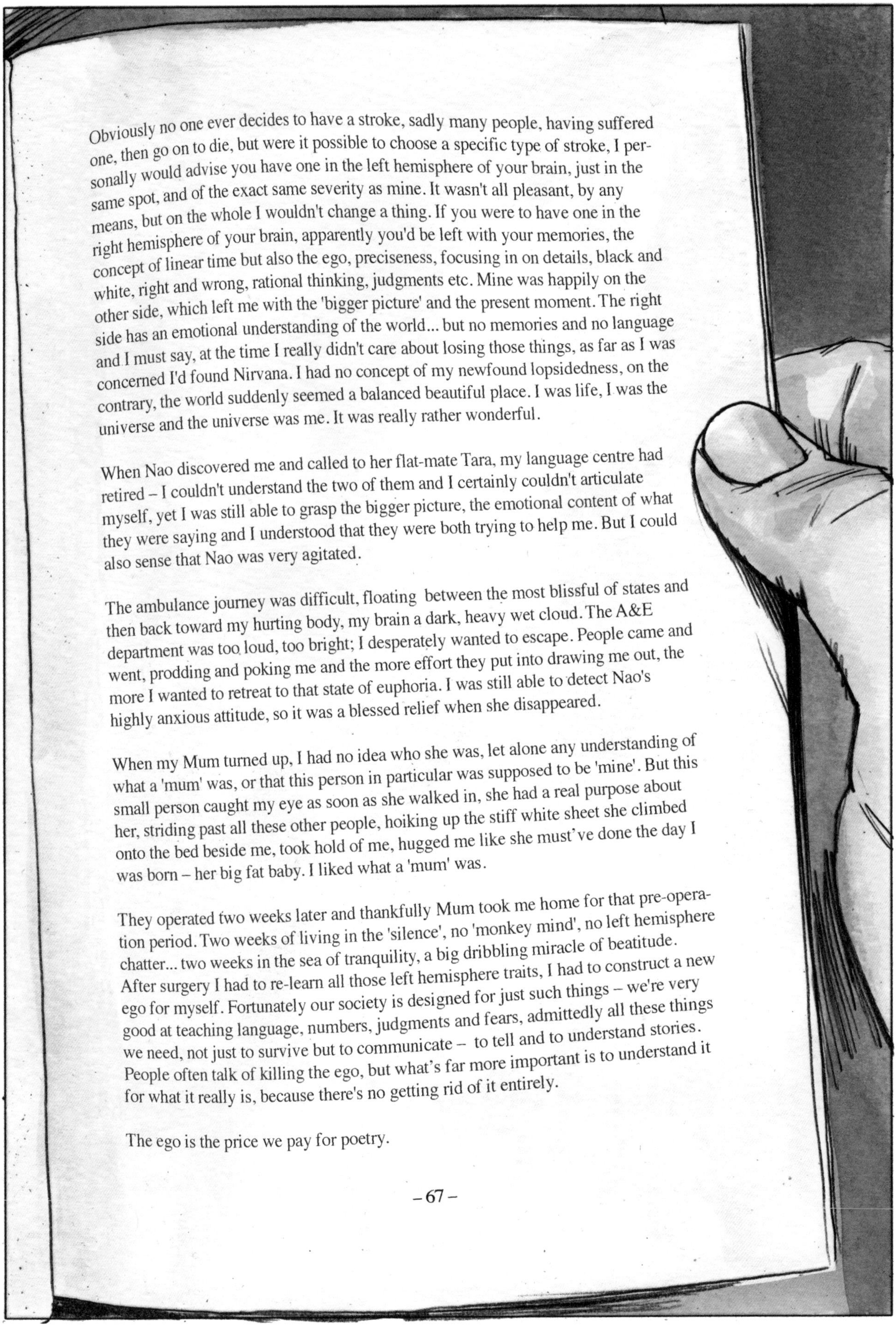

Obviously no one ever decides to have a stroke, sadly many people, having suffered one, then go on to die, but were it possible to choose a specific type of stroke, I personally would advise you have one in the left hemisphere of your brain, just in the same spot, and of the exact same severity as mine. It wasn't all pleasant, by any means, but on the whole I wouldn't change a thing. If you were to have one in the right hemisphere of your brain, apparently you'd be left with your memories, the concept of linear time but also the ego, preciseness, focusing in on details, black and white, right and wrong, rational thinking, judgments etc. Mine was happily on the other side, which left me with the 'bigger picture' and the present moment. The right side has an emotional understanding of the world... but no memories and no language and I must say, at the time I really didn't care about losing those things, as far as I was concerned I'd found Nirvana. I had no concept of my newfound lopsidedness, on the contrary, the world suddenly seemed a balanced beautiful place. I was life, I was the universe and the universe was me. It was really rather wonderful.

When Nao discovered me and called to her flat-mate Tara, my language centre had retired – I couldn't understand the two of them and I certainly couldn't articulate myself, yet I was still able to grasp the bigger picture, the emotional content of what they were saying and I understood that they were both trying to help me. But I could also sense that Nao was very agitated.

The ambulance journey was difficult, floating between the most blissful of states and then back toward my hurting body, my brain a dark, heavy wet cloud. The A&E department was too loud, too bright; I desperately wanted to escape. People came and went, prodding and poking me and the more effort they put into drawing me out, the more I wanted to retreat to that state of euphoria. I was still able to detect Nao's highly anxious attitude, so it was a blessed relief when she disappeared.

When my Mum turned up, I had no idea who she was, let alone any understanding of what a 'mum' was, or that this person in particular was supposed to be 'mine'. But this small person caught my eye as soon as she walked in, she had a real purpose about her, striding past all these other people, hoiking up the stiff white sheet she climbed onto the bed beside me, took hold of me, hugged me like she must've done the day I was born – her big fat baby. I liked what a 'mum' was.

They operated two weeks later and thankfully Mum took me home for that pre-operation period. Two weeks of living in the 'silence', no 'monkey mind', no left hemisphere chatter... two weeks in the sea of tranquility, a big dribbling miracle of beatitude. After surgery I had to re-learn all those left hemisphere traits, I had to construct a new ego for myself. Fortunately our society is designed for just such things – we're very good at teaching language, numbers, judgments and fears, admittedly all these things we need, not just to survive but to communicate – to tell and to understand stories. People often talk of killing the ego, but what's far more important is to understand it for what it really is, because there's no getting rid of it entirely.

The ego is the price we pay for poetry.

– 67 –

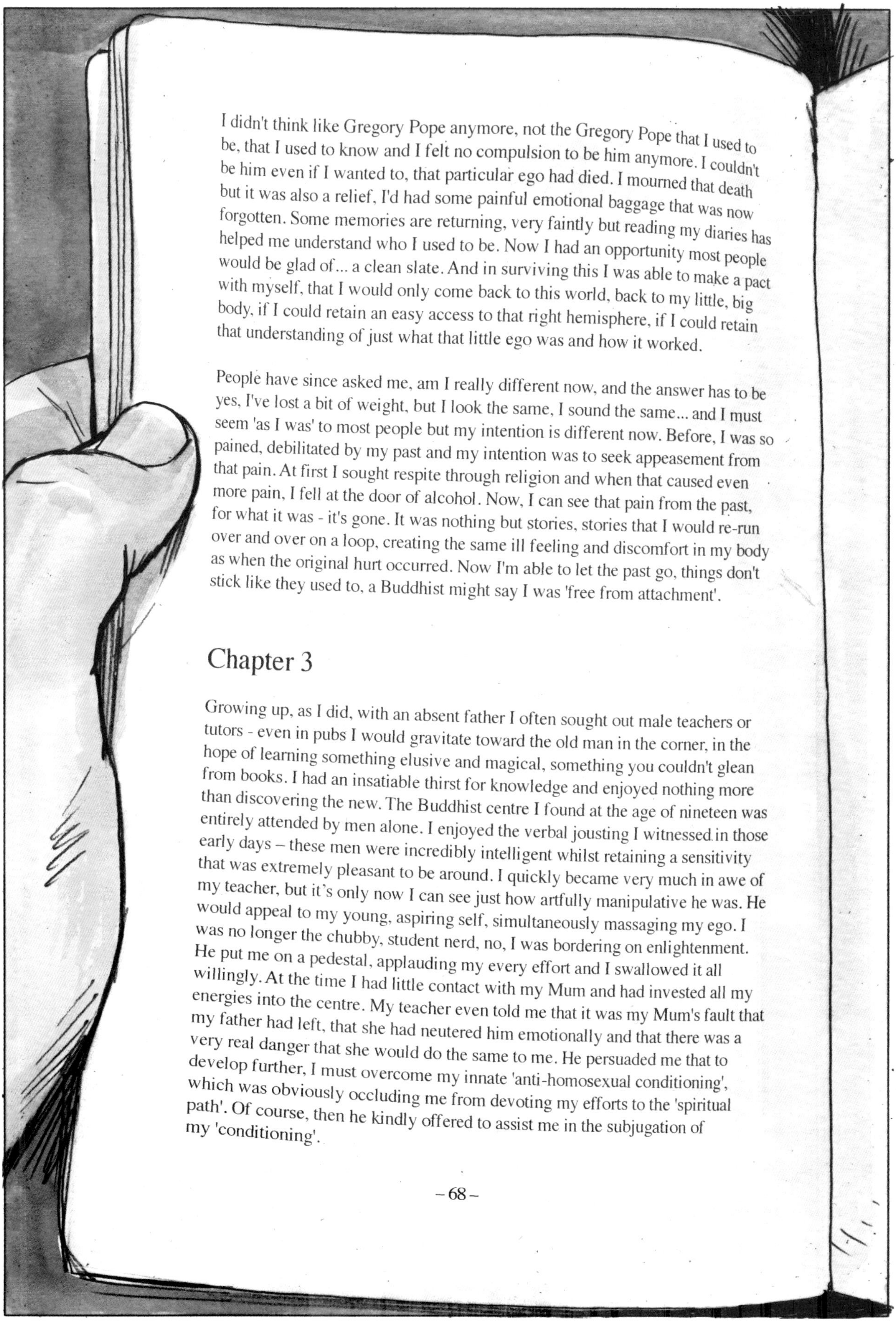

I didn't think like Gregory Pope anymore, not the Gregory Pope that I used to be, that I used to know and I felt no compulsion to be him anymore. I couldn't be him even if I wanted to, that particular ego had died. I mourned that death but it was also a relief, I'd had some painful emotional baggage that was now forgotten. Some memories are returning, very faintly but reading my diaries has helped me understand who I used to be. Now I had an opportunity most people would be glad of... a clean slate. And in surviving this I was able to make a pact with myself, that I would only come back to this world, back to my little, big body, if I could retain an easy access to that right hemisphere, if I could retain that understanding of just what that little ego was and how it worked.

People have since asked me, am I really different now, and the answer has to be yes, I've lost a bit of weight, but I look the same, I sound the same... and I must seem 'as I was' to most people but my intention is different now. Before, I was so pained, debilitated by my past and my intention was to seek appeasement from that pain. At first I sought respite through religion and when that caused even more pain, I fell at the door of alcohol. Now, I can see that pain from the past, for what it was - it's gone. It was nothing but stories, stories that I would re-run over and over on a loop, creating the same ill feeling and discomfort in my body as when the original hurt occurred. Now I'm able to let the past go, things don't stick like they used to, a Buddhist might say I was 'free from attachment'.

Chapter 3

Growing up, as I did, with an absent father I often sought out male teachers or tutors - even in pubs I would gravitate toward the old man in the corner, in the hope of learning something elusive and magical, something you couldn't glean from books. I had an insatiable thirst for knowledge and enjoyed nothing more than discovering the new. The Buddhist centre I found at the age of nineteen was entirely attended by men alone. I enjoyed the verbal jousting I witnessed in those early days – these men were incredibly intelligent whilst retaining a sensitivity that was extremely pleasant to be around. I quickly became very much in awe of my teacher, but it's only now I can see just how artfully manipulative he was. He would appeal to my young, aspiring self, simultaneously massaging my ego. I was no longer the chubby, student nerd, no, I was bordering on enlightenment. He put me on a pedestal, applauding my every effort and I swallowed it all willingly. At the time I had little contact with my Mum and had invested all my energies into the centre. My teacher even told me that it was my Mum's fault that my father had left, that she had neutered him emotionally and that there was a very real danger that she would do the same to me. He persuaded me that to develop further, I must overcome my innate 'anti-homosexual conditioning', which was obviously occluding me from devoting my efforts to the 'spiritual path'. Of course, then he kindly offered to assist me in the subjugation of my 'conditioning'.

– 68 –

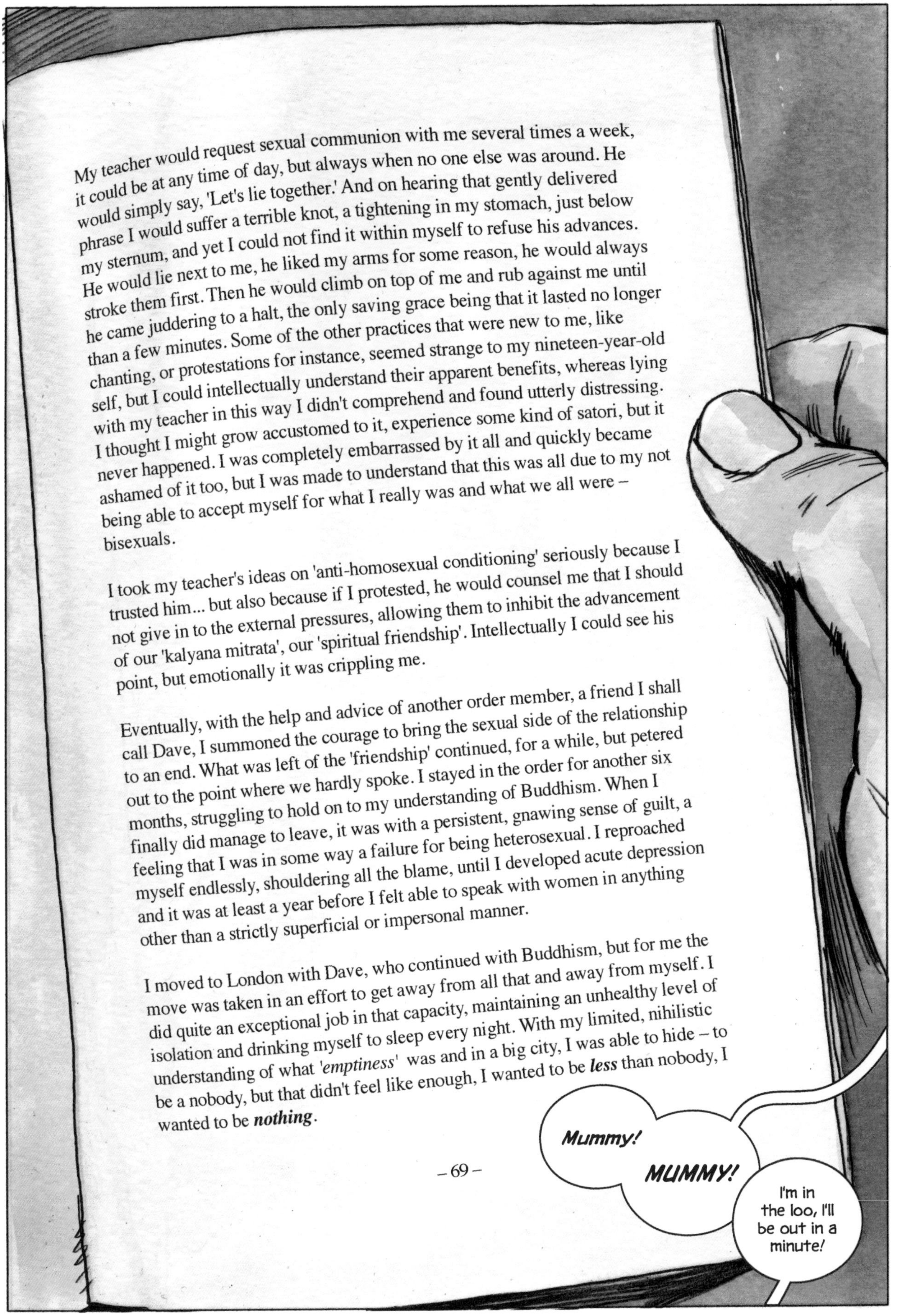

My teacher would request sexual communion with me several times a week, it could be at any time of day, but always when no one else was around. He would simply say, 'Let's lie together.' And on hearing that gently delivered phrase I would suffer a terrible knot, a tightening in my stomach, just below my sternum, and yet I could not find it within myself to refuse his advances. He would lie next to me, he liked my arms for some reason, he would always stroke them first. Then he would climb on top of me and rub against me until he came juddering to a halt, the only saving grace being that it lasted no longer than a few minutes. Some of the other practices that were new to me, like chanting, or protestations for instance, seemed strange to my nineteen-year-old self, but I could intellectually understand their apparent benefits, whereas lying with my teacher in this way I didn't comprehend and found utterly distressing. I thought I might grow accustomed to it, experience some kind of satori, but it never happened. I was completely embarrassed by it all and quickly became ashamed of it too, but I was made to understand that this was all due to my not being able to accept myself for what I really was and what we all were – bisexuals.

I took my teacher's ideas on 'anti-homosexual conditioning' seriously because I trusted him... but also because if I protested, he would counsel me that I should not give in to the external pressures, allowing them to inhibit the advancement of our 'kalyana mitrata', our 'spiritual friendship'. Intellectually I could see his point, but emotionally it was crippling me.

Eventually, with the help and advice of another order member, a friend I shall call Dave, I summoned the courage to bring the sexual side of the relationship to an end. What was left of the 'friendship' continued, for a while, but petered out to the point where we hardly spoke. I stayed in the order for another six months, struggling to hold on to my understanding of Buddhism. When I finally did manage to leave, it was with a persistent, gnawing sense of guilt, a feeling that I was in some way a failure for being heterosexual. I reproached myself endlessly, shouldering all the blame, until I developed acute depression and it was at least a year before I felt able to speak with women in anything other than a strictly superficial or impersonal manner.

I moved to London with Dave, who continued with Buddhism, but for me the move was taken in an effort to get away from all that and away from myself. I did quite an exceptional job in that capacity, maintaining an unhealthy level of isolation and drinking myself to sleep every night. With my limited, nihilistic understanding of what '*emptiness*' was and in a big city, I was able to hide – to be a nobody, but that didn't feel like enough, I wanted to be ***less*** than nobody, I wanted to be ***nothing***.

– 69 –

Mummy!
MUMMY!
I'm in the loo, I'll be out in a minute!

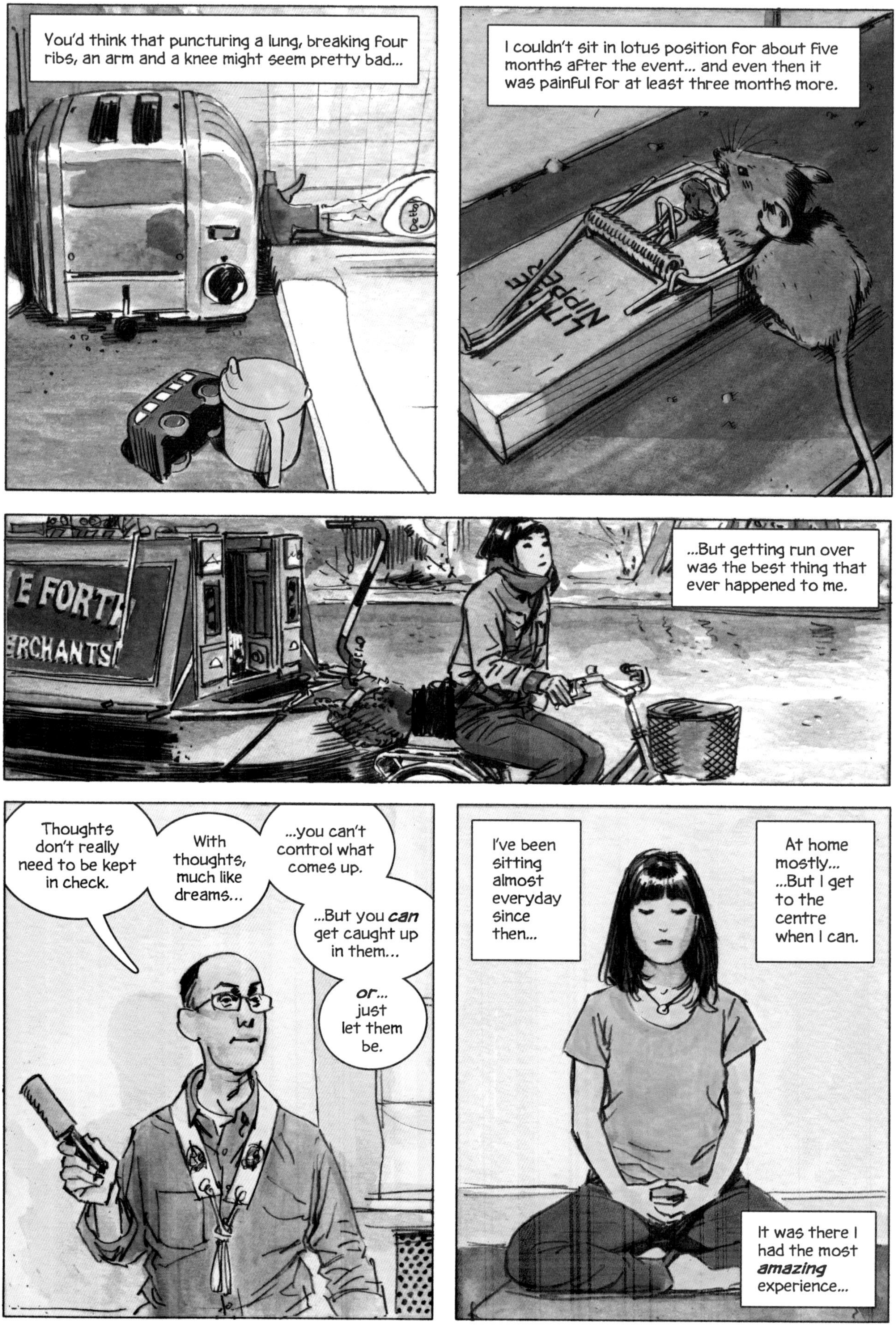
You'd think that puncturing a lung, breaking four ribs, an arm and a knee might seem pretty bad...
I couldn't sit in lotus position for about five months after the event... and even then it was painful for at least three months more.
...But getting run over was the best thing that ever happened to me.
Thoughts don't really need to be kept in check.
With thoughts, much like dreams...
...you can't control what comes up.
...But you *can* get caught up in them...
or... just let them be.
I've been sitting almost everyday since then...
At home mostly... ...But I get to the centre when I can.
It was there I had the most ***amazing*** experience...

I didn't imagine it, I didn't picture myself as this flower.

I ***was*** this flower, I truly was...

I felt it... as if all the atoms that usually held my shape... for a moment... they changed their mind...

...it ***was*** the reality of that moment.

It felt so... ***precious***...

So ***delicate***...

I was struck dumb, in awe...

I held my breath, as if somehow that might freeze the moment... so I could enjoy it...

...hold on to it, a bit longer. . .

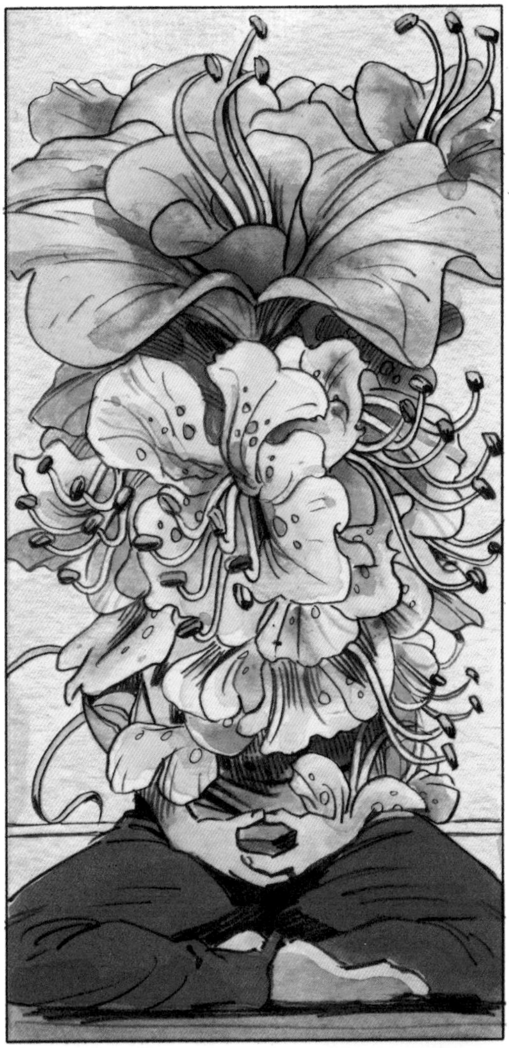

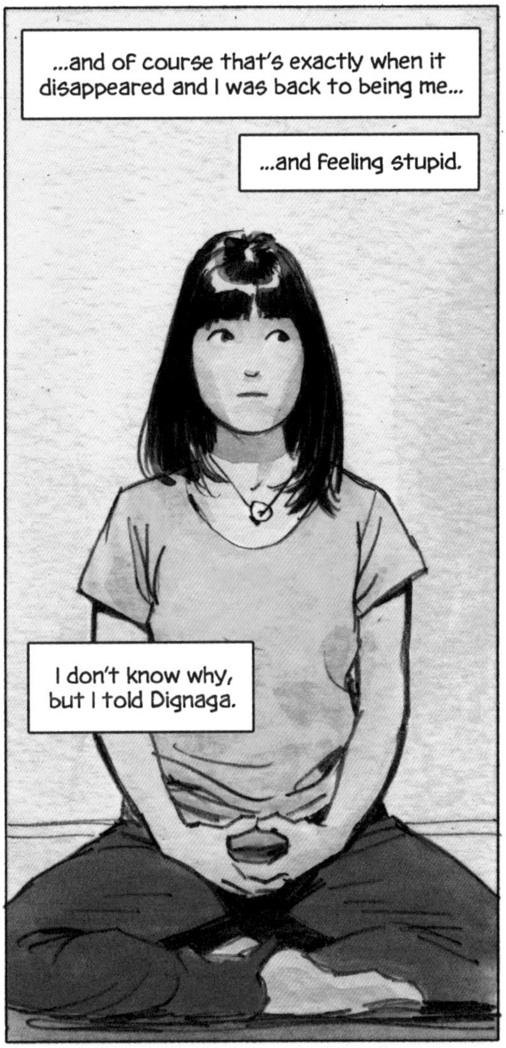
...and of course that's exactly when it disappeared and I was back to being me...
...and feeling stupid.
I don't know why, but I told Dignaga.

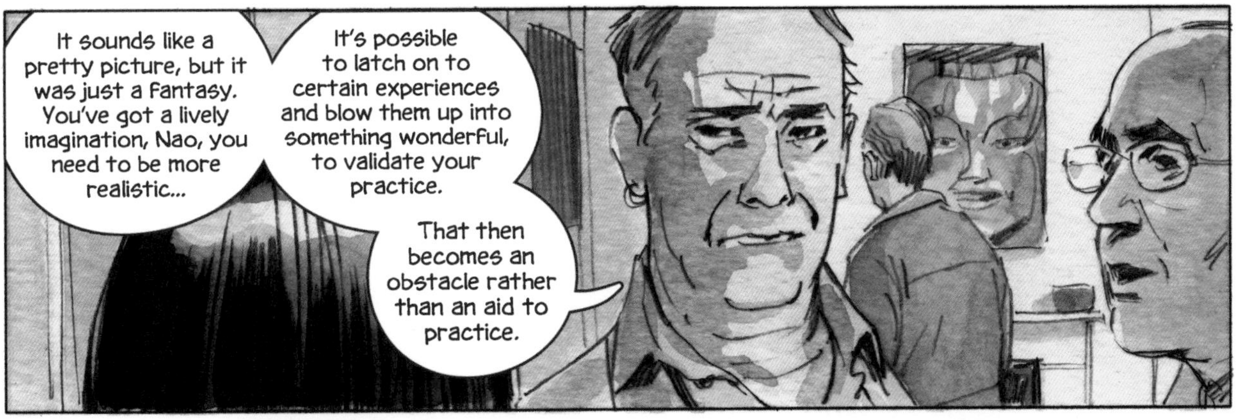
It sounds like a pretty picture, but it was just a fantasy. You've got a lively imagination, Nao, you need to be more realistic...
It's possible to latch on to certain experiences and blow them up into something wonderful, to validate your practice.
That then becomes an obstacle rather than an aid to practice.

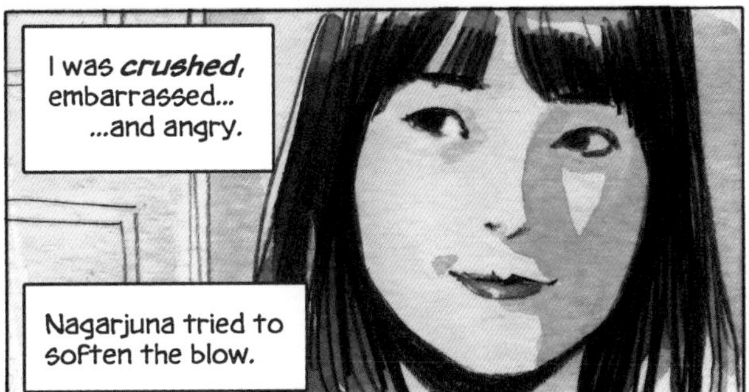
I was *crushed*, embarrassed... ...and angry.
Nagarjuna tried to soften the blow.

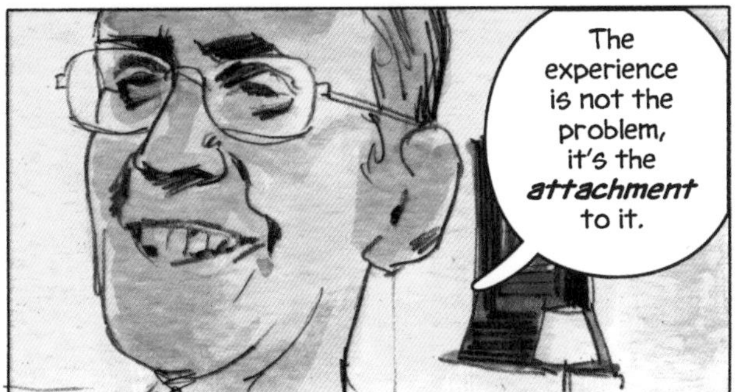
The experience is not the problem, it's the *attachment* to it.

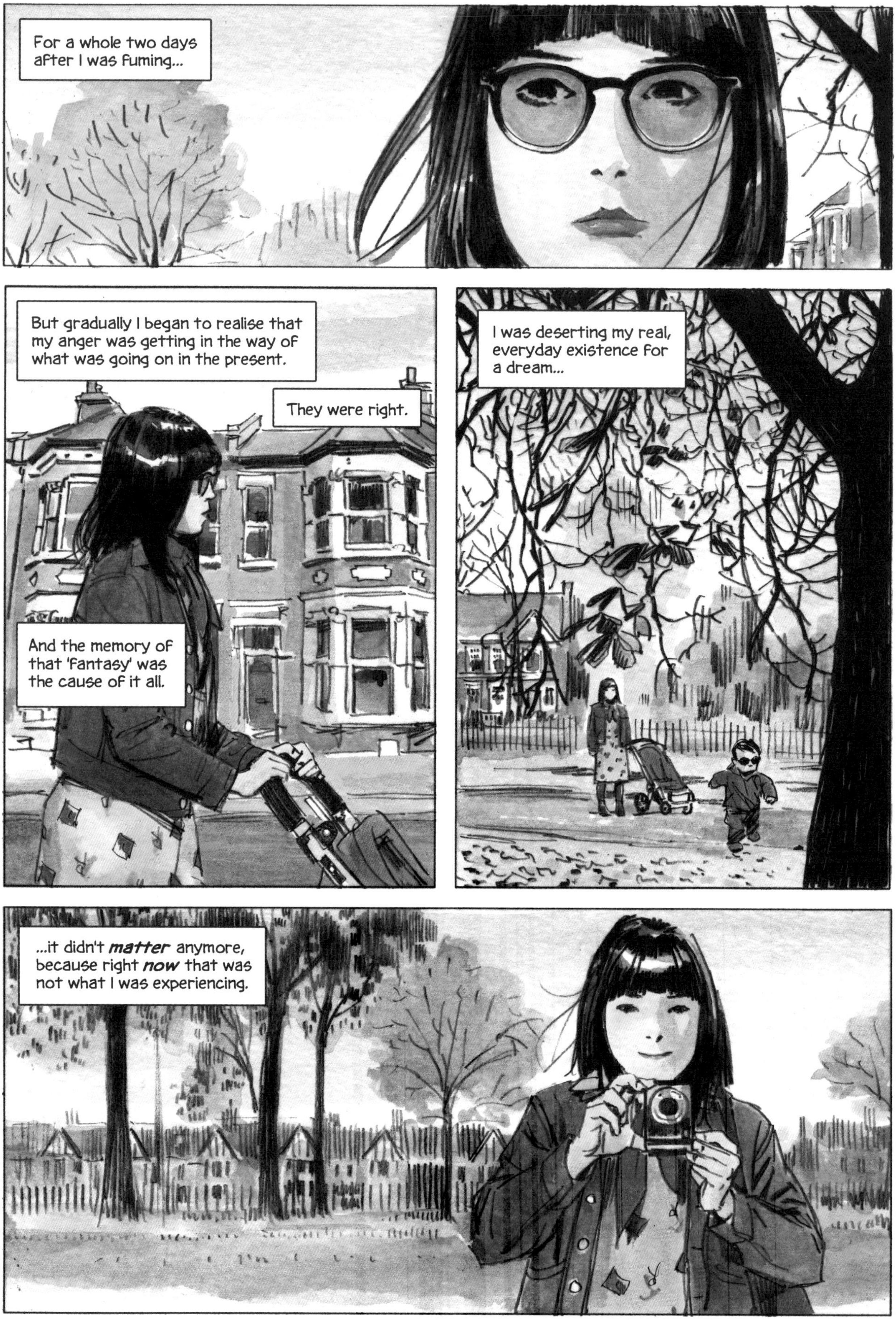
For a whole two days after I was fuming...
But gradually I began to realise that my anger was getting in the way of what was going on in the present.
They were right.
And the memory of that 'fantasy' was the cause of it all.
I was deserting my real, everyday existence for a dream...
...it didn't *matter* anymore, because right *now* that was not what I was experiencing.

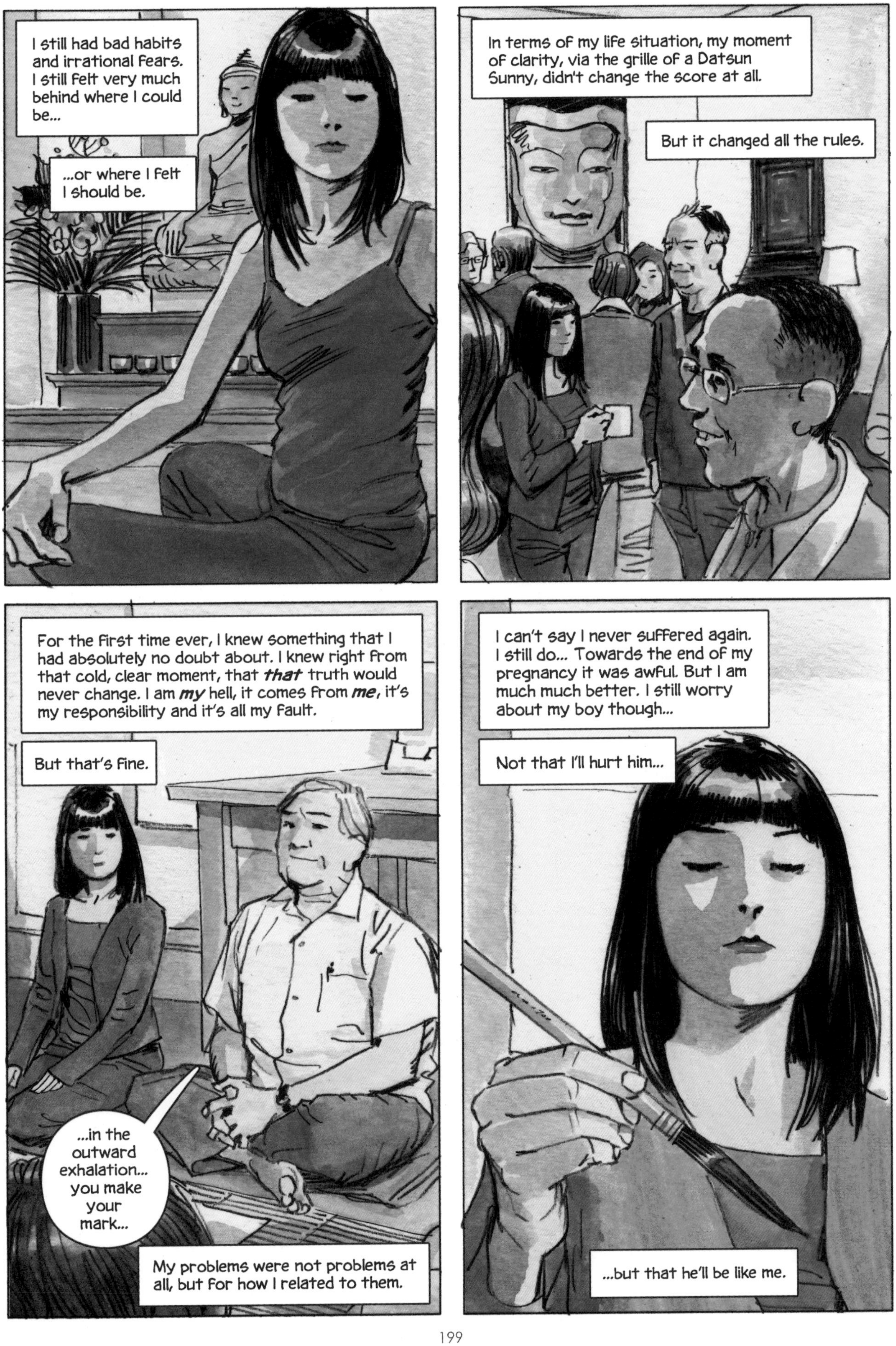
I still had bad habits and irrational fears. I still felt very much behind where I could be...
...or where I felt I should be.
In terms of my life situation, my moment of clarity, via the grille of a Datsun Sunny, didn't change the score at all.
But it changed all the rules.
For the first time ever, I knew something that I had absolutely no doubt about. I knew right from that cold, clear moment, that ***that*** truth would never change. I am ***my*** hell, it comes from ***me***, it's my responsibility and it's all my fault.
But that's fine.
...in the outward exhalation... you make your mark...
My problems were not problems at all, but for how I related to them.
I can't say I never suffered again. I still do... Towards the end of my pregnancy it was awful. But I am much much better. I still worry about my boy though...
Not that I'll hurt him...
...but that he'll be like me.

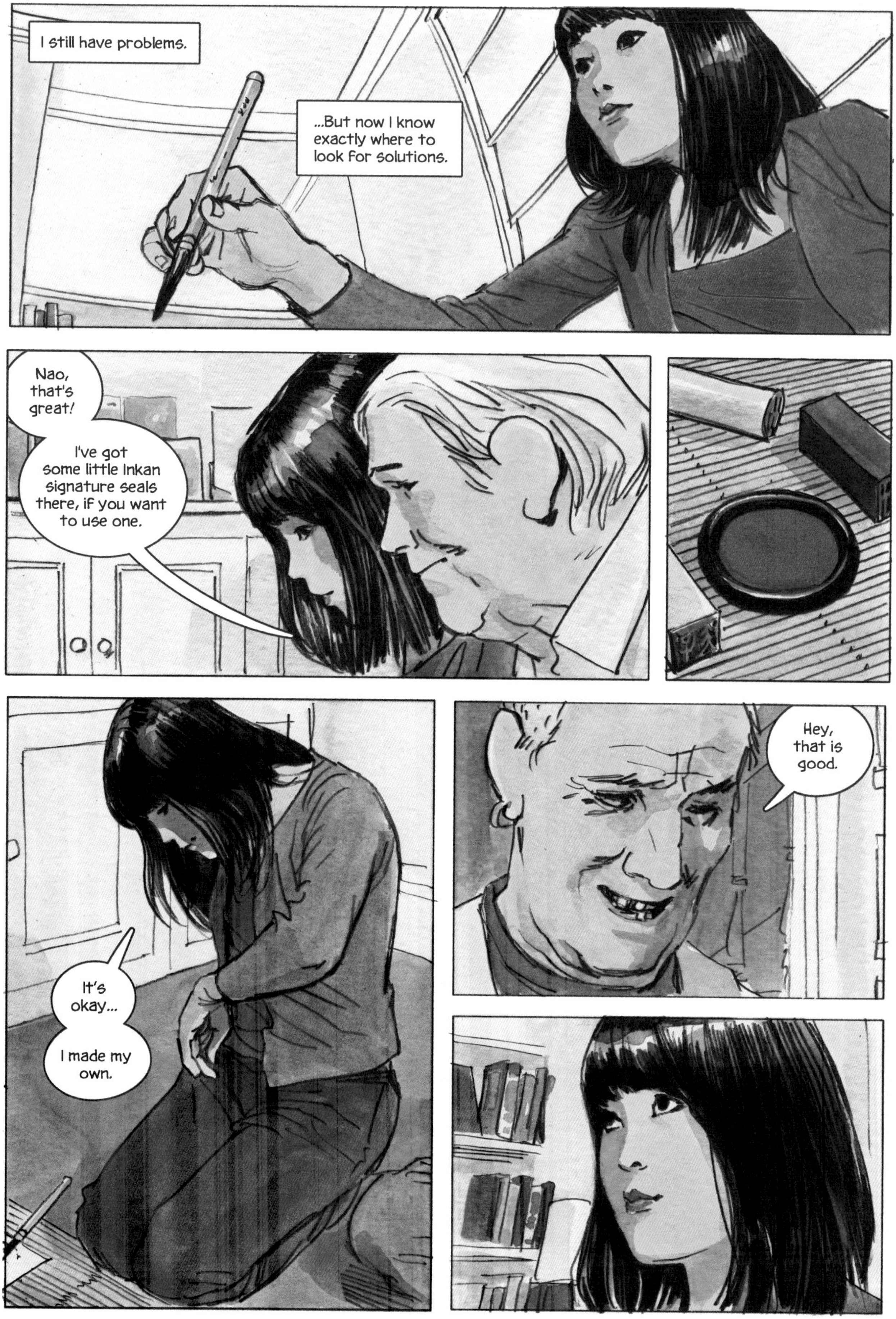
I still have problems.
...But now I know exactly where to look for solutions.
Nao, that's great!
I've got some little Inkan signature seals there, if you want to use one.
It's okay...
I made my own.
Hey, that is good.

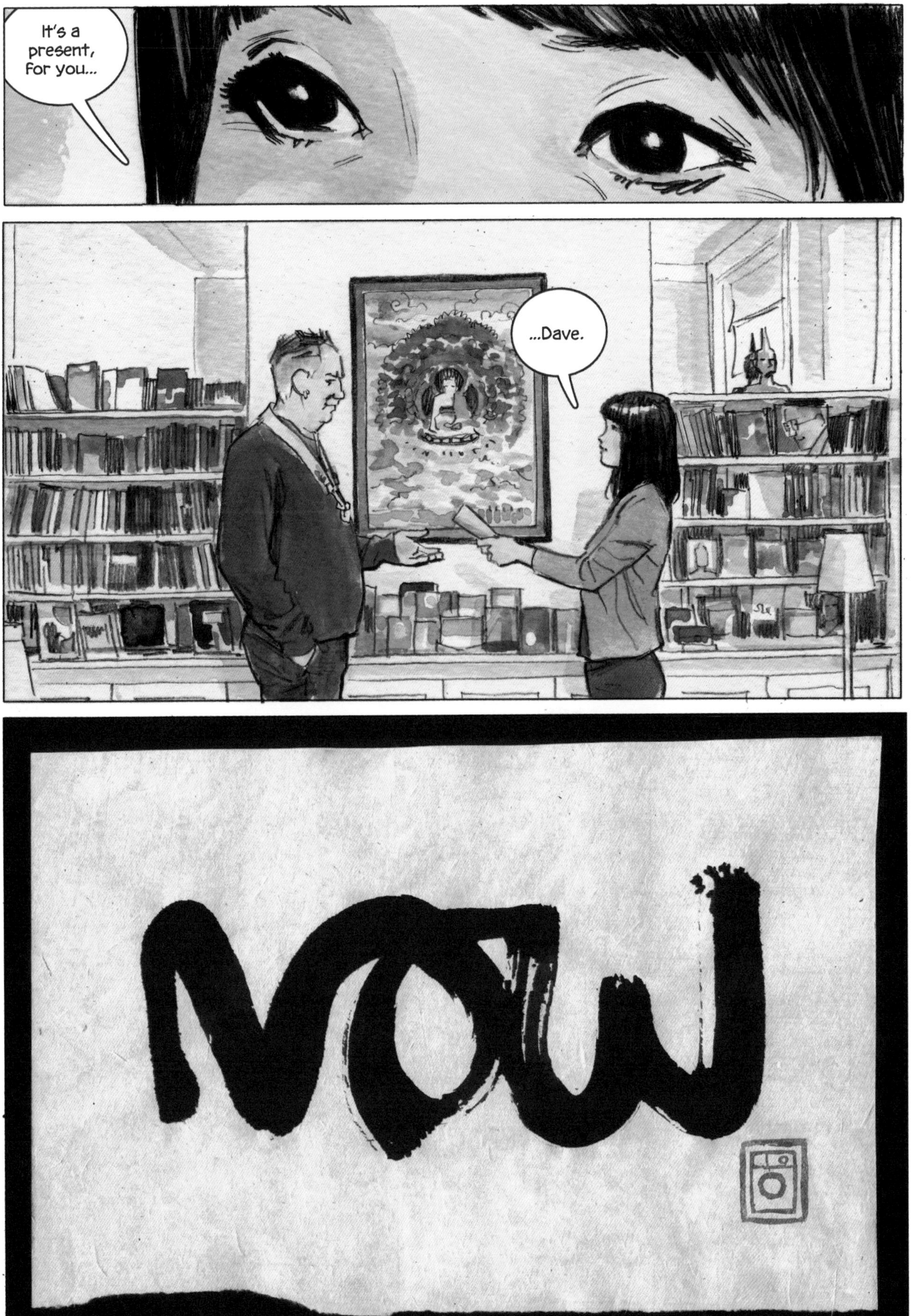
It's a present, for you...
...Dave.
NOW

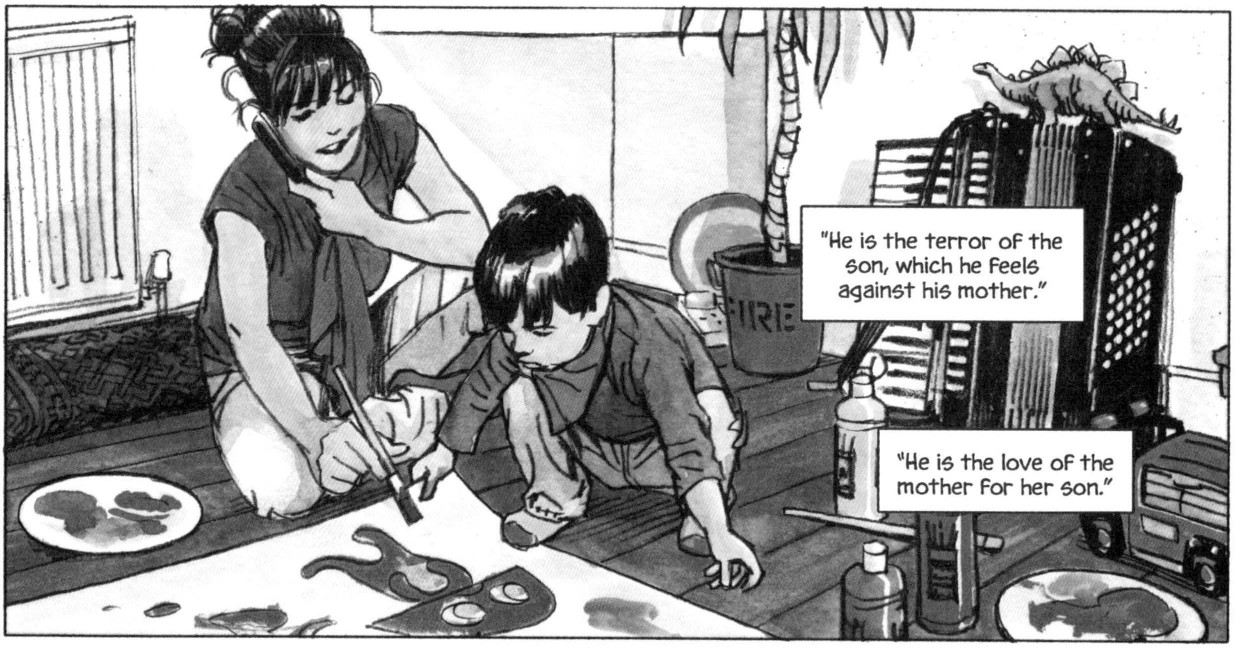
"He is the terror of the son, which he feels against his mother."
"He is the love of the mother for her son."

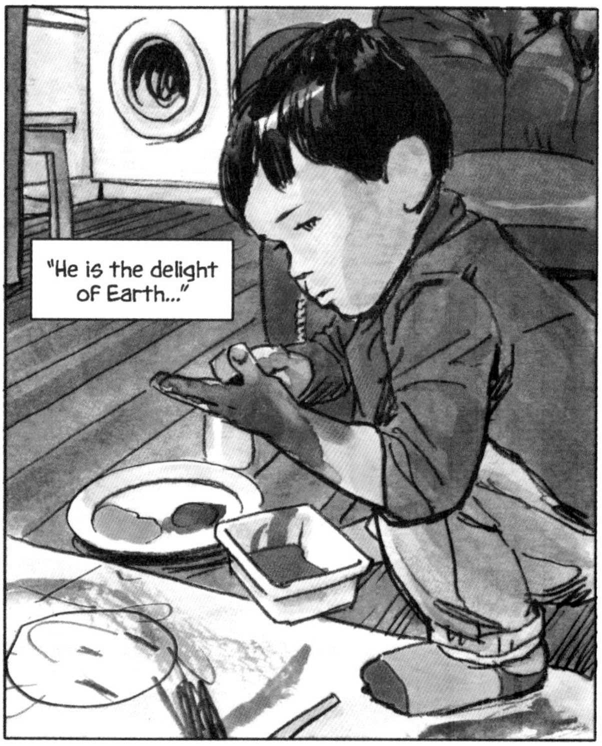
"He is the delight of Earth..."

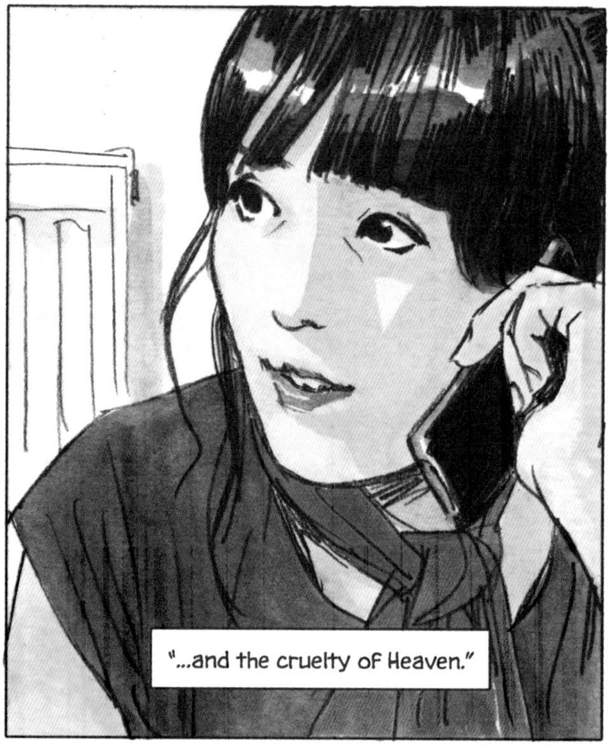
"...and the cruelty of Heaven."

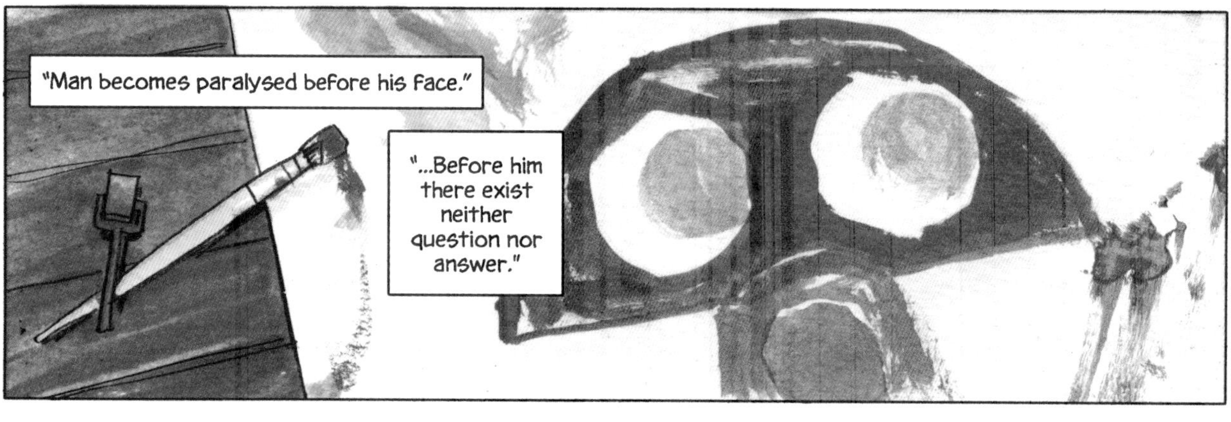
"Man becomes paralysed before his face."
"...Before him there exist neither question nor answer."

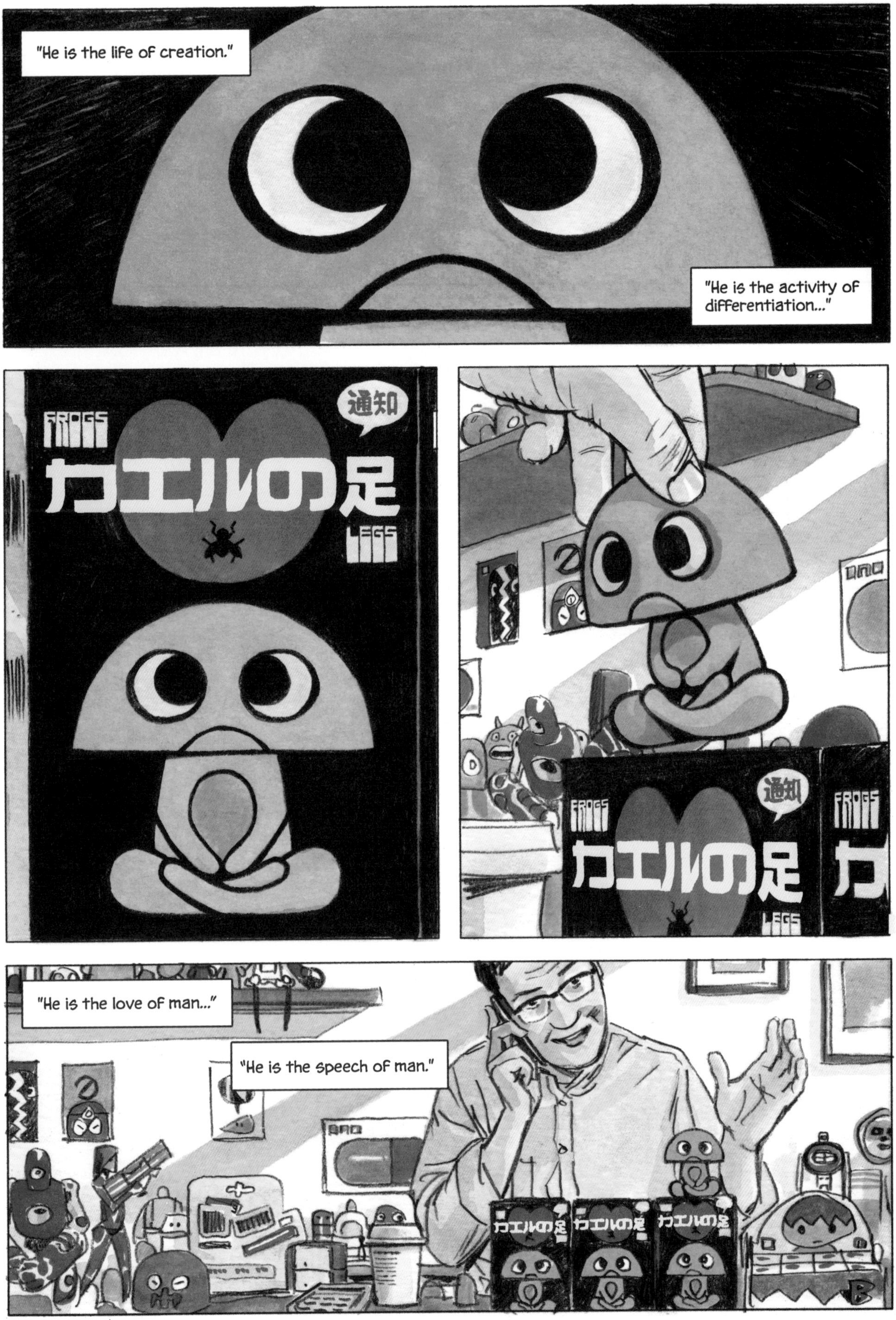
"He is the life of creation."
"He is the activity of differentiation..."
FROGS
通知
カエルの足
LEGS
通知
FROGS
カエルの足
LEGS
FROGS
"He is the love of man..."
"He is the speech of man."
カエルの足
カエルの足
カエルの足

"He is both the radiance and the dark shadow of man."

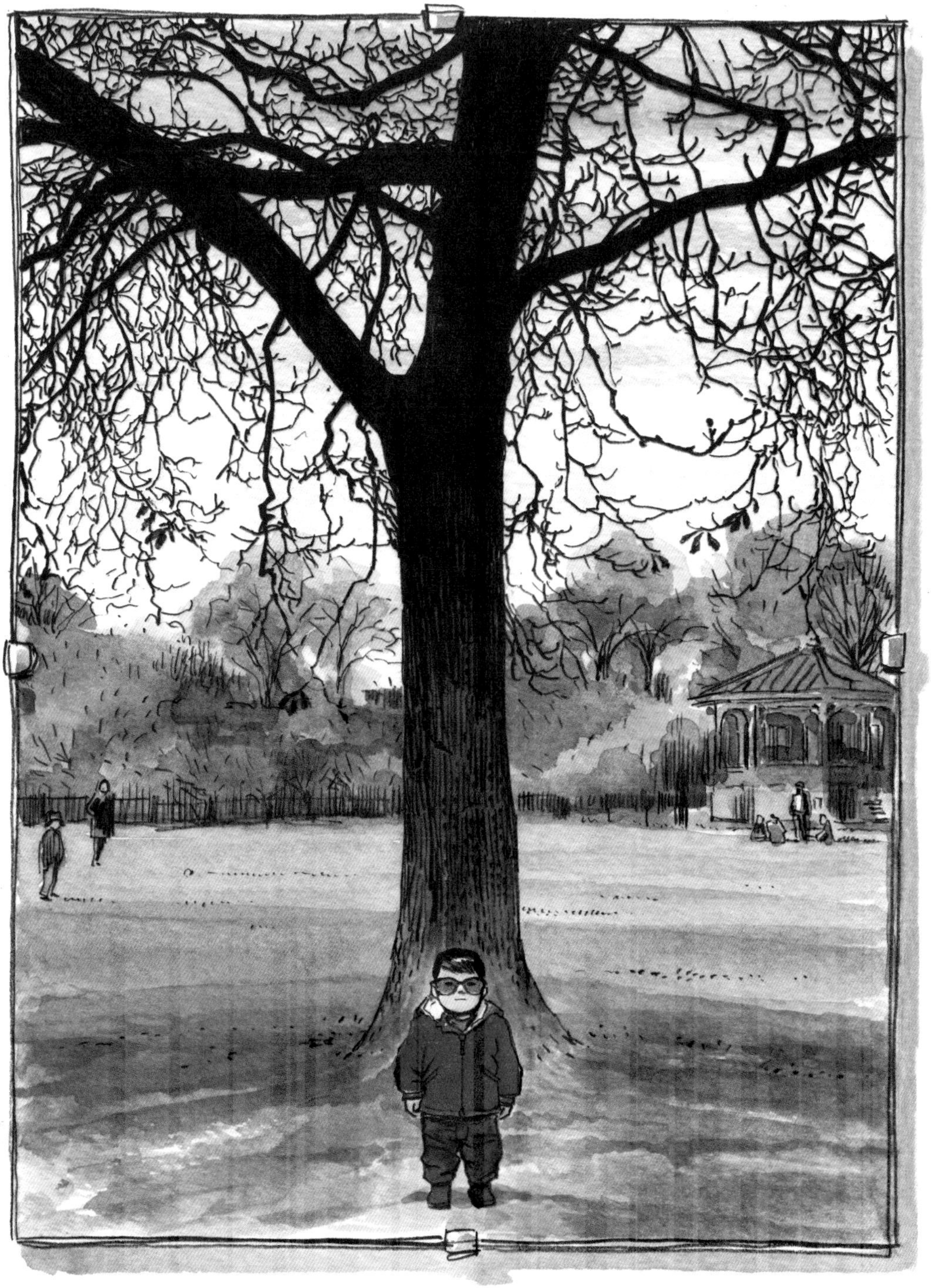

"He is deceitful reality."

ACKNOWLEDGMENTS

Although there's only my name on the spine, there would be no book at all without the love & support of my wife, Siobhan - Thank you.

I'd also like to give special thanks to my boys Ro and Hal for bringing a daily dose of joy, especially when things were hard.

I cannot thank my Mum & Dad enough for their unending love and support, they are without doubt the best parents ever.

All my family have been great but extra special thanks goes to Mark Dillon for all the work he put in.

For their support, encouragement and witting or unwitting contributions to the creation of this book I'd like to thank.

Emma Hayley • Doug Wallace • Lizzie Kaye • Alan Martin • Rob Bliss • Al Murphy • Harry Gwinner • Lilian Galvin • Si Spencer • Jamie Hewlett • Jessica Hynes • Liz Taylor • Frank Wynne • James Coore • Seb Monk • Damon Albarn • Stephen Sedgwick • Jason Cox • Steve Mackey • Steve Dillon • Philip Bond • Mat Wakeham • Kate McLauchlan • Mike Robinson • Matt Watkins • Lucy McLauchlan • Anthony Dillon • Cara Speller • Tim Watkins • Kersti Bergstrom • Stacy Wall • Laurence Dunmore • Chizuko Takagi • Simon Wright • Yuriko Pasieka • Haruka Kuroda • Faz Choudhury • Richard Martin • Ashley Wood • Aidan Onn • Chent • Ratnapraba • Paramananda • Tarakarunya • Jinananda • Sthiracitta • Vilasamani • Mark Dunlop • Jill Bolte Taylor • C. G. Jung • Hal Hartley • Ricky White • The Govers • Alec Jagodzinski

Jean Giraud Moebius

And to all the people on the internet who've expressed their support, a really big thank you.

For more information about Obsessive Compulsive Disorder
http://www.ocduk.org/

Other websites of interest
www.naobrown.com & www.ichi-anime.jp